The Pension Answer Book

Special Supplement
Fiduciary Responsibility Under ERISA

Jacob I. Freidman, Esq.
Rory Judd Albert, Esq.
Neal S. Schelberg, Esq.

THE PENSION ANSWER BOOK SERIES

**A PANEL PUBLICATION
ASPEN PUBLISHERS, INC.**

This publication is designed to provide accurate and authoritative information in regard to the subject matter covered. It is sold with the understanding that the publisher is not engaged in rendering legal, accounting or other professional services. If legal advice or other professional assistance is required, the services of a competent professional person should be sought.

—From a Declaration of Principles jointly adopted by a Committee of the American Bar Association and a Committee of Publishers and Associations.

Copyright © 1993

by
PANEL PUBLISHERS
A division of Aspen Publishers, Inc.
A Wolters Kluwer Company

36 West 44th Street
Suite 1316
New York, NY 10036
(212) 790-2000

ISBN 1-56706-048-X

All rights reserved. No part of this book may be reproduced in any form or by any means without permission in writing from the publisher.

Printed in the United States of America

About Panel Publishers

Panel Publishers derives its name from a panel of business professionals who organized in 1964 to publish authoritative, timely books, information services, and journals written by specialists to assist accountants, tax practitioners, attorneys, and other business professionals; human resources, compensation and benefits, and pension and profit-sharing professionals; and owners of small to medium-sized businesses. Our mission is to provide practical, solution-based "how-to" information to business professionals.

The Panel line of products, designed to assist the practitioner in providing pension, tax and related advice, includes the following titles:

The Pension Answer Book
401(k) Answer Book
Nonqualified Deferred Compensation Answer Book
The S Corporation: Planning & Operation
Executive Compensation
Individual Retirement Account Answer Book
The Pension Answer Book: Forms & Worksheets
Journal of Pension Planning & Compliance
Journal of Pension Benefits
Pension Benefits Newsletter

PANEL PUBLISHERS
A Division of Aspen Publishers, Inc.
Practical Solutions for Business Professionals

SUBSCRIPTION NOTICE

This Panel product is updated on a periodic basis with supplements to reflect important changes in the subject matter. If you purchased this product directly from Panel Publishers, we have already recorded your subscription for this update service.

If, however, you purchased this product from a bookstore and wish to receive future updates and revised or related volumes billed separately with a 30-day examination review, please contact our Customer Service Department at 1-301-698-9342 or send your name, company name (if applicable), address, and the title of the product to:

PANEL PUBLISHERS
A division of Aspen Publishers, Inc.
A Wolters Kluwer Company

7201 McKinney Circle
Frederick, MD 21701

Dedications and Acknowledgments

We dedicate this book to three of our outstanding colleagues at Proskauer, Matthew L. Eilenberg, Esq., Andrea S. Rattner, Esq., and Bernard Weinreb, Esq. We are indebted to them for their talented efforts and the enormous amount of time that they devoted to helping us complete this book. They tackled this project with great devotion and sacrificed many nights and weekends in the process. We also wish to acknowledge the invaluable assistance of our other partners, associates, and paralegals.

To Rick Kravitz, our publisher, we express thanks for encouraging us to take on this project and to Corinne Henning-Sachs, Esq., our editor, we offer appreciation for her constructive comments and helpful suggestions.

Hannah, Nancy, and Ruth deserve our everlasting thanks for their love, patience, support, and encouragement. Now that this project has been completed, perhaps we will get to see them a bit more often.

Preface

This *Special Supplement to the Pension Answer Book—Fiduciary Responsibility Under ERISA* was designed to answer questions that arise every day regarding the duties and liabilities of advisers, administrators, accountants, attorneys, in-house pension benefit professionals, and employee benefit plan fiduciaries under ERISA. This Supplement is intended to provide clear guidance for all pension professionals and to cover hundreds of questions arising on a day-to-day basis regarding fiduciary responsibility.

It is now almost two decades since the Employee Retirement Income Security Act (ERISA) was enacted in 1974. In reaction to certain perceived and actual abuses of plan assets and participants' entitlement to benefits, ERISA ushered in a new era of governmental protection of benefit plan assets and participants. The linchpin of that protective scheme was the enactment of a comprehensive set of guidelines governing the conduct of those charged with the duty of administering benefit plans.

ERISA's definition of fiduciary is very broad and covers many people who might not even realize that they *are* fiduciaries under ERISA. These people, and others who may or may not be fiduciaries, include:

- Participants and beneficiaries,
- Administrators and recordkeepers,
- Service providers,
- Attorneys, accountants, plan auditors, and consultants,

- Members of investment, pension, or other administrative committees, and
- Employers and corporate officers who sponsor, maintain, or contribute to plans.

These people and groups need the guidance that this *Special Supplement—Fiduciary Responsibility Under ERISA* provides.

While there have been numerous changes to the non-fiduciary provisions of ERISA, the fiduciary provisions have remained fundamentally the same since enactment. Yet the standard of behavior for fiduciaries and the scope of their liabilities have only in recent years started receiving widespread review by the judicial system.

A review of the facts in many of the decided cases reveals an astonishing lack of substantive knowledge by fiduciaries of their responsibilities under ERISA. This book explains, in plain English, the fundamental rules that every benefit plan fiduciary and associated advisors must know to satisfy the fiduciary's legal obligations and avoid personal liability. Since the ERISA fiduciary standard is that of the prudent expert and a "pure heart and empty mind" is no defense, it behooves every fiduciary and consultant to become intimately familiar with the statutory, regulatory, and common law fiduciary obligations.

Jacob I. Friedman
Rory Judd Albert
Neal S. Schelberg

September 1, 1993

How to Use This Book

This *Special Supplement to The Pension Answer Book—Fiduciary Responsibility Under ERISA* is designed as a guide for pension committee members, investment managers, accountants, attorneys, and others charged with administering or advising pension and welfare plans. It provides quick, authoritative answers to hundreds of questions dealing with fiduciary responsibility and liability under ERISA in simple, straightforward language and avoids technical jargon whenever possible. The question-and-answer format, with its breadth of coverage and plain-language explanations, effectively conveys the complex and essential subject matter of fiduciary duties relating to employee benefit plans. In addition, the book provides extensive appendix material gleaned from years of legal practice as well as Internal Revenue Service and Department of Labor forms and rulings.

List of Questions. A detailed List of Questions is designed to help the reader locate specific areas of immediate interest. Subheadings help to group and organize the questions by topic within each chapter.

Appendices. For the subscriber's convenience, a glossary, several checklists, and relevant regulations and ERISA sections are included in appendices at the end of the book.

Index. An index is provided as an aid to locating specific information. All references are to question numbers rather than page numbers.

About the Authors

Jacob I. Friedman, Esq. is a partner in the Tax Department of Proskauer Rose Goetz & Mendelsohn. Mr. Friedman advises Proskauer's exempt organization, banking, telecommunications, manufacturing, and financial clients on employee benefits, fiduciary, and tax issues. He advises clients with respect to all aspects of investments made by pension plans, unrelated business income tax ramifications, and employee benefit consequences of mergers and acquisitions. Mr. Friedman has extensive experience in consultation and litigation relating to ERISA fiduciary issues. Mr. Friedman received his Bachelor of Arts degree *cum laude* from Brooklyn College and his Juris Doctor degree *cum laude* from New York Law School, where he served as an Associate Editor of the *New York Law Review*. Mr. Friedman also received his Masters of Law degree (in Taxation) from New York University Law School. Mr. Friedman has lectured at seminars sponsored by *The New York Law Journal*, New York University, The New York State Bar Association, the International Association of Financial Planners, and various tax-exempt associations on areas such as real estate investment, tax credits, unrelated business taxable income, ERISA, and negotiating strategy with the IRS.

Rory Judd Albert, Esq. is a partner in Proskauer's Labor and Employment Law Department and practices in the area of employee benefits and executive compensation law. He advises clients regularly with respect to the design, implementation, and operation of defined benefit, defined contribution, profit sharing, 401(k), annuity, employee stock ownership, executive compensation, and other types of deferred compensation plans, as well as numerous health and welfare plans. Mr. Albert is frequently called upon to render advice on a wide variety of legal matters, such as ERISA's complex fiduciary responsibility, plan asset, trusteeship, exclusive benefit, prudence, diversification, and prohibited transaction rules, the intricate provisions of the Internal Revenue Code governing tax-qualified benefit plans (as well as rules relating to nonqualified plans), and other state and federal status affecting the operation of benefit plans (such as COBRA, ADEA, and securities laws). Mr. Albert is a member of the New York State Bar and is admitted to practice before the United States District Courts for the Southern and Eastern Districts of New York. He received his Juris Doctor degree from Columbia Law School, where he was the Managing Editor of the *Columbia Journal of Law and Social Problems*, and his Bachelor of Science degree from the Massachusetts Institute of Technology.

Neal S. Schelberg, Esq. is a partner in Proskauer's Labor and Employment Law Department, where he practices exclusively in the employee benefits area. He provides legal counsel to single employer and multiemployer pension and welfare funds and their sponsors. Mr. Schelberg has been involved in all phases of employee benefits practice. He provides day-to-day legal advice involving the entire spectrum of ERISA issues confronting plan sponsors and plan fiduciaries. Mr. Schelberg also has had extensive experience structuring, drafting, and negotiating the employee benefit aspects of purchases, sales, mergers, leveraged buyouts and other forms of business acquisitions, consolidations and reorganizations, and the formation of limited partnerships. His practice also encompasses ERISA litigation of fiduciary and prohibited transaction issues. Mr. Schelberg is a member of the New York and District of Columbia Bars. He received his Masters of Laws degree from Georgetown University Law Center, his Juris Doctor degree from Hofstra University School of Law, where he was a Notes and Comments Editor of *The Hofstra Law Review*, and his Masters and Bachelor of Arts degree from Brooklyn College. Mr. Schelberg frequently writes and speaks on employee benefits law topics. He is currently serving as Chair of the Arbitration Committee of the International Foundation of Employee Benefit Plans. Mr. Schelberg is co-author of the "Cases and Rulings" column for *Pension World* magazine and has published articles for many other journals. He has taught courses on employee benefits law at New York University and Fordham University Law School.

About the Authors

Proskauer Rose Goetz & Mendelsohn has, for more than a century, provided legal services to individuals and businesses of all sizes and in a multitude of industries. One of the largest law firms in the United States today, it has offices throughout the country and abroad. Proskauer's nationally recognized Employee Benefits Law Group is comprised of approximately two dozen attorneys whose range of experience and skills covers the entire spectrum of employee benefits and executive compensation law.

The Employee Benefits Law Group's clientele includes many of the most prominent local, national and international businesses, as well as public employers, not-for-profit entities and public-interest groups. It also represents over 200 single-employer, multiemployer and collectively bargained pension and welfare plans.

The Employee Benefits Law Group regularly advises employers, trustees, administrators, boards of directors, and other plan fiduciaries on ERISA, Internal Revenue Code, and other matters relating to every type of employee benefits plan as well as transactions impacting plans. The Employee Benefits Law Group advises clients with respect to proceedings before, and issues involving, the Department of Labor, Internal Revenue Service, Pension Benefit Guaranty Corporation, Securities and Exchange Commission and other government agencies. Several of the Group's attorneys practice exclusively in employee benefits litigation.

Contents

List of Questions xvii

CHAPTER 1
Introduction 1-1

CHAPTER 2
Who Is a Fiduciary? 2-1

CHAPTER 3
Fiduciary Duties Under ERISA 3-1

CHAPTER 4
Allocation and Delegation of Fiduciary Responsibility 4-1

CHAPTER 5
Prohibited Transactions 5-1

CHAPTER 6
Fiduciary Liability 6-1

Fiduciary Responsibility Answer Book

CHAPTER 7
Investment Issues 7-1

CHAPTER 8
Plan Trusts and Plan Assets 8-1

APPENDIX A A-1

APPENDIX B B-1

GLOSSARY GL-1

TABLES T-1

INDEX I-1

List of Questions

Chapter 1 Introduction

Q 1:1	What is a fiduciary?	1-2
Q 1:2	What laws govern the conduct of fiduciaries?	1-2
Q 1:3	Which plans are subject to ERISA's fiduciary rules?	1-3
Q 1:4	Who enforces the fiduciary rules?	1-6
Q 1:5	When must a fiduciary become knowledgeable about the fiduciary rules?	1-7
Q 1:6	Can a fiduciary be personally liable for a violation of fiduciary responsibility?	1-8
Q 1:7	Do the ERISA fiduciary rules differ from the common law fiduciary rules?	1-8
Q 1:8	Must a person consent to be a fiduciary to be treated as a fiduciary?	1-10
Q 1:9	Can a fiduciary be liable for an unwitting violation of ERISA's fiduciary duties?	1-10

Chapter 2 Who Is a Fiduciary?

Determining Fiduciary Status

Q 2:1	Who is a fiduciary under ERISA?	2-1
Q 2:2	What types of persons can be fiduciaries under ERISA?	2-2
Q 2:3	Does a person's title or function govern fiduciary status?	2-5
Q 2:4	What types of activities will typically render a person a fiduciary of a plan under ERISA?	2-6

Fiduciary Responsibility Answer Book

Q 2:5	What types of offices or positions result in fiduciary status?	2-6
Q 2:6	When can a person be a fiduciary only for a limited purpose?	2-7
Q 2:7	Can a person ever be a fiduciary if the person does not perform one or more of the fiduciary functions described in Section 3(21)(A) of ERISA?	2-8
Q 2:8	Must an employee benefit plan have a specified number of fiduciaries?	2-9

Named Fiduciaries

Q 2:9	What is a named fiduciary?	2-9
Q 2:10	What are the duties of a named fiduciary?	2-10
Q 2:11	Who can be appointed a named fiduciary?	2-10
Q 2:12	What is the purpose of having a named fiduciary?	2-10
Q 2:13	How are named fiduciaries designated in the plan document?	2-11
Q 2:14	What is the liability of a named fiduciary?	2-11

Plan Trustees

Q 2:15	What is a plan trustee?	2-11
Q 2:16	When is a plan trustee a fiduciary?	2-12
Q 2:17	Is a bank that acts as a custodian for plan assets a fiduciary under ERISA?	2-12

Plan Sponsors

Q 2:18	What is the plan sponsor?	2-13
Q 2:19	Is the plan sponsor a plan fiduciary?	2-14
Q 2:20	Are members of a plan sponsor's board of directors plan fiduciaries?	2-15
Q 2:21	Can individuals who are officers or employees of a plan sponsor be plan fiduciaries?	2-16

Plan Administrators

Q 2:22	What is the plan administrator?	2-16
Q 2:23	Who is the plan administrator if the plan document does not designate a plan administrator?	2-17

List of Questions

Investment Managers
Q 2:24	What is an investment manager under ERISA?	2-17
Q 2:25	Is an investment manager a fiduciary under ERISA?	2-18

Broker-Dealers
Q 2:26	Is a broker-dealer a fiduciary under ERISA?	2-18

Professional Service Providers
Q 2:27	When are attorneys, accountants, actuaries, consultants, and other professionals who provide services to a plan ("professional service providers") considered plan fiduciaries?	2-19
Q 2:28	If a professional service provider who is a member of a professional firm renders services to a plan in a fiduciary capacity, can the other members of the professional firm be considered fiduciaries?	2-21
Q 2:29	When can an in-house professional service provider be considered a plan fiduciary?	2-21
Q 2:30	May other plan fiduciaries serve as professional service providers?	2-22

Third-Party Administrators
Q 2:31	When is a third-party administrator a fiduciary under ERISA?	2-22

Insurance Companies and Brokers
Q 2:32	When is an insurance company a fiduciary under ERISA?	2-23
Q 2:33	When is an insurance broker a fiduciary under ERISA?	2-24
Q 2:34	What does it mean to "render investment advice" for the purpose of determining fiduciary status?	2-24

Plan Participants
Q 2:35	When can plan participants' control over plan assets relieve fiduciaries of liability?	2-25

Fiduciaries for Collectively Bargained Plans
Q 2:36	Does a collectively bargained plan have special fiduciaries?	2-25

Chapter 3 Fiduciary Duties Under ERISA

Q 3:1	What are the primary fiduciary duties under ERISA?	3-1

Exclusive Benefit

Q 3:2	What is required for a fiduciary to satisfy the "exclusive benefit" requirement?	3-2
Q 3:3	Is it a violation of the exclusive benefit requirement if the fiduciary's action also benefits the employer?	3-2

Prudence

Q 3:4	What must a fiduciary do to satisfy the prudence requirement?	3-3
Q 3:5	What is the legal standard for determining whether a fiduciary's acts are prudent?	3-3
Q 3:6	Are a fiduciary's actions judged by the standard of an ordinary person or that of an expert?	3-3
Q 3:7	Does a fiduciary have an obligation to seek the assistance of an expert to satisfy the prudence requirement?	3-4
Q 3:8	What is the difference between "substantive prudence" and "procedural prudence"?	3-4
Q 3:9	What substantive factors must a fiduciary consider in connection with plan investments?	3-5
Q 3:10	What is procedural prudence in the context of investing plan assets?	3-5

Diversification

Q 3:11	What is required for a fiduciary to satisfy the diversification requirement?	3-6
Q 3:12	What are the primary factors for prudent diversification?	3-6

Adherence to Plan Documents

Q 3:13	What is required for a fiduciary to discharge his or her responsibilities in accordance with plan documents?	3-7

To Whom Is Duty Owed

Q 3:14	To whom does a plan fiduciary owe a fiduciary duty?	3-8
Q 3:15	Who is a plan participant?	3-8
Q 3:16	Who is a plan beneficiary?	3-9

List of Questions

Q 3:17	Can a plan fiduciary have obligations to persons other than plan participants and beneficiaries?	3-9

Settlor Functions Versus Fiduciary Activities

Q 3:18	What is a "settlor function?"	3-10
Q 3:19	What are the most common settlor functions?	3-10
Q 3:20	When can a fiduciary perform a settlor function?	3-11
Q 3:21	To what extent is a fiduciary's implementation of a settlor function exempt from the rules on fiduciary responsibility?	3-13

Responsibility of Co-Fiduciaries

Q 3:22	In general, when is a fiduciary responsible for a breach of fiduciary responsibility by a co-fiduciary?	3-13
Q 3:23	What special rules apply to a trustee for a breach of fiduciary responsibility by a co-trustee?	3-14
Q 3:24	May fiduciary responsibilities be allocated among fiduciaries, or delegated to persons other than named fiduciaries?	3-14

Special Rules

Q 3:25	Are there special fiduciary rules that apply to a plan holding qualifying employer real property (QERP) or qualifying employer securities (QES), or to an employee stock ownership plan (ESOP)?	3-15
Q 3:26	What special fiduciary rules apply when an investment manager has been appointed for a plan?	3-15
Q 3:27	May a fiduciary maintain indicia of ownership of any plan assets outside the United States?	3-15
Q 3:28	Are there special fiduciary rules that apply when a pension plan participant or beneficiary exercises control over the assets in his or her individual account?	3-16
Q 3:29	What special fiduciary standards apply to benefit plans covering only partners or other self-employed persons?	3-16
Q 3:30	Are there special fiduciary rules that apply in connection with the termination of a single-employer pension plan?	3-17
Q 3:31	What special fiduciary rules apply in the context of acquisitions and dispositions of businesses?	3-17
Q 3:32	When does ERISA preempt other rules of law?	3-18
Q 3:33	Are there exceptions in ERISA to the preemption rules?	3-19

Fiduciary Responsibility Answer Book

Q 3:34	What special fiduciary standards apply to public employee plans sponsored by federal, state, or municipal governments?	3-19
Q 3:35	Is there a fiduciary duty to give accurate tax information to plan participants?	3-20
Q 3:36	Can there be a fiduciary duty to reject an employer's contribution of property?	3-21
Q 3:37	Can a third-party administrator have a fiduciary duty to give an accounting to an employer as plan sponsor?	3-22

Chapter 4 Allocation and Delegation of Fiduciary Responsibility

How to Allocate or Delegate Fiduciary Responsibility

Q 4:1	May fiduciary duties be allocated among fiduciaries and delegated by fiduciaries to other fiduciaries?	4-2
Q 4:2	May fiduciary duties be delegated to or allocated among nonfiduciaries?	4-2
Q 4:3	What are trustee responsibilities?	4-3
Q 4:4	May a named fiduciary delegate trustee responsibilities to a person other than a trustee?	4-5
Q 4:5	How are fiduciary duties allocated among named fiduciaries and delegated to other fiduciaries?	4-5
Q 4:6	Does the allocation or delegation of fiduciary duties relieve the allocating or delegating fiduciary of any fiduciary duties under ERISA?	4-5
Q 4:7	What is the fiduciary duty to monitor?	4-6
Q 4:8	Can a delegating fiduciary be relieved of its duty to monitor the performance of those individuals to whom fiduciary responsibilities have been delegated?	4-7

Co-Fiduciary Liability

| Q 4:9 | Is a fiduciary who participates or conceals an act or omission of another fiduciary liable for the acts or omissions of the other fiduciary? | 4-8 |
| Q 4:10 | Is a fiduciary who knows of a breach of fiduciary responsibility by another fiduciary liable for the acts or omissions of the other fiduciary? | 4-9 |

List of Questions

Q 4:11	Are there any other circumstances under which a fiduciary could be liable for the acts or omissions of another fiduciary?	4-10
Q 4:12	What action must a fiduciary take if the fiduciary knows of a co-fiduciary's breach of fiduciary duty?	4-11

Investment Managers

Q 4:13	May a named fiduciary delegate investment duties?	4-13
Q 4:14	Who is responsible for appointing an investment manager?	4-13
Q 4:15	May fiduciaries, other than named fiduciaries, appoint an investment manager?	4-14
Q 4:16	May nonfiduciaries appoint an investment manager?	4-14
Q 4:17	What are the responsibilities of an investment manager?	4-14
Q 4:18	Must investment managers follow the directions of a named fiduciary of a plan?	4-14
Q 4:19	May other plan fiduciaries serve as investment managers?	4-15
Q 4:20	Is anyone precluded from serving as an investment manager under ERISA?	4-15
Q 4:21	How is fiduciary responsibility shared under ERISA when there are multiple plan investment managers?	4-15
Q 4:22	Is the operator of a collective, common, or group trust or of a separate account an investment manager with respect to a plan that invests in such a vehicle?	4-16
Q 4:23	Are trustees and investment managers required to exercise proxies or other rights associated with plan securities?	4-17
Q 4:24	Can an entity that otherwise would not be an investment manager become one merely by exercising proxies or other rights associated with plan securities over which they have responsibility?	4-17
Q 4:25	What is a QPAM?	4-17
Q 4:26	Is a qualified professional asset manager an investment manager?	4-18

Participant-Directed Plan Investments

Q 4:27	What is the purpose of ERISA Section 404(c) regarding participant-directed plan investments?	4-19
Q 4:28	Must a plan comply with the requirements of Section 404(c) of ERISA?	4-19

Fiduciary Responsibility Answer Book

Q 4:29	What is an "ERISA Section 404(c) plan"?	4-20
Q 4:30	How does an ERISA Section 404(c) plan provide a participant or beneficiary an opportunity to exercise control over assets in his or her account?	4-20
Q 4:31	What does it mean to afford a participant or beneficiary a reasonable opportunity to give investment instructions?	4-21
Q 4:32	What are "core alternatives" under an ERISA Section 404(c) plan?	4-22
Q 4:33	How does an ERISA Section 404(c) plan offer a broad range of investment alternatives?	4-22
Q 4:34	May an ERISA Section 404(c) plan offer investment alternatives in addition to the core alternatives?	4-25
Q 4:35	What must a Section 404(c) plan provide if, due to the volatility of the market, a participant is allowed to transfer assets out of any investment alternative more than once in a three-month period?	4-26
Q 4:36	When has a participant or beneficiary exercised independent control with respect to decisions regarding assets in his or her individual account under an ERISA Section 404(c) plan?	4-28
Q 4:37	May a participant or beneficiary exercise independent control if the transaction involves a fiduciary?	4-28
Q 4:38	Is a plan considered to be an ERISA Section 404(c) plan if the plan permits a participant to exercise control over certain assets of the plan but not over others?	4-29
Q 4:39	Must a participant give a plan fiduciary affirmative investment instructions for the fiduciary to be relieved of liability under Section 404(c) of ERISA?	4-30
Q 4:40	What types of information and documents must be supplied automatically to participants and beneficiaries to give them the opportunity to obtain sufficient information to make informed investment decisions under an ERISA Section 404(c) plan?	4-31
Q 4:41	What types of information must be furnished to participants and beneficiaries upon request to enable them to make informed investment decisions under an ERISA Section 404(c) plan?	4-34
Q 4:42	Who is responsible for providing the information described in Questions 4:40 and 4:41?	4-36
Q 4:43	What other duties are the responsibility of an identified plan fiduciary under an ERISA Section 404(c) plan?	4-36

List of Questions

Q 4:44	Must an identified plan fiduciary of an ERISA Section 404(c) plan always comply with the investment instructions of a participant or beneficiary?	4-37
Q 4:45	Under what circumstances will a plan fiduciary be relieved of liability for any loss that results from a participant's or beneficiary's exercise of control with respect to the acquisition or sale of employer securities?	4-38
Q 4:46	Does a plan fiduciary have an obligation to provide investment advice to a participant or beneficiary? . . .	4-39
Q 4:47	What types of fiduciary responsibilities does a plan fiduciary continue to retain although a plan satisfies the requirements of Section 404(c) of ERISA?	4-39
Q 4:48	If a participant under a Section 404(c) plan engages in a prohibited transaction under ERISA and the Internal Revenue Code, will the participant be liable?	4-40
Q 4:49	How is co-fiduciary liability limited under Section 404(c) of ERISA?	4-41

Chapter 5 Prohibited Transactions

In General

Q 5:1	What is a prohibited transaction?	5-2
Q 5:2	May a plan fiduciary receive a benefit from the plan? . .	5-3
Q 5:3	May a person serve as a plan fiduciary if he or she is involved in a different capacity with a party in interest?	5-3
Q 5:4	Who is a party in interest or a disqualified person with respect to a plan?	5-4
Q 5:5	What are the differences between the prohibited transaction rules under the Code and ERISA?	5-5
Q 5:6	What plans are covered by the prohibited transaction rules?	5-5

Liability and Penalties

Q 5:7	When is a fiduciary liable for engaging in a prohibited transaction under ERISA and the Code?	5-5
Q 5:8	What are the penalties for engaging in a prohibited transaction?	5-6
Q 5:9	Can a nonfiduciary be subject to liability for a prohibited transaction?	5-7

Q 5:10	Can a single event result in several prohibited transactions?	5-9
Q 5:11	Is the full excise tax imposed on each disqualified person who participates in a prohibited transaction?	5-9

Sales, Exchanges or Leases

Q 5:12	What types of transactions are included in the prohibition against sales, exchanges, or leases between a plan and a party in interest?	5-10
Q 5:13	Does an employer's contribution of property to a plan result in a prohibited transaction?	5-12

Loans or Extensions of Credit

Q 5:14	What types of transactions are included in the prohibition against lending money or the extension of credit between a plan and a party in interest?	5-13
Q 5:15	Under what circumstances are loans from a plan to participants and beneficiaries permissible?	5-15
Q 5:16	Who may *not* borrow without obtaining an individual prohibited transaction exemption?	5-16
Q 5:17	To whom must plan loans be made available?	5-16
Q 5:18	May plans require a minimum loan?	5-17
Q 5:19	What written information must be provided to participants regarding a loan program?	5-17
Q 5:20	What interest rate must be charged by a plan for loans?	5-18
Q 5:21	How must plan loans be secured?	5-19

Goods, Services, and Facilities

Q 5:22	What types of transactions are included in the prohibition against furnishing goods, services, and facilities between plans and parties in interest?	5-20
Q 5:23	May a party in interest ever furnish goods and services to a plan?	5-20
Q 5:24	What is a "reasonable contract or arrangement" for furnishing goods, services, and facilities between a plan and a party in interest?	5-21
Q 5:25	What is a "necessary service" that a party in interest may provide under a reasonable contract?	5-22
Q 5:26	What is "reasonable compensation" that a party in interest may receive for providing necessary services?	5-23

List of Questions

Q 5:27	May a fiduciary who receives full-time pay from a sponsoring employer, employer association, or union receive compensation for his or her services to a plan?	5-23
Q 5:28	When may a fiduciary who receives full-time pay from a sponsoring employer, employer association, or a union receive reimbursement or advances for expenses incurred on behalf of the plan?	5-23

Employer Securities and Employer Real Property

Q 5:29	What is the prohibition against the acquisition on behalf of a plan of employer securities and employer real property?	5-24

Self-Dealing

Q 5:30	What is the prohibition against a fiduciary dealing with plan assets in his or her own interest or for his or her own account?	5-25
Q 5:31	May a fiduciary deal with assets of a plan in which he or she has an account?	5-26
Q 5:32	Under what circumstances may a fiduciary receive compensation or other consideration for furnishing office space or providing services to a plan without violating ERISA's prohibition against self-dealing?	5-26
Q 5:33	May a fiduciary provide multiple services to a plan?	5-27

Asset Transfers

Q 5:34	What is included in the prohibition against the transfer to, or use by, a party in interest of plan assets?	5-28

Parties With Adverse Interests

Q 5:35	What is the prohibition against a fiduciary acting in any transaction involving the plan on behalf of a party (or representing a party) whose interests are adverse to the interests of the plan?	5-29

Kickbacks

Q 5:36	What is the prohibition against the receipt of kickbacks by fiduciaries?	5-30

Corrections and Exemptions

Q 5:37	Can a prohibited transaction be corrected?	5-30
Q 5:38	May a plan purchase insurance to cover any losses to the plan resulting from a prohibited transaction? . . .	5-31
Q 5:39	Are there any statutory exceptions to the prohibited transaction provisions?	5-31
Q 5:40	May administrative exemptions to the prohibited transaction rules be granted by the DOL?	5-32
Q 5:41	May a prohibited transaction exemption be granted retroactively?	5-32
Q 5:42	Can a prohibited transaction exemption be used to benefit the owner of a closely held corporation?	5-33
Q 5:43	What is a prohibited transaction class exemption? . . .	5-33
Q 5:44	What is an individual prohibited transaction exemption?	5-35
Q 5:45	May plan expenses be paid out of the plan?	5-35
Q 5:46	Under what circumstances may the sponsor of a single employer plan receive a refund of contributions it made to the plan?	5-36
Q 5:47	Under what circumstances may an employer participating in a multiemployer plan receive a refund of contributions it made to the plan?	5-37

Chapter 6 Fiduciary Liability

Personal Liability

Q 6:1	Can a fiduciary be held personally liable for a breach of duty?	6-2
Q 6:2	Is a fiduciary liable for a breach not occurring during the fiduciary's term in office?	6-2
Q 6:3	Is there a duty to remedy a fiduciary breach committed by a predecessor fiduciary?	6-3
Q 6:4	Does a successor fiduciary have any obligation if the successor does not have knowledge of an actual breach, but only knows of a possible breach by a predecessor fiduciary?	6-3

Equitable Remedies

Q 6:5	What types of remedies can be imposed on a fiduciary for a breach of fiduciary duty?	6-4

List of Questions

Q 6:6	Are there restrictions on the use of equitable remedies for a fiduciary's breach?	6-5
Q 6:7	Are any equitable remedies available as an alternative to the removal of a fiduciary for breach of duty?	6-6
Q 6:8	What other types of equitable remedies are available?	6-6

Damages: Plan Losses

Q 6:9	What losses may a fiduciary be liable to restore?	6-7
Q 6:10	What is the measure of a plan's loss to be restored as a remedy for a fiduciary breach?	6-8
Q 6:11	Can any gains offset a loss resulting from a fiduciary's breach?	6-9

Damages: Fiduciary Profits

| Q 6:12 | What profits may a fiduciary be liable to disgorge? | 6-9 |

Punitive Damages

| Q 6:13 | May a participant or beneficiary recover punitive damages for a breach of fiduciary duty? | 6-10 |
| Q 6:14 | May a plan recover punitive damages for a breach of fiduciary duty? | 6-11 |

20 Percent Penalty

| Q 6:15 | What is the 20 percent penalty for breach of fiduciary duty? | 6-11 |
| Q 6:16 | Are there any set-offs for the 20 percent penalty? | 6-12 |

Excise Taxes & Penalties

| Q 6:17 | What excise taxes and other penalties may apply to a fiduciary breach? | 6-12 |

Criminal Liability

Q 6:18	May a fiduciary face criminal liability for a breach of fiduciary duty?	6-12
Q 6:19	Are there other laws imposing criminal liability on a fiduciary?	6-13
Q 6:20	Do any federal crimes specifically apply to employee benefit plans?	6-13

Fiduciary Responsibility Answer Book

Interference with ERISA Rights

Q 6:21 May a fiduciary face civil liability for interference with rights protected under ERISA? **6-14**

Q 6:22 If an employer changes the terms of a health insurance plan, making it self-insured, and sharply reducing the lifetime limit for expenses related to AIDS and related illnesses, after a participant has been diagnosed with AIDS, does the change constitute interference with the exercise of rights under a plan or ERISA Section 510? **6-15**

Protecting Against the Risk of Liability

Q 6:23 May a plan release a fiduciary from liability? **6-15**

Q 6:24 May a fiduciary be relieved from his or her fiduciary duties by delegating duties with respect to a plan to another individual? **6-16**

Q 6:25 May a plan fiduciary indemnify its employees who actually perform the fiduciary services for the plan? **6-17**

Q 6:26 What is the effect of a provision in a plan that purports to free a fiduciary from liability for breaching his or her fiduciary duties? **6-17**

Q 6:27 Is a release from a plan participant that frees a fiduciary from liability for fiduciary breaches valid? **6-17**

Fiduciary Liability Insurance

Q 6:28 May a plan purchase insurance for itself or for plan fiduciaries to cover liability or losses resulting from the acts or omissions of plan fiduciaries? **6-18**

Q 6:29 May a fiduciary or an employer purchase insurance for the plan fiduciary to cover liability or losses resulting from the acts or omissions of the plan fiduciary? . . . **6-18**

Q 6:30 May plan fiduciaries purchase, from the same insurance company that insures the plan against fiduciary breaches, a policy that protects the fiduciary from recourse lawsuits that the insurer can bring against the fiduciary? **6-19**

Indemnity by Sponsor

Q 6:31 May an employer who sponsors a plan, or an employee organization whose members are covered by the plan, indemnify a fiduciary? **6-19**

xxx

List of Questions

Co-Fiduciaries and Contribution

Q 6:32 Does a fiduciary who is sued for a breach of fiduciary duty have an implied right of contribution and/or indemnity against a co-fiduciary who participated in the breach? ... 6-20

Q 6:33 Does a fiduciary who is sued for a breach of fiduciary duty have an implied right of contribution and/or indemnity against a nonfiduciary who participated in a breach? . 6-21

Attorneys' Fees

Q 6:34 May a plan reimburse a fiduciary's legal expenses incurred in defending a lawsuit charging breach of fiduciary duties? ... 6-22

Q 6:35 If a fiduciary is found liable for breaching his or her fiduciary duties, can the fiduciary be held liable for attorneys' fees? ... 6-22

Q 6:36 May attorneys' fees be recovered by a defendant in an ERISA action? ... 6-24

Q 6:37 May attorneys' fees be awarded to a losing party in an ERISA action? ... 6-25

Q 6:38 How is the amount of attorneys' fees to be awarded in an ERISA action determined? ... 6-25

Standard of Judicial Review

Q 6:39 What standard does a court use in reviewing a fiduciary's actions? ... 6-25

Q 6:40 In general, does a court apply a de novo standard or the arbitrary and capricious standard? ... 6-27

Q 6:41 What exceptions are there to the general rule under the *Firestone* case? ... 6-27

Q 6:42 Can plan documents be drafted to raise the standard of deference that a court will give to a fiduciary's determination of a benefit claim? ... 6-28

Steps to Reduce Risks

Q 6:43 How can maintaining records and minutes reduce the risk of fiduciary liability? ... 6-28

Q 6:44 How can maintaining records and minutes reduce the risk of co-fiduciary liability? ... 6-29

Q 6:45 Does consulting an expert reduce the risk of fiduciary liability? ... 6-29

Q 6:46	How do fiduciaries protect themselves from decisions or actions that would constitute a fiduciary breach?	6-29
Q 6:47	Under what circumstances can recusal be a better alternative than resignation?	6-30
Q 6:48	How should a recusal be documented?	6-31
Q 6:49	Is a fiduciary ever required to do more than recuse himself or herself?	6-31
Q 6:50	How can delegation of one's fiduciary duty reduce the risk of fiduciary liability?	6-33

Compliance with Claims Procedure

Q 6:51	What is a benefits claim?	6-33
Q 6:52	When is a benefits claim deemed filed?	6-33
Q 6:53	How are benefit claim decisions typically made?	6-33
Q 6:54	Does a plan need explicit, written procedures for processing claims for benefits and reviewing the denial of claims?	6-34
Q 6:55	When must a claimant be informed that a benefits claim has been denied?	6-35
Q 6:56	What information must a claim denial contain?	6-35
Q 6:57	What are a claimant's procedural rights on an appeal of a claim denial?	6-36
Q 6:58	When must an appeal be decided?	6-36
Q 6:59	What information must a decision on appeal contain?	6-36
Q 6:60	Can a fiduciary's compliance with claims procedures reduce the risk of fiduciary liability?	6-37
Q 6:61	Are any plans exempt from the requirement of providing a reasonable claims procedure?	6-37
Q 6:62	What special rules for claims procedures apply to health maintenance organizations (HMOs)?	6-38
Q 6:63	What special rules for claims procedures apply to collectively bargained plans?	6-38

Nonfiduciary Liability

Q 6:64	Can a nonfiduciary be held liable for a fiduciary breach of duty?	6-39
Q 6:65	Can a nonfiduciary be liable for a prohibited transaction?	6-39
Q 6:66	Can the 20 percent penalty tax be imposed against nonfiduciaries in connection with a fiduciary breach?	6-40

List of Questions

Chapter 7 Investment Issues

How to Select an Investment Manager Under ERISA

Q 7:1	What is the proper method of selecting an investment manager qualified to invest plan assets under ERISA?	7-2
Q 7:2	How should a fiduciary responsible for appointing an investment manager investigate the investment manager's experience, qualifications, and investment approach?	7-3
Q 7:3	What specific types of information should plan fiduciaries solicit in the process of selecting investment managers?	7-5
Q 7:4	What factors should plan fiduciaries consider in developing investment guidelines or other plan objectives for investment managers?	7-9
Q 7:5	Is an investment manager obligated to follow the investment guidelines agreed to between the manager and the plan?	7-10
Q 7:6	How should a plan fiduciary negotiate the investment management agreement?	7-11

How to Monitor an Investment Manager Under ERISA

Q 7:7	Once a plan fiduciary selects an investment manager, is the appointing fiduciary relieved of ERISA fiduciary duty with respect to the delegated investment duties?	7-13
Q 7:8	What specific actions should the appointing fiduciary undertake in monitoring the investment performance of investment managers?	7-14

Investments

Q 7:9	Are plan fiduciaries prohibited from making certain types of investments under ERISA?	7-16
Q 7:10	What factors must a plan fiduciary consider when investing plan assets?	7-16
Q 7:11	How does a fiduciary design an investment strategy for plan assets?	7-17
Q 7:12	What does it mean for a fiduciary to act prudently in connection with investment decisions impacting plan assets?	7-18

Fiduciary Responsibility Answer Book

| Q 7:13 | Must a fiduciary retain an expert when evaluating investments for a plan? | 7-19 |
| Q 7:14 | Must a plan fiduciary follow industry investment standards with respect to its investment decisions? | 7-20 |

Purchasing Annuities

Q 7:15	What is the relevance of selecting an insurance product such as an annuity?	7-21
Q 7:16	How should a plan fiduciary select an annuity provider (e.g., insurance company)?	7-22
Q 7:17	Under what circumstances may a pension plan purchase annuity contracts?	7-23
Q 7:18	Does the purchase of an annuity contract in connection with either the termination of a plan or distribution of benefits from an ongoing plan relieve the plan and its fiduciaries of liability regarding the payment of benefits?	7-24
Q 7:19	Is the Pension Benefit Guaranty Corporation (PBGC) responsible for the payment of benefits after the plan purchases an annuity contract from an insurance company?	7-26
Q 7:20	Are there other special considerations that apply when a plan purchases an annuity contract in connection with a plan termination?	7-26

Guaranteed Investment Contracts (GICs) and Bank Investment Contracts (BICs)

Q 7:21	What is a "guaranteed investment contract" (GIC), and what is a "bank investment contract" (BIC)?	7-28
Q 7:22	What factors should a plan fiduciary consider when selecting a GIC?	7-29
Q 7:23	What factors should a plan fiduciary consider when selecting a BIC?	7-30
Q 7:24	What actions may a plan fiduciary take in connection with a plan investment—such as a GIC—that is issued by a troubled insurance company?	7-30
Q 7:25	How should plan fiduciaries communicate the special nature of GICs to the plan participants?	7-31
Q 7:26	What information regarding a GIC should a plan fiduciary provide to participants?	7-32

List of Questions

Employer Securities and Employer Real Property

Q 7:27	May a plan invest in employer securities or employer real property?	7-33
Q 7:28	What are qualifying employer securities (QES)?	7-34
Q 7:29	What is "qualifying employer real property" (QERP)?	7-37
Q 7:30	What is an "eligible individual account plan"?	7-38
Q 7:31	Are there any restrictions on an eligible individual account plan's investment in QES or QERP?	7-38
Q 7:32	What is an employee stock ownership plan (ESOP)?	7-42
Q 7:33	How does an ESOP acquire employer securities?	7-42
Q 7:34	What does it mean for a plan to purchase or sell QES for "adequate consideration" from a party-in-interest?	7-42
Q 7:35	How are the shares of QES that are allocated to participants' accounts voted in an ESOP?	7-43
Q 7:36	What should a fiduciary do if an ESOP participant does not vote the shares of QES that are passed through to such participant?	7-45
Q 7:37	How does a fiduciary vote the shares of QES held in the ESOP's loan suspense account that are not allocated to participants?	7-48
Q 7:38	What must a fiduciary of a plan that contains QES do when confronted with a tender offer, hostile takeover, corporate control contest, or other potential conflict of interest?	7-48

Social Investing

Q 7:39	What is "social investing"?	7-50
Q 7:40	What are examples of social investing?	7-50
Q 7:41	May fiduciaries of a plan implement an investment policy that has social underpinnings?	7-51
Q 7:42	Is a plan prohibited from investing in a single geographic area?	7-53
Q 7:43	What type of plans have generally followed a strategy of social investing?	7-54

Other Investments

Q 7:44	Are there any restrictions on a plan's investment in securities?	7-55

Fiduciary Responsibility Answer Book

Q 7:45	Are there special considerations or restrictions that apply to a plan's investment in real estate?	7-56
Q 7:46	Are there special considerations or restrictions that apply to a plan's investment in a bank?	7-57
Q 7:47	May a plan fiduciary invest in futures?	7-59
Q 7:48	Are there special considerations and restrictions on investing in foreign securities?	7-60
Q 7:49	Are there any special concerns that apply to investments made by very large pension plans?	7-61
Q 7:50	Are there any special rules that apply to investments by small plans?	7-61

Chapter 8 Plan Trusts and Plan Assets

Plans Subject to ERISA Fiduciary Rules

Q 8:1	In general, what types of plan are subject to fiduciary rules under ERISA?	8-2
Q 8:2	What other fiduciary rules apply if an employee benefit arrangement is not subject to the ERISA fiduciary responsibility rules?	8-2
Q 8:3	Is a plan without common law employees subject to the ERISA fiduciary rules?	8-2
Q 8:4	What is an employee pension benefit plan?	8-3
Q 8:5	Is a severance pay plan a pension plan or a welfare plan subject to ERISA or is it a non-ERISA plan?	8-3
Q 8:6	Is an individual retirement account or annuity (IRA) a pension plan subject to the fiduciary rules of ERISA?	8-5
Q 8:7	When is a tax-sheltered annuity program maintained by a tax-exempt employer under Section 403(b) of the Code a pension plan subject to the fiduciary rules of ERISA?	8-5
Q 8:8	What is an employee welfare benefit plan that is subject to ERISA's fiduciary rules?	8-6
Q 8:9	Are payroll practices treated as welfare plans subject to the fiduciary rules of ERISA?	8-7
Q 8:10	What types of fringe benefits or welfare programs are not treated as welfare plans?	8-8
Q 8:11	Are dependent care assistance programs (DCAPs) welfare plans subject to the fiduciary rules of ERISA?	8-10

List of Questions

Q 8:12	Do ERISA's fiduciary responsibility rules apply if a plan is not maintained by an employer or an employee organization?	8-10
Q 8:13	Are any employee pension or welfare benefit plans not subject to ERISA?	8-11
Q 8:14	Are any employee pension or welfare benefit plans that are subject to ERISA exempt from ERISA's fiduciary responsibility rules?	8-13

Plan Assets

Q 8:15	Of what significance is it whether a plan's investment in another entity is a plan asset?	8-13
Q 8:16	In general, when are participant contributions considered plan assets?	8-14
Q 8:17	Are participant contributions to a cafeteria plan or contributory welfare plan treated as plan assets?	8-15
Q 8:18	May plan expenses be paid out of plan assets?	8-15
Q 8:19	What are the consequences if plan assets are used to pay improper expenses?	8-16
Q 8:20	What are settlor expenses?	8-16
Q 8:21	Should the plan documents provide that plan expenses may be paid out of plan assets?	8-16
Q 8:22	What are direct plan expenses?	8-16
Q 8:23	Can a part of an insurance policy be a plan asset for fiduciary purposes, even though it is not a plan asset for prohibited transaction purposes?	8-17

Plan in Writing

Q 8:24	Can an unwritten policy be an ERISA plan?	8-17
Q 8:25	Can informal documents provide the terms of a plan?	8-17
Q 8:26	What risks are there if there is no written plan document?	8-18
Q 8:27	Does the employer bear the risk that written descriptions of plan benefits are incorrect or not up-to-date?	8-18

General Trust Requirements

Q 8:28	What is ERISA's trust requirement?	8-19
Q 8:29	When must assets of employee benefit plans be held in trust?	8-19
Q 8:30	What is ERISA's trust exemption relating to plan assets consisting of insurance contracts or policies?	8-20

Fiduciary Responsibility Answer Book

Q 8:31	What is ERISA's trust exemption relating to plan assets of or that are held by an insurance company?	8-21
Q 8:32	Are the underlying assets of an insurance company that issues group annuity contracts in which plans invest considered plan assets?	8-21
Q 8:33	What is ERISA's trust exemption relating to mutual fund investments treated as tax-favored annuity contracts?	8-23
Q 8:34	What is ERISA's trust exemption relating to assets of Keogh plans and individual retirement accounts? . . .	8-23
Q 8:35	Must cafeteria plans and contributory welfare plans hold participant contributions in trust?	8-24
Q 8:36	May ERISA plans use custodial accounts instead of a trusteed accounts?	8-24
Q 8:37	Who may act as a trustee of an ERISA plan?	8-25
Q 8:38	How are plan trustees appointed?	8-26
Q 8:39	What rules govern the trust agreement, and what are examples of provisions that should be addressed in a trust agreement?	8-26
Q 8:40	May securities owned by a plan be held in a street name or in the name of a nominee?	8-28

Powers and Duties of Trustees

Q 8.41	What are the powers of a trustee as to the management and control of plan assets under ERISA?	8-29
Q 8:42	What is the trustee's responsibility with respect to plan assets if the trustee is subject to the direction of a named fiduciary?	8-30
Q 8:43	What is the trustee's responsibility with respect to plan assets if the authority to manage, acquire, or dispose of plan assets is delegated to an investment manager? .	8-31
Q 8:44	May the responsibilities of a trustee be allocated or delegated?	8-32

Exclusive Benefit and Anti-Inurement

Q 8:45	What are ERISA's exclusive benefit and anti-inurement rules governing plan assets?	8-33
Q 8:46	What are the exceptions to ERISA's exclusive benefit rule?	8-33
Q 8:47	What are the rules governing the reversion of residual plan assets to the employer following the termination of a single employer pension plan?	8-34

List of Questions

Q 8:48	What is the rule that permits the transfer of excess pension assets to a retiree health account?	8-35
Q 8:49	How are plan assets allocated following the termination of a pension plan?	8-36
Q 8:50	How are plan assets distributed following the termination of a welfare plan?	8-36

Look-Through Rule

Q 8:51	What is the look-through rule?	8-37
Q 8:52	When does the look-through rule apply?	8-37
Q 8:53	What is an equity interest?	8-38
Q 8:54	What is a publicly offered security?	8-38
Q 8:55	Which equity investments are generally exempt from the look-through rule?	8-39
Q 8:56	What types of investments fall within an unsafe harbor and are never exempt from the look-through rule?	8-39
Q 8:57	When is equity participation in an entity by benefit plan investors considered to be significant?	8-40
Q 8:58	What is a benefit plan investor?	8-41

Operating Companies

Q 8:59	What is an operating company?	8-42
Q 8:60	What is a real estate operating company (REOC)?	8-43
Q 8:61	What is a venture capital operating company (VCOC)?	8-45
Q 8:62	Can an operating company (including a REOC or a VCOC) ever be subject to the look-through rule?	8-47

Joint Ownership and Investment Pools

Q 8.63	In determining what are plan assets, how must an asset owned jointly by a plan and other parties be counted?	8-47
Q 8:64	In determining what are plan assets, how must an equity interest whose value relates to identified property owned by the entity be counted?	8-48
Q 8.65	If a plan acquires a guaranteed governmental mortgage pool certificate, are the underlying mortgages plan assets?	8-49

Miscellaneous Plan Asset Issues

Q 8:66	Is a stop-loss insurance policy purchased by an employer sponsoring a welfare benefit plan considered a plan asset?	8-49
Q 8:67	Is the cash value portion of a split dollar life insurance policy considered a plan asset?	8-50

Bonding

Q 8:68	What is ERISA's bonding requirement?	8-51
Q 8:69	What are the exceptions to ERISA's bonding requirements?	8-51

Chapter 1

Introduction

The Employee Retirement Income Security Act of 1974, as amended (ERISA) imposes a vast array of technical and complex rules with which employee benefit plans must comply. Overlaying these rules are the principles regarding the fiduciary's standard of conduct that guide trustees, administrators, and other managers of employee benefit plans. This book explains ERISA's fiduciary duties and responsibilities pertaining to the administration of employee benefit plans and the management of plan assets. It also assists plan fiduciaries in understanding ERISA's fiduciary requirements and provides them with the knowledge necessary to discharge their responsibility and avoid liability. Any person with a relationship to an employee benefit plan (whether pension or welfare plan) should read this book in order to better understand the technical and complex fiduciary rules under ERISA that apply to a plan and plan fiduciaries. These persons include, for example:

- Plan participants and beneficiaries
- Plan administrators
- Plan trustees
- Investment managers
- Service providers for plans
- Members of plan committees (e.g., investment committees, administrative committees)

- Employers who sponsor, maintain, or contribute to plans, and those employers' boards of directors
- Attorneys, accountants, consultants, actuaries, and other professionals who advise plans, plan fiduciaries, and sponsoring employers.

Q 1:1 What is a fiduciary?

The term "fiduciary" is broadly defined under ERISA to encompass any person or entity that:

1. Exercises any discretionary authority or control with respect to management of an employee benefit plan, or exercises any authority or control with respect to the management or disposition of its assets;
2. Renders investment advice as to the plan's assets for a fee or other compensation, or has any authority or responsibility to do so; or
3. Has any discretionary authority or responsibility in the administration of the plan.

[ERISA § 3(21)(A)]

This definition generally includes plan trustees, plan administrators, members of plan investment or administrative committees, investment managers, and any person who selects or appoints such individuals. The term fiduciary is intentionally broad so that the standard of conduct prescribed under ERISA (known as ERISA's fiduciary duties) applies to a broad range of individuals in order to hold them responsible for the misuse of plan assets, losses to the plans arising out of the fiduciary's violation of ERISA, or other wrongdoings relating to the plans. (See, generally, Chapter 2 regarding who is a fiduciary.)

Q 1:2 What laws govern the conduct of fiduciaries?

ERISA sets forth a standard of conduct that a plan fiduciary is bound to follow. In discharging his or her duties with respect to a plan, a fiduciary must do the following:

1. Act solely in the interest of plan participants and their beneficiaries;
2. Act for the exclusive purpose of providing benefits to plan participants and their beneficiaries and defraying reasonable expenses of administering the plan;
3. Exercise the same care, skill, prudence, and diligence that a prudent person acting in a like capacity and familiar with such matters would exercise in the conduct of an enterprise of a like character and with like aims;
4. If the fiduciary is involved in investing plan assets, diversify plan investments so as to minimize the risk of large losses (unless it is clearly not prudent to do so under the circumstances); and
5. Act in accordance with the documents and instruments governing the plan (insofar as the documents and instruments are consistent with ERISA).

[ERISA § 404(a)(1)] (See, generally, Chapter 3 regarding fiduciary duties under ERISA).

Although ERISA is the primary statute that governs the conduct of fiduciaries, a fiduciary must also be familiar with relevant provisions of other laws that may apply to his or her conduct. These include, for example, the Internal Revenue Code (Code) (particularly in the case of tax-qualified pension plans); various labor laws (e.g., the Age Discrimination in Employment Act (ADEA), the Americans with Disabilities Act of 1990 (ADA), Family and Medical Leave Act (FMLA), and the Labor-Management Relations Act of 1947 (LMRA or Taft-Hartley Act)); certain securities laws (e.g., the Securities Act of 1933, the Securities and Exchange Act of 1934, the Investment Advisors Act of 1940, and the Investment Company Act of 1940); state laws that are not preempted by ERISA; banking laws (e.g., FDIC regulations); insurance requirements; and certain federal criminal statutes. If a fiduciary is not familiar with the requirements of the relevant laws, he or she is obligated to consult with others who are knowledgeable in such laws.

Q 1:3 Which plans are subject to ERISA's fiduciary rules?

ERISA's fiduciary rules reach and impact a broad range of plans. The term "plan" under ERISA includes "any plan, fund, or program

Q 1:3 **Fiduciary Responsibility Answer Book**

. . . established or maintained by an employer or by an employee organization, or by both" to provide benefits—either in the form of pension or welfare benefits—to its participants and beneficiaries. [ERISA §§ 3(1) and 3(2)] A pension plan includes any plan, fund, or program that provides retirement income to employees or results in the deferral of income by employees for periods extending to or beyond the termination of employment. [ERISA § 3(2)(A)] A welfare plan includes any plan, fund, or program that provides virtually any benefit other than a pension benefit. Welfare plans may provide, through the purchase of insurance or otherwise, medical, surgical, or hospital care or benefits; benefits in the event of sickness, accident, disability, death, or unemployment; vacation benefits; apprenticeship or other training programs; day-care centers; scholarship funds; prepaid legal services; or any benefit described in Section 302(c) of the Labor Management Relations Act of 1947 (29 USCS § 186(c)) (other than pensions on retirement or death, and insurance to provide such pensions). [ERISA § 3(1)]

Certain arrangements are excluded from ERISA's definitions of pension plan, welfare plan, or plan (whether pension or welfare). For example, bonus programs that do not systematically defer income to or beyond an employee's termination of employment or that do not provide retirement income, individual retirement accounts, certain tax-sheltered annuities under Section 403(b) of the Code, and certain supplemental payment plans are *not* ERISA pension plans. [DOL Reg § 2510.3-2(c), (d), (f), and (g)]

Specifically excluded from the definition of welfare plan under ERISA are payroll practices that are:

1. Payments by an employer of compensation on account of work performed by an employee (including compensation that exceeds the employees normal rate of compensation, such as overtime pay and shift, holiday, or weekend premiums);

2. Payments of an employee's normal compensation, out of the employer's general assets, due to the employee's disability (i.e., the employee is physically or mentally unable to perform his or her duties, or is otherwise absent for medical reasons (e.g., pregnancy, physical examination, or psychiatric treatment)); and

3. Payment of compensation out of the employer's general assets when the employee performs no duties due to, for example, vacation, holiday, military leave, jury duty, training, or education. [DOL Reg § 2510.3-1(b)]

In addition, a welfare plan under ERISA does not include certain on-premises facilities (e.g., recreation, dining, first aid or other facilities (other than day-care centers)); holiday gifts (e.g., turkeys at Thanksgiving); sales to employees; hiring hall facilities; remembrance funds; strike funds; industry advancement programs; certain group insurance programs (i.e., voluntary programs for employees that are not endorsed by or contributed to by an employer, and where the employer's sole functions are to permit the insurer to publicize the program, to collect premiums through payroll deductions or dues checkoffs, and to remit them to the insurer); and unfunded scholarship programs. [DOL Reg § 2510.3-1(c) through (k)]

Although ERISA requires a plan to be in writing, no written plan document need exist for there to be a plan for ERISA purposes. The courts have generally interpreted the term plan broadly to include very informal employment arrangements and practices, even if unwritten. [*See, e.g.*, Adams v Avondale Indus, Inc, 905 F2d 943 (6th Cir), *cert denied*, 498 US 984 (1990) (ERISA coverage is not necessarily avoided by the failure to put the plan in writing); Williams v Wright, 927 F2d 1540 (11th Cir 1991) (Although no formal plan document existed other than a letter describing the retirement-type benefits to be paid to an employee out of the company's general assets, this letter created a plan subject to ERISA's fiduciary requirements)] However, certain one-time severance-type payments may not necessarily constitute a plan subject to ERISA. [*See, e.g.*, Fort Halifax Packing Co v Coyne, 482 US 1 (1987)]

Basically, ERISA's fiduciary rules reach all pension and welfare plans except:

- Governmental plans
- Church plans (where no election to be covered by ERISA has been made under Section 410(d) of the Code)
- Plans maintained outside the United States primarily for the benefit of nonresident aliens

- Plans maintained solely to comply with workers' compensation, unemployment compensation, or disability insurance laws
- Excess benefit plans (unfunded plans maintained solely to provide benefits to certain employees in excess of the limitations on contributions and benefits under Section 415 of the Code)

[ERISA §§ 4(b), 3(36)]

In addition, plans that do not cover employees are not subject to ERISA. [DOL Reg § 2510.3-3(b)] Therefore, plans that cover only sole proprietors and their spouses, owners and their spouses (provided that the employer is wholly owned by the owner or by the owner and his or her spouse), or only partners are not subject to ERISA since these individuals are not considered employees. [DOL Reg §§ 2510.3-3(b), 2510.3-3(c); Schwartz v Gordon, 761 F2d 864 (2d Cir 1985) (Self-employed physician who maintained own Keogh plan, where he was the sole participant, could not assert breach of fiduciary duty under ERISA against the bank who was the custodian of the plan assets and against the broker who invested the plan assets. This was because the Keogh plan was not a plan under ERISA since it did not cover an employee. The court found that while the Keogh plan received similar tax treatment to other plans, ERISA's protections were unnecessary because the self-employed physician had control of the funds and over the plan.)] (See Qs 8:1 through 8:14 regarding what is a plan under ERISA.)

Q 1:4 Who enforces the fiduciary rules?

The U.S. Department of Labor (DOL) plays the major role in the enforcement of the fiduciary rules of ERISA. For example, ERISA grants investigative authority to the Secretary of Labor to make investigations, require the production of books and records, and take certain other actions (e.g., enter places, inspect books and records, question persons) as the Secretary deems necessary to determine if a violation of ERISA's fiduciary rules has occurred. [ERISA § 504] The Secretary of Labor is also authorized to coordinate employee benefit plan responsibility and enforcement with other governmental agencies, and to share information with these agencies. [ERISA § 506]

The Secretary of Labor also enforces ERISA's fiduciary rules in certain situations by assessing penalties on plans, their administrators, and other persons. For example, the DOL may assess a civil penalty of 20 percent of the amount payable pursuant to a court order or settlement agreement with the DOL for a breach of fiduciary duty (or knowing participation therein). [ERISA § 502(l)(1)] (See Qs 6:15 and 6:16 regarding the 20 percent civil penalty.)

The DOL also enforces the prohibited transaction rules, grants exemptive relief from these provisions, and, with respect to non-qualifed pension plans or welfare plans, imposes a civil penalty for their violation. The Internal Revenue Service (IRS), however, may also enforce these rules (which apply solely to tax-qualified pension plans and individual retirement accounts as opposed to all ERISA plans) by imposing penalties (excise taxes) on disqualified persons for prohibited transactions. (See Q 5:8 regarding penalties for prohibited transactions.)

Nevertheless, despite the DOL's enforcement authority, the determinations of whether a person is a fiduciary, whether a plan is subject to ERISA, and whether a person breaches his or her fiduciary duties—as well as most other questions under ERISA—are ultimately left to the federal courts. A lawsuit to establish the liability of a fiduciary under ERISA may be brought by the Secretary of Labor, any plan participant or beneficiary, or by another plan fiduciary (e.g., with respect to the enforcement of the co-fiduciary liability requirements). [ERISA § 502(a)]

In actions brought by participants or beneficiaries (other than to cover benefits due under a plan) and in all actions brought by fiduciaries, copies of the complaint in a lawsuit must be served by certified mail upon both the Secretary of Labor and the Secretary of Treasury. Each then has the discretion to intervene in the proceeding (except that the Secretary of Treasury may not intervene in an action under Part 4 of Title I of ERISA relating to fiduciary duties). [ERISA § 502(h)]

Q 1:5 When must a fiduciary become knowledgeable about the fiduciary rules?

Once a person becomes a fiduciary under ERISA, that person is bound to follow the statutory responsibilities setting forth the standard of conduct that the fiduciary must maintain. Because these rules apply immediately upon becoming a fiduciary, the person who becomes a fiduciary should understand them prior to becoming a fiduciary or, at the very latest, when the person actually becomes a fiduciary. ERISA does not authorize a grace period for a fiduciary to get up to speed on understanding the fiduciary rules.

Q 1:6 Can a fiduciary be personally liable for a violation of fiduciary responsibility?

Yes. If a fiduciary breaches any of the responsibilities, obligations, or duties imposed upon him or her under ERISA as a fiduciary, he or she will be personally liable to reimburse the plan for any losses resulting from the breach. [ERISA § 409(a)] The fiduciary will be responsible for restoring to the plan any profits that he or she made through the use of plan assets. A civil action may be brought by a participant or beneficiary, or by another fiduciary. [ERISA § 502(a)(2)] In addition, the fiduciary will be subject to equitable or remedial relief as a court may deem appropriate, such as removal of the fiduciary. [ERISA § 409(a); Oscar A Samos, MD, Inc v Dean Witter Reynolds, Inc, 772 FSupp 715 (D RI 1991)] (See, generally, Chapter 6 regarding fiduciary liability.) Even if a fiduciary delegates his fiduciary duties to others, he does not completely relieve himself of his fiduciary duties—he is obligated to monitor the performance of those to whom the duties have been delegated. (See Qs 4:1 and 4:4 through 4:8 regarding the delegation of ERISA fiduciary duties and the duty to monitor.)

The U.S. Supreme Court held that a nonfiduciary who does not profit from a breach of fiduciary duty is not liable for monetary damages resulting from his or her actions. [Mertens v Hewitt Assocs 124 LEd 2d 161 (1993)] (See Q 5:9 regarding nonfiduciary liability.)

Q 1:7 Do the ERISA fiduciary rules differ from the common law fiduciary rules?

Yes, to a certain extent they do. While Congress acknowledged that the fiduciary responsibility provisions of ERISA incorporated various principles of the fiduciary rules under the common law of trusts, it also modified the common law of trusts in a manner that was appropriate for employee benefit plans. [S Rep No 127, 93d Cong, 1st Sess 30 (1973); HR Rep No 533, 93d Cong, 1st Sess 11 (1973); HR Rep No 1280, 93d Cong, 2d Sess 301 (1974)] Under ERISA preemption, the ERISA fiduciary duty requirements generally supersede the common law of trusts and exclusively set forth the standard of conduct for fiduciaries. [ERISA § 514(a)] (See Qs 3:32 and 3:33 regarding ERISA preemption.)

For example, the standard of care imposed on fiduciaries under ERISA is generally stricter than the usual "prudent person" rule embodied in the common law of trusts. In general, the common law of trusts requires trustees to meet the standard of care, skill, and caution of a prudent person, without regard to a specialized level of expertise, while ERISA requires trustees (as well as other fiduciaries) to meet the standard of a "prudent expert"—that is, someone familiar with matters relating to employee benefit plans. (See Qs 3:6 and 3:7 regarding the prudent expert standard.)

Another distinction may be found with respect to the diversification requirement. Although ERISA expressly requires diversification of plan assets, the common law of trusts has historically not imposed upon trustees the duty to diversify (although there is a growing consensus in the common law that the duty of prudence includes the duty to diversify). [III Scott, *Law of Trusts* §§ 227 and 228] (See Q 3:11 regarding the diversification requirement.)

In the case of sanctions for breaches of fiduciary duty, some courts have looked to traditional trust law for guidance in interpreting the equitable nature of certain ERISA actions, whether equitable relief is appropriate, or whether a fiduciary has an implied right of contribution and/or indemnity against a co-fiduciary. (See Q 6:32 regarding the right of contribution or indemnity against co-fiduciaries.) On the other hand, other courts have rejected traditional trust law in instances where to follow it would expressly violate ERISA. [*See, e.g.*, Guidry v Sheet Metal Workers Nat Pension Fund, 493 US 365 (1990) (where the court found it inappropriate to use the equitable relief provision under ERISA and allow the use of a constructive trust, because it would weaken ERISA's prohibition on the assignment or alienation

Q 1:8   Fiduciary Responsibility Answer Book

of pension benefits)] (See, generally, Qs 6:5 through 6:8 regarding equitable remedies.)

Q 1:8   Must a person consent to be a fiduciary to be treated as a fiduciary?

Generally, no. ERISA does not require a person to consent to be a fiduciary, except that an investment manager and qualified professional asset manager (QPAM) must each consent to be a fiduciary in order to qualify as such under ERISA. Because fiduciary status is determined by a person's function rather than title, in most instances, a person will become a fiduciary if he or she performs duties that are fiduciary in nature regardless of whether the person consents to becoming a fiduciary. (See Qs 2:3 through 2:7 regarding fiduciary status and fiduciary functions.)

If fiduciary duties such as investment responsibilities are exercised by plan participants and beneficiaries with respect to their own individual accounts, they, unlike other persons exercising such responsibilities, will not be deemed to be fiduciaries under ERISA. (See Qs 4:27 through 4:49 regarding participant-directed investments under Section 404(c) of ERISA.)

However, an ERISA-qualified investment manager must acknowledge in writing that it is a fiduciary with respect to a plan. [ERISA § 3(38)] (See Qs 2:24, 2:25, and 4:14 through 4:24 regarding investment managers.) Similarly, a QPAM—generally a fiduciary, since it has the power to manage plan assets—must also acknowledge in writing that it is a fiduciary. [PTCE 84-14, 49 FR 9494, as amended by 50 FR 41430] (See Qs 4:25, 4:26, and 5:14 regarding QPAMs.) If an investment manager or a QPAM does not acknowledge that it is a fiduciary, it will not be an ERISA-qualified investment manager or QPAM. It may, however, still be a fiduciary if it performs fiduciary functions (e.g., investing plan assets).

Q 1:9   Can a fiduciary be liable for an unwitting violation of ERISA's fiduciary duties?

Yes, even if a fiduciary is unaware that he or she is violating ERISA's fiduciary duties, the fiduciary may still be liable for the violation. The

ERISA standard of conduct is an objective one—good faith is not sufficient. [See, e.g., *Katsoras v Cody*, 744 F2d 270, 279 (2d Cir), *cert denied*, 469 US 1072 (1984) (A fiduciary's lack of familiarity with investments is no excuse; under an objective standard, a fiduciary must be judged according to the standards of others acting in a like capacity and familiar with such matters. If the fiduciary cannot adequately and objectively judge the merits of a particular course of action, the fiduciary is not off the hook simply because it did not know that it breached ERISA duties. In this instance, the fiduciary has an obligation to seek outside assistance.)]

However, in certain cases of co-fiduciary liability, the fiduciary must be aware that it is involved in a breach of fiduciary duty. For instance, co-fiduciary liability will be imposed if the fiduciary participates knowingly in, knowingly undertakes to conceal, or has knowledge of an act or omission of another fiduciary that is a breach of fiduciary duty, unless he or she makes reasonable efforts under the circumstances to remedy the breach. [ERISA § 405(a)(1) and (3)] (See Qs 4:9 through 4:12 regarding co-fiduciary liability.)

Chapter 2

Who Is a Fiduciary?

Individuals and entities that deal with plans may, as a result of their duties, position, or status, be fiduciaries with respect to an ERISA employee benefit plan. This chapter discusses how to determine when these individuals or entities are plan fiduciaries.

Determining Fiduciary Status	2-1
Named Fiduciaries	2-9
Plan Trustees	2-11
Plan Sponsors	2-13
Plan Administrators	2-16
Investment Managers	2-17
Broker-Dealers	2-18
Professional Service Providers	2-19
Third-Party Administrators	2-22
Insurance Companies and Brokers	2-23
Plan Participants	2-25
Fiduciaries for Collectively Bargained Plans	2-25

Determining Fiduciary Status

Q 2:1 Who is a fiduciary under ERISA?

A person is a fiduciary of a plan under ERISA to the extent such person:

1. Exercises any discretionary authority or discretionary control over management of the plan;
2. Exercises any authority or control over the management or disposition of its assets;
3. Renders investment advice for a fee or other compensation, direct or indirect, with respect to any moneys or other property of the plan, or has any authority or responsibility to do so; or
4. Has any discretionary authority or responsibility in the administration of the plan.

[ERISA § 3(21)(A)]

Example 1. An auditing firm limited the services it provided to a plan, serving only as an independent outside auditor for annual audits. The firm failed to inform the plan's retirement board that the plan's investment advisors were trading in "naked options," a type of investment that violated plan guidelines. These investments ultimately resulted in large losses. Even if the retirement board relied on the audits, the auditing firm was not a fiduciary, because it had no control over plan assets and had not performed in any capacity beyond that of independent outside auditor. [Pension Plan of Public Serv Co of New Hampshire v KPMG Peat Marwick, 815 FSupp 52 (D NH 1993)]

Example 2. An employer's accountants, as well as its controlling shareholders and its directors, engaged in complex commercial transactions and acts of self-dealing by reason of their control of the assets of the plan. The accountants were fiduciaries, and breached their fiduciary duty. [Martin v Feilen, 965 F2d 660 (8th Cir 1992), *cert denied* 113 SCt 979 (1993)]

Q 2:2 What types of persons can be fiduciaries under ERISA?

The term "person" includes, for example, an individual, partnership, corporation, joint venture, trust, estate, unincorporated organization, association, or employee organization. [ERISA § 3(9)]

A person may become a fiduciary either by being named as a fiduciary in a plan document (or pursuant to a procedure specified in the plan document), or by performing any of the fiduciary functions listed in Question 2:1.

Example 1. Abbey participated in a fully insured retirement plan sponsored by a professional association in which his employer, an accounting firm, was a participating employer. Abbey left the firm in October 1983. When Abbey applied for payment, the insurer informed him that no funds would be released to him until the employer delivered a "Notice of Change" form, which the insurer then sent to the employer. Despite repeated requests by Abbey and his attorney, the employer did not complete the form until May 1985, after Abbey sued. The employer was a fiduciary under ERISA. In delaying the completion of the form, it exercised actual control over the disposition of plan assets. Fiduciary status "must be determined by focusing on the function performed, rather than on the title held." [Blatt v Marshall & Lassman, 812 F2d 810, 812 (2d Cir 1987)]

Example 2. Wanda Jo was never formally appointed as a fiduciary or trustee of a pension plan, yet she repeatedly signed documents that identified her as a trustee or administrator of the plan. Specifically, Wanda Jo signed a deed as trustee conveying land held by the plan. She also was listed on numerous federal forms and returns as trustee or administrator. Wanda Jo was a fiduciary; formal appointment was not a prerequisite to fiduciary liability. [Donovan v Mercer, 747 F2d 304 (5th Cir 1984)]

Example 3. Edward D. Jones & Co. was a brokerage firm. Jack was the sales representative for Jones and sold investments to the trustees of a profit-sharing plan. Jack regularly met with the trustees and presented a choice among a few securities recommended by him specifically for the plan. The trustees would confer privately and then advise Jack whether they had decided to buy any of the recommended securities. When Jack was transferred to another office, Gary took over the account, increasing the share of the plan's investment purchased through Jones from 50 percent to 99 percent. Gary provided the trustees with portfolio summaries for the investments purchased through Jones (but not for investments purchased elsewhere), even after the trustees lost confidence in Gary and ceased buying through Jones. Later, the plan lost money on some of the investments recommended by Gary and purchased through Jones. Jones was not a fiduciary. Neither it, nor Jack nor Gary had any discretion with respect to the disposition of assets, and there was no understanding that Jones's sales pitches would be the primary basis for plan investments. [Farm King Supply, Inc Integrated Profit Sharing Plan & Trust v Edward D Jones & Co, 884 F2d 288 (7th Cir 1989)]

Each individual member of a board or plan committee is a fiduciary to the extent he or she actually exercises any authority or otherwise has discretion to act with respect to a plan.

Example. Gary was the trustee of an employer's qualified employee stock ownership plan, and bore responsibility for the investment of plan assets. Gary also was the corporate secretary and senior vice president of the employer. Harris was the president, the CEO and a more-than-10-percent shareholder of the employer. Wesley was one of several members of the employer's board of directors.

The plan documents authorized the board of directors to select the trustees and appoint a successor, directed the appointment of a retirement committee to administer the plan and directed the establishment of a funding policy and its communication to the trustee. The trustee had responsibility for periodically valuing the plan assets at fair market value.

Gary and Harris caused the plan to acquire stock of the employer from themselves and other directors at prices in excess of fair market value. Moreover, the plan made a loan to Harris, even though the loan did not satisfy the conditions imposed by the plan documents.

The board of directors, including Wesley, unanimously approved the appointment of Gary as trustee. Gary had no training or experience in managing an employee plan or investing plan assets. The board never reviewed the performance of the plan investments or otherwise monitored Gary's performance as trustee, and in fact ignored an internal auditor's report and comments of a state regulatory authority indicating irregularities in the investment of plan assets.

The United States Department of Labor (DOL) sued Gary, Harris and the directors for breach of fiduciary duty. DOL reached a settlement with all parties except Wesley. The court found that Wesley was a fiduciary as a member of the board of directors, and was jointly and severally liable for any losses resulting from the fiduciary breach. [Martin v Harline, 15 EBC(BNA) 1138 (D Utah 1992)]

Planning Pointer. When an individual is appointed as a fiduciary (or as a member of a plan committee that is a fiduciary), the new fiduciary should be made aware that he or she is assuming fiduciary functions, with the risk of fiduciary liability. The individual should also be made generally aware of any fiduciary insurance coverage that has been provided, and limitations on that coverage. The person or entity appointing the new fiduciary may wish to furnish this information in writing at the time of appointment, and obtain a written acknowledgment from the new fiduciary.

A person who has been convicted of any of a wide range of crimes, including robbery, bribery, extortion, and fraud, is not permitted to serve as a fiduciary for a period of 13 years after the conviction or the end of imprisonment for the crime, whichever is later. [ERISA § 411(a)] In addition, equitable remedies for egregious breaches of fiduciary duty have included temporarily or permanently barring individuals from serving as fiduciaries. [ERISA § 409(a); Martin v Feilen, 965 F2d 660 (8th Cir 1992), *cert denied*, 113 SCt 979 (1993) (permanent bar)] (See the discussion of equitable remedies for fiduciary breaches at Qs 6:5 through 6:8.)

Q 2:3 Does a person's title or function govern fiduciary status?

Under ERISA's broad definition of "fiduciary," fiduciary status is determined by the person's function rather than title. Under this functional approach, any person will be a fiduciary if he or she actually exercises any authority or otherwise has discretion to act with respect to a plan. The term "fiduciary" can encompass plan sponsors (whether an employer or employee organization), boards of directors of companies sponsoring plans, plan committees (such as investment or administrative committees), bank or individual trustees, investment managers (which include registered investment advisers, banks, trust companies, and insurance carriers), administrative service providers, employees, consultants, attorneys, accountants, plan professionals, and plan employees (and each person who selects, appoints, and supervises or monitors the performance of any of these persons). [DOL Reg §§ 2509.75-5 & 2509.75-8]

In particular, a plan committee (often called a benefits committee, a retirement committee, a retirement board, a plan investment committee or the like) appointed by the governing board of the employer may very well constitute a fiduciary by reason of having discretion to act with respect to a plan. Moreover, the individual members of such a committee are most likely fiduciaries if the committee is a fiduciary. [See Martin v Harline, 15 EBC(BNA) 1138 (D Utah 1992) (individual member of the board of directors)]

Q 2:4 What types of activities will typically render a person a fiduciary of a plan under ERISA?

Any activity performed by a person that is within the scope of the functions described in Question 2:1 will render a person a fiduciary with respect to the plan. Any person becomes a fiduciary if he or she performs (or has the authority or responsibility to perform) any activity relating to the management, investment, or administration of a plan. These activities include, for example:

- Appointing other plan fiduciaries,
- Delegating responsibility to or allocating duties among other plan fiduciaries,
- Selecting and monitoring plan investment vehicles,
- Acquiring or disposing of plan assets,
- Interpreting plan provisions, and
- Making decisions under the plan.

A person who only performs activities of a purely ministerial nature (such as calculating benefits, processing claims, and maintaining records) generally is not a fiduciary of a plan under ERISA. (See the discussion of purely ministerial acts that are not fiduciary in nature at Q 2:7.)

Q 2:5 What types of offices or positions result in fiduciary status?

Some offices or positions of an employee benefit plan, by their very nature, require persons who hold them to perform one or more of the fiduciary functions described in Question 2:1. For example, a plan administrator of a plan must, by the very nature of his or her position, have discretionary authority or discretionary responsibility in the administration of the plan. Persons who hold such positions will therefore be fiduciaries.

Other offices and positions should be examined, on a case-by-case basis, to determine whether they involve the performance of any of the functions described in Question 2:1. For example, a plan might designate as a "benefit supervisor" a plan employee whose sole function is to calculate the amount of benefits to which each plan participant is entitled in accordance with a mathematical formula contained in the written instrument pursuant to which the plan is maintained. The benefit supervisor, after calculating the benefits, would then inform the plan administrator of the results of his or her calculations, and the plan administrator would authorize the payment of benefits to a particular plan participant. Since the benefit supervisor does not exercise any *discretionary* authority in performing the benefit computation, or any of the other functions described in Question 2:1, the benefit supervisor *would not* be a plan fiduciary. [DOL Reg § 2509.75-8, D-3]

However, the plan might designate as a "benefit supervisor" a plan employee who has the final authority to authorize or disallow benefit payments in cases where a dispute exists as to the interpretation of plan provisions relating to eligibility for benefits. Under these circumstances, the benefit supervisor *would* be a plan fiduciary, since the benefit supervisor exercises discretionary authority in the administration of the plan and exercises control over the disposition of plan assets. [DOL Reg § 2509.75-8, D-3]

Q 2:6 When can a person be a fiduciary only for a limited purpose?

A person can be a fiduciary for a limited purpose only, such as having responsibility for managing a limited portion of the plan assets, or for delegating fiduciary responsibility to another person. [ERISA § 405(b); DOL Reg § 2509.75-8, D-4] For example, an investment manager, as described in Questions 2:24 and 2:25, might have responsibility for only a portion of plan assets.

If the plan so provides, any person or group of persons may serve in more than one fiduciary capacity (including, for example, serving both as trustee and administrator). [ERISA § 402(c)(1)] Fiduciary responsibilities that do not involve the management and control of plan assets may be allocated among named fiduciaries, and named fiduciaries may designate persons other than named fiduciaries to carry out fiduciary responsibilities (if the plan document expressly provides procedures for such allocation or designation). In these circumstances, the person delegating fiduciary responsibility to another has direct fiduciary responsibility only for the prudence of the initial delegation and for prudently monitoring the continued delegation. (See the discussion of co-fiduciary liability at Qs 4:9 through 4:12.) [ERISA § 405; DOL Reg § 2509.75-8, D-4, FR-12, & FR-16]

Q 2:7 Can a person ever be a fiduciary if the person does not perform one or more of the fiduciary functions described in Section 3(21)(A) of ERISA?

Generally, no. Unless a person is a named fiduciary, the person will be a fiduciary only if the person performs one or more of the fiduciary functions described in Section 3(21)(A) of ERISA, as set forth in Question 2:1. (See the discussion of named fiduciaries at Qs 2:9 through 2:14.)

Those performing purely ministerial functions within guidelines established by others are not plan fiduciaries. DOL regulations list the following functions as ministerial and, therefore, nonfiduciary in nature:

1. Application of rules to determine eligibility for participation or benefits;
2. Calculation of service and compensation for benefit purposes;
3. Preparing employee communications material;
4. Maintaining participants' service and employment records;
5. Preparing reports required by government agencies;
6. Calculating benefits;
7. Explaining the plan to new participants and advising participants of their rights and options under the plan;
8. Collecting contributions and applying them as specified in the plan;
9. Preparing reports covering participants' benefits;
10. Processing claims; and

11. Making recommendations to others for decisions with respect to plan administration.

[DOL Reg § 2509.75-8, D-2]

Planning Pointer. An individual who performs only these ministerial duties and who does not have or exercise any fiduciary powers may still have to be bonded, as required under Section 412 of ERISA, if he or she handles funds of the plan. (See the discussion of bonding at Qs 8:68 and 8:69.)

Q 2:8 Must an employee benefit plan have a specified number of fiduciaries?

No. There is no minimum or maximum required number of fiduciaries that an employee benefit plan must have. Each plan, however, must have at least one named fiduciary who serves as plan administrator and, if plan assets are held in trust, the plan must have at least one trustee. (See the discussion of when plan assets must be held in trust at Qs 8:28 through 8:35.) If these requirements are met, a plan is not limited in the number of its fiduciaries and may, therefore, have as few or as many fiduciaries as are necessary for the plan's prudent operation and administration. [DOL Reg § 2509.75-8, FR-12]

Named Fiduciaries

Q 2:9 What is a named fiduciary?

A named fiduciary is a fiduciary who is either designated in the plan document (or summary plan description) as the named fiduciary or designated as such by an employer and/or employee organization pursuant to a procedure specified in the plan. Common examples of named fiduciaries are the sponsoring employer, the employer's board of directors, a joint board of union and management trustees, and independent professionals (such as a bank or insurance company).

A plan governed by ERISA must provide for one or more named fiduciaries. [ERISA § 402(a)]

Q 2:10   Fiduciary Responsibility Answer Book

Q 2:10   What are the duties of a named fiduciary?

A named fiduciary is jointly and severally responsible with co-fiduciaries for controlling and managing the operation and administration of a plan. A named fiduciary must appoint trustees who have responsibility over plan assets, unless the plan document designates the trustees. [ERISA § 403(a)] A named fiduciary also has the responsibility to hear benefit and claims appeals of participants and beneficiaries under the plan's claim procedures. [ERISA § 503(2)] (See the discussion of the claim procedures required under ERISA at Qs 6:51 through 6:63.)

Plan documents may provide for the allocation of responsibilities (other than trustee responsibilities relating to the management or control of plan assets, unless such authority is delegated to an investment manager) among named fiduciaries, and may authorize named fiduciaries to delegate non-trustee fiduciary responsibilities to others. [ERISA § 405(c)(1)]

Q 2:11   Who can be appointed a named fiduciary?

A named fiduciary may be an individual, employee organization, corporation, unincorporated organization, association, partnership, joint venture, mutual company, joint stock company, trust or estate. If a plan document designates a corporation or other entity that is not an individual as a named fiduciary, it should provide for the designation of specified individuals or other persons to carry out specified fiduciary responsibilities under the plan. [ERISA §§ 3(9), 3(21)(A); DOL Reg § 2509.75-5, FR-3]

Q 2:12   What is the purpose of having a named fiduciary?

The purpose of designating a named fiduciary is to enable employees and other interested persons to ascertain who is responsible for operating the plan. The advantage of designating a named fiduciary is to focus liability for mismanagement with a measure of certainty by limiting the exposure of liability to that named person. Thus, in the absence of conduct that falls within the rules governing co-fiduciary liability, the liability of a fiduciary who is not a "named fiduciary" is generally limited to the functions the fiduciary performs with respect to the plan, and the fiduciary will not be personally liable for all phases of the management and administration of the plan.

[DOL Reg § 2509.75-8, FR-16; Birmingham v SoGen-Swiss Int'l Corp Retirement Plan, 718 F2d 515, 521-522 (2d Cir 1983)]

Q 2:13 How are named fiduciaries designated in the plan document?

The plan document should explicitly designate the plan's named fiduciaries. [DOL Reg § 2509.75-5, FR-1] However, the named fiduciary requirement can also be satisfied without making specific reference to the term "named fiduciary." If the plan document clearly identifies one or more persons by name or title, combined with a statement that such person or persons have authority to control and manage the operation and administration of the plan, the requirement is satisfied. Thus, a plan document may provide that the plan committee (identified by name or title) will control and manage the operation and administration of the plan or a union-negotiated employee benefit plan document may provide that the joint board on which employees and employers are equally represented will control and manage the operation and administration of the plan. [DOL Reg § 2509.75-5, FR-1, FR-2]

Q 2:14 What is the liability of a named fiduciary?

If responsibilities are prudently allocated among named fiduciaries according to plan procedures designed for that purpose, a named fiduciary will not be liable for the acts and omissions of other named fiduciaries, except as provided in ERISA's co-fiduciary rules. [DOL Reg § 2509.75-8, FR-13] Similarly, named fiduciaries will not be liable for the acts and omissions of a person who is not a named fiduciary in carrying out the responsibilities delegated to such person provided, of course, that the named fiduciary prudently selects and monitors the actions of such individual. [DOL Reg § 2509.75-8, FR-14]

Plan Trustees

Q 2:15 What is a plan trustee?

A trustee is the individual or entity who holds the assets of the plan in trust. A plan may have one or more trustees.

Q 2:16 **Fiduciary Responsibility Answer Book**

Trustees are either designated in the plan instrument or are appointed by a named fiduciary. Members of a plan committee can be trustees if specifically and individually designated or appointed. (See the discussions of named fiduciaries at Qs 2:9 through 2:14, and the discussion of when plan assets must be held in trust at Qs 8:28 through 8:35.)

A trustee has exclusive authority and discretion over the management and control of plan assets (and, thus, is a fiduciary with respect to the management and control of such assets) unless (i) the plan expressly provides that the trustees are subject to the direction of a named fiduciary, or (ii) the named fiduciary in charge of control or management of plan assets delegates such control to one or more investment managers. [ERISA § 403(a)] (See the discussion of investment managers at Qs 2:24 & 2:25 and 4:13 through 4:26.)

In one case, trustees were held not to be fiduciaries since they lacked discretion over the investment of plan assets when the plan itself designated required investments. [Arakelian v National Western Life Ins Co, 755 FSupp 1080 (D DC 1990)]

Planning Pointer. There are typically three different types of trustees: officers as trustees, directed trustees, and discretionary trustees. Some plan sponsors appoint officers of the plan sponsor as trustees. This is more often found in defined contribution plans. Others appoint a bank as trustee. Depending on the desires of the plan sponsor, the trustee is either "directed" or "custodial," i.e., either the plan sponsor or the plan administrator directs the trustee how to invest plan assets or the trustee makes the investment decisions ("discretionary" trustee).

Q 2:16 When is a plan trustee a fiduciary?

A trustee who has authority or control over the management or disposition of plan assets is a plan fiduciary. [ERISA § 3(21)(A)] However, a trustee who is merely a custodian who holds legal title to plan assets, but is under the direction of others regarding the management and disposition of plan assets, has only limited fiduciary responsibility.

Q 2:17 Is a bank that acts as a custodian for plan assets a fiduciary under ERISA?

A bank is not necessarily a fiduciary under ERISA simply by acting as a custodian of pension fund assets, if the bank does not exercise "discretionary authority and control" with respect to such assets. [Useden v Acker, 947 F2d 1563 (11th Cir 1991) (clear standards circumscribed bank's discretion)]

When a bank is merely a servicing agent for a particular investment, and is never itself involved with the administration or management of the plan's funds itself or in making its investment policies and decisions, but is only required to fulfill various ministerial functions respecting one investment, including making advances to the borrower and remitting loan repayments, the bank is not a fiduciary. [Robbins v First American Bank, 514 FSupp 1183, 1190 (ND Ill 1981)]

When a bank receives employer payments, pays out administrative fees to the plan fund, and transfers funds from savings accounts to commercial accounts, and the agreement between the bank and the plan trustees specifies that the bank is to provide various other services, all of which are clearly detailed by the trustees and do not require the bank to exercise its judgment, the services are ministerial, and the bank is not a fiduciary. [Hibernia Bank v Int'l Bhd of Teamsters, 411 FSupp 478 (ND Cal 1976)]

Where a bank's duties are otherwise custodial services, and the bank also offers a daily cash "sweep service," whereby a third party determines how much uninvested cash will be "swept" into one of several specified money market funds overnight, the bank generally will not be deemed a fiduciary. [DOL Adv Op Ltr No 88-2A (Feb 2, 1988)]

However, a custodian may be a fiduciary to the extent it exercises investment discretion over plan assets or has discretionary authority in the administration of plan assets. [DOL Adv Op Ltr No 88-09A (Apr 5, 1988); DOL Adv Op Ltr No 82-052A (Sept 28, 1982)]

Plan Sponsors

Q 2:18 What is the plan sponsor?

A plan sponsor is one of the following: (i) the employer, in the case of an employee benefit plan established or maintained by a single employer, (ii) the employee organization, in the case of a plan established or maintained by an employee organization, or (iii) the association, committee, joint board of trustees, or other similar group of representatives of the parties who establish or maintain the plan, in the case of a plan established or maintained by two or more employers or jointly by one or more employers and one or more employee organizations. [ERISA § 3(16)(B)]

Q 2:19 Is the plan sponsor a plan fiduciary?

A plan sponsor is a plan fiduciary only to the extent it retains responsibility for or exercises the functions described in Question 2:1. Officials of a company sponsoring an ERISA plan are fiduciaries when they retain authority for the selection and retention of plan fiduciaries because to that extent they have retained discretionary authority and control respecting management of the plan. [*See* Freund v Marshall & Ilsley Bank, 485 FSupp 629 (WD Wis 1979); DOL Reg § 2509.75-8, D-4] A court has held that a plan sponsor was considered to be exercising control over plan assets and became a fiduciary when it refused to execute a form that would have permitted the trustees to distribute vested benefits to a terminated employee. [Blatt v Marshall and Lassman, 812 F2d 810 (2d Cir 1987)] However, a plan sponsor is not a fiduciary with respect to the management of plan assets, and the management and administration of the plan, unless it retains authority over these functions on a day-to-day basis. [Leigh v Engle, 727 F2d 113 (7th Cir 1984) *remanded*, 669 FSupp 1390 (ND Ill 1985), *aff'd*, 858 F2d 361 (7th Cir 1988), *cert denied*, 489 US 1078 (1989)] An employer whose only responsibility to a health plan was to pay premiums was not deemed a fiduciary where it exercised no administrative authority or discretionary control under the plan. [St Mary Medical Ctr v Cristiano, 724 FSupp 732 (CD Cal 1989)]

A plan sponsor does not become a fiduciary solely as a result of the establishment, amendment, or termination of a plan. These so-called settlor functions are not subject to the ERISA fiduciary rules. [DOL letter to Kirk F Maldonado, dated March 2, 1987, reprinted in *BNA Pension Reporter*, April 6, 1987; Payonk v HMW Indus, 883 F2d 221 (3d Cir 1989)] (See the discussion of settlor functions at Qs 3:18 through 3:21.)

Q 2:20 Are members of a plan sponsor's board of directors plan fiduciaries?

Members of the board of directors of an employer that maintains an employee benefit plan will be fiduciaries only to the extent that they have responsibility for the functions described in Question 2:1. For example, the board of directors may be responsible for the selection and retention of the plan administrator and/or plan fiduciaries. In such a case, members of the board of directors exercise discretionary authority or discretionary control respecting management of such plan and are, therefore, fiduciaries with respect to the plan. A plan covering employees of a corporation may designate the corporation as the named fiduciary. In such a case, the plan should provide for the designation of specified persons (by name or by title) to carry out specified fiduciary functions under the plan. [ERISA § 405(c)(1)(B); DOL Reg § 2509.75-5, FR-3] In the absence of such a designation, the corporation's board of directors (and each individual member) can be treated as a fiduciary, since the board has retained discretionary authority and control respecting management of the plan. [DOL Reg § 2509.75-8, D-4; Martin v Harline, 15 EBC(BNA) 1138 (D Utah 1992) (individual member of the board of directors); Newton v Van Otterloo, 756 FSupp 1121, 1132 (ND Ind 1991) (power to appoint and remove fiduciaries makes company's board of directors fiduciaries)]

However, if the responsibility of board members is limited to the selection and retention of fiduciaries, then the liability of board members is limited to that extent (apart from co-fiduciary liability arising under circumstances described in Qs 4:9 through 4:10). [Batchelor v Oak Hill Medical Group, 870 F2d 1446 (9th Cir 1989)]

The plan sponsor's board of directors may also be designated as named fiduciaries. However, if the directors are made named fiduciaries of the plan, their liability may be limited pursuant to a procedure provided for in the plan document for the allocation of fiduciary responsibilities among named fiduciaries or for the designation of persons other than named fiduciaries to carry out fiduciary responsibilities, as discussed in Question 2:6. (See the discussion of co-fiduciary liability at Qs 4:9 through 4:12.)

Q 2:21 Can individuals who are officers or employees of a plan sponsor be plan fiduciaries?

Yes. Individuals who are employees of a plan sponsor are plan fiduciaries if they have authority and control regarding the management and administration of the plan or the disposition of plan assets. For example, an individual who has authority and control regarding the appointment of a plan administrator or trustee is a fiduciary for this purpose. This individual must act prudently in making these selections in order to fulfill his or her fiduciary duties. (See the discussion of selecting fiduciaries at Qs 2:19 and 2:22.) However, officers or employees of a plan sponsor are not fiduciaries if they do not perform fiduciary functions.

Plan Administrators

Q 2:22 What is the plan administrator?

The plan administrator manages the day-to-day affairs of the plan. Among the responsibilities of the plan administrator are the hiring of attorneys, accountants, actuaries, and other plan professionals, determining plan eligibility and other rights of participants, ruling on benefit claims, preparing reports to be filed with governmental agencies, preparing reports for participants, and maintaining plan records.

The plan administrator is generally specifically designated by the plan document as the plan administrator. The document may designate a plan administrator:

- By name
- By reference to the person or group holding a named position
- By reference to a procedure for designating an administrator
- By reference to the person or group charged with the specific responsibilities of plan administrator.

A plan may provide for the allocation of specific responsibilities of plan administration among named persons and for named persons to designate others to carry out such responsibilities.

Q 2:23 Who is the plan administrator if the plan document does not designate a plan administrator?

If no person or group is designated, the following is the plan administrator:

(i) The employer (in the case of a plan maintained by a single employer),

(ii) The employee organization (in the case of a plan maintained by an employee organization), or

(iii) The group representatives of parties who maintain a plan, such as a joint board of trustees (in the case of a plan maintained by two or more employers, or jointly by one or more employers and one or more employee organizations).

[ERISA § 3(16)(A)]

If a plan administrator cannot be determined under the rules set forth in this answer, the plan administrator is the person or persons actually responsible for control, disposition, or management of the property received by the plan. [ERISA § 3(16)(A); IRC § 414(g); Treas Reg § 1.414(g)]

Investment Managers

Q 2:24 What is an investment manager under ERISA?

An investment manager is a person registered under the Investment Advisors Act of 1940, a bank or trust company, or an insurance company. An investment manager must have the power to manage, acquire, or dispose of any plan assets, and must acknowledge in writing that it is an ERISA fiduciary with respect to the plan. [ERISA § 3(38)] Investment authority over plan assets can be delegated, under limited circumstances, to one or more qualified investment managers, if the plan document expressly provides for such delegation. [ERISA §§ 402(c)(3), 405(d)] (See the discussion of delegation of investment authority at Qs 4:13 through 4:18.)

Q 2:25 Is an investment manager a fiduciary under ERISA?

Yes. An investment manager must acknowledge in writing that it is a fiduciary with respect to a plan. [ERISA § 3(38)] If an investment manager fails to comply with fiduciary standards, the investment manager will be liable for any losses to the plan resulting from the breach of fiduciary duty and may be required to disgorge any profits derived from the breach. Under certain circumstances, if the plan document expressly provides that the trustee is subject to the direction of a named fiduciary (other than the trustee), the investment manager will be subject to proper directions of the named fiduciary, if those directions are consistent with the plan and ERISA. [ERISA § 402(b)(1); DOL Reg § 2509.75-8, FR-15]

> **Example.** The plan document for a pension plan provides that an investment committee is the named fiduciary for purposes of investing plan assets. The plan document also provides that the investment committee may issue a funding policy governing what types of assets may be acquired or retained for investment by the plan. The investment committee duly adopts a resolution limiting plan investments in equity securities to 65 percent of the overall value of plan assets. As long as that policy is not otherwise contrary to ERISA (for example, if such a limit were imprudent as an investment policy at a given time), then the trustee and an investment manager to whom investment responsibilities had been delegated would be subject to that policy in investing plan assets.

Broker-Dealers

Q 2:26 Is a broker-dealer a fiduciary under ERISA?

Generally, no. A broker or dealer who is registered under the Securities Exchange Act of 1934, a reporting dealer in US Government securities, or a supervised bank that executes securities transactions on behalf of a plan in the ordinary course of its business as a broker, dealer, or bank is not deemed to be a fiduciary solely because of those transactions, provided that the following conditions are met:

1. The broker-dealer is not affiliated with a plan fiduciary.

2. An authorized plan fiduciary specifies the following:
   a. the security to be purchased or sold;
   b. a price range within which the security is to be purchased or sold;
   c. a time span (not more than five business days) during which the security may be purchased or sold; and
   d. the minimum or maximum quantity of the security that may be purchased or sold within the price range.

[DOL Reg § 2510.3-21(d)(1)]

The broker-dealer is not treated as a fiduciary regarding any plan assets over which the broker-dealer does not have any discretionary authority, control, or responsibility, subject to the rules on co-fiduciary liability and the rules governing prohibited transactions. [DOL Reg § 2510.3-21(d)(2)]

A broker's practice of recommending investments as part of the broker's usual course of business does not make the broker a fiduciary in the absence of an agreement, arrangement, or understanding that the advice will serve as a primary basis for plan investment decisions and that the advice will be based on the particular investment needs of the plan. [Farm King Supply, Inc Integrated Profit Sharing Plan & Trust v Edward D Jones & Co, 884 F2d 288 (7th Cir 1989)]

A broker can become a plan fiduciary if the broker engages in unauthorized acquisitions or dispositions of plan assets. [Olson v EF Hutton & Co Inc, 957 F2d 622 (8th Cir 1992)]

Professional Service Providers

Q 2:27 When are attorneys, accountants, actuaries, consultants, and other professionals who provide services to a plan ("professional service providers") considered plan fiduciaries?

A professional service provider can become a fiduciary of a plan if he or she has or exercises discretionary authority, control, or responsibility with respect to the plan, its assets, or its administra-

Q 2:27   **Fiduciary Responsibility Answer Book**

tion, even if such activities are not authorized by the named fiduciaries or other fiduciaries. [ERISA § 3(21)(A); DOL Reg § 2509.75-5, D-1; Olson v EF Hutton & Co, 957 F2d 622 (8th Cir 1992) (broker)]

When professional service providers are not fiduciaries, they generally will not have fiduciary liability for compensatory money damages, even if they are knowing participants in a fiduciary breach. [Mertens v Hewitt Assocs, 61 USLW 4510 (US 1993)] However, if they knowingly participate in a "prohibited transaction," they may be liable for excise taxes and penalties, and they may be required to take corrective actions to undo the prohibited transaction. [IRC § 4975(a) and (b)] (excises on prohibited transactions); ERISA § 502(i) (penalty for prohibited transaction)] (See the discussion of prohibited transactions at Chapter 5.)

Where a professional service provider effectively exercises control over the assets of an employee plan in complex commercial transactions, or engages in acts of self-dealing, the relationship has been held to result in fiduciary status. [Martin v Feilen, 965 F2d 660 (8th Cir 1992), *cert denied* 113 SCt 979 (1993) (accountants as well as controlling stockholders and directors engaged in transactions that destroyed the company and wiped out the employees' stock ownership plan)]

A professional service provider is not considered a plan fiduciary solely by reason of rendering professional services. Most recent cases have held that professional service providers acting in their usual professional functions do not thereby possess or exercise the necessary discretionary authority, control, or responsibility in connection with the employee benefit plan to cause them to be fiduciaries under ERISA. [Mertens v Hewitt Assocs, 124 LEd 2d 161 (1993) (actuaries); Useden v Acker, 947 F2d 1563, 1577-78 (11th Cir 1991) (law firm and bank not fiduciaries); Pappas v Buck Consultants, Inc, 923 F2d 531 (7th Cir 1991) (actuaries); Anoka Orthopaedic Assocs, PA v Lechner, 910 F2d 514 (8th Cir 1990) (attorneys and consultants); Painters of Philadelphia Dist Council No 21 Welfare Fund v Price Waterhouse, 879 F2d 1146 (3d Cir 1989) (accountants); Nieto v Ecker, 845 F2d 868 (9th Cir 1988) (attorney); Yeseta v Baima, 837 F2d 380 (9th Cir 1988) (attorney and accountant)]

Who Is a Fiduciary? Q 2:29

Q 2:28 If a professional service provider who is a member of a professional firm renders services to a plan in a fiduciary capacity, can the other members of the professional firm be considered fiduciaries?

The other members of the professional firm can be considered fiduciaries, depending on the circumstances. If the other members directly or indirectly have or exercise discretionary authority, control, or responsibility with respect to the plan, its assets, or its administration, the other members will be considered fiduciaries. [*See* Useden v Acker, 947 F2d 1563, 1577-78 (11th Cir 1991) (law firm not fiduciary)]

> **Planning Pointer.** It is not uncommon for the corporate secretary of a plan sponsor to be an attorney. Moreover, the attorney's law firm commonly serves as counsel to the employer and the employee benefit plans sponsored by the employer. These roles do not automatically make the law firm a fiduciary. If the corporate secretary-attorney also serves as trustee or named fiduciary, however, in order to limit the possibility that the law firm would be treated as a fiduciary, the corporate secretary-attorney should avoid taking an active role in rendering legal advice with respect to the plan.

Q 2:29 When can an in-house professional service provider be considered a plan fiduciary?

To the extent the in-house professional service provider possesses or exercises any of the fiduciary functions described above, he or she will be considered a plan fiduciary. The offices and positions of an in-house professional service provider could include the functions of plan administrator or trustee, which are generally fiduciary functions. Other offices and positions should be examined to determine whether they involve the performance of any of the fiduciary functions described above. The title of the designation is not determinative. (See the discussion of offices and positions that can result in fiduciary status at Q 2:3.) In-house professional service providers (such as in-house counsel) who effectively have the final authority to approve benefit payments in cases where a dispute exists as to the interpretation of plan provisions relating to eligibility for plan benefits are fiduciaries within the meaning of ERISA. [DOL Reg § 2509.75-8, D-3]

Q 2:30   May other plan fiduciaries serve as professional service providers?

Generally, yes. Any person may serve a plan in both a fiduciary and non-fiduciary capacity, or in more than one fiduciary capacity. [ERISA § 402(c)(1)] However, the accountant retained by an employee benefit plan for purposes of auditing and rendering an opinion on the financial information that may be required to be included in the annual report (Form 5500) filed with DOL must in fact be independent of the plan for which the accountant renders an opinion. [ERISA § 103(a)(3)(A); DOL Reg § 2509.75-9]

Third-Party Administrators

Q 2:31   When is a third-party administrator a fiduciary under ERISA?

A person who is independent of the plan sponsor, the named fiduciary, and other fiduciaries of a plan may agree to perform various functions related to the administration of the plan. These functions often include recordkeeping, tax reporting, coordination with payroll records, and similar functions. Such persons are commonly referred to as third-party administrators. A third-party administrator is not a fiduciary unless it performs a fiduciary function as described in Question 2:1, or is a named fiduciary, as described in Questions 2:9 through 2:14. By contrast, as described in Question 2:7, a person performing ministerial functions within guidelines established by others is not a plan fiduciary. [DOL Reg § 2509.75-8, D-2.]

> **Example.** An employer had a self-insured health plan. An independent third-party administrator had discretion over payment of claims under the plan. The employer purchased excess loss (stop loss) insurance coverage from an insurance company. The insurer neither paid claims to participants nor reviewed the denial of claims. Its duties were strictly limited to reimbursing the employer for benefits in excess of the policy deductible by the terms of the excess loss insurance policy.

The employer, through its third-party administrator, paid a claim not covered under the plan. The excess loss insurer denied the employer's claim for reimbursement. The employer sued the insurer for breach of fiduciary duty. The Ninth Circuit held that the excess loss insurer did not exercise sufficient discretion over the claim payments or over the plan's assets to be considered an ERISA fiduciary. [Kyle Railways, Inc v Pacific Administration Services Inc, 16 EBC(BNA) 2032 (9th Cir 1993)]

Insurance Companies and Brokers

Q 2:32 When is an insurance company a fiduciary under ERISA?

An insurance company may provide the investment vehicles for funding the benefits under a plan, may agree to serve as named fiduciary, may serve as third-party administrator, or may directly or indirectly perform any number of functions in connection with a plan. If the insurance company in performing those functions, performs (or has the authority or responsibility to perform) any activity relating to the management, investment, or administration of a plan, the insurance company will become a fiduciary, unless those acts are purely ministerial acts, as described in Question 2:7. The insurer may be deemed a fiduciary if it has discretion over the administration of the plan. [DOL Reg § 2509.75-8, D-3; American Federation of Unions v Equitable Life Assurance Soc, 841 F2d 658, 664 (5th Cir 1988) (an insurance company's "urging the purchase of its own products" does not result in fiduciary status, since the sales pitch was not intended as the primary basis for investment of plan assets); Sixty-Five Security Plan v Blue Cross & Blue Shield of New York, 583 FSupp 380 (SDNY 1984), *reh'g denied, certif granted*, 588 FSupp 119 (SDNY 1984) (insurer assessed reasonableness of hospital stay, denied and granted claims, and negotiated hospital rates)]

> **Example.** An insurance company entered into a written agreement with the named fiduciary (the administrator) of a plan providing insured medical benefits. The agreement stated that the intention of the parties was that the insurance company would *not* be a fiduciary under ERISA. In fact, employees of the insurance company effectively exercise the final authority to authorize or disal-

low benefit payments in cases where a dispute exists as to the interpretation of plan provisions relating to eligibility for benefits. Under these circumstances, the insurance company would be a fiduciary under ERISA. [DOL Reg § 2509.75-8, D-3]

Q 2:33   When is an insurance broker a fiduciary under ERISA?

An insurance broker often will be retained by a plan to help select an insurance policy among insurance companies that will provide the benefits under the plan. In general, an insurance broker serving in that role will not be a fiduciary. However, if the insurance broker "renders investment advice," as described in Question 2:34, the person will be considered a fiduciary. This requires, however, that there must be an agreement that the advice will be the primary basis for the investment of plan assets. [DOL Reg § 2510.3-21(c)(1); American Federation of Unions v Equitable Life Assurance Society, 841 F2d 658, 664 (5th Cir 1988)(insurer's agent was fiduciary)]

Q 2:34   What does it mean to "render investment advice" for the purpose of determining fiduciary status?

A person is deemed to "render investment advice" to a plan only if the person:

1. Renders advice to a plan concerning the value of securities or other property or makes recommendations regarding the purchase or sale of securities or other property.
2. Directly or indirectly has discretionary authority or control over the purchase or sale of securities or other property for a plan or regularly renders advice on investment strategy, portfolio composition or diversification of investments pursuant to an agreement that the advice rendered will be the primary basis for the investment of plan assets.

[DOL Reg § 2510.3-21(c)(1)]

A person who renders investment advice for a fee need not be paid a fee directly. Instead, a person who renders investment advice (as defined above) will be considered to be a fiduciary if such person receives any benefit or compensation, whether directly or indirectly, as a result of such advice. [Farm King Supply, Inc Integrated Profit Sharing Plan & Trust v Edward D Jones & Co, 884 F2d 288 (7th Cir 1989)]

Plan Participants

Q 2:35 When can plan participants' control over plan assets relieve fiduciaries of liability?

Section 404(c) of ERISA provides rules for relieving a fiduciary of liability for investment decisions that are "passed through" to plan participants in certain individual account plans such as money purchase pension plans, profit sharing plans, 401(k) plans, etc.

Under Section 404(c), if a plan provides for individual accounts and permits an individual participant or beneficiary to exercise control over the assets in his or her account, and that individual actually exercises such control, then any other person who is otherwise a plan fiduciary, such as the named fiduciary, will not be liable for any loss resulting from the individual's exercise of control over his or her account. The individuals who exercise control over their accounts do not become fiduciaries. [ERISA § 404(c)] (*See* the discussion of participant-directed accounts at Qs 4:27 through 4:49.)

Fiduciaries for Collectively Bargained Plans

Q 2:36 Does a collectively bargained plan have special fiduciaries?

Yes. There are two types of collectively bargained plans: a single employer plan and a multiemployer plan. A collectively bargained single employer plan is generally a plan in which only one employer participates pursuant to a collective bargaining agreement. A multiemployer plan is generally a plan to which more than one employer is required to contribute and which is maintained pursuant to one or more collective bargaining agreements between one or more employer organizations and more than one employer. [ERISA § 3(37)]

The Labor Management Relations Act (LMRA) mandates that a plan created pursuant to a collective bargaining agreement (whether it is a multiemployer plan or a single employer plan) be equally represented in the administration of the fund by employer trustees and union trustees. [LMRA § 302(c)(5)(B)] Since the plan document of a collectively bargained plan must specifically identify members of a joint board of trustees of the plan, the members of the joint board of trustees are named fiduciaries of such plans. (See the discussion of named fiduciaries at Qs 2:9 through 2:14.)

Chapter 3

Fiduciary Duties Under ERISA

The primary fiduciary duties under ERISA are the "exclusive benefit," prudence, and diversification requirements and the requirement that the fiduciary act in accordance with plan documents. This chapter discusses the nature of these and other ERISA fiduciary duties.

Exclusive Benefit	3-2
Prudence	3-3
Diversification	3-6
Adherence to Plan Documents	3-7
To Whom Is Duty Owed	3-8
Settlor Functions Versus Fiduciary Activities	3-10
Responsibility of Co-Fiduciaries	3-13
Special Rules	3-15

Q 3:1 What are the primary fiduciary duties under ERISA?

The primary fiduciary duties under ERISA are to:

1. Act for the exclusive benefit of plan participants and beneficiaries;
2. Act prudently;
3. Diversify the investments of the plan assets; and
4. Act in accordance with plan documents. [ERISA § 404(a)(1)]

Exclusive Benefit

Q 3:2   What is required for a fiduciary to satisfy the "exclusive benefit" requirement?

To satisfy the exclusive benefit requirement, a fiduciary must act solely in the interest of the plan's participants and beneficiaries, and for the exclusive purpose of providing benefits to participants and their beneficiaries and defraying reasonable administrative expenses of the plan. [ERISA § 404(a)(1)(A)]

> **Example.** The controlling shareholders, directors and accountants of an employer (all related by blood and marriage) undertook complex commercial transactions and engaged in self-dealing using the assets of the employer's employee stock ownership plan (ESOP). These individuals were also fiduciaries of the ESOP by reason of their control of plan assets. They caused the employer to assume a high-interest loan obligation of a company partially owned by the accountants, in exchange for inadequate consideration. They also caused the ESOP to buy and sell shares of employer stock at prices less favorable to the ESOP than to others.
>
> Their actions impaired the value of the company's stock, a large part of which constituted plan assets. Their actions destroyed the company, and were contrary to the interests of the participants and beneficiaries of the plan. Although an ESOP fiduciary is permitted some dual loyalty, the actions of the fiduciaries were taken without investigation of alternatives and without reliance on outside advisors. Those acts of self-dealing accordingly violated the exclusive benefit rule as well as the duty of prudence. [Martin v Feilen, 965 F2d 660 (8th Cir 1992), *cert denied* 113 SCt 979 (1993)]

Q 3:3   Is it a violation of the exclusive benefit requirement if the fiduciary's action also benefits the employer?

A transaction may incidentally benefit the employer without resulting in a violation of the exclusive benefit rule if, after a careful, thorough, and impartial inquiry, the fiduciary reasonably concludes that the transaction is in the interest of plan participants and beneficiaries. [Donovan v Bierwirth, 680 F2d 263 (2d Cir), *cert denied*, 459 US 1069 (1987)]

Planning Pointer. Where a fiduciary sees the possibility of a conflict of loyalty between the plan participants and the beneficiaries on one hand, and another party to a transaction (such as the sponsoring employer) on the other hand, the fiduciary should promptly seek the advice of a competent, independent advisor. It may be necessary under such circumstances for the fiduciary to recuse himself or herself (i.e., formally withdraw) from participating in any decision that would potentially present such a conflict of loyalty, or resign as a fiduciary before being called upon to participate in the decision. [DOL Adv Op Ltr No 84-09A, n.2 (Feb 16, 1984); DOL Adv Op Ltr No 79-42A (July 5, 1979); DOL Reg § 2550.408b-2(e)(2) and 2(f)(Ex 7)]

Prudence

Q 3:4 What must a fiduciary do to satisfy the prudence requirement?

To satisfy the prudence requirement, a fiduciary must act "with the care, skill, prudence, and diligence under the circumstances then prevailing that a prudent man acting in a like capacity and familiar with such matters would use in the conduct of an enterprise of a like character and with like aims." [ERISA § 404(a)(1)(B)]

Q 3:5 What is the legal standard for determining whether a fiduciary's acts are prudent?

The standard for prudence depends on the circumstances. "The scope of the fiduciary's duty of prudence is . . . limited to those factors and circumstances that a prudent person having similar duties and familiar with such matters would consider relevant, whether the context is one of plan investments or otherwise." [44 Fed Reg 37,222-23 (July 20, 1979) (DOL release accompanying DOL Reg § 2550.404a-1(b))]

Q 3:6 Are a fiduciary's actions judged by the standard of an ordinary person or that of an expert?

Particularly in the context of investing plan assets, a fiduciary charged with an investment decision must act as a prudent expert would under similar circumstances, taking into account all relevant substantive factors, as they appeared at the time of the investment decision, not in hindsight. This standard under ERISA "is not that of a prudent lay person, but rather of a prudent fiduciary with experience dealing with similar enterprises." [Whitfield v Cohen, 682 FSupp 188, 194 (SD NY 1988), quoting Marshall v Snyder, 1 EBC (BNA) 1878, 1886 (ED NY 1979)]

The fiduciary's conduct is to be judged against generally accepted conduct in the investment industry. "The prudence standard charges fiduciaries with a high degree of knowledge. The standard measures the decisions of plan fiduciaries against the decisions that would be made by experienced investment advisers." [Joint Comm'n on Tax'n, Overview of the Enforcement and Administration of the Employee Retirement Income Security Act of 1974, at 12 (JCX-16-90) (June 6, 1990)]

Q 3:7 Does a fiduciary have an obligation to seek the assistance of an expert to satisfy the prudence requirement?

Yes. Not all plan fiduciaries can be expert in all phases of employee benefit plan investments and administration, nor can they have knowledge in the entire range of activities integral to the operation of a plan. Therefore, fiduciaries have an affirmative duty to seek the advice and counsel of independent experts when their own ability is insufficient under the circumstances. For example, pension plan trustees breached the prudence standard in connection with a $2 million loan to a bank when they considered only the information presented by the interested parties who sought the loan and failed to conduct an independent investigation. [Katsaros v Cody, 744 F2d 270, 279 (2d Cir), *cert denied*, 469 US 1072 (1984)]

> **Planning Pointer.** A fiduciary who lacks the expertise needed to address an issue prudently should promptly seek, and retain, a professional who has the expertise to assist the fiduciary in the decision.

Q 3:8 What is the difference between "substantive prudence" and "procedural prudence"?

The DOL, the courts, and commentators have distinguished between two types of prudence: substantive and procedural prudence.

The former refers to the merits of the decision made by the fiduciary; the latter addresses the process through which the fiduciary reaches his or her decision.

As long as there is no conflict of interest that would impair the fiduciary's exercise of independent judgment, a fiduciary who considers the appropriate substantive factors ("substantive prudence") and does so using proper procedures ("procedural prudence") will satisfy the prudence requirement. [Katsaros v Cody, 744 F2d 270, 279 (2d Cir), *cert denied*, 469 US 1072 (1984)]

Q 3:9 What substantive factors must a fiduciary consider in connection with plan investments?

To satisfy the statutory obligation of prudence in connection with plan investments, a fiduciary must give "appropriate consideration" to the following substantive factors:

1. The investment must be evaluated as part of the plan's overall portfolio;
2. The design of the portfolio, including the investment, must be reasonable for the purposes of the plan;
3. The risk of loss and opportunity for gain (or other return) must be favorable, relative to alternative investments;
4. The investment must take into consideration the diversification of the portfolio;
5. The investment must take into consideration the liquidity and current return of the entire portfolio relative to anticipated cash flow requirements of the plan; and
6. The investment must take into consideration the projected return of the portfolio relative to the funding objectives of the plan. [DOL Reg § 2550.404a-1(b)]

Q 3:10 What is procedural prudence in the context of investing plan assets?

To satisfy procedural prudence in the context of investing plan assets, the fiduciary must:

1. Employ proper methods to investigate, evaluate, and structure the investment, including the retention of a professional advisor if the fiduciary lacks the expertise himself or herself;
2. Act in a manner as would others who have a capacity and familiarity with such matters; and
3. Exercise independent judgment when making investment decisions.

[Lanka v O'Higgins, 810 FSupp 379 (NDNY 1992) (A "contrarian" investment advisor satisfied these requirements.)]

Diversification

Q 3:11 What is required for a fiduciary to satisfy the diversification requirement?

A fiduciary must diversify plan investments so as to minimize the risk of large losses unless, under the circumstances, it is clearly prudent not to do so. [ERISA § 404(a)(1)(C)]

In the case of a pension plan that is an "eligible individual account plan," the diversification requirement is not violated by the acquisition or holding of qualifying employer real property or qualifying employer securities. [ERISA § 404(a)(2)] (See the discussion of qualifying employer real property and qualifying employer securities at Qs 5:29 and 7:27 through 7:38.)

Q 3:12 What are the primary factors for prudent diversification?

The seven factors to be considered for prudent diversification are:

1. The purposes of the plan;
2. The amount of the plan assets;
3. Financial and industrial conditions;
4. The type of investment, whether mortgages, bonds, shares of stock, or otherwise;
5. Distribution as to geographical location;

6. Distribution as to industries; and
7. The dates of maturity.

[H Rep No 1280, 93d Cong, 2d Sess (1974), reprinted in [1974] US Code Cong & Ad News 5038, at 5084-85]

Adherence to Plan Documents

Q 3:13 What is required for a fiduciary to discharge his or her responsibilities in accordance with plan documents?

A fiduciary must act in accordance with the documents governing the plan to the extent the documents are consistent with Titles I and IV of ERISA, which include the provisions on fiduciary responsibility, and plan termination insurance. [ERISA § 404(a)(1)(D)]

Example. A pension plan participant informed Company A in February 1987 that he was undergoing a divorce. As required by the rules under ERISA and the IRC, the plan contained formal written procedures for determining whether a domestic relations order qualifies. These procedures specified that upon receipt of an order, the plan administrator would notify the participant and place a "hold" on the participant's account pending a decision whether the order was qualified.

On August 26, 1987, following an informal, unwritten procedure, the plan administrator placed a hold on the participant's account after the ex-wife's attorney informed the administrator that the divorce had been granted, that the settlement provided for payment of $80,000 to the ex-wife from the participant's account, and that an order was forthcoming.

The participant was unable to complete a sale of Company A shares in his plan account planned for September 23, 1987. The stock market crashed on October 19, 1987, causing losses in the participant's account. The plan actually received the divorce order in November 1987, and then transferred $87,500 from the participant's account to his ex-wife.

On appeal, the court found a violation of the fiduciary duty to administer the plan in conformity with written plan documents because the written procedures would impose a hold only after receipt of the divorce order. [Schoonmaker v Employee Savings Plan of Amoco Corp and Participating Companies, 987 F2d 410 16 EBC (BNA) 1646 (7th Cir 1993)]

To Whom Is Duty Owed

Q 3:14 To whom does a plan fiduciary owe a fiduciary duty?

In general, a plan fiduciary owes a fiduciary duty to plan participants and plan beneficiaries. [ERISA § 404(a)(1)(A)]

A plan fiduciary generally does not owe a fiduciary duty to employees of the employer as employees, unless they are participants, beneficiaries, or members of a group with a reasonable possibility of becoming participants (or beneficiaries). [Belade v ITT Corp, 909 F2d 736 (2d Cir 1990)] In addition, a plan fiduciary generally owes no fiduciary duty to the employer. [Tuvia Convalescent Center v. National Union of Hospital and Health Care Employees, 717 F2d 726, 730 (2d Cir 1983)] One court has recently ruled, however, that a third-party administrator has a fiduciary duty under the federal common law of trusts to furnish an accounting to the employer on demand. [Libbey-Owens-Ford Co v Blue Cross & Blue Shield Mut of Ohio, 982 F2d 1031 (6th Cir 1993)] (See the discussion of disclosure and reporting obligations at Q 3:17.)

Q 3:15 Who is a plan participant?

A participant is an employee or former employee of an employer (or a member or former member of a employee organization), who is or may become eligible to receive any benefit from a plan covering employees of the employer (or members of the organization), or whose beneficiaries may be eligible to receive such a benefit. [ERISA § 3(7)]

The "may become eligible" language of ERISA Section 3(7) applies to former employees only if they have a reasonable expectation of returning to covered employment, or a colorable claim to vested benefits. [Firestone Tire & Rubber Co v Bruch, 489 US 101 (1989)]

The term "employee" as used in Section 3(6) of ERISA incorporates traditional agency law criteria for identifying the master-servant relationship. [Nationwide Mutual Ins Co v Darden, 112 SCt 1344 (1992)]

Q 3:16 Who is a plan beneficiary?

A beneficiary is a person designated by a plan participant, or by the terms of a plan, who is or may become entitled to a benefit under the plan. [ERISA § 3(8)]

Q 3:17 Can a plan fiduciary have obligations to persons other than plan participants and beneficiaries?

In addition to the duties owed to participants and beneficiaries, and indirectly to co-fiduciaries, a plan fiduciary may have disclosure and reporting obligations to other persons. These obligations include:

1. Summary plan descriptions and summaries of material modifications must be furnished to participants and beneficiaries, and also must be filed with the United States Department of Labor (DOL). [ERISA § 101(a) and (b)]
2. Annual reports, summary annual reports, terminal reports, and supplementary reports must be furnished to participants and beneficiaries, and also must be filed with the DOL, and in some cases, with the Internal Revenue Service. [ERISA § 101(b) and (c); IRC §§ 6039D, 6058]
3. Notice of failure to meet minimum funding standards must also be furnished to participants and beneficiaries, and must be filed with the Pension Benefit Guaranty Corporation (PBGC) [ERISA § 101(d)]
4. Notice of transfer of excess pension assets into a health benefits account must be furnished to participants and beneficiaries, and also to the DOL, the Internal Revenue Service, and each employee organization (i.e., labor union) representing participants. [ERISA § 101(e)]

Failure to meet these obligations can result in a substantial penalty for a fiduciary. For example, failure to file a timely Annual Report on IRS Form 5500 can result in a $1,000 per day penalty imposed by the DOL. [ERISA § 502(c)(2)] In addition, the fiduciary may be liable to individual participants and beneficiaries. [ERISA § 502(c)(1) and (3)]

Planning Pointer. Because these substantial penalties may be imposed on individuals if they are fiduciaries, many employee plan documents designate the sponsoring company as named fiduciary and plan administrator, rather than naming an individual. The documents should also expressly permit delegation of the functions by the company to committees or individuals (specified by title or position, not by name). [DOL Reg § 2509.75-5, FR-1 and FR-3]

Settlor Functions Versus Fiduciary Activities

Q 3:18 What is a "settlor function?"

A "settlor function" is an action or decision made by the sponsoring employer (or in the case of a collectively bargained plan, the employers and the employee representatives), rather than by a fiduciary exercising discretion. ERISA only imposes fiduciary obligations on the trustees and fiduciaries of a plan; nonfiduciaries are not bound by these provisions. In this regard, the DOL, the courts, and (in recent legislative history) Congress have recognized a distinction between "settlor" (or "grantor") functions—which are not subject to the fiduciary provisions of ERISA, and fiduciary activities, which must conform to ERISA. This distinction is based on the common law of trusts. Just as a settlor (grantor) of a trust is not performing a fiduciary role in deciding to create the trust, so the sponsoring employer of an ERISA plan is not performing a fiduciary role in designing an ERISA plan.

Q 3:19 What are the most common settlor functions?

The most common settlor functions are "design" decisions concerning the establishment of the plan, the benefits to be provided, the classes of employees to be included or excluded, and the amendment and termination of the plan.

Where an employer decided to implement an early retirement program at selected facilities only, as part of (and as an amendment to) an existing retirement benefits plan that applied to all of the employer's facilities, neither the employer nor the Retirement Board that administered its retirement programs violated any of ERISA's fiduciary duties. The determination of who would be eligible for the early retirement program was "purely a corporate management decision," and such design decisions may be made by the employer without reference to ERISA's fiduciary obligations. [Trenton v Scott Paper Co, 832 F2d 806 (3d Cir 1987), *cert denied*, 485 US 1022 (1988)]

> **Planning Pointer.** Plan documents should expressly provide mechanisms for amending and terminating each plan. Many sponsoring employers provide that the board of directors or a named committee is responsible for amending and terminating the plan. Plan communications should clearly state who has authority to take these actions, and that they expressly reserve the right to do so. When a design decision of the board or a committee is required, minutes or other written records should clearly show that the decision is a design decision, and that the board or committee was exercising reserved powers of a nonfiduciary nature.

Q 3:20 When can a fiduciary perform a settlor function?

Any person may simultaneously act in a fiduciary capacity and in a nonfiduciary capacity as an agent of the sponsoring employer. [NLRB v Amax Coal Co, 453 US 322, 338 (1981)] (See the discussion of officers and employees of a plan sponsor at Q 2:21.) The nonfiduciary role, however, must in no respect affect the discharge of the fiduciary duties with respect to the plan. [DOL Adv Op Ltr No 81-30A (Mar 16, 1981)]

> **Example 1.** An employer's pension committee is the named fiduciary and plan administrator of its overfunded defined benefit pension plan, and acts on behalf of the board of directors in making design decisions. The pension committee decides to terminate the pension plan, to purchase and distribute annuity contracts, and to

establish a successor money purchase (defined contribution) plan. The pension committee is a fiduciary and is subject to fiduciary standards in allocating surplus assets and in choosing an insurer to issue annuity contracts. By contrast, settlor functions include the decision to establish a successor plan and the design of such a plan after a valid termination of the prior plan. The pension committee is not subject to fiduciary standards in performing these settlor functions. [Letter from Dennis M. Kass of the PWBA to John M. Erlenborn of the ERISA Advisory Council (March 13, 1986)]

Example 2. Company *A* divested itself of a number of subsidiaries. Employees of the subsidiaries were permitted to withdraw their benefits from Company *A*'s overfunded pension plan, for which Company *A* was also administrator. Shortly after that, Company *A* decided to terminate its pension plan, and gave remaining participants the 10-day PBGC notice required under the law then in effect. The remaining participants received a portion of the plan surplus upon plan termination. The employees of the divested subsidiaries did not receive any portion of the surplus, and asserted a fiduciary violation by Company *A* as plan administrator in not notifying the employees of the subsidiary that the plan would soon be terminated. The Court of Appeals held that Company *A* had no fiduciary obligation to notify the employees of the subsidiary in advance of the 10-day PBGC notice requirement. Company *A* also had no obligation to take any other action relating to plan termination. The decision to terminate the plan was a design decision and a matter of business corporate management to be made and effectuated by Company A acting as employer and not as fiduciary. Company *A* as plan administrator lacked the authority to terminate the plan, and lacked definitive information that the plan would be terminated until Company *A* as employer made the final decision. [Payonk v HMW Industries, Inc, 883 F2d 221 (3d Cir 1989)]

Even if the sponsoring employer (or the employers and employee representatives, in the case of a collectively bargained plan) makes a design decision that constitutes a settlor function, plan fiduciaries, such as trustees or plan administrators, may be called upon to implement the decision. Such implementation may remain a fiduciary function. [101st Cong, 2d Sess, Statement of the

Managers, Revenue Reconciliation Act of 1990, at 170, 172 (October 26, 1990)]

Q 3:21 To what extent is a fiduciary's implementation of a settlor function exempt from the rules on fiduciary responsibility?

A fiduciary's implementation of a settlor function is exempt from the rules on fiduciary responsibility to the extent that the fiduciary is merely implementing the design decision of the sponsoring employer (or, in the case of a collectively bargained plan, the employers and the employee representatives) without exercising discretion.

> **Example.** An employer sponsored a retirement plan for its salaried employees, and a subsidized early retirement program for certain classes of its salaried employees. The employer's retirement committee served as the managing board of the retirement plan. Salaried employees participating in the retirement plan asserted a breach of fiduciary duty by reason of being excluded from the early retirement program. The decision to restrict benefits under the early retirement program was a design decision not itself subject to fiduciary standards. Accordingly, actions by the retirement committee as fiduciary that were taken to implement that decision (i.e., setting up the program so as to exclude the salaried employees participating in the retirement plan) were also not subject to fiduciary standards. [Trenton v Scott Paper Co, 832 F2d 806 (3d Cir 1987), *cert denied* 485 US 1022 (1988)]

Responsibility of Co-Fiduciaries

Q 3:22 In general, when is a fiduciary responsible for a breach of fiduciary responsibility by a co-fiduciary?

A fiduciary is responsible for a breach of fiduciary responsibility by a co-fiduciary:

1. If the fiduciary participates knowingly in (or knowingly undertakes to conceal) an act or omission of the co-fiduciary, knowing it is a breach [ERISA § 405(a)(1)];
2. If the fiduciary fails to satisfy any of the basic fiduciary duties (exclusive benefit, prudence, diversification or conforming to plan documents consistent with ERISA), and this failure enables the co-fiduciary to commit the breach [ERISA § 405(a)(2)]; and
3. If the fiduciary has knowledge of the breach and does not make reasonable efforts under the circumstances to remedy the breach. [ERISA § 405(a)(3)]

Q 3:23 What special rules apply to a trustee for a breach of fiduciary responsibility by a co-trustee?

If plan assets are held in a single trust by more than one trustee, each trustee must use reasonable care to prevent a breach by a co-trustee. In addition, the co-trustees must jointly manage, control, and bear responsibility for all plan assets, except to the extent that the co-trustees have agreed pursuant to the trust agreement to allocate specific responsibilities among themselves, subject to the rules generally applicable to co-fiduciary liability. [ERISA § 405(b)(1), (2), and (3)] (See the discussion of co-fiduciary liability at Qs 4:9 through 4:12.)

Q 3:24 May fiduciary responsibilities be allocated among fiduciaries, or delegated to persons other than named fiduciaries?

Yes. Plan documents may expressly provide procedures for allocating fiduciary responsibilities (other than trustee functions) among named fiduciaries or procedures under which named fiduciaries may designate persons to carry out fiduciary responsibilities (other than trustee functions). However, in the absence of an express plan provision, any such allocation or designation will not be effective. [ERISA § 405(c)(1)] (See the discussion of allocation of fiduciary duties and designation of persons to carry out fiduciary duties at Qs 4.1 through 4.8.)

Special Rules

Q 3:25 Are there special fiduciary rules that apply to a plan holding qualifying employer real property (QERP) or qualifying employer securities (QES), or to an employee stock ownership plan (ESOP)?

Yes. The diversification requirement is not violated to the extent that an eligible individual account plan (generally, any defined contribution pension plan, other than a money purchase pension plan, but including an ESOP) holds QERP or QES. [ERISA § 404(a)(2)] Moreover, an eligible individual account plan may acquire and hold more than 10 percent of the value of the assets of the plan in QERP and QES. [ERISA § 407(b)(1)] By contrast, the amount of QERP and QES that a plan other than an eligible individual account plan may acquire and hold is not more than 10 percent of the value of the assets of the plan. [ERISA § 407(a)(1) and (2)] (See the discussion of qualifying employer real property and qualifying employer securities at Qs 5:29 and 7:27 through 7:38.)

Q 3:26 What special fiduciary rules apply when an investment manager has been appointed for a plan?

If an investment manager has been appointed for a plan, no trustee is liable for the acts or omissions of the manager, and no trustee is under an obligation to invest or otherwise manage those plan assets that are managed by the investment manager. [ERISA § 405(d)(1)] Nevertheless, a trustee is not relieved of responsibility for his or her own actions. [ERISA § 405(d)(2)] (See the discussion of investment managers at Qs 4.13 through 4.26 and 7:1 through 7:8.)

Q 3:27 May a fiduciary maintain indicia of ownership of any plan assets outside the United States?

Generally not. Except as authorized by the United States Department of Labor by regulation, no fiduciary may maintain the indicia of ownership of any plan assets outside the jurisdiction of the United States. [ERISA § 404(b)] The indicia of ownership are the bonds, stock certificates, or other evidence of ownership of plan assets. [DOL Adv Op Ltr No 75-80 (Feb 13, 1975)] The rule is not intended to prohibit all plan investments outside the United States. [H Rep No 1280, 93d Cong, 2d Sess (1974), reprinted in [1974] US Code Cong & Ad News 5038, at 5086-87] Rather, it is the evidence of ownership of such foreign investments that must generally be held in the United States.

The DOL has issued regulations allowing a fiduciary to maintain evidence of ownership of plan assets outside the United States under limited circumstances. The assets must be specified types of securities or currency, and must be in the control or possession of a U.S. institution having adequate capitalization. [DOL Reg § 2550.404b-1(a)] This control or possession can be exercised indirectly by a U.S. bank's use of a foreign clearing agency that acts as a securities depository, if certain conditions are met. [DOL Adv Op Ltr No 91-28A (July 19, 1991)]

Q 3:28 Are there special fiduciary rules that apply when a pension plan participant or beneficiary exercises control over the assets in his or her individual account?

Yes. When a pension plan participant or beneficiary exercises control over the assets in his or her individual account, such person is not deemed to be a plan fiduciary, and a person who would otherwise be a fiduciary with respect to such account is not liable for any loss, or by reason of any breach resulting from the participant's exercise of control. [ERISA § 404(c); DOL Reg § 2550.404c-1] (See the discussion of participant-directed investments at Qs 4.27 through 4.49.)

Q 3:29 What special fiduciary standards apply to benefit plans covering only partners or other self-employed persons?

A benefit plan covering only partners or other self-employed persons is not a plan subject to the fiduciary responsibility rules of ERISA, because no "employees" participate. This would include many "Keogh" or "H.R. 10" plans, but not if there are any participants who are common-law employees. [DOL Reg § 2510.3-3(b)]

For these purposes, an individual and his or her spouse are not "employees" of a trade or business (including a partnership or corporation) wholly owned by the individual or by the individual and spouse. [DOL Reg § 2510.3-3(c)(1)] A partner and his or her spouse are not "employees" of the partnership for this purpose. [DOL Reg § 2510.3-3(c)(2)]

Example. Helene owns all the stock of a corporation that operates a franchise business. The corporation pays her and her husband wages as employees; there are no other employees. Helene has set up a qualified profit-sharing plan and a qualified pension plan covering herself and her husband. These two plans are not subject to the fiduciary responsibility rules of ERISA, because the plans do not cover any "employees." The result would be the same if Helene operated her business as a sole proprietorship, or if her husband owned any portion of the business as a partner or shareholder.

Q 3:30 Are there special fiduciary rules that apply in connection with the termination of a single-employer pension plan?

Yes. If a single-employer pension plan expressly provides for reversion of plan assets to the employer upon plan termination (after payment of plan benefits and expenses), the employer may take such a reversion. If there is such an employer reversion, the employer must pay a penalty tax of 50 percent of the reversion, which is reduced to 20 percent if the employer establishes a "qualified replacement plan" or elects to provide certain benefit increases upon termination. [IRC § 4980] ERISA contains a specific fiduciary obligation to comply with the requirements for a qualified replacement plan or for a qualifying increase in benefits, as the case may be. [ERISA § 404(d)(1)]

In addition, the plan administrator of a single-employer defined benefit pension plan must file a Notice of Intent to Terminate with the PBGC at least 60 days before a proposed termination. [ERISA § 4041(a)(2); PBGC Reg § 2616.3] The obligation to give such notice is not a fiduciary duty. (See Example 2 at Q 3:20.)

Q 3:31 What special fiduciary rules apply in the context of acquisitions and dispositions of businesses?

In the context of acquisitions and dispositions of businesses, a fiduciary's potential conflict of loyalties as plan fiduciary and agent of the employer is exacerbated. The circumstances often include tender offers, corporate restructurings, hostile takeovers, and various forms of control contests. (See the discussion of officers or employees of plan sponsors as plan fiduciaries at Q 2:21 and of settlor functions at Qs 3:18 through 3:21.) In particular, a corporate officer may be in the position of negotiating what benefits (under various plans subject to ERISA) will be extended to employees affected by the corporate transaction. In general, such a negotiation is a settlor function, although the corporate officer may be serving simultaneously as a plan fiduciary. If so, measures must be instituted to eliminate the conflict, including resignation or recusal. (See the discussion of resignation or recusal to satisfy the "exclusive benefit" requirement at Q 3:3.)

Q 3:32 When does ERISA preempt other rules of law?

The fiduciary requirements of ERISA generally preempt all state laws "insofar as they may . . . relate to any employee benefit plan. . . ." [ERISA § 514(a)] This means that ERISA generally supersedes the common law of trusts, as well as state tort and contract law.

However, ERISA does not preempt state law in connection with a severance pay arrangement if it is not an "employee benefit plan."

Example. In May 1990, an employer informed employees at one location that the employer would consolidate operations, and would discharge employees at that location. On September 15, 1990, the employer orally announced that employees who continued to work until the consolidation was complete would receive 60 days' additional pay following their last day of work. On November 15, 1990, the employer cancelled the arrangement. Employees were told they could continue to work for 60 days more at their regular pay. All employees were terminated on January 15, 1991.

The employees asserted state law claims for breach of contract, negligent misrepresentation and wage violations, as well as a federal claim of ERISA violations.

The Second Circuit Court of Appeals held that state law was not preempted, because the offer of 60 days' severance pay did not constitute an employee welfare plan under ERISA. According to the court, the employer did not have to engage in any "ongoing administrative program" to make the severance payments. [James v Fleet/Norstar Financial Group, No 92-7946, 1993 US App LEXIS (2d Cir 1993), quoting Fort Halifax Packing Co v Coyne, 482 US 1, 11 (1987)]

Q 3:33 Are there exceptions in ERISA to the preemption rules?

Yes. Exceptions apply in the case of "any law of any State which regulates insurance, banking, or securities," and any "generally applicable criminal law." [ERISA § 514(b)(2) and (4)] State tax laws "relating to" employee benefit plans are preempted by ERISA. [ERISA § 514(a); H Conf Rep No 97-984, 97th Cong, 2d Sess, 18, reprinted in 1982 US Code Cong & Ad News 4598, 4603] A tax on gains derived from real property transfers—a tax of general application—was recently found to "relate to" an employee benefit plan in more than a tenuous, remote or peripheral way, requiring preemption. [Morgan Guaranty Trust Co v Tax Appeals Tribunal, 80 NY2d 44 (1992)] A local real estate tax, however, was found not to be preempted by ERISA. [*In re* Am Fed of Musicians' & Employers' Pension Fund, NYLJ (March 10, 1993), at 21 (NY Sup Ct 1993)]

Q 3:34 What special fiduciary standards apply to public employee plans sponsored by federal, state, or municipal governments?

Public employee plans are creatures of state legislatures and are not subject to ERISA. The distinct fiduciary standards applicable to public employee plans derive from state statutes (increasingly modeled after ERISA) and common law.

The contrast with ERISA is evidenced in the context of "social investing." Social investing has been defined as investing where the principal impetus is not maximization of investment returns to benefit plan participants or their beneficiaries but to further some other policy or goal. (See the discussion of social investing at Qs 7:39 through 7:43.)

Some states have enacted statutes requiring social investing of pension assets. Moreover, standards under state laws that govern fiduciaries of such state plans may be less restrictive than ERISA.

Thus, public employee funds generally have a freer hand than ERISA funds to consider socially useful investments.

The current position of the DOL is that, under ERISA, fiduciaries may select an investment course that reflects non-economic factors, so long as application of such factors follows primary consideration of a broad range of investment opportunities that are equally economically advantageous.

Q 3:35 Is there a fiduciary duty to give accurate tax information to plan participants?

Generally not. There is generally no obligation for a fiduciary to give a participant or beneficiary any tax information, except as specifically provided by other statutes. [See IRC § 402(f) (rollover notice)] Any such obligation is not a fiduciary obligation. However, once a fiduciary undertakes to provide tax information, the information must be provided in a reasonable and prudent fashion.

> **Example.** An employer adopted a "five-plus-five" early retirement window for its pension plan. In addition, eligible participants could elect to receive a special, additional lump sum benefit. Written materials described the programs, and contained a prominent warning urging readers to consult their tax advisors. A toll-free phone number was made available to answer questions. The employer's benefits coordinator conducted a live video program, at which he answered several questions about rolling over the "qualified portion" of distributions in order to postpone income tax and avoid an excise tax on early distributions.
>
> Some participants elected the early retirement package, including the additional lump sum payments, and discovered that a portion of the lump sum payments could not be rolled over, because that portion exceeded the limits under IRC Section 415. The portion that could not be rolled over was subject to immediate taxation. The written materials that had been distributed did not address Section 415 limitations. The aggrieved participants asserted a breach of the duty of care and prudence.
>
> The fiduciaries' decision not to address Section 415 limitations in the written materials was held not to be a breach of fiduciary duty. Their decision fell within the prudent person standard and the

general duty to act in the interests of plan participants. [Farr v US West, Inc, 815 FSupp 1364 (D Ore 1992)]

Q 3:36 Can there be a fiduciary duty to reject an employer's contribution of property?

Yes. ERISA contains the exclusive benefit requirement, whereby a fiduciary is bound to pursue the advantage of the plan, for the benefit of participants and beneficiaries. [ERISA § 404(a)(1)(A)] ERISA also imposes an obligation to avoid transactions that the fiduciary knows or should know will constitute prohibited transactions. [ERISA § 406(a)]

The United States Supreme Court has ruled that a sponsor's contribution of unencumbered property (other than qualifying employer securities or qualifying employer real property) to a defined benefit pension plan in satisfaction of its funding obligation is a sale or exchange that is subject to the excise tax on prohibited transactions under IRC Section 4975. [United States v Keystone Consol Indus, Inc, No 91-1677 (1993)]

Justice Stevens noted in his dissent that a plan trustee or other fiduciary has the duty to reject property transfers that are disadvantageous to the plan. The Supreme Court has now clarified, that an employer's transfer of unencumbered property (other than qualifying employer securities or qualifying employer real property) to a pension plan in satisfaction of a funding obligation constitutes a prohibited transaction and is subject to an excise tax. Accordingly, such a transfer would plainly not be in the interest of the plan, and plan fiduciaries would also have specific duty not to permit the transfer to take place.

The Supreme Court's reasoning would support a similar duty to reject contributions of property (other than qualifying employer securities or qualifying employer real property) in the following circumstances:

1. Unencumbered property contributed as required contributions to money purchase pension plans;

2. Unencumbered property contributed as required matching contributions to employee stock ownership plans, profit-sharing plans, or stock bonus plans; and
3. Encumbered property under all circumstances.

The carrier was a fiduciary of an ERISA welfare benefit plan, because it had discretionary authority to grant or deny claims. Moreover, the carrier had a fiduciary duty to provide an accounting on demand, not because ERISA Section 404 or the plan documents required it, but because general principles of trust law as incorporated into ERISA required it. The employer was entitled to review a reasonable number of the carrier's records for the plan within reasonable time limits. [Libbey-Owens-Ford Co v Blue Cross & Blue Shield Mut of Ohio, 982 F2d 1031 (6th Cir 1993)]

Q 3:37 Can a third-party administrator have a fiduciary duty to give an accounting to an employer as plan sponsor?

Yes. ERISA does not expressly impose upon a third-party administrator a fiduciary duty to give an accounting on demand to an employer as plan sponsor. Nevertheless, a federal common law of trusts applies, including the rule that a fiduciary must furnish financial information to its principal on demand.

Example. An employer self-insured its health benefit plan. An insurance carrier administered claims as a third-party administrator. The employer deposited funds with the carrier to cover about two months' worth of claims and administrative fees. The carrier used the deposits to pay claims on behalf of the plan. The carrier issued administrative manuals to govern the processing of claims, retaining the authority to grant or deny claims and to resolve all disputes regarding coverage.

The carrier received rebates from hospitals and did not credit them to the employer. The carrier also improperly paid a number of invalid nursing home claims.

Chapter 4

Allocation and Delegation of Fiduciary Responsibility

Under ERISA, certain fiduciary duties may be allocated among named fiduciaries or delegated to other persons. Many of these duties relate to the administration of a plan or the investment of plan assets and may be delegated to persons such as administrators, trustees, investment managers, and, in certain instances, to plan participants and beneficiaries. This chapter examines the procedures by which plan fiduciaries may allocate or delegate their fiduciary duties, the types of duties that may be delegated, and the extent to which fiduciaries nevertheless retain certain fiduciary responsibilities for supervising and monitoring the actions and performance of those to whom fiduciary duties are delegated (including potential exposure for co-fiduciary liability).

How to Allocate or Delegate Fiduciary Responsibility	4-2
Co-Fiduciary Liability	4-8
Investment Managers	4-13
Participant-Directed Plan Investments	4-18

How to Allocate or Delegate Fiduciary Responsibility

ERISA provides a specific method for allocating fiduciary duties among plan fiduciaries and for delegating fiduciary duties to other persons. Certain powers are delegable; others are not. In order for a fiduciary to relieve himself or herself of responsibility for powers that are allocated or delegated, the method of allocation or delegation must be accomplished pursuant to the terms of the plan document. The following section addresses the various methods by which fiduciary duties may be allocated or delegated.

Q 4:1 May fiduciary duties be allocated among fiduciaries and delegated by fiduciaries to other fiduciaries?

Yes, fiduciary duties (other than so-called trustee duties, relating to the management or control of plan assets) may be allocated or delegated pursuant to authority contained in the plan document authorizing the allocation or delegation. Certain fiduciary duties may be allocated among named fiduciaries, and named fiduciaries may designate persons other than named fiduciaries to carry out certain fiduciary duties (if the plan expressly provides procedures for allocation or designation). [ERISA § 405(c)(1)] If the plan instrument does not provide for a procedure for the allocation of fiduciary responsibilities among named fiduciaries, any allocation that the named fiduciaries may make among themselves will not relieve a named fiduciary of liability for the performance of fiduciary responsibilities allocated to other named fiduciaries. [DOL Reg § 2509.75-8 at FR-13] Special restrictions apply to the allocation or delegation of duties relating to the management or control of plan assets (i.e., trustee responsibilities). (See Qs 4:3 and 4:4.)

Q 4:2 May fiduciary duties be delegated to or allocated among nonfiduciaries?

Generally not. If a person performs (or has the authority or responsibility to perform) functions relating to the management, investment, or administration of a plan, he or she will become a fiduciary with respect to the plan. (See, generally, Chapter 2.) Because a person performing fiduciary duties is deemed to be a fiduciary

Allocation and Delegation of Fiduciary Responsibility   Q 4:3

(regardless of his or her title), fiduciary duties may only be delegated to fiduciaries. In addition, fiduciary duties may only be allocated among named fiduciaries and cannot be allocated among (1) fiduciaries other than named fiduciaries or (2) nonfiduciaries. [ERISA § 405(c)(1)]

Planning Pointer. Since the determination of fiduciary status is based on the individual's function rather than title, a nonfiduciary will automatically become a fiduciary if fiduciary duties are delegated to the nonfiduciary. The one exception to this rule relates to the delegation of investment responsibility to a plan participant or beneficiary with respect to his or her individual account, pursuant to Section 404(c) of ERISA (see Qs 4:27 et seq). Despite the delegation of responsibility for their own investment choices, participants will not be deemed to be fiduciaries under ERISA.

Q 4:3   What are trustee responsibilities?

Trustee responsibilities include those responsibilities provided in a plan's trust instrument (if any) to manage or control the assets of a plan, other than a power under the trust instrument of a named fiduciary to appoint an investment manager. [ERISA § 405(c)(3)]

Planning Pointer. Examples of trustee responsibilities generally include the following duties (most of which relate to the investment and disposition of plan assets and, therefore, are subject to ERISA's fiduciary duties):

1. To invest and reinvest the assets of the plan in various types of securities and other property. Examples of such investments would include, but not necessarily be limited to, some or all of the following:
   - common and preferred stock;
   - convertible securities;
   - obligations of the United States Government or any government of a State of the United States (and each of their agencies and instrumentalities);
   - corporate obligations and other forms of indebtedness (e.g., bonds, notes, debentures, commercial paper);

Q 4:3   **Fiduciary Responsibility Answer Book**

- qualifying employer securities (see Q 7:28);
- qualifying employer real property (see Q 7:29);
- savings and time deposits;
- guaranteed investment contracts (GICs), annuity contracts, insurance policies, and other arrangements sponsored by insurance carriers (see Qs 7:15 through 7:20 regarding annuities and 7:21 through 7:26 regarding GICs);
- certain types of foreign securities, provided that the conditions under Section 404(b) of ERISA and DOL Reg § 2550-404(b)-1 (relating to the maintenance of the indicia of ownership of plan assets outside the jurisdiction of the United States district courts) are satisfied (see Qs 7:27 and 7:48); and
- certain types of options and warrants.

The foregoing list does not represent all of the types of securities and other property that plan trustees and investment managers of a plan may invest in under ERISA, but is representative of the general types of securities and other property that plan trustees and investment managers may invest in under ERISA. For example, many plans subject to the fiduciary rules of ERISA invest in real property, or interests in real property, either directly or through real property collective or group trusts or limited partnerships (see Qs 7:45, 8:56 and 8:58).

2. To exercise all rights appurtenant to plan assets, such as the power to exercise proxies, participate in voting rights, mergers, consolidations, reorganizations or liquidations. (See Q 4:23 for further details on the ERISA fiduciary responsibilities relating to the voting of proxies.)
3. To compromise, contest, litigate, arbitrate or abandon claims or demands in connection with plan assets.
4. To pool all or a portion of plan assets in one or more collective, commingled, or group trusts (see Q 4:22).
5. To lend plan assets to broker/dealers and other borrowers of securities, provided that certain rules are complied with and/or to borrow such sums as may be prudent and in the best interest of the plan.
6. To hold all plan assets in safekeeping.

Allocation and Delegation of Fiduciary Responsibility   Q 4:6

7. Generally, to perform all other acts that the fiduciary deems necessary and prudent for the protection of the assets of the plan.

This list does not include all trustee powers, but merely sets forth examples of the powers generally exercised by plan trustees. The plan's trustee or named fiduciary may delegate some or all of the foregoing powers to an ERISA-qualified investment manager. (See Qs 2:24 and 2:25, describing the qualifications and general authority of an ERISA investment manager.)

Q 4:4 May a named fiduciary delegate trustee responsibilities to a person other than a trustee?

Generally, a named fiduciary may not delegate trustee responsibilities to any person other than a trustee. [ERISA § 405(c)(1)] Investment authority may be delegated, however, to an investment manager under ERISA (see Q 2:24, defining an investment manager) if the plan document provides that the named fiduciary (responsible for control and management of plan assets) has the power to appoint an investment manager. If investment authority is delegated to an investment manager (and not to a trustee), the trustee will generally not be liable for the acts or omissions of the investment manager and will be relieved of the obligation to invest plan assets under the control of the investment manager. [ERISA §§ 402(a)(3); 403(a)(2); 405(d)(1)] Investment authority may, under certain limited circumstances, be delegated to a plan participant or beneficiary pursuant to Section 404(c) of ERISA (see Qs 4:27 et seq).

Q 4:5 How are fiduciary duties allocated among named fiduciaries and delegated to other fiduciaries?

Fiduciary duties must be allocated and delegated in a prudent manner in accordance with plan procedures designed for that purpose (see generally, Qs 3:4 through 3:10 regarding the prudence requirement).

Q 4:6 Does the allocation or delegation of fiduciary duties relieve the allocating or delegating fiduciary of any fiduciary duties under ERISA?

Yes, but only in certain situations and only to a certain extent. If responsibilities are allocated prudently among named fiduciaries in accordance with plan procedures, a named fiduciary will not be liable for the acts and omissions of other named fiduciaries, except as provided in ERISA's co-fiduciary rules (see Qs 4:9 through 4:12 for a discussion of these rules). [DOL Reg § 2509.75-8 at FR-13] Similarly, a named fiduciary will not be liable for the acts and omissions of a person who is not a named fiduciary in carrying out the responsibilities delegated to such person, provided that the named fiduciary prudently selects and monitors his or her actions (see Qs 7:1 through 7:8 regarding selecting and monitoring investment managers) and also has not violated ERISA's co-fiduciary rules (see Qs 4:9 through 4:12). If the plan instrument does not provide for a procedure for allocating fiduciary responsibilities among named fiduciaries, any allocation that the named fiduciaries may make among themselves will not relieve a named fiduciary of responsibility or liability. [DOL Reg § 2509.75-8 at FR-13 and FR-14]

Q 4:7 What is the fiduciary duty to monitor?

A fiduciary's duties with regard to the delegation of certain fiduciary responsibilities does not end once the fiduciary has delegated its duties to another person. A fiduciary's duty to monitor the actions of those individuals to whom fiduciary responsibilities have been delegated generally requires the appointing fiduciary to review and evaluate, at reasonable intervals, the performance of other fiduciaries to whom fiduciary responsibilities are delegated. Such review should be accomplished in a manner that may be reasonably expected to ensure that the performance of the fiduciaries to whom the delegation is made has complied with the terms of the plan and all statutory standards, including ERISA's exclusive benefit, prudence, diversification, and prohibited transaction rules. (See generally, Chapters 3 and 5.)

There is no single procedure that will be appropriate in all cases. The procedure adopted may vary with the nature of the plan and other facts and circumstances relevant to the choice of the procedure. [DOL Reg § 2509.75-8; Whitfield v Cohen, 682 FSupp 188, 196 (SDNY 1988) (A "fiduciary must ascertain within a reasonable time whether an agent to whom he has delegated a trust power is properly carrying out his responsibilities.")]

Planning Pointer. The appointing fiduciary should establish procedures to enable it to monitor the performance of the fiduciaries

Allocation and Delegation of Fiduciary Responsibility Q 4:8

to whom it has delegated fiduciary responsibilities. Such procedures could include, for example, a requirement that the appointed fiduciary furnish written reports and oral presentations to the appointing fiduciary at regular intervals (e.g., quarterly, semi-annually, or other time period as may be appropriate for the relevant circumstances). (See Qs 7:7 and 7:8 regarding the monitoring of investment managers.)

Example. The Board of Directors of *ABC* Corporation appointed *N* as trustee of the corporation's employee stock ownership plan (ESOP). *N*, who was also a vice president of *ABC* Corporation, had no prior training or experience managing an employee benefit plan or investing its assets and was not present at the board meeting when he was appointed. The board neither questioned *N*, reviewed the performance of plan investments made by *N*, nor otherwise monitored the performance of *N* as a trustee. The board did not request any annual reports from the plan committee and, in fact, never appointed a committee. The board did not require *N* to value the ESOP at fair market value on an annual basis as provided in the plan document (*N* made an annual valuation using book value). The board's failure to conduct any independent investigation into *N*'s qualifications to serve as a fiduciary, and its failure to conduct periodic reviews of *N*'s performance after his appointment, constitute breaches of the duty of prudence. The board and the directors, individually, imprudently neglected to monitor the administration and investment of plan assets by *N*; imprudently permitted *N* to continue to make plan purchases in excess of fair market value; and imprudently failed to remove *N* or take appropriate steps to prevent *N* from continuing to violate ERISA in connection with the management of the plan. [Martin v Harline, 1992 US Dist LEXIS 8778 (D Utah 1992)] (See, generally, Qs 3:4 through 3:10, regarding the prudence requirement, Qs 4:9 through 4:12, regarding co-fiduciary liability and Qs 7:1 through 7:8 regarding selecting and monitoring investment managers.)

Q 4:8 Can a delegating fiduciary be relieved of its duty to monitor the performance of those individuals to whom fiduciary responsibilities have been delegated?

No. The delegation of fiduciary responsibilities does not relieve the delegating fiduciary of the duty to monitor periodically the performance of the individuals to whom such responsibilities have been delegated.

Co-Fiduciary Liability

In addition to being responsible (and personally liable) for his or her own fiduciary breaches, ERISA imposes obligations on all plan fiduciaries to guard against breaches of fiduciary responsibilities by other plan fiduciaries. Generally, a fiduciary will be liable for an act or omission of his or her co-fiduciary only if he or she participates in such breach, i.e., if by failing to comply with ERISA's standard of care rules, he or she has enabled the co-fiduciary to breach ERISA, or if the fiduciary has knowledge of a breach by a co-fiduciary and fails to make reasonable efforts under the circumstances to correct it. The following section provides further details on how a plan fiduciary can become liable for certain actions of his or her co-fiduciaries.

Q 4:9 Is a fiduciary who participates or conceals an act or omission of another fiduciary liable for the acts or omissions of the other fiduciary?

A fiduciary will be liable for the acts or omissions of another fiduciary if a fiduciary *knowingly* participates in, or *knowingly* undertakes to conceal, an act or omission of another fiduciary, *knowing* such act or omission to be a breach of fiduciary responsibility. [ERISA § 405(a)(1); Fink v National Savings & Trust Co., 772 F2d 951, 958 (DC Cir 1985)] If a fiduciary does not possess knowledge of his or her participation or concealment of a breach of fiduciary duty, the fiduciary lacking such knowledge will not necessarily be liable for the acts or omissions of another fiduciary. [*See* Davidson v Cook, 567 FSupp 225, 233 (ED Va 1983), *aff'd*, 734 F2d 10 (4th Cir), *cert denied*, 469 US 899 (1984) (where the court found that both ERISA Sections 405(a)(1) and 405(a)(3) (see Q 4:10) require actual knowledge that a breach of fiduciary duty is occurring or has occurred. Although finding that "in many instances at least some of the fiduciaries should have known of breaches," the court declined to impose any fiduciary liability on certain plan trustees who did not possess actual knowledge.)]

Example. *A* and *B* are co-trustees of a trust under a plan. *B* invests in commodity futures in violation of the trust instrument. If *B* tells *A* of this investment, and *A* alters the plan's financial records to conceal this investment, *A* will be liable under the co-fiduciary rules for knowingly concealing the breach. [ERISA Conf Comm Rep]

Q 4:10 Is a fiduciary who knows of a breach of fiduciary responsibility by another fiduciary liable for the acts or omissions of the other fiduciary?

Generally, yes, unless the fiduciary takes reasonable steps under the circumstances to remedy the breach of fiduciary duty. A fiduciary will be considered to have breached his or her co-fiduciary duties if he or she has knowledge of a breach by such other fiduciary and fails to make reasonable efforts under the circumstances to remedy the breach. [ERISA § 405(a)(3); Freund v Marshall & Ilsley Bank, 485 FSupp 629, 640-41 (WD Wisc 1979) (A plan administrator who merely resigned, rather than taking constructive action to remedy the breach, was held liable for a successor's breaches of which he had actual knowledge.)] Section 405(a) of ERISA imposes a duty on a fiduciary to take affirmative actions to remedy breaches by other fiduciaries.

Planning Pointer. A fiduciary who knows of a breach of fiduciary duty by a co-fiduciary and fails to take corrective measures, cannot merely resign from his or her fiduciary position in protest of the co-fiduciary's action or omission and escape co-fiduciary liability. Mere resignation, without more, does not satisfy the co-fiduciary's affirmative obligation to take specific action to remedy a breach of fiduciary duty. [DOL Reg § 2509.75-5, FR-10; Freund v Marshall & Ilsley Bank, 485 FSupp at 641] At the very least, the resigning fiduciary should consider notifying the appropriate government agencies of the breach (e.g., the U.S. Department of Labor). Under certain circumstances, the fiduciary may determine that it is necessary to proceed to court for an injunction (or similar relief) to prevent an imminent action that would result in a breach of fiduciary responsibility by a co-fiduciary.

Q 4:11 Are there any other circumstances under which a fiduciary could be liable for the acts or omissions of another fiduciary?

Yes. A fiduciary is liable for a breach of fiduciary responsibility of another fiduciary if he or she, by failing to fulfill his or her own fiduciary responsibilities, has enabled the other fiduciary to commit a breach of fiduciary duty. [ERISA § 405(a)(2); Free v Briody, 732 F2d 1331 (7th Cir 1984) (a trustee of an ERISA plan breached his fiduciary duties by failing to assert control over plan assets, thereby allowing his co-fiduciaries to use plan assets improperly, resulting in plan losses. After signing the plan instrument, the fiduciary failed to exercise care, skill, and prudence in dealing with the plan assets. The failure to assert control over, and protect plan assets, enabled his co-fiduciary to misuse them, resulting in significant plan losses.)]

Example 1. Plan X has two trustees, Y and Z, who are both responsible for the investment of Plan X's assets. Y does not monitor Z, and Z invests all of the assets of Plan X in a very risky investment, in which he has a personal interest. The investment fails and Plan X loses a significant amount of its assets. Y's negligence (failure to monitor Z) allowed Z to commit the breach and as a result, Y is liable to Plan X under ERISA's co-fiduciary rules.

Example 2. Trustee A of Multiemployer Plan Y pled guilty to federal charges of theft and embezzlement of over $2.59 million of Plan Y's assets. As part of the embezzlement scheme, Trustee A purchased a certificate of deposit for himself and deposited plan assets into his own account (instead of purchasing investments for Plan Y) and drafted false safekeeping receipts to give to Plan Y's administrator. The co-trustees of Trustee A had very little involvement in the management of Plan Y assets. For example, the trustees never conducted an independent investigation to verify whether Plan Y's assets were protected. There was also no procedure implemented to review checks that Plan Y had issued. In addition, the trust document required two signatures on all instruments executed on behalf of Plan Y—one of an employer trustee, and one of a union trustee. There was no procedure in place to verify whether the two-signature rule was being followed.

Allocation and Delegation of Fiduciary Responsibility   Q 4:12

The co-trustees violated the co-fiduciary duty rules under Section 405(a)(2) of ERISA since their failure to act prudently with respect to the management of Plan Y's assets enabled Trustee A to commit a breach of fiduciary duty (i.e., theft and embezzlement). The co-trustees did nothing to oversee Trustee A—some co-trustees did nothing but attend meetings. Despite the co-trustees' reliance on experts (e.g., Plan Y's lawyer and accountant), the co-trustees, in breaching their own fiduciary duties, enabled Trustee A to embezzle funds from Plan Y. [Mazur v Gaudet, 14 EBC (BNA) 2844 (ED La 1992)]

Planning Pointer. Individuals should be wary of becoming a figurehead fiduciary of a plan without really getting involved in plan management. In *Mazur*, described above, the defendant trustees had little involvement in the management of the plan. Uninvolved trustees could be held liable as co-fiduciaries for failure to satisfy their prudence obligation. A trustee is obligated to do more than simply attend meetings. He or she has an independent duty to comply with ERISA. A "pure heart and an empty head [is] not good enough." [Mazur v Gaudet, 14 EBC (BNA) 2844 (ED La 1992)]

Q 4:12   What action must a fiduciary take if the fiduciary knows of a co-fiduciary's breach of fiduciary duty?

As noted in Q 4:10, a fiduciary must act affirmatively and take direct action to make reasonable efforts to remedy the breach. Also, every fiduciary must exercise prudence to prevent his or her co-fiduciaries from committing a breach of fiduciary responsibility and must jointly manage and control plan assets unless specific duties have been allocated among them. [ERISA § 405(b)(1)(B)] However, a trustee will not be liable for following the proper directions of a named fiduciary if such directions are authorized by the terms of the plan and are not contrary to ERISA.

Example 1. A plan is considering the construction of a building to house its administrative offices. One trustee has proposed that the building be constructed on a cost-plus basis by a particular contractor without competitive bidding. When the trustee was questioned by another trustee as to the basis for the choice of the contractor, the impact of the construction on administrative costs,

Q 4:12 **Fiduciary Responsibility Answer Book**

and on other issues relating to the proposed construction, the trustee who made the proposal could not provide any satisfactory reasons. Several trustees feel that they would violate their general fiduciary duties if they entered into the proposed contract. Despite their position, the majority of trustees appears to be ready to vote to enter into the proposed contract.

If the minority trustees do not take any affirmative action to prevent the potential breach of fiduciary duty by the majority trustees, they will have breached their fiduciary duties under the co-fiduciary liability rules. Therefore, the minority trustees must take all reasonable and legal steps to prevent the action. Such steps might include:

- Notifying the U.S. Department of Labor;
- Publicizing the vote if the decision to proceed occurs as proposed; or
- As a last resort, attempting to obtain an injunction from a federal district court to prevent the action.

As noted in Q 4:10, mere resignation without taking appropriate steps to prevent the imprudent action will not suffice for the minority trustees to avoid liability once they have knowledge that the imprudent action is under consideration. [DOL Reg § 2509.75-5, FR-10]

Example 2. A trustee suggests to a co-trustee that the plan should invest a large percentage of its assets in shares of stock of one company, which the trustee believes will increase in value in a short time. The co-trustee, without any inquiry as to the trustee's stock recommendation, but being somewhat uncomfortable as to the significant amount of assets used to purchase the stock, nonetheless takes no action to prevent the trustee from purchasing the stock for the plan. After the plan purchases the stock, the co-trustee realizes that the purchase may have been a breach of the fiduciary duty to diversify plan assets.

Here, the co-trustee is probably liable for a breach of co-fiduciary duty by knowingly participating in the trustee's breach by acquiescing in the stock purchase. However, it may be possible to mitigate the co-trustee's liability if, after the co-trustee realizes a breach may have occurred once the stock is actually purchased,

Allocation and Delegation of Fiduciary Responsibility   Q 4:14

the co-trustee makes a reasonable effort to remedy the breach. Such steps might include reviewing the current price of the stock and subsequently deciding to prudently liquidate all or a portion of this investment and invest in other vehicles that would satisfy, among other things, ERISA's diversification requirement.

Investment Managers

One of the primary and most popular methods employed by plan fiduciaries to lessen their responsibility for the investment of plan assets is delegating authority and control over the management of plan assets to an ERISA-qualified investment manager. This section reviews the circumstances under which this delegation can be accomplished (provided, of course, that the delegating fiduciary is prudent in appointing, and periodically monitoring the investment performance of, such manager). (See Qs 7:7 and 7:8 regarding selecting and monitoring an investment manager.)

Q 4:13   May a named fiduciary delegate investment duties?

Generally, a named fiduciary may not delegate authority or discretion to manage or control plan assets to others, unless the plan documents allow delegation of such authority to another named fiduciary or to persons who are investment managers under ERISA. (See Q 2:24, defining the term "investment manager" under ERISA.) In addition, the named fiduciary must appoint trustees who have the authority to manage and control assets, unless the plan document designates such trustees. [ERISA § 403(a)] Therefore, the only entities that may invest plan assets are named fiduciaries, trustees, and investment managers and, in certain limited instances, plan participants and beneficiaries (see Qs 4:27 et seq).

Q 4:14   Who is responsible for appointing an investment manager?

The named fiduciary, who is responsible for the control and management of plan assets, is responsible—if it so chooses—for appointing investment managers under ERISA and for delegating such control and management to them. [ERISA § 402(c)(3)] However, a named fiduciary is not *required* to delegate investment duties to an investment manager and, instead, may decide to retain and exercise such responsibilities unilaterally.

Q 4:15 May fiduciaries, other than named fiduciaries, appoint an investment manager?

No, for the reasons discussed in Q 4:14.

Q 4:16 May nonfiduciaries appoint an investment manager?

No, for the reasons discussed in Q 4:14.

Q 4:17 What are the responsibilities of an investment manager?

As a result of the delegation of investment authority, the investment manager is responsible for the control and management of plan assets. Responsibilities of an investment manager for the management and control of plan assets generally are set forth in an investment management agreement between the manager and the named fiduciary of the plan. The agreement must acknowledge, among other things, that the manager has accepted the responsibility and is a fiduciary of the plan. Responsibilities could include many of the same investment powers generally afforded to trustees (see Q 4:3 and Q 7:6 regarding investment management agreements).

Q 4:18 Must investment managers follow the directions of a named fiduciary of a plan?

Generally not, unless the named fiduciary issues investment guidelines to the investment manager (see Q 7:5). Once a named fiduciary properly delegates the authority or discretion to manage or control plan assets to an investment manager, the named fiduciary will no longer have any fiduciary responsibility for the investment of such assets, provided that the named fiduciary prudently selects and periodically monitors the actions of the investment manager, and provided that the named fiduciary has not violated ERISA's co-

Allocation and Delegation of Fiduciary Responsibility   Q 4:21

fiduciary rules in performing such selection or monitoring duties. (See Qs 7:1 through 7:8.)

Q 4:19 May other plan fiduciaries serve as investment managers?

Yes. Any fiduciary, *other than a trustee or named fiduciary*, who satisfies the ERISA requirements to be an investment manager, may serve as an investment manager. (See Qs 2:24 and 4:20.)

Q 4:20 Is anyone precluded from serving as an investment manager under ERISA?

Yes. The only persons who may be appointed an investment manager are those who are investment managers under ERISA—namely, banks (as defined in the Investment Advisors Act of 1940); insurance companies qualified under the laws of more than one state to manage, acquire, and dispose of plan assets; or persons registered as investment advisors under the Investment Advisors Act of 1940. [ERISA § 3(38); DOL Reg § 2509.75-5, FR-6] (See Q 2:24.) For example, an investment manager that is neither a bank nor an insurance company, and that is not registered under the Investment Advisors Act of 1940 in reliance on an exemption from registration provided in such Act, may not be an investment manager under ERISA. In addition, even if an investment advisor's application for registration is pending, such advisor may not function as an investment manager under ERISA prior to the effective date of registration under the Investment Advisors Act. [DOL Reg § 2509.75-5, FR-6, FR-7] Also, a broker-dealer registered under the Securities and Exchange Act of 1934 cannot act as an investment manager unless it is an investment advisor, bank, or insurance company as defined in ERISA. [DOL Adv Op Ltr No 76-20 (Mar 30, 1976)]

Q 4:21 How is fiduciary responsibility shared under ERISA when there are multiple plan investment managers?

Except in instances of co-fiduciary liability, the liability of a fiduciary who is not a "named fiduciary" is generally limited to the functions delegated to such fiduciary by a named fiduciary. Absent co-fiduciary liability, such a fiduciary will not be personally liable for

Q 4:22 **Fiduciary Responsibility Answer Book**

any phases of management or administration of the plan that have not been delegated to him or her. [DOL Reg § 2509.75-8 at FR-16] Because investment managers are solely responsible for the investment of plan assets under their own management and control, each investment manager—in situations where there are multiple investment managers—does not share fiduciary responsibility with other investment managers who do not have the authority to manage or control the same pool of assets. Thus, the investment manager has fiduciary responsibility only for the allocable portion of plan assets over which such manager is specifically delegated investment management responsibility. It is possible, however, for an investment manager to breach ERISA's fiduciary duties with respect to plan assets *other than the portion over which such manager has control* in instances where such manager breached the co-fiduciary duty rules (e.g., by permitting a co-fiduciary, such as the trustee, to commit a breach of fiduciary duty). (See Qs 4:9 through 4:12.)

Q 4:22 Is the operator of a collective, common, or group trust or of a separate account an investment manager with respect to a plan that invests in such a vehicle?

Generally, yes, provided that the operator of the collective, common, or group trust satisfies the definition of an investment manager under ERISA, that is, it is a bank, insurance company, or investment advisor and acknowledges that it is a fiduciary with respect to the plan. (See Q 2.24, defining the term "investment manager" under ERISA.) Generally, the assets held in a collective or common trust fund of a bank, a group trust, and certain separate accounts of an insurance company (subject to certain exceptions) are considered to be plan assets. In instances where such funds are plan assets and where the "operators" (i.e., the sponsor) of such funds have discretionary control and authority with respect to the investment of plan assets, the operators are considered to be plan fiduciaries. Further, in instances where such operators are banks, insurance companies, or investment advisors, and such operators acknowledge in writing that they are fiduciaries with respect to the plan, they are also considered to be investment managers. [*See* DOL Reg § 2510.3-101(h)(1) and Qs 8:32 and 8:56 regarding instances where group, collective, and

Q 4:23 Are trustees and investment managers required to exercise proxies or other rights associated with plan securities?

Generally, yes. Because the exercise of proxies is an act of plan asset management, ERISA generally requires that the trustee have the exclusive authority to vote proxies except in certain situations (e.g., where investment authority for plan assets has been transferred to an investment manager). The investment manager generally has the responsibility to vote the proxies unless (1) the trustee reserves the right to vote proxies; or (2) the plan specifies that the trustee must follow the directions of a named fiduciary who is not a trustee. In voting proxies, the investment manager must follow ERISA's fiduciary requirements, including analyzing the issues and determining which course of action is in the best interests of plan participants and beneficiaries. For example, an investment manager generally cannot be passive regarding the exercising of proxies. (See Qs 7:35 through 7:37 regarding the fiduciary requirements applicable to proxy voting under employee stock ownership plans.) [DOL Letter to Robert A. G. Monks, Institutional Shareholder Services, Inc. (Jan 23, 1990); DOL Letter to Helmuth Fandl, Chairman of Retirement Board of Avon Products, Inc (Feb 23, 1988)]

Q 4:24 Can an entity that otherwise would not be an investment manager become one merely by exercising proxies or other rights associated with plan securities over which they have responsibility?

Generally, no. However, such an entity could become a fiduciary with respect to the exercise of proxy voting, unless the right to vote proxies is passed through to participants under Section 404(c) of ERISA. (See Qs 4:36, 4:40 (items 7 and 9), and 4:43.)

Q 4:25 What is a QPAM?

A QPAM is a qualified professional asset manager that has discretionary management authority over an investment fund and satisfies certain other standards. A QPAM may be a bank, savings and loan association, insurance company, or investment advisor, and must acknowledge in writing that it is a fiduciary. The use of a QPAM permits various parties in interests who are related to employee benefit plans to engage in transactions involving plan assets that would otherwise be prohibited transactions under ERISA, if, among other conditions, the assets are managed by a QPAM that is independent of the parties in interest and that meet specified financial conditions. [Prohibited Transaction Class Exemption (PTCE) 84-14; see Q 5:14 regarding QPAMs and prohibited transactions]

Q 4:26 Is a qualified professional asset manager an investment manager?

Generally, yes. Because a QPAM has the power to manage plan assets, typically is a registered investment advisor, bank, or insurance company, and acknowledges in writing that it is a fiduciary, a QPAM satisfies the definition of an investment manager under Section 3(38) of ERISA. In fact, in describing the proposed prohibited transaction class exemption relating to QPAMs, the DOL recognized that the QPAM requirements follow the general pattern of the definition of an investment manager under ERISA and that each category is subject to regulation by federal or state agencies. A financial entity does not achieve QPAM status with regard to a plan unless it enters into a written management agreement or issues a contract that delineates its management authority over plan assets and contains a statement acknowledging that it is a fiduciary. However, to the extent that a QPAM is a savings and loan association that is not a bank under the Investment Advisors Act of 1940, a QPAM would not be an investment manager under ERISA (but it would still be a fiduciary and qualify as a QPAM). [PTCE 84-14]

Participant-Directed Plan Investments

In addition to insulating a plan fiduciary from plan investment responsibilities and potential liabilities by appointing an ERISA-qualified investment manager, under certain limited circumstances, a plan fiduciary can also limit exposure to such liability by delegating

Allocation and Delegation of Fiduciary Responsibility Q 4:28

responsibility for investment decisions to plan participants or their beneficiaries. This section details the conditions under which fiduciary responsibilities can be delegated to participants or beneficiaries, thereby alleviating the delegating fiduciary, and also the participant or beneficiary, from ERISA investment responsibilities and possible liabilities.

Q 4:27 What is the purpose of ERISA Section 404(c) regarding participant-directed plan investments?

The purpose of Section 404(c) and the regulations promulgated by the Department of Labor is to set forth detailed rules under which a plan fiduciary may be insulated from investment responsibility (and, therefore, personal liability) arising from participants' exercise of control over their accounts in individual account plans (such as money purchase pension, profit sharing, 401(k), and 403(b) plans). Normally, plan fiduciaries are generally considered to have breached their fiduciary duties in instances where the plans for which they are responsible incur losses as a result of their acts or omissions. Section 404(c) provides for a limited exception to ERISA's general fiduciary duties in certain instances where a participant or beneficiary exercises control over assets in his or her individual account.

If an individual account plan satisfies the rules set forth in the Section 404(c) regulations, and if a participant actually exercises control over the assets in his or her account, the plan fiduciary (e.g., the named fiduciary, plan administrator, trustee) will be relieved of any liability resulting from the participant's investment decision with respect to his or her account, and the participant will not be deemed a fiduciary under ERISA. The plan fiduciary will, however, retain the fiduciary responsibility for, among other things, prudently selecting and periodically monitoring the performance of the investment alternatives made available to the plan's participants by the fiduciary. [DOL Reg § 2550.404c-1(a)(1)] (See the discussion of the fiduciary responsibilities a fiduciary retains under a Section 404(c) plan at Q 4:47.)

Q 4:28 Must a plan comply with the requirements of Section 404(c) of ERISA?

No. ERISA does not mandate that pension plans comply with the requirements of Section 404(c) of ERISA. Instead, these rules merely provide a method through which plan fiduciaries can insulate themselves from certain fiduciary liabilities relating to participant-directed investments under an individual account plan.

Q 4:29 What is an "ERISA Section 404(c) plan"?

An ERISA Section 404(c) plan is an individual account plan, such as a money purchase pension, profit sharing, 401(k), or 403(b) plan, that provides an opportunity for a participant or beneficiary to (1) exercise control over the assets in his or her individual account; and (2) choose, from among a broad range of investment alternatives, the manner in which some or all of the assets in his or her account are invested. [DOL Reg § 2550.404c-1(b)(1)] An individual account plan is a retirement plan that provides an individual account for each participant. Under such a plan, benefits are based solely upon the amounts contributed to the participant's account, and any income, expenses, gains, losses, and forfeitures of accounts of other participants that may be allocated to such a participant's account. [ERISA § 3(34)]

Q 4:30 How does an ERISA Section 404(c) plan provide a participant or beneficiary an opportunity to exercise control over assets in his or her account?

An ERISA Section 404(c) plan provides a participant or beneficiary an opportunity to exercise control over assets in his or her account only if the participant or beneficiary has a reasonable opportunity to (1) give investment instructions to an identified plan fiduciary, and (2) obtain sufficient information to make informed investment decisions. [DOL Reg § 2550.404c-1(b)(2)(i)(A) and (B)] In affording participants and beneficiaries the right to give investment instructions, such instructions may be given in writing, electronically, or telephonically. However, participants and beneficiaries must have the option to receive from the plan fiduciary written confirmation of the instructions.

> **Planning Pointer.** The specific manner by which participants may give investment instructions must be communicated to participants in written procedures that may be (but are not required to be) described in the plan documents. It may be most convenient

Allocation and Delegation of Fiduciary Responsibility   Q 4:31

for a plan to include the various investment alternatives, and the means by which investment instructions are to be communicated to the identified plan fiduciary, in a separate appendix to the plan. In this way, the plan document itself need not be amended and updated every time a new fiduciary is appointed.

Q 4:31   What does it mean to afford a participant or beneficiary a reasonable opportunity to give investment instructions?

An ERISA Section 404(c) plan must give a participant or beneficiary a reasonable opportunity to give investment instructions. To be relieved of liability for investment decisions concerning a participant's account, a fiduciary is required to implement prudently the participant's investment instructions. Since the participant is the decision maker with regard to the investment of assets in his or her account, the fiduciary's primary responsibility is to ensure that the instructions of participants are carried out. There are instances, however, in which a fiduciary is excused from implementing the instructions of a participant (see Q 4:44).

An ERISA Section 404(c) plan is not necessarily required to allow participants to direct the investments on a daily basis. Instead, the plan may impose reasonable restrictions on the frequency with which participants may give investment instructions. Restrictions are reasonable only if they permit participants to issue investment instructions with a frequency that is appropriate in light of the volatility of particular investment vehicles. (See Q 4:35 regarding the application of the volatility requirement to "core alternatives" and additional investment alternatives.) At a minimum, participants must be able to transfer their account from one core alternative (as defined in Q 4:32) to another at least once every three months. [DOL Reg § 2550.404c-1(b)(2)(B)(2)(ii)(c)]

Example 1. A profit-sharing plan allows participants to transfer funds among three investment vehicles that constitute a broad range of investments, every January 1, April 4, July 1, and October 1. Under these facts, this plan is not an ERISA Section 404(c) plan because there is a three-month period (i.e., January 2 through April 3) during which control cannot be exercised by participants and beneficiaries. [DOL Reg § 2550.404c-1(f)(3)]

Example 2. The plan described in Example 1 is revised to allow investment instructions by participants and beneficiaries with respect to each investment during the first 10 days of each calendar quarter (i.e., January 1-10, April 1-10, July 1-10, and October 1-10). This plan satisfies the condition that instructions must be permitted not less frequently than once within any three-month period, since there is no three-month period during which control cannot be exercised. [DOL Reg § 2550.404c-1(f)(2)]

Q 4:32 What are "core alternatives" under an ERISA Section 404(c) plan?

Under an ERISA Section 404(c) plan, a participant must at a minimum be able to choose from among at least three investment alternatives. [DOL Reg § 2550.404c-1 (b)(3)(i)(B)] The three investment alternatives, which must constitute a broad range of alternatives, are called "core alternatives." Each core alternative must be diversified and have materially different risk and return characteristics.

Q 4:33 How does an ERISA Section 404(c) plan offer a broad range of investment alternatives?

An ERISA Section 404(c) plan satisfies the requirement to offer a broad range of investment alternatives if it gives participants and beneficiaries a reasonable opportunity to:

1. Materially affect the potential return on assets over which the participants and beneficiaries exercise investment control;
2. Choose from at least three investment alternatives, each of which is diversified and has materially different risk and return characteristics (core alternatives);
3. Enable a participant or beneficiary to achieve a portfolio with risk and return characteristics at any point within the "range normally appropriate" by choosing among the core alternatives; and
4. Diversify investments so as to minimize the risk of large losses.

Allocation and Delegation of Fiduciary Responsibility Q 4:33

For a plan to have a broad range of investments, each core alternative must be diversified within itself and among the other core alternatives. If assets over which an individual has control are sufficiently small, so that the only prudent means by which to achieve diversification is by utilizing a "look-through" investment vehicle, a plan must offer a look-through vehicle (e.g., mutual funds, common, or collective trust fund, pooled investment funds, fixed rate investment contracts of a bank or insurance company, pooled insurance company separate accounts, etc.). [DOL Reg § 2550.404c-1(b)(3)(i)(C)] In determining whether look-through investment vehicles are sufficiently diversified, the underlying investments of such vehicles will be considered. [DOL Reg § 2550.404c-1(b)(3)]

Planning Pointer. It is probably not necessary for an ERISA Section 404(c) plan to offer either a very conservative or a very risky alternative in order to have materially different risk and return characteristics. The DOL has indicated that the regulations merely require that each of the investments have materially different risk and return characteristics, without specification as to the nature of the risks. [Preamble to DOL Reg § 2550.404c-1] While the regulations require that the available investment alternative enable participants to achieve a portfolio with aggregate risk and return characteristics at any point within the range "normally appropriate for participants," it is unclear what is intended by this phrase.

Planning Pointer. Fiduciaries who select the various core alternatives for an ERISA Section 404(c) plan should recognize that the Department of Labor has not provided for a "safe harbor" where plans would automatically satisfy Section 404(c) of ERISA by offering certain "preapproved" investments. Instead, plan fiduciaries must evaluate investment vehicles on a case-by-case basis, perhaps with the assistance of professional investment advisors or consultants.

Example 1. A profit-sharing plan allows plan participants to invest any portion of their individual accounts in the following three investment vehicles:

- Fund A—a mutual fund, known as a "balanced" fund, that invests between 50 and 60 percent of its assets in equities of a diversified classification of companies, between 20 and

Q 4:33   **Fiduciary Responsibility Answer Book**

40 percent of its assets in government and corporate bonds (generally of intermediate to longer maturities), and between 0 and 30 percent of its assets in cash, cash equivalents, and other short-term vehicles;
- Fund B—a money market mutual fund; and
- Fund C—a mutual fund that invests predominantly in stocks of companies in the utility industry.

Under these facts, the profit-sharing plan is probably not an ERISA Section 404(c) plan since Fund C, which invests in securities of companies concentrated in a single industry (utilities), is not sufficiently diversified.

Example 2. A 401(k) plan allows plan participants to invest in the following three funds:
- Fund A—an aggressive mutual fund that invests in stocks and attempts to mirror the general trends of the Standard and Poor's 500 with an emphasis on growth (as opposed to income);
- Fund B—a "balanced" income mutual fund consisting of equities seeking income (i.e., dividends) rather than growth, government and corporate bonds, and a small percentage of cash and cash equivalents; and
- Fund C—which provides a blended interest rate tied to GICs of three different insurance companies and bank investment contracts of two different banks (all such contracts investment grade rated with at least an A minus rating by Standard and Poor's and an Aaa rating by Moody's).

Under these facts, the 401(k) plan probably offers a broad range of investment alternatives. Here, each fund, as a look-through investment vehicle, is adequately diversified, materially different from the others in terms of risk and return (the least conservative investment—the equity fund—offers potentially the highest return and is materially different from the other funds), is diversified in combination with all core alternatives, and probably achieves a risk and return within a "range normally appropriate."

Example 3. A money purchase pension plan offers the following investment alternatives to participants:

4-24

Allocation and Delegation of Fiduciary Responsibility   Q 4:34

- A fund that invests predominantly in foreign currencies of many different countries;
- A portfolio of real property concentrated in a single geographic area; and
- A junk bond fund.

This plan does not offer a broad range of investment alternatives. The three funds, all of which may achieve a relatively high return, are significantly risky and, therefore, do not have materially different risk and return characteristics. In addition, the second alternative—the portfolio of real property concentrated in a single geographic area—is probably not sufficiently diversified. In any event, the selection of these investment vehicles may raise general prudence issues with respect to each particular investment vehicle, given the relatively high risk inherent in each vehicle.

Planning Pointer. Although employer securities might offer significantly different risk and return options, an employer security may never be a core alternative because it would not meet the diversification requirement. [Preamble to DOL Reg § 2550.404c-1 regulations] (See Q 4:45.)

Q 4:34 May an ERISA Section 404(c) plan offer investment alternatives in addition to the core alternatives?

Yes. An ERISA Section 404(c) plan may offer investment vehicles in addition to core alternatives, provided that the plan makes available at least three core alternatives. However, in order for Section 404(c) insulation to apply, the volatility requirement—that is, that participants must be afforded the opportunity to give investment instructions with a frequency that is appropriate in light of the volatility of the market—must be applied to both core alternatives and additional investment alternatives.

Planning Pointer. If a plan meets all of the Section 404(c) requirements, except that one of the additional investment alternatives does not meet the volatility requirement, the plan may still be considered an ERISA Section 404(c) plan. The fiduciary will not, however, receive any insulation from liability as to the assets invested in the alternative that does not meet the volatility requirement. The participant will not be deemed to have sufficient control, since he or she will not be able to transfer assets in light of the volatility of the market. In such an instance, the fiduciary will remain responsible for any losses that are incurred in connection with that alternative. [Preamble to DOL Reg § 2550.404c-1]

Q 4:35 What must a Section 404(c) plan provide if, due to the volatility of the market, a participant is allowed to transfer assets out of any investment alternative more than once in a three-month period?

In such circumstances, either one of the core alternatives (e.g., a more stable core alternative) or a low-risk cash equity fund must accept the transfer of those assets with the same frequency. [DOL Reg § 2550.404c-1(b)(2)(ii)(C)(2)]

If the plan allows the participant to transfer the assets into one of the more stable core investment alternatives, the core investment need only be established to allow the transfer of funds into it, rather than to allow the participant to transfer assets into and out of it. [Preamble to DOL Reg § 2550.404c-1]

If the plan instead chooses to satisfy the volatility requirement by allowing the participant to transfer the assets into an "income producing, low risk, liquid fund, subfund or account," such transfer must be permitted to be made as often as the participant is permitted to give instructions for a volatile investment alternative transfer (which allows investment instructions to be given more often than once within a three-month period). Essentially, such a fund would serve as a temporary "cash equivalency" vehicle into which a participant may place assets to be transferred to another investment alternative when the next scheduled investment opportunity occurs.

The participant must then be given the opportunity to transfer assets out of the low-risk fund into the other core investments as often as those core alternatives normally allow instructions to be accepted. [DOL Reg § 2550.404c-1(b)(2)(ii)(C)(2)(ii)]

Allocation and Delegation of Fiduciary Responsibility   Q 4:35

Planning Pointer. A plan sponsor maintains the right to alter the investment vehicle into which a participant may transfer assets so long as the plan documents are properly amended and plan participants are given reasonable notice of the change.

Example 1. A plan offers a broad range of three diversified core alternatives (Funds A, B, and C). In addition, it offers a high-risk equity fund. In light of the volatility of the market and the risk involved, the equity fund allows participants to issue investment instructions once in every four-week period. Once in every four-week period, the plan must allow the participant to either transfer assets from the equity fund into one of either Fund A, B, or C or into a low-risk cash equivalency fund.

Example 2. A plan offers the same funds as described under Example 1 (core alternatives—Funds A, B, and C, a high-risk equity fund and a low-risk cash equivalency fund). In addition, the plan also offers a one year, fully insured certificate of deposit (CD) as an additional investment alternative which, based on the volatility of the market, investment instructions could prudently be offered less frequently than once in a three-month period. Under this plan, the participant could not transfer the assets of the CD into the low-risk fund, since the low-risk cash fund alternative is available only to high-risk investments (e.g., the high-risk equity fund). Therefore, plan sponsors must make arrangements for the period between a participant's withdrawal of assets from a low-risk investment and the next available date on which the participant may provide investment instructions.

Planning Pointer. Nothing precludes the assessment of a penalty or valuation adjustment for early or premature withdrawals from an investment alternative contract (e.g., a CD, guaranteed insurance contract, or a bank investment contract). However, if the penalties or adjustments are too high, they may have the effect of discouraging transfers and would, therefore, deprive participants of their right to exercise control. The reasonableness of the penalties or adjustments is to be assessed by the plan fiduciary in light of the investment alternative, the rate of return, market forces, and similar factual considerations. [Preamble to DOL Reg § 2550.404c-1]

Q 4:36 When has a participant or beneficiary exercised independent control with respect to decisions regarding assets in his or her individual account under an ERISA Section 404(c) plan?

A participant or beneficiary will be deemed to have exercised independent investment control with respect to the investment of assets and the exercise of voting, tender, and similar rights associated with the participant's or beneficiary's ownership interest in an investment vehicle if:

1. The participant's or beneficiary's investment in the investment alternative was itself the result of an exercise of control;
2. The participant or beneficiary was provided a reasonable opportunity to give instructions; and
3. The participant's or beneficiary's control must be "independent."

Whether a participant or beneficiary has exercised independent control depends upon the facts and circumstances of each case. However, such exercise of control will not be independent if:

1. The participant or beneficiary is subject to improper influence by a plan fiduciary or plan sponsor with respect to the transaction;
2. The plan fiduciary concealed material, nonpublic facts regarding the investment (unless the disclosure would have violated a federal or state law that was not preempted by ERISA); or
3. The participant or beneficiary is legally incompetent and the responsible plan fiduciary accepts the instructions of the participant or beneficiary knowing him or her to be legally incompetent.

[DOL Reg § 2550.404c-1(c)(1) and (2)]

Q 4:37 May a participant or beneficiary exercise independent control if the transaction involves a fiduciary?

It depends. It may be possible for a participant or beneficiary to exercise independent control even if a fiduciary is involved in the transaction. A fiduciary may be involved in a transaction with a participant under an ERISA Section 404(c) plan provided that the transaction is fair and reasonable to the participant or beneficiary. For these purposes, a transaction will be fair and reasonable if the participant or beneficiary pays no more than, or receives no less than, adequate consideration in connection with the transaction (see Q 7:34 for a discussion of adequate consideration). However, a participant or beneficiary will not be deemed to exercise independent control in the case of a sale, exchange, or lease of property (other than certain permissible transactions involving an investment in employer securities set forth in Q 4:45) between an ERISA Section 404(c) plan and a plan fiduciary or affiliate, or in the case of a loan to a plan fiduciary or affiliate, unless the transaction is fair and reasonable to the participant or beneficiary. [DOL Reg § 2550.404c-1(c)(3)]

Q 4:38 Is a plan considered to be an ERISA Section 404(c) plan if the plan permits a participant to exercise control over certain assets of the plan but not over others?

A plan may be an ERISA Section 404(c) plan even though it only permits participants to exercise control over a specified portion of their account balances. However, the insulation from liability under Section 404(c) of ERISA will not apply to transactions involving assets over which the participant is not permitted to exercise control and, in such instances, the plan fiduciaries are subject to all of the fiduciary requirements under ERISA with respect to these assets. [Preamble to DOL Reg § 2550.404c-1]

> **Example 1.** A profit-sharing plan has a 401(k) feature where participants may invest their pre-tax (401(k)) contributions among a broad range of investment alternatives. The profit-sharing plan also provides for an employer-matching contribution that is invested solely by the plan's investment manager. Assuming that the plan meets all other requirements of Section 404(c) of ERISA, the plan is an ERISA Section 404(c) plan, except that, with respect to investment of employer matching contributions, the protection of Section 404(c) of ERISA will not apply.

Q 4:39 Must a participant give a plan fiduciary affirmative investment instructions for the fiduciary to be relieved of liability under Section 404(c) of ERISA?

Generally, yes. A plan fiduciary will not be relieved of responsibility for investment decisions, unless those decisions have been affirmatively made by a participant or beneficiary. [ERISA § 404(c)(1)(i)] Until an affirmative instruction is given, no relief is available under Section 404(c).

Planning Pointer. For example, a fiduciary may not simply allow assets to remain uninvested if a participant refuses to exercise control over those assets. The fiduciary remains responsible for prudently investing those assets and will be personally liable for any losses that occur as a result of their failure to earn income. [Preamble to DOL Reg § 2550.404c-1] In such an instance, a plan may contain a so-called default provision stating that assets will be automatically invested in a particular investment vehicle (e.g., a short-term "money market" fund) or in a specified manner (e.g., certain percentages in designated investment vehicles), until the participant affirmatively instructs the plan fiduciary as to the investment of assets in his or her account. Under such circumstances, however, protection under Section 404(c) would still be unavailable, and the plan fiduciary would have to monitor (and possibly change) the investment in accordance with ERISA's general fiduciary duties. (In fact, the DOL decided not to reinstate the default option set forth in its 1987 proposed regulations—which permitted the use of a "safe/default" fund in the absence of an affirmative election—because the DOL believed that the use of such vehicles would reduce flexibility in plan design and investments.) [Preamble to DOL Reg § 2550.404c-1]

Planning Pointer. A plan may treat an affirmative election as effective until it is affirmatively revoked, provided that the participant is given the opportunity to transfer the assets or to alter his or her election. [Preamble to DOL Reg § 2550.404c-1] Thus, in order to maximize the amount of affirmative elections made by participants, plans should be drafted in a manner that automatically honors the most recent affirmative investment election by a participant, until and unless a subsequent election is made. If, for example, a plan is drafted in a manner that requires an affirmative investment election each year (rather than automatically carrying

Allocation and Delegation of Fiduciary Responsibility Q 4:40

forward the most recent election), plan fiduciaries will continue to retain fiduciary responsibility for the investment of assets in a participant's account until the participant makes an affirmative election.

Q 4:40 What types of information and documents must be supplied automatically to participants and beneficiaries to give them the opportunity to obtain sufficient information to make informed investment decisions under an ERISA Section 404(c) plan?

The following information and documents must be furnished automatically to all participants and beneficiaries:

1. *Notice of Limited Liability.* Participants and beneficiaries must receive an explanation that the plan is an ERISA Section 404(c) plan (i.e., that it complies with ERISA Section 404(c) and Title 29 of the CFR § 2550.404c-1) and that the plan fiduciaries may be relieved of liability for any losses that result from the participant's or beneficiary's investment instructions.

2. *Description of All Investment Alternatives.* A description of investment alternatives available under the plan must be supplied to participants and beneficiaries, including a general description of the investment objectives, risk and return characteristics, and the types and diversification of assets comprising each investment alternative.

Planning Pointer. If a plan does not limit the investment alternatives available to participants and allows participants to invest in *any* asset administratively feasible for the plan to hold, a general statement to that effect will be a sufficient description. However, participants should be encouraged to obtain and review materials relating to any potential investment prior to actually making an investment. [Preamble to DOL Reg. § 2550.404c-1]

3. *Identification of Investment Managers.* Designated investment managers must be identified.

Planning Pointer. While there is no guidance regarding the extent of the information necessary for identification of an investment manager, a brief description of the investment manager, including

Q 4:40 Fiduciary Responsibility Answer Book

its prior investment performance, will most likely suffice. If desired, additional detailed information about the investment manager could be provided to participants.

   4. *Investment Instructions and Restrictions.* Participants and beneficiaries must receive an explanation of how to give investment instructions, including any limits imposed on these instructions, such as transfers to or from a designated investment alternative or restrictions on voting, tender, and similar rights.

Planning Pointer. If, for example, a penalty will be assessed or valuation adjustment made if a participant or beneficiary withdraws assets from an alternative before the maturity date of that investment alternative, the participant or beneficiary must be informed of that possibility. [Preamble to DOL Reg § 2550.404c-1] CDs, GICs, and other fixed-rate investment contracts are typical examples of where a penalty or an adjustment may apply. Such investments typically have "equity-wash" restrictions (i.e., where transfers to and from a fixed-rate investment contract are made through an equity fund where the funds must remain for a specified period of time), prohibitions on direct transfers from such contracts to competing funds, requirements that investments remain in a GIC for a certain minimum period, and a fee or charge for premature redemption or a market value adjustment for suspension of a contract.

   5. *Transaction Fees.* A description of transaction fees and expenses charged directly to the participant's account (such as commissions, sales loads, deferred sales charges, or redemption or exchange fees) must be automatically provided to participants and beneficiaries. This requirement does not relate to all fees, charges, and expenses, but only those that arise in connection with the purchase or sale of any interest in an investment alternative. The description need not include expenses, fees, or commissions incurred in the operation or management of the investment alternative. [Preamble to DOL Reg § 2550.404c-1] A typical example of an expense not required to be disclosed is a mutual fund's management fee. Although certain charges (such as management fees) are not required to be supplied automatically to participants and beneficiaries, they must be supplied to participants and beneficiaries upon request.

Allocation and Delegation of Fiduciary Responsibility Q 4:40

6. *Provider of Information.* Participants and beneficiaries must be furnished with a description of the additional information available upon request (see Q 4:41) and the name, address, and telephone number of the plan fiduciary responsible for providing that information.

7. *Confidentiality Procedures.* If a plan provides for investment in employer securities, participants and beneficiaries must automatically receive a description of the procedure established to provide for confidentiality of participants' and beneficiaries' directions relating to the purchase, holding, and sale of employer securities and the exercise of the voting, tender, and similar rights, and identification of the plan fiduciary responsible for monitoring compliance with those procedures.

8. *Prospectuses.* Participants and beneficiaries must automatically receive, immediately following their initial investment in an investment alternative for which a prospectus is required under the Securities Act of 1933 (Securities Act) (i.e., securities offered for public sale), a copy of the most recent prospectus, unless it was furnished immediately prior to the investment.

Planning Pointer. A mutual fund is a typical example of an investment alternative that is subject to the Securities Act and for which a prospectus is required. It appears that this requirement extends solely to an investment alternative subject to the Securities Act and not to each underlying investment (i.e., all "securities" as broadly defined by the Securities and Exchange Commission (SEC)) within an investment alternative. Since interests in an insurance company separate account or in a bank collective trust fund generally are not subject to the Securities Act, participants (in addition to any other investor in such interests) are not entitled to a prospectus. Despite the requirements of ERISA Section 404(c), the staff of the SEC has made recommendations favoring legislation to provide employees in participant-directed defined contribution plans with additional disclosure. The SEC recommendations contain a proposal to amend Section 3(a)(2) of the Securities Act to remove the exception for interests in collective trusts and separate accounts in which participant-directed defined contribution plans invest. The gist of the proposal is that a unit of participation in, for instance, a bank pooled fund or insurance company separate account offered to a plan participant ought to

4-33

be considered a security just like a mutual fund offering. If this legislative change is made, plans will be required under Section 404(c) to provide participants with a prospectus for these types of investments.

9. *"Pass-Through" Proxy Materials.* Participants and beneficiaries must automatically receive, subsequent to an investment, any materials provided to the plan relating to the exercise of voting, tender, or similar rights, to the extent such rights are passed through to participants and beneficiaries. (In the case of investments in employer securities, such rights must be passed through to participants and beneficiaries along with all other shareholders.) [DOL Reg § 2550.404c-1(b)(2)(i)(B)(1)]

Planning Pointer. It is not sufficient that the fiduciary provide participants and beneficiaries with a referral for obtaining information. Rather, the fiduciary must ensure that participants and beneficiaries have basic information concerning the investment alternatives under the plan. Participants and beneficiaries must be given enough information and enough time to make informed investment decisions to exercise the rights incident to the ownership of those assets. [Preamble to DOL Reg § 2550.404c-1]

Q 4:41 What types of information must be furnished to participants and beneficiaries upon request to enable them to make informed investment decisions under an ERISA Section 404(c) plan?

The following information must be furnished to a participant or beneficiary on request:

1. *Operating Expenses.* A description of the annual operating expenses of each designated investment alternative (e.g., investment management fees, administrative fees, transaction costs, and other costs that reduce a participant's rate of return).

2. *Other Information.* Copies of any prospectuses, financial statements and reports, and other information relating to investment alternatives that is furnished to the plan.

3. *List of Assets.* A list of the assets comprising the portfolio of each designated investment alternative that constitute plan

Allocation and Delegation of Fiduciary Responsibility   Q 4:41

assets (see the discussion regarding plan assets at Qs 8:15 through 8:24 and 8:51 through 8:58), the value of each asset, and, with respect to each asset that is a fixed-rate investment contract issued by a bank, savings and loan association, or insurance company, the name of the issuer of the contract, the term of the contract, and the rate of return on the contract.

Planning Pointer. Since, under ERISA's annual reporting rules, this information must be reported on Form 5500, in most cases little additional work will need to be done by plan fiduciaries to supply this information to participants and beneficiaries. If, however, changes that materially affect the investment portfolio have occurred since the last annual report was issued, simply supplying the latest annual report may not give the participant enough information to make an informed decision. In this circumstance, the plan fiduciary will not receive Section 404(c) liability protection.

4. *Overall Investment Performance.* Participants and beneficiaries are entitled to receive information concerning the value, as well as past or current performance, of the shares in any designated investment alternative.

5. *Individual Investment Performance.* Participants and beneficiaries are also entitled to receive information concerning the value of shares or units in designated investment alternatives held in the participant's or beneficiary's account (although plans may establish reasonable procedures limiting requests for account balance information). [DOL Reg § 2550.404c-1(b)(2)(i)(B)(2)]

Planning Pointer. While it would be permissible to include the information described in Questions 4:40 and 4:41 in either the summary plan description or in a separate statement, in most cases a separate statement to participants and beneficiaries may be preferable. This will avoid frequent amendments to the summary plan description to conform to modifications to the plan's investment alternatives. In any event, for plans invested in mutual funds, most of the information will be included in the mutual funds' prospectuses. Also, inquiries to the plan administrator can be minimized if the participants are provided with the toll-free numbers of the available investment funds.

Q 4:42 Who is responsible for providing the information described in Questions 4:40 and 4:41?

The identified plan fiduciary, or a person designated by the plan fiduciary to act on his or her behalf, is responsible for providing the information delineated in Questions 4:40 and 4:41 to participants and beneficiaries. A plan need not name a specific person as the plan fiduciary, but may instead designate the title or position of the fiduciary, such as plan administrator or trustee. However, participants and beneficiaries must have an identifiable source from whom to obtain information. [Preamble to DOL Reg § 2550.404c-1]

Q 4:43 What other duties are the responsibility of an identified plan fiduciary under an ERISA Section 404(c) plan?

In addition to providing information to participants and beneficiaries, the identified plan fiduciary must also:

1. Comply with the investment instructions of a participant or beneficiary;

2. Ensure that the confidentiality procedures and information relating to the purchase, holding, and sale of employer securities, as well as the exercise of voting, tender, and similar rights with respect to employer securities are followed; and

3. Ensure that an independent fiduciary is appointed to carry out activities relating to any situation that involves a potential for undue employer influence upon participants and beneficiaries with regard to the direct or indirect exercise of shareholder rights.

[DOL Reg §§ 2550.404c-1(b)(2)(i)(A); 2550.404c-1(b)(2)(i)(B)(1); 2550.404c-1(d)(2)(ii)(E)(4)(vii); 2550.404c-1(d)(2)(ii)(E)(4)(viii); and 2550.404c-1(d)(2)(ii)(E)(4)(ix); Preamble to DOL Reg § 2550.404c-1d; Leigh v Engle, 727 F2d 113 (7th Cir 1984), *remanded*, 669 FSupp 1390 (ND Ill 1985), *aff'd*, 858 F2d 361 (7th Cir 1988), *cert denied*, 489 US 1078 (1989) (when the trustees of a plan are faced with a conflict of interest resulting from a corporate control contest, the trustees may be unable to carry out their duties with the sole interest of plan beneficiaries in mind, and should seriously consider appointing neutral fiduciaries (at least temporarily) to avoid any undue influence).]

Q 4:44 Must an identified plan fiduciary of an ERISA Section 404(c) plan always comply with the investment instructions of a participant or beneficiary?

Generally, yes. An identified plan fiduciary must follow the investment instructions of a participant or beneficiary, except that such fiduciary may decline to follow participant and beneficiary instructions (as well as instructions specified in the plan) which, if implemented:

1. Would result in a prohibited transaction (see generally, Chapter 5);
2. Would generate income that would be taxable to the plan;
3. Would jeopardize the plan's tax-qualified status under the Internal Revenue Code;
4. Would not be in accordance with the plan documents and instruments (insofar as they are consistent with ERISA);
5. Would cause a fiduciary to maintain the indicia of ownership of any assets of the plan outside the jurisdiction of the district courts of the United States (other than as permitted by Section 404(b) of ERISA and DOL Reg § 2550.404b-1; see Qs 3:27 and 7:48);
6. Could result in a loss in excess of a participant's or beneficiary's account balance; or
7. Would result in a direct or indirect:
   - sale, exchange, or lease of property between a plan sponsor or any affiliate of the sponsor and the plan (except for certain transactions that are exempt under Section 408(e) and meet other requirements under the Section 404(c) regulations);
   - loan to a plan sponsor or any affiliate of the sponsor;
   - acquisition or sale of any employer real property; or
   - acquisition or sale of any employer security, except in certain circumstances (see Q 4:45 for a discussion of the exceptions).

Q 4:45 Fiduciary Responsibility Answer Book

[DOL Reg §§ 2550.404c-1(b)(2)(ii)(B) and 2550.404c-1(d)(2)(ii)]

Q 4:45 Under what circumstances will a plan fiduciary be relieved of liability for any loss that results from a participant's or beneficiary's exercise of control with respect to the acquisition or sale of employer securities?

A plan fiduciary will not be liable for losses resulting from a participant's or beneficiary's exercise of control with respect to the acquisition or sale of employer securities if, in addition to the general requirements that apply to ERISA Section 404(c) plans, the following conditions are satisfied:

1. The securities are "qualifying employer securities" (see Q 7:28 for a definition of qualifying employer securities);
2. The securities are stock or an equity interest in a publicly traded partnership;
3. The securities are publicly traded on a national exchange or other generally recognized market;

Planning Pointer. The standard for determining if a market is sufficiently established to qualify for this provision is whether it ensures that participants can dispose of employer securities in a manner that is not subject to the influence of the employer. [Preamble to DOL Reg § 2550.404c-1]

4. The securities are traded with sufficient frequency and in sufficient volume to assure that participant and beneficiary directions to buy or sell the security may be acted upon promptly and efficiently;

Planning Pointer. If a fiduciary exercises discretion in the timing of the execution of transactions concerning employer securities, the fiduciary will remain liable for any losses that are sustained under ERISA Title 1, part 4. [Preamble to DOL Reg § 2550.404c-1]

5. Information provided to shareholders of such securities is provided to participants and beneficiaries with accounts holding such securities;

Allocation and Delegation of Fiduciary Responsibility   Q 4:47

6. Voting, tender, and similar rights are passed through to participants and beneficiaries with accounts holding such securities;
7. Participants and beneficiaries are given information relating to the confidentiality procedures (for the purchase, holding, and sale of employer securities and the exercise of voting, tender, and similar rights) and identification of the plan fiduciary responsible for monitoring compliance with those procedures; and
8. An independent fiduciary is appointed to carry out activities where there is the potential for undue employer influence on participants and beneficiaries with regard to the direct or indirect exercise of shareholder rights.

[DOL Reg § 2550.404c-1(d)(2)(ii)(E)(4)]

Q 4:46 Does a plan fiduciary have an obligation to provide investment advice to a participant or beneficiary?

No. A plan fiduciary has no obligation to provide investment advice to a participant or beneficiary under an ERISA Section 404(c) plan. [DOL Reg § 2550.404c-1(c)(4)]

Q 4:47 What types of fiduciary responsibilities does a plan fiduciary continue to retain although a plan satisfies the requirements of Section 404(c) of ERISA?

Even though a plan satisfies the requirements of Section 404(c) of ERISA and relieves plan fiduciaries of liability for violations of fiduciary duties resulting from participant-directed investments, a plan fiduciary remains responsible for, among other things, the following:

- The prudent selection and monitoring of plan investment alternatives;
- The proper and timely implementation of participants' investment decisions;
- The timely dissemination of required information; and

- The avoidance of prohibited transactions (i.e., transactions between the plan and certain parties in interest or transactions involving a conflict of interest among, or self-dealing by, fiduciaries) (see, generally, Chapter 5).

For example, if a participant gives an investment instruction to a plan fiduciary and, due to the imprudence of the fiduciary, a loss is sustained by the participant's account, the fiduciary will remain liable because the loss was the result of the fiduciary's breach of his or her duties rather than as a result of the instructions of the participant. [Preamble to DOL Reg § 2550.404c-1]

Planning Pointer. Since plan fiduciaries retain certain fiduciary responsibilities, it is important for fiduciaries to determine at the outset whether the insulation afforded by Section 404(c) outweighs the administrative costs and burdens that accompany compliance with its requirements. If a plan does not satisfy Section 404(c), it is still possible for it to maintain a prudently managed, well diversified portfolio and thereby comply with the fiduciary duty requirements under ERISA. Neither Section 404(c) nor the DOL regulations set forth, by implication or otherwise, standards for all ERISA-covered plans requiring the types of investments a fiduciary must make in order to maintain a prudent or well-diversified portfolio.

Q 4:48 If a participant under a Section 404(c) plan engages in a prohibited transaction under ERISA and the Internal Revenue Code, will the participant be liable?

Probably no, under the prohibited transaction rules of ERISA, but, probably yes, under the prohibited transaction rules of the Code.

If a participant engages in a transaction with a party in interest with respect to the plan (which is prohibited under the Code and ERISA), such plan complies with Section 404(c), and the participant actually exercises independent control over plan assets, he or she will not violate the prohibited transaction rules under ERISA. [Preamble to DOL Reg. § 2550.404c-1] If a participant exercises independent control over the assets in his or her individual account in accordance with the regulations, that participant will not be considered a fiduciary of the plan. [DOL Reg § 2550.404c-1(d)(1)] Further, Section

Allocation and Delegation of Fiduciary Responsibility Q 4:49

404(c) of ERISA expressly states that where a plan participant exercises independent control over the assets in his or her own account, no fiduciary will be liable under Part 4 of Title I of ERISA, which contains the prohibited transaction rules.

However, such a transaction may violate the prohibited transaction rules under the Internal Revenue Code. Since there is no provision in the Internal Revenue Code corresponding to Section 404(c) of ERISA, there is no statutory exemption from the excise taxes imposed by the Code on prohibited transactions involving an ERISA Section 404(c) plan.

Example. A participant, P, independently exercises control over assets in his individual account plan by directing a plan fiduciary, F, to invest 100 percent of his account balance in the stock of one company. In addition, P directs F to purchase the stock from B, who is a party in interest with respect to the plan. Neither P nor F has engaged in a transaction prohibited under Section 406 of ERISA: P, because he is not a fiduciary with respect to the plan by reason of his exercise of control, and F, because he is not liable for any breach of part 4 of Title I that is the direct and necessary consequence of P's exercise of control. However, a prohibited transaction under Section 4975(c) of the Code may have occurred, and, in the absence of an exemption, tax liability may be imposed. [DOL Reg § 2550.404c-1(f)(6)]

Q 4:49 How is co-fiduciary liability limited under Section 404(c) of ERISA?

If the plan complies with Section 404(c), no other person who is otherwise a fiduciary shall be liable for any loss or for any breach of ERISA Title I, part 4 that is the direct and necessary result of the participant's exercise of control. [DOL Reg § 2550.404c-1(d)(2)(i)]

Example 1. A participant, P, independently exercises control over assets in his individual account plan by directing a plan fiduciary, F, to invest 100 percent of his account balance in the stock of one company. P is not a fiduciary with respect to the plan by reason of his exercise of control, and F will not be liable for any losses that necessarily result from P's investment instruction. [DOL Reg § 2550.404c-1(f)(5)]

One effect of this provision is that it relieves plan fiduciaries of liability as co-fiduciaries under Section 405 of ERISA. [Preamble of DOL Reg § 2550.404c-1]

Example 2. If a participant gives an investment instruction that may be carried out in more than one way, (e.g, purchase certain securities in an unspecified manner), and the fiduciary chooses a method of implementing the instructions that results in a breach of fiduciary duty (e.g., the fiduciary purchases the securities from a party in interest), the fiduciary will remain liable for any resulting losses or consequences of the breach of his or her duties. [Preamble to DOL Reg § 2550.404c-1]

Example 3. A participant, P, independently exercises control over assets in his individual account plan by directing a plan fiduciary, F, to invest 100 percent of his account balance in the stock of one company. P does not specify that the stock be purchased from B, a party in interest, and F chooses to purchase the stock from B. In the absence of an exemption, F has engaged in a transaction prohibited by Section 406(a) of ERISA because the decision to purchase the stock from B is not a direct or necessary result of P's exercise of control. [DOL Reg § 2550.404c-1(f)(7)]

Chapter 5

Prohibited Transactions

To discharge his or her fiduciary obligations to a plan, every fiduciary must be familiar with the laws prohibiting various transactions between a plan and various related parties. These "prohibited transaction" provisions supplement and amplify the minimum standards of fiduciary conduct prescribed by ERISA. They generally preclude a fiduciary from causing a plan to engage in certain transactions with "parties in interest." This chapter discusses the types of transactions that are considered prohibited transactions, the exceptions to the prohibited transaction rules, and the consequences to a fiduciary of entering into a prohibited transaction.

In General	5-2
Liability and Penalties	5-5
Sales, Exchanges or Leases	5-10
Loans or Extensions of Credit	5-13
Goods, Services, and Facilities	5-20
Employer Securities and Employer Real Property	5-24
Self-Dealing	5-25
Asset Transfers	5-28
Parties With Adverse Interests	5-29
Kickbacks	5-30
Corrections and Exemptions	5-30

In General

Q 5:1 What is a prohibited transaction?

ERISA and the Internal Revenue Code (Code) prohibit certain transactions between plans and specified persons (called "disqualified persons" in ERISA and "parties in interest" in the Code). These transactions are referred to as prohibited transactions. ERISA places the responsibility for prohibited transactions on the fiduciary, whereas the Code places the responsibility for prohibited transactions on the party in interest who participates in the prohibited transaction. [ERISA § 406; IRC § 4975(a)]

A fiduciary (defined in Chapter 2) may not knowingly cause the plan to engage in any of the following prohibited transactions:

1. The sale, exchange, or lease of any property between the plan and a party in interest (see the discussion of who is a party in interest at Q 5:4);
2. Lending money or extending credit between the plan and a party in interest;
3. Furnishing goods, services, or facilities between the plan and a party in interest;
4. Transfer of plan assets to a party in interest or use of plan assets by or for the benefit of a party in interest; or
5. The acquisition or holding on behalf of the plan of any "employer security" or "employer real property" (see the discussion of what is an "employer security" or "employer real property" at Q 5:29) in excess of the ERISA section 407 limits.

Further, a fiduciary of a plan may not:

1. Deal with the assets of the plan in his or her own interest or for his or her own account (i.e., self-dealing);
2. Act in a transaction involving the plan on behalf of a party whose interests are adverse to the interest of the plan, its participants or its beneficiaries (i.e., engage in potential conflicts of interest); or

3. Receive any consideration from any party dealing with the plan in connection with a transaction involving plan assets (i.e., kickbacks).

A transaction between a plan and a party in interest is a prohibited transaction; (a) even if such transaction would normally be considered prudent [Leib v Comm'r, 88 TC 1474 (1987)]; and (b) even if the plan, its participants, or its beneficiaries do not incur a loss as a result of the transaction and the parties acted in good faith. [Cutaiar v Marshall, 590 F2d 523 (3d Cir 1979)]

Note. The prohibited transaction rules are intended to set forth *per se* prohibitions. Congress did not want to permit any of the listed transactions, regardless of whether they were good for the plan. Accordingly, the fact that the plan made a profit on the transaction is not a defense.

Each of these prohibited transactions is discussed in this chapter, as are the statutory and administrative exemptions to these prohibited transaction rules.

Q 5:2 May a plan fiduciary receive a benefit from the plan?

Yes. Section 408(c) of ERISA provides that the prohibited transaction rules are not to be construed as prohibiting any fiduciary from receiving any benefit to which the fiduciary may be entitled as a participant or beneficiary in the plan, as long as the benefit is computed and paid on a basis that is consistent with the terms of the plan as applied to all other participants and beneficiaries.

Q 5:3 May a person serve as a plan fiduciary if he or she is involved in a different capacity with a party in interest?

Yes. Section 408(c) of ERISA provides that a person may act as a fiduciary even if he or she is an officer, employee, agent, or other representative of a party in interest.

Planning Pointer. A fiduciary who wears two hats must use extra care to assure that he or she satisfies the loyalty and other fiduciary requirements when he or she acts on behalf of the plan.

Q 5:4 Who is a party in interest or a disqualified person with respect to a plan?

A party in interest with respect to a plan is one of the following:

1. A fiduciary of a plan (see the discussion in Chapter 2);
2. Counsel to an employee benefit plan;
3. An employee of an employee benefit plan;
4. A person providing services to the plan;
5. An employer whose employees are covered by the plan;
6. An employee organization whose members are covered by the plan;
7. A direct or indirect owner of 50 percent or more of either
   (a) the combined voting power of all classes of corporate stock,
   (b) the total value of shares of all classes of such corporation's stock,
   (c) the capital or profit interests of a partnership, or
   (d) the beneficial interest of a trust or unincorporated enterprise;
8. A relative (i.e., a spouse, ancestor, lineal descendent, or spouse of a lineal descendent) of any of the above-described persons;
9. A corporation, partnership, trust, or estate at least 50 percent owned or controlled by the above-described persons;
10. An employee, officer, director, or at least 10 percent owner of the entities described in 4 through 7 and 9 above; and
11. A joint venturer or partner owning at least a 10 percent interest in any of the entities described in 4 through 7 and 9 above.

The determination of who is a party in interest is nearly identical under ERISA and the Code. The Code, however, uses the nomenclature "disqualified person" instead of party in interest. [ERISA § 3(14); IRC § 4975(e)(2)]

Q 5:5 What are the differences between the prohibited transaction rules under the Code and ERISA?

The prohibited transaction rules under ERISA and the Code are very similar. The main distinctions between the prohibited transaction rules under ERISA and the Code relate to the plans covered, the sanctions for violating the prohibited transaction rules, and the establishment of liability for violating a prohibited transaction. [ERISA §§ 401 and 406; IRC § 4975(e)]

Plans covered by ERISA's prohibited transaction rules are discussed at Q 5:6. The different penalties under ERISA and the Code for violating the prohibited transaction rules are discussed in Q 5:8.

Q 5:6 What plans are covered by the prohibited transaction rules?

ERISA's prohibited transaction rules apply to all plans subject to ERISA—that is, in general, most pension benefit plans and most welfare benefit plans (see the discussion of what is a pension benefit plan and a welfare benefit plan subject to ERISA at Qs 8:4 through 8:14). By contrast, the Code's prohibited transaction rules apply only to tax-qualified plans (i.e., plans that are granted tax-favored status by meeting the detailed rules under IRC § 401), qualified annuities (i.e., annuity contracts purchased by an employer for an employee under a plan that meets the requirements of IRC § 404(a)(2) and are granted tax-favored status under the Code), IRAs, and individual retirement annuities. Also, the Code rules continue to apply even if the plan later loses its tax qualification. [ERISA Conf Comm Rep]

Liability and Penalties

Q 5:7 When is a fiduciary liable for engaging in a prohibited transaction under ERISA and the Code?

Under ERISA, a fiduciary is liable for engaging in a prohibited transaction if the fiduciary knew or should have known that he or she caused the plan to engage in a prohibited transaction. A fiduciary is liable for losses to the plan arising from a prohibited transaction in which the plan engaged if the fiduciary would have known that the transaction involving the particular party in interest was prohibited had the fiduciary acted as a prudent person. Prudence is determined based on the particular facts and circumstances of the case. In general, for a fiduciary to be prudent in the case of a significant transaction, the fiduciary must make a thorough investigation of the other party's relationship to the plan to determine whether the party is a party in interest. In the case of a normal and insubstantial day-to-day transaction, it may be sufficient to check the identity of the other party against a roster of parties in interest that is periodically updated. [ERISA Conf Comm Rep]

ERISA's knowledge requirement is not included in the Code. Thus, a disqualified person is subject to the excise tax imposed by the Internal Revenue Service (see Q 5:8) without proof of knowledge. [ERISA Conf Comm Rep]

In general, a transaction will not be a prohibited transaction under either ERISA or the Code if the transaction is an ordinary "blind" purchase or sale of securities through an exchange where neither the buyer nor the seller (nor the agent of either) knows the identity of the other party involved. Thus, a fiduciary (or party in interest) will not be liable merely because, by chance, the other party turns out to be a party in interest (or plan). [ERISA Conf Comm Rep]

Q 5:8 What are the penalties for engaging in a prohibited transaction?

ERISA imposes traditional trust law remedies, such as damages and either criminal or civil penalties, for the fiduciary's breach of his or her duties under ERISA. [ERISA §§ 501 and 502]

The Code imposes a mandatory excise tax on a disqualified person or party in interest who participates in a prohibited transaction involving a qualified plan. [IRC § 4975] ERISA provides for the imposition of a civil penalty on a disqualified person or party in interest who participates in a prohibited transaction involving an ERISA plan that is either a non-qualified plan or a welfare plan. [ERISA § 502(i)]

Note. The excise tax or penalty is the personal liability of the disqualified person or party in interest. The plan may not indemnify the disqualified person or party in interest for the excise taxes he or she incurs as a result of entering into a prohibited transaction.

Although fiduciaries are disqualified persons, they are subject to the excise tax only if they act in a prohibited transaction in a capacity other than that of fiduciary. This tax is equal to 5 percent of the "amount involved" in the prohibited transaction for each year (or part thereof) in the "taxable period." [IRC § 4975(a) and (b)] The amount involved is the greater of the fair market value of the property (and money) given, or the fair market value of the property (and money) received. The valuation date for purposes of calculating the 5 percent excise tax is the date on which the prohibited transaction occurred. [IRC § 4975(f)(4)] The taxable period is the period beginning with the date on which the prohibited transaction occurred and ending on the earlier of the date of mailing by the Secretary of the Treasury of a notice of deficiency as to the 5 percent tax, the date the 5-percent tax is assessed, or the date on which the "correction" of the prohibited transaction is completed. A separate 5 percent tax is imposed for each year or part of a year in the taxable period until the correction is completed. [IRC § 4975(f)(2)]

If the transaction is not corrected within the "correction period," a tax equal to 100 percent of the amount involved is imposed. (See Q 5:37 for rules regarding how to correct a prohibited transaction.)

Q 5:9 Can a nonfiduciary be subject to liability for a prohibited transaction?

Yes. If the nonfiduciary is a disqualified person, he or she is subject to an excise tax imposed by the Internal Revenue Service (with respect to tax qualified plans) or to a penalty imposed by the Department of Labor (with respect to ERISA plans that are not tax qualified plans) for participating in a prohibited transaction violation. [IRC § 4975 and ERISA § 502(i)] Further, ERISA imposes a 20 percent civil penalty upon any person who knowingly participates in fiduciary breaches or other violations by a fiduciary of Part 4 of Title I of ERISA (including prohibited transactions). [ERISA § 502(1)] The scope of this 20 percent civil penalty provision will be discussed below. Also, as will be discussed below, the U.S. Supreme Court held that monetary damages cannot be recovered from nonfiduciaries who

Q 5:9   **Fiduciary Responsibility Answer Book**

knowingly participate in a breach of fiduciary duty under ERISA where the nonfiduciary did not have any monetary gain from the breach. [Mertens v Hewitt Assoc, S Ct Dkt No 91-1671 (1993)]

Until recently there was a split in authority as to whether a nonfiduciary party may be subject to monetary damages under ERISA for engaging in a prohibited transaction. For example, in *McDougall v Donovan,* 539 FSupp 596 (ND Ill 1982), the court held that, since ERISA grants the Secretary of Labor broad authority to bring actions under ERISA, equitable enforcement authority is not limited solely to actions against fiduciaries for their participation in prohibited transactions. Therefore, the Secretary also has the authority to seek restitution to recover ill gotten gains from nonfiduciary parties in interest. Several circuit courts have agreed with this position. [*See also,* Thorton v Evans, 692 F2d 1064 (7th Cir 1982) (district court erred in dismissing a complaint alleging conspiracy to defraud a pension fund on the ground that defendants were not fiduciaries, since nonfiduciaries who aided fiduciaries in breaching their fiduciary duty may be sued and may be liable to the extent they have profited from the breach).] The Supreme Court did not resolve this issue.

Courts had gone even further and held that monetary damages may be recovered from a nonfiduciary even in situations where the nonfiduciary did not profit from his or her participation in the breach. Thus, in *Foltz v US News & World Report, Inc.* [627 FSupp 1143, 1167-68 (D DC 1986)], the court permitted a recovery of damages by former employees against an appraiser retained by the plan where the employees were harmed by the appraiser's undervaluation of employer stock held by the plan. [*See also* dicta in Thorton v Evans, 692 F2d 1064, 1078 (7th Cir 1982) (the court stated that it is the participation in the breach—and not profit—by the nonfiduciary which is the predicate for liability).] However, in *Nieto v Ecker,* [845 F2d 868 (9th Cir 1988)], the court rejected the reasoning of *Foltz* and held that a nonfiduciary cannot be liable for a breach of fiduciary duty under ERISA where the third party did not profit from the breach. This issue was resolved by the U.S. Supreme Court.

The Supreme Court, in a 5-to-4 decision in *Mertens v Hewitt Assoc* [61 USLW 4510 (US 1993)] reviewed this issue and held that a nonfiduciary who does not profit from a breach is not liable for monetary damages resulting from his or her actions. In *Mertens,* an actuarial firm failed to change the plan's actuarial assumptions to reflect the plan's additional costs attributable to an employer's early retirement incentive program. As a result of Hewitt's failure, the plan became underfunded and it was ultimately terminated by the Pension Benefit Guaranty Corporation. Following the termination, participants received only the benefits guaranteed by ERISA, which was lower than their full benefit due under the plan. The Court held that only remedies that are traditionally viewed as equitable can be recovered from a nonfiduciary. Therefore, compensatory damages resulting from the undervaluation of plan costs could not be recovered from the actuarial firm.

> Note: The Court expressed uncertainty as to whether ERISA affords a cause of action of any sort against nonfiduciaries who participate in a fiduciary breach. Thus, it was unclear to the Court whether restitution of ill-gotten gains can be recovered from a nonfiduciary under ERISA. The Court expressed the view that the ERISA § 502(1) provision that imposes a 20 percent civil penalty on *any person* who knowingly participates in a fiduciary breach can be interpreted as referring to co-fiduciaries, who are expressly liable for their knowing participation under ERISA § 405(a).

Q 5:10 Can a single event result in several prohibited transactions?

Yes. A single event can result in several prohibited transactions subjecting a disqualified person to separate excise taxes for each prohibited transaction. For example, where several corporate officers and directors, who were also plan participants, sold jointly owned property to the plan, those participants were held to be liable for the excise tax for each of the following prohibited transactions: (1) the sale of property to the plan, (2) the plan's assumption of the mortgage on the property, and (3) the participant's issuance of a promissory note to the plan. [Rutland v Comm'r, 89 TC 1137, 1146 (1987)]

Q 5:11 Is the full excise tax imposed on each disqualified person who participates in a prohibited transaction?

No. Even if more than one disqualified person participates in a prohibited transaction, only one excise tax will be imposed. However, all the disqualified persons participating in the prohibited transaction will be jointly and severally liable for its payment. [IRC § 4975(a) and (f)(1)]

Sales, Exchanges or Leases

Q 5:12 What types of transactions are included in the prohibition against sales, exchanges, or leases between a plan and a party in interest?

The direct or indirect sale, exchange, or lease of any property between a plan and a party in interest is a prohibited transaction whether instituted by the plan or the party in interest. It also does not matter whether the property is owned by the plan or the party in interest. [ERISA § 406(a)(1)(A); IRC § 4975(c)(1)(A); ERISA Conf Comm Rep]

Further, a party in interest to a plan may not transfer real or personal property to the plan if the property is:

1. Subject to a mortgage or lien that the plan assumes, or
2. If the property is subject to a mortgage or lien that a party in interest placed on the property within the 10-year period ending on the date of the transfer. [ERISA § 406 and IRC § 4975(c)(1)]

Note. A party in interest's transfer of property to a plan is a prohibited transaction if the plan assumes any lien on the property, even if the lien is not placed on the property by the party in interest. Further, a transaction is prohibited if the party in interest placed a lien on the property within the 10-year period ending on the date of transfer, even if the plan did not assume the lien.

Examples of transactions found to be in violation of this prohibited transaction include:

- The acquisition by a mutual fund of property from a party in interest as part of an arrangement under which the plan invests or retains its investment in the mutual fund [ERISA Comm Rep]; and

- The indirect acquisition of a jet plane by the plan from a union (a party in interest), when the jet plane belonged originally to the union, was traded in for another aircraft, and was ultimately sold to the plan for slightly more than its trade-in value. [McDougall v Donovan, 552 FSupp 1206 (ND Ill 1982)]

Exceptions to the prohibition against sales include the following:

1. A plan's exercise of a securities conversion privilege is exempt from the prohibited transaction rules to the extent provided in the DOL regulations, but only if the plan receives adequate consideration pursuant to such conversion [ERISA § 408(b)(7)] The Conference Committee's report explains that this exemption is needed since a plan may hold or acquire certain employer securities and some of these securities may be convertible (from bonds to stock, for example). Pursuant to the Committee's report, the conversion is permitted if all the securities of the class held by the plan are subject to the same terms, and if the terms are determined in an arm's-length transaction so that the conversions cannot be tailored to apply only to a particular plan. Similarly, a conversion generally will not be permitted if all but an insignificant percentage of unrelated holders of such securities do not exercise the conversion privilege. Also, any acquisition of employer securities pursuant to a conversion privilege must be within the limits established by the general rules governing the acquisition and holding of employer securities [ERISA Comm Rep] (see Qs 5:29, 7:28 for a discussion regarding the legal limitations on a plan's acquisition of employer securities); and

2. A plan's acquisition, sale, or lease of "qualifying employer securities" is exempt from the prohibition if the transaction is for adequate consideration and no broker's commission is charged. [ERISA § 408(e)] (See Qs 5:29 and 7:27 through 7:38 for a discussion regarding plan investments in qualifying employer securities.)

Q 5:13 Does an employer's contribution of property to a plan result in a prohibited transaction?

Yes. The Supreme Court recently decided that even the transfer of unencumbered property to a pension plan is a prohibited transaction. [Comm'r v Keystone Consol Indus, Inc, S Ct No 91-1677 (1993)] However, the transfer of unencumbered property to a profit-sharing plan appears to be permissible. [DOL Opinion Ltr 90-05A]

The Supreme Court's decision confirmed the position of the DOL regarding contributions to a pension plan (e.g., a defined benefit or money purchase pension plan). The Court also inferred that it would agree with the DOL's position regarding contributions to discretionary profit sharing plans. According to the DOL, the contribution of property to a pension plan is a prohibited transaction because the contribution discharges the employer's legal obligations to contribute cash to the plan. On the other hand, if the plan is not a pension plan (e.g., if it is a discretionary profit sharing plan), the contribution of property is not a prohibited transaction because the contribution is entirely voluntary and does not relieve the employer of an obligation to make cash contributions to the plan. [DOL Opinions Ltrs 81-69A and 90-05A]

Prior to *Keystone,* the courts were split on the issue of contributing unencumbered property to a pension plan. The Fourth Circuit Court of Appeals held that an employer's contribution of a third-party promissory note to satisfy the plan's funding obligation is a sale or exchange and is therefore a prohibited transaction. [Wood v Comm'r, 955 F2d 908 (4th Cir 1992), *rev'g* 95 TC 364 (1990)] By contrast, the Fifth Circuit had held that an employer did not engage in a prohibited transaction when it transferred unencumbered property to its qualified retirement plan in satisfaction of its funding obligations because the transfer of unencumbered property was not a sale or exchange. [Keystone Consol Indus, Inc v Comm'r, 951 F2d 76 (5th Cir 1992), *aff'g* 60 TCM (CCH) 1423 (1990)]

It should be noted that the transfer of *encumbered* property to any ERISA plan, including a profit sharing plan, would be treated as a sale or exchange. (*See* Q 5:12 regarding the transfer of property subject to a lien.)

Loans or Extensions of Credit

Q 5:14 What types of transactions are included in the prohibition against lending money or the extension of credit between a plan and a party in interest?

This prohibition applies to direct and indirect loans and extensions of credit. Accordingly, a third-party loan to a plan guaranteed by a party in interest would generally be a prohibited transaction. [ERISA § 406(a)(1)(B) and IRC § 4975 (c)(1)(B); ERISA Conf Comm Rep]

> **Note.** An employer may generally not fund a plan with the employer's debt obligation, since this is an indirect loan from the plan to the employer. Also, a plan may not invest in a loan made by a third party to a party in interest. Further, a plan may not acquire a debt investment under which a party in interest is the obligor. [ERISA Conf Comm Rep]

Examples of transactions found to be in violation of this prohibited transaction include:

- A loan from the plan to a union that is a party in interest. [Whitfield v Tomasso, 682 FSupp 1287 (EDNY 1988)];
- Loans from the plan sponsor to the plan. [Brock v Citizens Bank of Clovis, 841 F2d 344 (10th Cir), *cert denied* 488 US 829 (1988)]; and
- Loans by the plan to a corporation wholly owned by the fiduciary. [Brock v Gillikin, 677 FSupp 398 (EDNC 1987)].

As a result of this prohibition, it would generally be impermissible for a plan to lend money to employees of the plan sponsor since such employees are parties in interest to the plan. (See Q 5:4, subparagraph 10.) However, there is a statutory exemption permitting plan loan programs if certain conditions are met. This statutory exemption is discussed in Qs 5:15 through 5:21.

There are also other statutory and administrative exemptions to this prohibited transaction. These include the following:

1. Loans to an employee stock ownership plan (i.e., a plan that is designed to invest primarily in stocks and marketable obliga-

tions and that meets certain other IRS requirements) if the loan is primarily for the benefit of plan participants and beneficiaries and is made at an interest rate not in excess of a "reasonable" rate. The exemption applies only to loans (and guarantees) used to leverage the purchase of qualifying employee securities. [ERISA § 408(b)(3), and IRC § 4975(d)(3); ERISA Conf Comm Rep]

2. Interest-free loans to plans by parties in interest; however, the proceeds of the loan may be used only for: (a) the payment of ordinary operating expenses of the plan, including the payment of benefits, in accordance with the terms of the plan, and of periodic premiums under an insurance or annuity contract; or (b) a three-day period, for a purpose incidental to the ordinary operation of the plan. In addition, the loan must be unsecured and not made by an employee benefit plan. [PTCE 80-26]

3. Loans secured by residential mortgages. [PTCE 88-59] This exemption provides relief for several categories of residential mortgage financing transactions in which plans participate. The decision to enter into such a transaction must be made on behalf of the plan by a "qualified real estate manager" who is independent of the plan and any contributing employer to the plan or union whose members are participants in the plan. Any mortgage loan to be acquired must be eligible for purchase by one of the three U.S. governmental agencies purchasing mortgages (e.g., FNMA) and must be originated by an independent "established mortgage lender." Certain other conditions must also be met to satisfy this exemption.

4. Transactions between parties in interest and investment funds managed by a qualified professional asset manager (QPAM). The QPAM must be independent of the parties in interest and must satisfy certain financial standards, including a minimum amount of assets it manages. The QPAM may be a bank, savings and loan association, insurance company, or an investment adviser, and must acknowledge in writing that it is a fiduciary. The investment fund managed by the QPAM may be any account or fund (including a single customer account) subject to the QPAM's discretionary management authority. The ex-

emption sets forth several additional conditions that must be met by the QPAM and the party in interest to satisfy this exemption. [PTCE 84-14; *see* Qs 4:25 and 4:26 for additional information regarding QPAMs.]

5. Investment by certain plans (in general, defined contribution plans) in bonds, debentures, notes, and other marketable obligations of the employer, if the acquisition is for adequate consideration and if no commission is charged with respect thereto. [ERISA §§ 407(d)(5) and 408(e)] (See Qs 5:29 and 7:27 through 7:38 for a discussion of plan investments in qualifying employer securities.)

Q 5:15 Under what circumstances are loans from a plan to participants and beneficiaries permissible?

Both the Code and ERISA contain provisions that permit plan loans under certain conditions.

Generally, loans are not treated as prohibited transactions if, in addition to being bona fide loans and not disguised distributions (see IRC Section 72(p)(1)(a)), they:

1. Are available to participants and beneficiaries on a reasonably equivalent basis;
2. Are not made available to highly compensated employees in an amount greater than the amount made available to other employees;
3. Are made in accordance with specific provisions that are set forth in the plan;
4. Bear a reasonable rate of interest; and
5. Are adequately secured.

[ERISA § 408(b)(1)]
These requirements are discussed in Qs 5:17 through 5:21.

Section 72(p) of the Code limits the amount of the permitted loan and sets forth other criteria to avoid the loan being treated as an impermissible plan distribution. In addition, Section 4975 of the Code and Section 408(b) of ERISA set forth requirements that must be satisfied if a plan loan is not to be treated as a prohibited transaction and to avoid violation of the anti-alienation provisions of the Code.

Q 5:16 Who may *not* borrow without obtaining an individual prohibited transaction exemption?

The exemption in Q 5:15 does not apply to loans to "owner-employees" of partnerships, "shareholder-employees" of S corporations, and sole proprietors and certain of their relatives. These persons must obtain individual exemptions from the DOL on a case-by-case basis (see Q 5:44). [ERISA § 408(d); DOL Reg § 2550.408b-1(a)(2)]

An owner-employee is an employee who:

(a) Owns the entire interest in an unincorporated trade or business, or

(b) In the case of a partnership, is a partner who owns more than 10 percent of either the capital interest or the profits interest in such partnership. [IRC § 401(c)(3)]

A shareholder-employee is an employee or officer of an electing "S" corporation who owns (or is considered as owning), on any day during the taxable year of such corporation, more than 5 percent of the outstanding stock of the corporation.

Q 5:17 To whom must plan loans be made available?

Loans must be made available to all participants and beneficiaries who are active employees. While a plan may make loans available to all vested terminees and beneficiaries, it is only required to make them available to vested terminees and beneficiaries who are parties in interest. [DOL Reg § 2550.408b-1(a)(1)(i); DOL Opinion Ltr 89-30A]

Note. Persons who are both vested terminees or beneficiaries and parties in interest will in most cases be extremely limited and consist only of 10 percent shareholders and certain corporate directors (since any other vested terminee is no longer an employee of a contributing employer).

Although the regulations require that loans be made available both to participants who are active employees and to participants who are no longer active employees and to beneficiaries of such participants, the regulations permit loans to nonemployee participants and beneficiaries to be on such different terms and conditions as would be considered by commercial lenders. [Preamble to DOL Reg § 2550.408b]

The availability of loans, of course, must not be based on an individual's race, color, religion, age, sex, or national origin. Factors, such as creditworthiness, that would be consistent with practices of a commercial lender, may be considered. In addition, financial need may be considered. [DOL Reg § 2550.408b-1(b)] Guiding the foregoing is that, under ERISA Section 404, the plan administrator is a fiduciary and, hence, must administer the loan programs in accordance with its general fiduciary responsibilities, including prudence.

The same maximum percentage of the vested account balance may be made available to all borrowers even though this will result in different dollar amounts being made available. Alternatively, there can be a maximum dollar limitation. Variations may be permissible in order to comply with the adequate security requirements. [DOL Reg § 2550.408b-1(c); preamble to DOL Reg § 2550.408b]

Q 5:18 May plans require a minimum loan?

Yes. However, plan loan programs may generally not require a minimum loan in excess of $1,000. [DOL Reg § 2550.408b-1(b)]

Q 5:19 What written information must be provided to participants regarding a loan program?

All loan programs must be established pursuant to specific authority provided in a plan document. This authority must include:

(a) The identity of the persons authorized to administer the participant loan program;
(b) A procedure for applying for loans;
(c) The basis on which loans will be approved or denied;

Q 5:20   **Fiduciary Responsibility Answer Book**

    (d) Limitations (if any) on the types and amounts of loans offered;

    (e) The procedures under the program for determining a reasonable rate of interest;

    (f) The types of collateral that may secure a participant loan; and

    (g) The events constituting default and the steps that will be taken to preserve plan assets in the event of such default.

The provisions do not have to be in the plan itself, but can be in a separate written document forming part of the plan. [DOL Reg § 2550.408b-1(d)]

Q 5:20 What interest rate must be charged by a plan for loans?

The plan must charge a reasonable rate. A reasonable rate of interest is one that provides the plan with a return commensurate with the prevailing interest rate charged on similar commercial loans by persons in the business of lending money. [DOL Reg § 2550.408b-1(e)]

> **Note.** The DOL refused to set a "safe harbor" interest rate or method of calculation (such as treasury bills or prime) and, accordingly, plan administrators must rely on changing commercial standards for similar loans.

> **Planning Pointer.** It may be difficult for many plans to determine an appropriate rate to be charged. In practice, plans will have to look at the rates being charged by a group of banks in the local region for similar types of loans. One particular problem may be in identifying the appropriate type of loan or credit risk comparable to the plan loan. For example, the DOL has indicated, informally, that plan loans secured by plan accounts are probably not analogous to passbook loans since plan loans generally cannot be immediately foreclosed on default because of tax law limitations on in-service distributions.

> One approach may be to structure the loan security and repayment procedure and then survey several banks as to what interest rate or factors they would use on a similar loan. Surveying one bank may not be adequate evidence of the commercially prevailing rate.

> Generally, interest rates may not be set on a national basis unless the plan is administered on this basis.

Q 5:21 How must plan loans be secured?

Loans must be adequately secured. Securing the loan by a portion of the participant's vested accrued account is deemed adequate security. No more than 50 percent of the present value of a participant's vested accrued benefit may be used as security for participant loans and taken into account in determining whether the security is adequate, leaving the remaining account balance unencumbered. [DOL Reg § 2550.408b-1(f)] Thus, lending a participant's full vested accrued benefit to the participant will require additional security under the DOL regulations.

In the case of individual accounts, where the investment experience of the assets is credited solely on a per-participant basis, any participant who has a vested accrued benefit may borrow up to 50 percent of the present value of the vested accrued benefit secured by that 50 percent of the vested account balance. Additional security would be required in a defined benefit plan or an individual account plan with shared investment experience. [Preamble to DOL Reg § 2550.4086]

Regulations provide that the adequacy of security is determined in light of the type and amount of security that would be required in the case of an otherwise identical transaction in a normal commercial setting between unrelated parties dealing at arm's length. [DOL Reg § 2550.408b-1(f)(1)] Although not entirely free from doubt, it would appear that the guaranteed nature of an investment (such as a guaranteed investment contract) should be a factor to be considered in determining the adequacy of the security. This would apparently also be a factor in determining whether the interest rate on the loan is reasonable. (The preamble indicates that the opportunity for gain and the risk of loss are proper criteria to consider when determining the reasonableness of the interest rate.)

Planning Pointer. The DOL has left to the plan administrator the determination of what is adequate security in these situations. While, in theory, the security may vary for active and inactive participants (see Q 5.17), the variance would have to be in accordance with commercial practices. Otherwise, the ability to borrow may not be available on a reasonably equivalent basis.

According to the preamble to the DOL regulations, a plan may delay foreclosing on the borrower's vested accrued benefit under the plan, which serves as security, as long as no loss of principal or income results from the delay of such enforcement.

Goods, Services, and Facilities

Q 5:22 What types of transactions are included in the prohibition against furnishing goods, services, and facilities between plans and parties in interest?

This prohibited transaction applies to both the direct and indirect furnishing of goods, services, and facilities between a plan and a party in interest. For example, it is a prohibited transaction for a plan to furnish personal living quarters to a party in interest. [ERISA § 406(a)(1)(C); IRC § 4975(c)(1)(C); ERISA Conf Comm Rep] A pension fund trustee who allowed the pension fund to pay for his personal criminal defense expenses participated in a prohibited transaction and was subject to the excise tax imposed by the Code. [O'Malley v Comm'r, 972 F2d 150 (7th Cir 1992)]

Q 5:23 May a party in interest ever furnish goods and services to a plan?

Yes. A specific statutory exemption allows a plan to make a reasonable contract or arrangement (see Q 5:24) with a party in interest (including a fiduciary) for office space, or for services that are necessary (see Q 5:25) for the establishment or operation of the plan, if no more than reasonable compensation (see Q 5:26) is paid. [ERISA § 408(b)(2)] As mentioned in Q 5:4, a person who provides services to a plan is a party in interest with respect to the plan. Thus, were it not for an exemption, a plan would never be permitted to receive services, even if the services are needed to run the plan properly, since any provider of services would be by a party in interest.

It is crucial to note that, although a fiduciary is also a party in interest and is subject to the exemption pertaining to the leasing of office space and the provision of services to a plan, this exemption does not always shelter the fiduciary engaging in such transactions. For example, if the fiduciary uses any of the "authority, control, or responsibility which makes him or her a fiduciary" to cause the plan to pay the fiduciary a fee for services rendered (or to a person in whom the fiduciary has an interest which may affect the exercise of his or her best judgment as a fiduciary), then the fiduciary has per se violated the fiduciary prohibitions set forth in ERISA § 406(b). [DOL Reg § 2550.408b-2(e)]

> **Planning Pointer.** If a plan needs certain goods or services that a fiduciary is competent to provide, but she cannot retain herself to provide them because she is in a position where the exercise of her best judgment as a fiduciary may be compromised, she should recuse herself from any decision regarding the individual or entity to be retained. If the plan then decides to retain her services, the provision of these additional services will generally not be considered a prohibited transaction. [See DOL Reg § 2550.408b-2(f)]

See Q 5:33 for a discussion regarding the prohibition against the provisions of multiple services by plan fiduciaries. Also, see Q 5:27 for special rules that must be met by fiduciaries to permit them to receive compensation from a plan.

Q 5:24 What is a "reasonable contract or arrangement" for furnishing goods, services, and facilities between a plan and a party in interest?

Although the regulations do not explain what is meant by a reasonable contract or arrangement, reasonableness will be determined based on all the facts and circumstances.

To come within the statutory exemption for leasing office space and the providing services to a plan (as described in Q 5:23), the plan must be able to terminate the contract or arrangement on reasonably short notice without penalty. The purpose of this requirement is to prevent the plan from becoming locked into an arrangement that has become disadvantageous to it. [DOL Reg § 2550.408b-2(c)]

> **Example 1.** A long-term lease entered into between a plan and a party in interest is generally not an unreasonable arrangement merely because of its long term, if the lease may be terminated by the plan without penalty.

Example 2. A minimal fee in a service contract that is charged to the plan to allow recoupment of reasonable startup costs is not a penalty. Similarly, a provision in a lease for a termination fee charged to the plan that covers reasonably foreseeable expenses relating to the vacancy and reletting of the office space upon early termination of the lease is not a penalty. Thus, a lessor or service provider may charge the plan a fee to compensate the lessor or provider for the loss it incurs as a result of the plan's early termination of the contract, arrangement, or lease. However, these arrangements may not provide for compensation in excess of the loss incurred by the provider. Further, such arrangements must provide for the mitigation of damages (i.e., the provider must, as much as possible, attempt to minimize the extent of his or her loss resulting from the plan's breach). [DOL Reg § 2550.408b-2(c)]

Planning Pointer. A lease between a plan and its lessor should provide that if the plan breaks the lease, the lessor will use reasonable efforts to find a replacement tenant before the lease term expires. If the market is such that the lessor should be able to find a suitable tenant to replace the plan after two months, the lessor's recovery of damages from the plan for breaking the lease will generally be limited to only two months' rent, since the lessor should, with reasonable effort, have found a replacement lessee during that period.

Q 5:25 What is a "necessary service" that a party in interest may provide under a reasonable contract?

A service is necessary if it is appropriate and helpful to the plan in carrying out the purposes for which the plan was established and is maintained. [DOL Reg § 2550.408b-2(6)]

Planning Pointer. The regulations do not specify what is meant by "appropriate and helpful" services. It is clear that legal, accounting, actuarial, and administrative services are needed by the plan. However, there are other types of services that are not clearly appropriate and helpful (for example, whether the fund office should be painted every year). In case of doubt, advice from legal counsel or the DOL should be sought.

Moreover, a person providing a necessary service to a plan may furnish goods that are necessary for establishing or operating the plan in the course of, and incidental to, furnishing the necessary service to the plan. [DOL Reg § 2550.408b-2(b)]

Q 5:26 What is "reasonable compensation" that a party in interest may receive for providing necessary services?

The determination of whether compensation for the provision of services is reasonable is based on all the facts and circumstances. [DOL Reg § 2550.408c-2(b)(1)] Compensation that may not be deducted by an employer on its tax return as an ordinary and necessary business expense because such compensation is considered excessive under the Code is not considered "reasonable" compensation under the DOL statutory exemption for the provision of services. [DOL Reg § 2550.408c-2(b)(5)] An attorney hired to provide professional services to a multiemployer plan may be found to have engaged in a prohibited transaction if he or she accepts payment for services he or she did not perform. [Nieto v Ecker, 845 F2d 868 (9th Cir 1988)]

Q 5:27 May a fiduciary who receives full-time pay from a sponsoring employer, employer association, or union receive compensation for his or her services to a plan?

No. However, the fiduciary may be reimbursed for "direct expenses" (see Q 5:28) properly and actually incurred and not otherwise reimbursed. [DOL Reg § 2550.408c-2(b)(2)]

Q 5:28 When may a fiduciary who receives full-time pay from a sponsoring employer, employer association, or a union receive reimbursement or advances for expenses incurred on behalf of the plan?

Fiduciaries may receive reimbursement of "direct expenses" properly and actually incurred on behalf of the plan and not otherwise reimbursed. [DOL Reg § 2550.408c-2(b)(2)] An expense is a direct expense if it would not have been sustained had the service not been provided and if it does not represent an allocable portion of overhead costs. [DOL Reg § 2550.408c-2(b)(3)]

A fiduciary may receive an advance to cover direct expenses that he or she will incur when performing duties for a plan if:

1. The amount of the advance is reasonable in relation to the amount of the direct expense that is likely to be incurred in the immediate future (such as during the next month); and
2. The fiduciary accounts to the plan at the end of the period covered by the advance for the expenses properly and actually incurred.

[DOL Reg § 2550.408c-2(b)(4)]

Employer Securities and Employer Real Property

Q 5:29 What is the prohibition against the acquisition on behalf of a plan of employer securities and employer real property?

A plan may not acquire or hold any "employer security" (i.e., a security issued by an employer that has employees covered by the plan) that is not a "qualifying employer security" (i.e., stock, "marketable obligations," or an interest in certain publicly traded partnerships). Further, a plan may not acquire or hold "employer real property" (i.e., realty leased by a plan to the sponsoring employer or its affiliate) that is not "qualifying employer real property." Also, a plan that is not an "eligible individual account plan" (i.e., in general, a defined contribution plan) may, generally, not acquire qualifying employer securities or qualifying employer real property if, immediately following the acquisition, the aggregate value of qualifying employer securities or qualifying employer real property held by the plan exceeds 10 percent of the fair market value of the assets of the plan. [ERISA § 407(a)(2)] Thus, a defined benefit plan may not invest more than 10 percent of its assets in qualifying employer securities or qualifying employer real property. [ERISA §§ 406(a)(1)(E) and 407] (See Qs 5:29 and 7:27 through 7:38 for additional rules regarding plan investments in qualifying employer securities and qualifying employer real property.)

A plan fiduciary engages in a prohibited transaction if he or she causes a plan *to acquire* employer securities or employer real property in violation of the rules set forth in the previous paragraph. [ERISA § 406(a)(1)(E)] Further, a fiduciary who controls plan assets enters into a prohibited transaction if he or she permits a plan *to hold* employer securities or employer real property in violation of the rules set forth in the previous paragraph. [ERISA § 406(a)(2)]

Self-Dealing

Q 5:30 What is the prohibition against a fiduciary dealing with plan assets in his or her own interest or for his or her own account?

This prohibited transaction forbids self dealing by fiduciaries.

Example 1. Plan trustees authorized monthly payments for themselves as compensation for services rendered to the plans when they were also receiving full-time pay from contributing employers and unions, and also authorized the plans to make plan contributions on their behalf to make them eligible for plan benefits. These activities were prohibited transactions. [Donovan v Daugherty, 550 FSupp 390 (SD Ala 1982)]

Example 2. A welfare fund trustee caused the fund to purchase certificates of deposits from an insurance company at the time that he and his wife received cash and loans from the founder of the company in violation of this prohibition. [McLaughlin v Tomasso, 9 EBC (BNA) 2438 (EDNY 1988)]

Example 3. Fund trustees of the same fund as in Example 2 authorized the union to retain for its own account employer contributions intended for the fund, caused the fund to reimburse the union as an administrative expense for time the trustees allegedly spent on fund business, and caused the fund to pay the union's taxes. These activities also violated the self-dealing prohibition. [McLaughlin v Tomasso, 9 EBC (BNA) 2438 (EDNY 1988)]

Example 4. If a trustee, who is a plan fiduciary, retains an administrator to provide administrative services to the plan and the administrator then retains the trustee to provide, for additional fees, actuarial services to the plan that the trustee is currently not providing, both the trustee and the administrator would be violating the prohibition against self-dealing. [DOL Reg § 2550.408b-2(f), Ex 5]

Example 5. If a plan fiduciary retains his son to provide administrative services to the plan, the fiduciary is engaging in a prohibited transaction because his son is a person in whom the fiduciary has an interest that may affect the fiduciary's best judgment as a fiduciary. [DOL Reg § 2550.408b-2(f), Ex 6]

Q 5:31 May a fiduciary deal with assets of a plan in which he or she has an account?

Yes. Although ERISA prohibits a fiduciary from dealing with plan assets in his or her own interest or for his or her own account, ERISA does not prohibit a fiduciary from dealing with assets of a plan in which he or she has an account when the dealings apply to all plan accounts without discrimination. [ERISA Conf Comm Rep]

Q 5:32 Under what circumstances may a fiduciary receive compensation or other consideration for furnishing office space or providing services to a plan without violating ERISA's prohibition against self-dealing?

If a fiduciary does not use any of the authority, control, or responsibility that makes him or her a fiduciary to cause a plan to pay him or her (or to a person in whom the fiduciary has an interest which may affect the fiduciary's best judgment) a fee for services he or she performs, there is no self-dealing violation by the fiduciary. [DOL Reg § 2550.408b-2(e)(2)]

The regulations give the following examples of situations that are not considered prohibited self-dealing by a fiduciary:

- A plan's investment advisor, who is a plan fiduciary, may be retained by another plan fiduciary to provide portfolio evaluation services in addition to the services the investment advisor currently provides. [See DOL Reg § 2550.408b-2(f), Ex 1]
- A bank, whose president is a trustee of a plan, may be retained by the plan to provide it administrative services *if* the trustee recuses himself from all consideration of the proposal to retain the bank *and* does not otherwise exercise the authority and control or responsibility that makes him a fiduciary to cause the plan to retain the bank. [DOL Reg § 2550.408b-2(f), Ex 7]

The DOL found no violation when a fiduciary, who was a general partner in a limited partnership for plan investments in a certain type of foreign security in which the plan was a limited partner, received investment management fees from the plan, since the fiduciary did not make the plan's purchase decisions. [DOL Op 92-08A]

Q 5:33 May a fiduciary provide multiple services to a plan?

In general, no. A party in interest who is a plan fiduciary is generally prohibited from providing multiple services to a plan. This rule was adopted because of the potential problems inherent in situations in which persons who can act on behalf of a plan are also in a position to personally benefit at the expense of the plan in exercising their authority. [ERISA Conf Comm Rep] For example, a brokerage house that provides investment advice to a plan for a fee could cause the plan to make investments to increase its fees if it were also allowed to provide brokerage services to the same plan.

The DOL regulations greatly ease this prohibition by providing that multiple services may be provided where the fiduciary does not use any of the authority, control, or responsibility that makes him or her a fiduciary to cause a plan to pay a fee for the services he or she performs. (See Q 5:32)

Parties in interest who are not fiduciaries (see Q 5:4) are not covered by this multiple-services prohibition. Also, ERISA provides a statutory exemption that permits a bank or similar financial institution supervised by a state or federal authority to provide multiple ancillary services to a plan under certain limited circumstances. [ERISA § 408(b)(6)]

Asset Transfers

Q 5:34 What is included in the prohibition against the transfer to, or use by, a party in interest of plan assets?

The rule under ERISA § 406(a)(1)(D) and IRC § 4975(c)(1)(D) prohibits direct and indirect plan asset transfers to, or for the benefit of, a party in interest. Also prohibited under this rule is the use of plan assets by, or for the benefit of, a party in interest. This prohibited transaction may occur even though there has been no transfer of money or property between the plan and the party in interest. [ERISA Comm Rep]

> **Example 1.** A multiemployer pension fund wished to purchase a retroactive retirement benefit for an individual who was an employee of the fund for 23 years, but who was not a participant in the plan during those years, in recognition of the employee's service to the fund. The DOL opined that these benefits were not part of the employee's "expectation of compensation" for his services to the fund for those years. Accordingly, the purchase of such retirement benefits would not constitute "reasonable compensation" under ERISA's statutory exemption that permits a plan to contract or make reasonable arrangements with a party in interest for the rendering of necessary services, and would therefore be a prohibited transaction. [DOL Opinion Ltr 89-08A]

> **Example 2.** A plan trustee transferred assets from the plan's trust account to his own personal account, allegedly to protect plan assets from an illicit scheme by plan participants. The trustee thus engaged in this prohibited transaction since violation of the prohibition does not require a culpable motive on the part of the plan fiduciary. [PBGC v Fletcher, 750 FSupp 233 (WD Tex 1990)]

> **Example 3.** A plan purchased and sold securities to manipulate the price of the security to the advantage of a party in interest.

This constituted a use by or for the benefit of a party in interest of assets of the plan. [ERISA Conf Comm Rep]

Parties With Adverse Interests

Q 5:35 What is the prohibition against a fiduciary acting in any transaction involving the plan on behalf of a party (or representing a party) whose interests are adverse to the interests of the plan?

This prohibited transaction under ERISA § 406(b)(2) prevents a fiduciary from engaging in potential conflicts of interest.

Note. This is not a prohibited transaction under the Code. Thus, a violation of this prohibited transaction will not result in an excise tax assessment by the Internal Revenue Service. [ERISA Conf Comm Rep]

Example 1. Plan trustees, who were officers of the companies sponsoring the plan, were held to have entered into a prohibited transaction by approving plan loans to the sponsoring companies. [Freund v Marshall & Ilsley Bank, 485 FSupp 629 (WD Wis 1979)]

Example 2. Identical trustees of two employee benefit plans, whose participants and beneficiaries were not the same, transacted loans between plans without first obtaining a prohibited transaction exemption. A court found that this violated section 406(b)(2) of ERISA. The court held that prohibited transactions under section 406(b)(2) are "adverse" in the technical sense, without a necessity for the transaction to exhibit fiduciary misconduct or harm to the beneficiaries before the statute is violated. [Cutaiar v Marshall, 590 F2d 523 (3d Cir 1979)]

Example 3. An investment manager invested plan assets in speculative ventures in which he had a substantial equity interest, resulting in losses to the plan. His conduct violated this prohibition. [Lowen v Tower Asset Management, 829 F2d 1209 (2d Cir 1987)]

Kickbacks

Q 5:36 What is the prohibition against the receipt of kickbacks by fiduciaries?

A plan fiduciary may not receive payments or other forms of compensation from individuals or entities dealing with the plan in connection with a transaction involving plan income or assets. [ERISA § 406(b)(3); IRC § 4975(c)(1)(F)]

The following are examples of transactions found to be in violation of this prohibited transaction:

- A plan fiduciary may not receive a commission from an insurance company for referring the plan to the insurance company. [DOL Reg § 2550.408b-2(e)(1)]
- Gratuities paid to plan trustees by plan service providers are prohibited. [Brink v DaLesio, 496 FSupp 1350 (D Md 1980), aff'd in part and rev'd in part, 667 F2d 420 (4th Cir 1981)]

Corrections and Exemptions

Q 5:37 Can a prohibited transaction be corrected?

Yes. A prohibited transaction can be corrected by undoing the transaction to the extent possible, but in any case placing the plan in a financial position no worse than the position it would have been in had the party in interest acted under the highest fiduciary standards. [IRC § 4975(f)(5) and ERISA § 502(i)]

> **Note.** This requirement may be even more severe than the imposition of the excise tax (or penalty) discussed in Q 5:8, as the "undoing" of a transaction may be far costlier than the amount of tax (or penalty) involved. The disqualified person, however, cannot choose between paying the tax (or penalty) and "undoing" the transaction, as the tax (or penalty) is continuously imposed for each year the prohibited transaction occurs, until it is corrected.

To avoid a 100 percent excise tax (or penalty), the prohibited transaction must be corrected in the period beginning with the date on which the prohibited transaction occurs and ending 90 days after the mailing of the notice of deficiency with respect to the 100 percent tax (or penalty). The Secretary of the Treasury (or Department of Labor) may grant an extension if he determines that the extension is "reasonable and necessary" to correct the prohibited transaction. [Treas Reg § 53.4963-1(e)(3)]

> **Example.** The 5 percent tax on prohibited transactions was imposed on a subsidiary that sold customer loans to its parent corporation's profit sharing plan (see Q 5:8 for a discussion of the 5 percent excise tax on prohibited transactions). The plan's trustee was the corporation's sole shareholder. The plan could not cure the prohibited transaction by retroactively appointing an unrelated co-trustee. [Westoak Realty and Investment Co, Inc, 63 TCM (CCH) 2502, 14 EBC (BNA) 2874 (1992)]

Q 5:38 May a plan purchase insurance to cover any losses to the plan resulting from a prohibited transaction?

Yes. A plan may carry insurance to protect itself from losses it incurs due to the misconduct of a fiduciary. A plan may not, however, contain a provision that would relieve a fiduciary of liability for a prohibited transaction. [ERISA § 410]

Q 5:39 Are there any statutory exceptions to the prohibited transaction provisions?

Yes. There are numerous statutory exceptions to the prohibited transaction provisions. Some of the most common are as follows:

1. Loans made by a plan to a plan participant or beneficiary, if the loan satisfies certain requirements (see Qs 5:15 through Q 5:21 for a discussion of these requirements).

2. Services rendered by a party in interest to a plan that are necessary for the establishment or operation of the plan if no more than reasonable compensation is paid (see Q 5:23).

3. A loan to an employee stock ownership plan (ESOP), provided the interest rate is not in excess of a reasonable interest rate.

4. Ancillary services provided by a federal- or state-supervised bank or similar financial institution that is a fiduciary to the plan, under certain circumstances.
5. The acquisition or sale by a plan of qualifying employer securities or the acquisition, sale, or lease by a plan of qualifying employer real property (see Q 5:29), under certain circumstances.

[ERISA § 408(b)]

Q 5:40 May administrative exemptions to the prohibited transaction rules be granted by the DOL?

Yes. DOL may grant an exemption from the prohibited transaction rules if the exemption is (1) administratively feasible, (2) in the interests of the plan, its participants and beneficiaries, and (3) protective of the rights of the plan's participants and beneficiaries. [ERISA § 408(a); IRC § 4975(c)(2)]

IRS has delegated to the DOL primary authority to issue rulings and regulations on, and grant exemptions from, the prohibited transaction restrictions. A specific statement explaining how the proposed exemption satisfies the requirements listed above and detailed information concerning the proposed transaction are required. The grant of an administrative exemption may be conditional or unconditional. [Reorganization Plan No 4, 43 Fed Reg 47713 (October 17, 1978)]

An administrative prohibited transaction exemption does not relieve a fiduciary of his or her basic fiduciary duties (including the duty to act prudently and solely in the interest of plan participants and beneficiaries) or from any other provisions of the act to which the exemption does not specifically apply. [DOL Reg §§ 2570.30 through 2570.52]

Q 5:41 May a prohibited transaction exemption be granted retroactively?

Yes. In general, most prohibited transaction exemptions are granted on a prospective basis. However, DOL may grant a retroactive exemption if the applicant acted in good faith and the safeguards necessary for the grant of a prospective exemption were in place when the prohibited transaction occurred. However, the DOL will generally not grant a retroactive exemption if the transaction resulted in a loss to the plan or was inconsistent with the general fiduciary responsibility provisions of ERISA Sections 403 and 404. [DOL Tech Rel 85-1]

Q 5:42 Can a prohibited transaction exemption be used to benefit the owner of a closely held corporation?

Yes. The fact that the corporation or a shareholder also benefits from the transaction will not preclude the granting of an exemption. For example, it may be possible for the corporation to borrow money from its qualified retirement plan or to sell assets to the plan to improve the corporation's cash flow without incurring a penalty. The following examples illustrate this answer.

Example 1. A sponsoring employer was granted an exemption that permitted its pension plan to make loans to the employer on a recurring basis over a five-year period. The proceeds of the loans were used by the employer to purchase automobiles. [PTE 82-125]

Example 2. The DOL permitted the plans of a professional corporation that had acquired medical facilities to lease such facilities to the professional corporation. The DOL determined that the terms of the lease were at least as favorable to the plans as those they could obtain from an unrelated party. [PTE 83-124]

Q 5:43 What is a prohibited transaction class exemption?

A prohibited transaction class exemption is an administrative exemption that applies to any parties in interest (see the discussion of party in interest at Q 5:4) within the class of parties in interest specified in the exemption who meet its conditions. [DOL Reg § 2570.31(b)]

Most prohibited transaction exemptions are issued by the DOL. However, the following types of prohibited transaction exemption request are handled by the Internal Revenue Service:

Q 5:43   **Fiduciary Responsibility Answer Book**

1. All requests regarding individual retirement accounts and individual retirement annuities;
2. All requests regarding directed investments that are exempt from the prohibited transaction provisions by virtue of ERISA section 404(c); and
3. All requests regarding leveraged employee stock ownership plans.

The following list sets forth some important class exemptions that have been granted:

- **PTCE 76-1**—Arrangements between multiple employer plans and contributing employers involving delinquent employer contributions. The exemption contains conditions under which extensions of time for making contributions, payment of less than the full amount due or a determination that a contribution is uncollectible would be permitted.
- **PTCE 77-10**—Sharing and leasing office space and administrative services and the sale or lease of goods by multiple employer plans to a participating employee organization, participating employer, or another multiple employer plan.
- **PTCE 80-26**—Interest free loans between plans and parties in interest (see Q 5:14 for a discussion of this exemption).
- **PTCE 80-51**—This exemption provides relief for certain transactions involving bank collective funds in which employee benefit plans invest.
- **PTCE 81-6**—Lending securities by employee benefit plans to broker-dealers and banks who are parties in interest.
- **PTCE 84-14**—Transactions involving plans whose assets are managed by a QPAM. (See Q 5:14 for a discussion of this exemption.)
- **PTCE 84-24**—Investment of plan assets in contracts or mutual fund shares by insurance agents and brokers who are parties in interest and their receipt of commissions in connection with such transactions.
- **PTCE 85-68**—The plan's acquisition, through sale or contribution by the employer, of customer notes that have been accepted

by the employer in the ordinary course of the employer's business.

Q 5:44 What is an individual prohibited transaction exemption?

An individual prohibited transaction exemption is an administrative exemption that applies only to the specific parties in interest named or otherwise defined in the exemption. No other individuals can rely on such exemption. [DOL Reg § 2570.31(e)]

Individual exemptions have been granted by the DOL in many areas, including the following:

- Commission payments to a party in interest
- The extension of credit between a plan and a party in interest
- Transactions involving collective investment funds, group trusts, insurance, and annuities
- Transactions between investment managers and parties in interest
- Leases
- Loans
- Sale, transfer, or use of plan assets
- Sales or contributions of real property
- Repurchase agreements
- Sales contribution or exchange of securities and notes
- Provision of services.

Q 5:45 May plan expenses be paid out of the plan?

Yes. Plan assets may be used to defray the reasonable expenses of administering the plan. [ERISA § 403(c)(1)] However, expenses for so-called settlor functions, such as expenses incurred in designing the plan, drafting the initial plan document, or terminating the plan (see discussion of settlor functions at Qs 3:18 through 3:21), may not be paid out of the plan. [DOL Letter to Kirk F. Maldonado, dated March 2, 1987]

Q 5:46 Under what circumstances may the sponsor of a single employer plan receive a refund of contributions it made to the plan?

A sponsor of a single employer plan may receive a refund of contributions it made to the plan in the following circumstances:

1. If a contribution was made to the plan by the employer by a mistake of fact (but not a mistake of law), the plan may permit a return of contributions to the employer within one year of the contribution.

2. If contributions to the plan were conditioned upon the initial tax qualification of the plan, and the plan receives from the IRS an adverse determination with respect to its initial qualification, the plan may permit return of contributions to the employer within one year of the IRS determination, if the application for determination was filed by the time prescribed under the IRC.

3. If a contribution to the plan was expressly made conditional upon its deductibility under section 404 of the Code, then, to the extent the deduction is disallowed, the employer may receive a return of contributions within one year of the disallowance of the deduction.

    Planning Pointer. The IRS has made it clear that, for the employer to obtain a refund from the plan under this rule, the plan or the board resolutions must explicitly state that contributions are conditioned on deductibility. For example, plan language stating that the nondeductible contributions *must* or *shall* be returned meet this requirement. However, plan language stating that nondeductible contributions *may* be returned to the employer would not suffice to permit a return of nondeductible contributions to the employer. [See Rev Proc 90-49]

4. An employer may receive a reversion of excess plan assets after a plan is terminated.

[ERISA § 403(c) and (d)]

Note. An employer receiving a reversion from a tax qualified pension plan is subject to income tax and a substantial excise tax. [IRC § 4980]

Q 5:47 Under what circumstances may an employer participating in a multiemployer plan receive a refund of contributions it made to the plan?

An employer participating in a multiemployer plan may receive a refund of contributions it made to the plan in the following circumstances:

1. If a contribution was made to the plan by the employer as a result of a mistake of fact or law (other than a mistake relating to the issue of whether the plan is tax qualified), the plan may permit the return of such contribution to the employer within six months after the plan administrator determines that the contribution was made by such a mistake.

2. If contributions to the plan were conditioned upon the *initial* tax qualification of the plan, and the plan receives an adverse determination with respect to the initial qualification from the IRS, the plan may permit the return of contributions to the employer within one year of the IRS determination, if the application for determination was filed by the time prescribed under the IRC.

3. If a contribution to the plan was expressly made conditional upon its deductibility under IRC section 404, then, to the extent the deduction is disallowed, the employer may receive a return of contributions within one year of the disallowance of the deduction.

4. If it is determined that the employer made an overpayment of a withdrawal liability payment, the plan may permit a return of such payment to the employer within six months of the date of such determination.

[ERISA § 403(b); IRC § 401(a)(2)]

Chapter 6

Fiduciary Liability

A fiduciary can be subject to civil and criminal liability for failure to discharge its duties under ERISA. This chapter discusses the scope of such liability and proposes steps to reduce the risk of incurring such liability.

Personal Liability	6-2
Equitable Remedies	6-4
Damages: Plan Losses	6-7
Damages: Fiduciary Profits	6-9
Punitive Damages	6-10
20 Percent Penalty	6-11
Excise Taxes & Penalties	6-12
Criminal Liability	6-12
Interference with ERISA Rights	6-14
Protecting Against the Risk of Liability	6-15
Fiduciary Liability Insurance	6-18
Indemnity by Sponsor	6-19
Co-Fiduciaries and Contribution	6-20
Attorneys' Fees	6-22
Standard of Judicial Review	6-25
Steps to Reduce Risks	6-28
Compliance with Claims Procedures	6-33
Nonfiduciary Liability	6-39

Personal Liability

Q 6:1 Can a fiduciary be held personally liable for a breach of duty?

Yes. A fiduciary who breaches the fiduciary requirements of ERISA is personally liable for any losses to the plan resulting from this breach. Any profits obtained by the fiduciary through the use of plan assets must be restored to the plan. [ERISA § 409(a)]

A civil action may be brought by a participant or beneficiary, or by another fiduciary. [ERISA § 502(a)(2)] The court may impose other appropriate relief, including removal of the fiduciary. [ERISA § 409(a)]

Q 6:2 Is a fiduciary liable for a breach not occurring during the fiduciary's term in office?

A fiduciary cannot be held liable for a breach committed before the fiduciary became a fiduciary or after the fiduciary ceased to be a fiduciary, only for a breach committed while a fiduciary. [ERISA § 409(b)]

Example 1. A bank began acting as trustee for a plan on February 1, 1975. Before the bank assumed the role of trustee, it had no involvement in the determination of whether individuals were or were not employees. Before February 1, 1975, the bank also had no knowledge or responsibility for any subsequent inaction relating to any individuals' entitlements under the plan. Where the bank's knowledge of these individuals' claims did not arise until litigation had already begun, the bank owed no fiduciary duty, and was not liable for a fiduciary breach, to individuals contesting determinations concerning their employee status. [Baeten v Van Ess, 446 FSupp 868 (ED Wis 1977)]

Example 2. Briody became trustee of a pension plan on March 12, 1979. On March 19, 1979, a co-trustee, Hodgman, committed a breach of fiduciary duty, by transferring $40,000 to an investment manager who had previously been involved in fiduciary breaches, of which Hodgman was aware. Briody did not know about Hodgman's breach until later. Nevertheless, because he had already assumed the position of trustee, Briody was liable for Hodgman's breach under the co-fiduciary liability rules. [Free v Briody, 732 F2d 1331 (7th Cir 1984)]

Example 3. James and Ramon were trustees of a profit-sharing plan, but resigned on April 15, 1983. After that date, they did not carry out any fiduciary functions. They therefore cannot be held liable for the successor trustee's acceptance on April 20, 1983 of an offer to purchase stock of the employer held by the plan, since it occurred after their resignations. [Anderson v Mortell, 722 FSupp 462 (ND Ill 1989)] If they had resigned without prudently providing for continuing management of the plan, the act of resigning would have been a fiduciary breach. [Freund v Marshall & Ilsley Bank, 485 FSupp 629, 641 (WD Wis 1979)]

Q 6:3 Is there a duty to remedy a fiduciary breach committed by a predecessor fiduciary?

Yes. If a successor fiduciary learns of a breach committed by a predecessor, the successor is obligated to take reasonable steps to remedy the situation as successor fiduciary. Failure to take such action constitutes a separate, current breach of fiduciary duty by the successor. [DOL Adv Op Ltr No 76-95 (Sept 30, 1976)]

Example. Allen, an existing trustee of a pension plan, has invested plan assets in a parcel of real estate. Sconnie becomes a trustee of the plan on December 1, 1976. When she becomes trustee, Sconnie learns that this would be a risky investment and involves conflicts of interest and self-dealing by Allen. Sconnie then has enough knowledge to determine that this investment violates ERISA. She has a duty to liquidate these improper investments upon assuming her fiduciary responsibilities, taking all reasonable steps as promptly as reasonably possible after becoming trustee. [Marshall v Craft, 463 FSupp 493 (ND Ga 1978)]

Q 6:4 Does a successor fiduciary have any obligation if the successor does not have knowledge of an actual breach, but only knows of a possible breach by a predecessor fiduciary?

Yes. A successor fiduciary who has enough knowledge to indicate that a breach of fiduciary duty may have taken place has a duty to notify the plan trustees or the DOL of the information it does have. The successor does not have a duty to investigate further, or to implement special procedures to evaluate circumstances solely for determining whether they constitute a breach. [DOL Adv Op Ltr No 77-79/80A (Oct 3, 1977)]

> **Example.** *E* Life Insurance Company was managing fiduciary and an investment manager of a multiemployer pension plan. *VP* Company was another investment manager of the plan. *E* and *VP* had no affiliation with the plan before June 30, 1977. *E* and *VP* were responsible, effective June 30, 1977, for the management of all real estate assets of the plan.
>
> For a number of years before June 30, 1977, the plan and its fiduciaries were the subject of investigation by the DOL, the IRS, and other government agencies, for alleged civil and criminal abuse in connection with management of plan assets. On June 30, 1977, the plan entered into an agreement with the DOL to correct prior problems, and to appoint independent fiduciaries to manage plan assets, and entered into agreements with *E* and *VP* as independent fiduciaries.
>
> The DOL issued an advisory opinion that *E* and *VP* would fully satisfy their fiduciary responsibility (including co-fiduciary responsibility) with respect to breaches by other plan fiduciaries occurring before June 30, 1977, if, as agreed, they would keep their records open for government inspection, provide requested materials to the plan trustees, and respond to occasional government questions. *E* and *VP* were not required to perform any general or special investigative functions with respect to any prior plan transactions or investments, other than as described above. [DOL Adv Op Ltr No 77-79/80A (Oct 3, 1977)]

Equitable Remedies

Q 6:5 What types of remedies can be imposed on a fiduciary for a breach of fiduciary duty?

A fiduciary found to be in breach of its duty under ERISA is subject to legal remedies, equitable remedies, or both. Legal remedies include money damages for restoration of plan losses or disgorgement of the

Fiduciary Liability   Q 6:6

fiduciary's profits. [ERISA § 409(a); Mertens v Hewitt Assocs, 124 LEd2d 161 (1993) (restoration of losses is not an equitable remedy)] Equitable remedies under ERISA specifically endorsed by its legislative history include injunctions, constructive trusts, and removal of a fiduciary. [S Rep No 383, 93d Cong, 1st Sess, 105-106 (1973); Amalgamated Clothing & Textile Workers Union v Murdock, 861 F2d 1406 (9th Cir 1988) (constructive trust); Katsaros v Cody, 744 F2d 270 (2d Cir), *cert denied*, 469 US 1072 (1984) (removal, with appointment of new investment managers and other trustees for fifteen months); Whitfield v Tomasso, 682 FSupp 1287 (ED NY 1988) (permanent injunction against acting as fiduciary of, or providing service to, any ERISA plan)]

Q 6:6 Are there restrictions on the use of equitable remedies for a fiduciary's breach?

Yes. The "spendthrift," or anti-assignment, provisions of ERISA generally limit the equitable powers of the courts in fashioning remedies for fiduciary breaches. However, if a fiduciary's actions harm the plan itself, the fiduciary's own plan benefits are subject to attachment or other remedies.

Example 1. A fiduciary was a participant in a pension plan and embezzled money from a third party. The third party was the union that the participant served as business manager and chief executive officer. The United States Supreme Court ruled that a constructive trust could not be imposed on the fiduciary's own benefits under the pension plan, in favor of the union or any other third party. [Guidry v Sheet Metal Workers Nat'l Pension Fund, 493 US 365 (1990)] The Court found it inappropriate in this circumstance to use the equitable relief provision under ERISA Section 409, because it would weaken ERISA's prohibition on the assignment or alienation of pension benefits. [ERISA § 206(d)] *Guidry* did not address whether plan benefits of a fiduciary who is also a participant could be reached where the harm has been suffered by the plan itself.

Example 2. Robert was a trustee of and a participant in a union pension plan. He was convicted of engaging in a RICO conspiracy to receive kickbacks in exchange for channeling $20 million from the pension plan's assets to a Florida-based mortgage company.

Prior to the indictment, the pension plan and its other trustees filed a civil case alleging ERISA and Racketeer Influenced and Corrupt Organization Act (RICO) violations. The district court entered a judgment against Robert for $25.5 million for losses resulting from ERISA fiduciary violations and $96.6 million for RICO violations. Later, the pension plan notified Robert that it would prospectively set off his liability to the plan against his benefits from the plan. The Court of Appeals for the Third Circuit held that this setoff was permitted. [Coar v Kazimir, 990 F2d 1413, 16 EBC (BNA) 1904 (3d Cir 1993)]

Q 6:7 Are any equitable remedies available as an alternative to the removal of a fiduciary for breach of duty?

Outright removal of a fiduciary can be avoided in some circumstances. For example, a court may permanently enjoin a breaching trustee and the sponsoring employer from engaging in future conduct that constitutes a breach of the trustee's fiduciary duty, and may permit the trustee to continue serving but order the appointment of a qualified investment manager. [Whitfield v Cohen, 682 FSupp 188 (SD NY 1988)] Alternatively, a breaching fiduciary can be suspended until the transaction constituting the breach has been corrected. [Marshall v Kelly, 465 FSupp 341 (WD Okla 1978) (repayment of improper loans)] Another alternative is the creation of a receivership. [Marshall v Snyder, 430 FSupp 1224 (ED NY 1977), aff'd 572 F2d 894 (2d Cir 1978)]

Q 6:8 What other types of equitable remedies are available?

Other equitable remedies have included rescission of a purchase of employer stock [Eaves v Penn, 587 F2d 453 (10th Cir 1978)]; rescission of a plan administrator's employment contract providing excessive compensation [Gilliam v Edwards, 492 FSupp 1255 (D NJ 1980)]; reformation of plan documents [*In re* Gulf Pension Litigation, 764 FSupp 1149 (SD Tex 1991) (reversing the merger of two inactive overfunded plans into the employer's principal plan)]; and transfer of a portion of a pension fund to another trust. [Trapani v Consolidated Edison Employees' Mutual Aid Society, Inc, 891 F2d 48 (2d

Cir 1989) (amounts attributable to employees no longer participating in the original fund))

Damages: Plan Losses

Q 6:9 What losses may a fiduciary be liable to restore?

A fiduciary may be liable to restore the entire amount of any loss suffered by the plan resulting from the fiduciary's breach. If the fiduciary's breach does not result in a monetary loss to the plan, ordinarily there is no damage award as a remedy for the breach, although equitable remedies may be imposed on the fiduciary. [ERISA § 409(a)]

Example 1. Mitchell is the named fiduciary of a profit-sharing plan, with responsibility for investing plan assets. Mitchell's neighbor, Sarah, gives Mitchell a "hot tip" on the stock of Cheesy Gadget Corporation, which is going to announce a contract with the state government on Friday, May 15. Without investigating further, Mitchell immediately sells 40 percent of the assets of the plan and buys stock of Cheesy Gadget Corporation on May 14. The contract with the state government is indeed announced on May 15, and the price of the stock triples.

On May 20, Mitchell sells the plan's shares of Cheesy Gadget Corporation, realizing a large gain far in excess of what the plan assets would have earned absent the purchase. He does not profit personally from the transaction. Even if Mitchell's purchase of the stock was imprudent, he would not be liable to plan participants and beneficiaries because there were no losses to the plan. However, he may be subject to equitable relief (e.g., suspension or removal). [Donovan v Cunningham, 716 F2d 1455 (5th Cir 1983), *cert denied*, 467 US 1251 (1984) (breaching fiduciary subject to equitable relief, without regard to whether the ESOP suffered a loss)]

Example 2. A fiduciary (an investment manager) failed to diversify a plan's portfolio of high-grade debt securities. The fiduciary's liability is measured by subtracting the actual value of the portfolio when the fiduciary was dismissed from a hypothetical value of the portfolio if the assets had been diversified, including diversification as to maturity. [GIW Indus, Inc v Trevor, Stewart, Burton & Jacobsen, Inc, 10 EBC (BNA) 2290 (SD Ga 1989), *aff'd*, 895 F2d 729 (11th Cir 1990)]

Example 3. A fiduciary (an investment manager) violated a 50 percent limit on equity investments set by agreement with the plan trustees. The fiduciary's liability is measured by subtracting the actual earnings on the excess equity holdings from hypothetical earnings on the excess holdings, as if the excess holdings had been invested in bonds, using the interest rates appearing on the Shearson/Lehman Brothers Government/Corporate Bond Index. [Dardaganis v Grace Capital Inc, 684 FSupp 1196 (SD NY 1988), *aff'd in part*, 889 F2d 1237 (2d Cir 1989)]

Q 6:10 What is the measure of a plan's loss to be restored as a remedy for a fiduciary breach?

A plan's loss caused by a fiduciary's breach is measured by comparing what the plan actually earned (or lost) as a result of the fiduciary's actions with what the plan would hypothetically have earned (or lost) had the fiduciary's actions not taken place. Where several hypothetical alternatives are available, a court should use the alternative most favorable to the affected participants and beneficiaries.

Example. John, Robert, and Carl were the trustees of Corporation G's pension plan, and were high-ranking officials of G. Corporation L made a tender offer for a controlling interest in G at a price of $45 per share. The plan owned 525,000 shares of G stock. The trustees determined not to tender any of the plan's shares, and indeed used plan funds to purchase 1,158,000 additional shares of G stock at the prevailing market price of $36 to $39.75 a share (the price having risen from $26.75 a share to $35.88 when the tender offer was announced). The tender offer was preliminarily enjoined in court, and ultimately failed. G stock dropped in price to approximately the pre-tender offer level of $23 per share.

Approximately 17 months after the stock was purchased, the trustees, with court permission, sold the newly purchased stock (and some of the prior holdings) for $47.55 per share, realizing a $13 million gain.

The Court of Appeals for the Second Circuit held that the plan may have sustained a loss, despite the $13 million earnings, and remanded to the district court for a determination of the losses. The measure of loss required a comparison of (a) what the plan actually earned on the investment in G stock with (b) what the plan would have earned had the funds been available for other plan purposes. If (a) was less than (b), the difference was the loss; if (a) was not less than (b), there was no loss. [Donovan v Bierwirth, 754 F2d 1049 (2d Cir 1985)]

Q 6:11 Can any gains offset a loss resulting from a fiduciary's breach?

Generally, no. Losses to the plan resulting from a transaction constituting a breach of fiduciary duty are not offset by gains resulting from any separate and distinct transaction.

Example. Nathaniel was a fiduciary of a profit-sharing plan. He caused the plan to invest in three entities in which he and other fiduciaries made substantial investments, before and after the plan invested in the three entities. Nathaniel and the other fiduciaries profited from the plan's investment. Viewed as a portfolio, the plan's investment in the three entities yielded 72 percent—a very favorable yield. Two of the three investments had very high yields; one yielded only 4 percent. The court ruled that plan participants were entitled to compare the 4 percent yield with hypothetical earnings on alternative investments; the shortfall of $6,700 constituted a loss under Section 409(a) of ERISA, without offset by the substantial gain on the two other investments. [Leigh v Engle, 669 FSupp 1390, 1405 (ND Ill 1985), *on remand from* 727 F2d 113 (7th Cir 1984) *aff'd*, 858 F2d 361 (7th Cir 1988), *cert denied*, 489 US 1078 (1989)]

Damages: Fiduciary Profits

Q 6:12 What profits may a fiduciary be liable to disgorge?

If a fiduciary uses plan assets in a breach of fiduciary duty and makes any profit as a result, the fiduciary must disgorge those profits, regardless of whether or not the plan suffered a loss. [ERISA § 409(a)]

Example 1. A plan trustee improperly caused the plan to pay him sales commissions, and to pay excessive construction costs to the employer sponsoring the plan (of which the trustee was a principal shareholder). The trustee is required to restore both these amounts. [Marshall v Kelly, 465 FSupp 341 (WD Okla 1978)]

Example 2. Fiduciaries charged a plan an excessive fee for services, and lent part of the plan's funds at a rate far below market interest. The fiduciaries must disgorge the excess portion of the fee, and in addition, must make up the shortfall in interest and post a bond to secure the plan against potential losses in connection with the loan. [Donovan v Mazzola, 716 F2d 1226 (9th Cir 1983), *cert denied,* 464 US 1040 (1984)]

Punitive Damages

Q 6:13 May a participant or beneficiary recover punitive damages for a breach of fiduciary duty?

No. Punitive damages are not available for a breach of fiduciary duty (and the liability for the breach that arises out of Section 409 of ERISA). Damages, a legal remedy, are limited to restoration of losses and disgorgement of profits. Punitive damages are not an equitable remedy. [Mertens v Hewitt Assocs, 124 LEd2d 161 (1993)]

Example. A plan administrator fails to process a beneficiary's claim in a timely manner. Punitive damages are not available to the beneficiary. Remedies against the administrator are limited to recovery of the benefits, clarification of the right to benefits (whether present or future), or removal of the fiduciary. [Massachusetts Mutual Life Ins Co v Russell, 473 US 134 (1985)]

The Supreme Court in *Russell* declined to determine whether a participant or beneficiary could recover punitive damages when fiduciary liability arises out of provisions of ERISA other than Section 409, or when the fiduciary violates the terms of the plan. Language in a subsequent Supreme Court opinion has prompted some courts to uphold punitive damages arising out of interference with ERISA rights under Section 510 (rather than breach of fiduciary duty under Section 409). [Ingersoll-Rand Co v McClendon, 498 US 133, 145

(1990) ("no basis . . . for limiting ERISA actions to only those which seek 'pension benefits.' "); Haywood v Russell Corp, 584 So2d 1291, 1297 (Ala 1991) (state claim preempted)]

Other courts have rejected punitive damages under ERISA generally. [*See, e.g.,* Gaskell v Harvard Coop Soc'y, 762 FSupp 1539 (D Mass 1991)]

Q 6:14 May a plan recover punitive damages for a breach of fiduciary duty?

In *Massachusetts Mutual Life Ins Co v Russell,* [473 US 134 (1985)] the Supreme Court expressly left open the issue of whether a plan—as opposed to a participant or beneficiary—could recover punitive damages even when fiduciary liability arises out of Section 409. Some courts have subsequently stated that a plan can recover punitive damages under such circumstances. [Schoenholtz v Doniger, 657 FSupp 899 (SD NY 1987)] Other courts have questioned whether even a plan can recover punitive damages in an action arising out of a breach of fiduciary duty under ERISA Section 409. [Diduck v Kaszycki & Sons Contractors, Inc, 737 FSupp 792, 805 (SD NY 1990), *aff'd in part* 974 F2d 270, 286 (2d Cir 1992)]

20 Percent Penalty

Q 6:15 What is the 20 percent penalty for breach of fiduciary duty?

A penalty of 20 percent of the amount payable pursuant to a court order or settlement agreement with the DOL is assessed by the DOL for breach of fiduciary duty (or knowing participation therein) on or after December 19, 1989. [ERISA § 502(l)(1)] The civil penalty may apply to a person other than a fiduciary if the nonfiduciary knowingly participates in the breach. The penalty may be waived or reduced if the fiduciary or other person (1) acted reasonably and in good faith, or (2) cannot otherwise be reasonably expected to be able to restore all plan losses without severe financial hardship. [ERISA § 502(l)(3); Prop DOL Reg § 2560.502l-1]

Q 6:16 Are there any set-offs for the 20 percent penalty?

Yes. The penalty imposed on a fiduciary or other person is to be reduced by the amount of any penalty or tax imposed with respect to a prohibited transaction under Sections 406 and 502(i) of ERISA or Section 4975 of the IRC. [ERISA § 502(l)(4)]

Excise Taxes & Penalties

Q 6:17 What excise taxes and other penalties may apply to a fiduciary breach?

A fiduciary breach may also constitute a prohibited transaction under ERISA Section 406, IRC Section 4975, or both. IRC Section 4975 imposes an excise tax equal to 5 percent of the amount involved in the prohibited transaction for each year or part thereof in which the transaction remains uncorrected. An additional tax equal to 100 percent of the amount involved is imposed if the prohibited transaction is not corrected. [IRC § 4975(a), (b)] ERISA imposes a similar penalty on plans not covered by the excise tax under the IRC. [ERISA § 502(i); DOL Reg § 2506.502i-1]

Criminal Liability

Q 6:18 May a fiduciary face criminal liability for a breach of fiduciary duty?

Yes. Any person who willfully violates any reporting or disclosure provision in Title I of ERISA is subject to a fine of $5,000 (or $100,000, in the case of a partnership or corporation), imprisonment for one year, or both. [ERISA § 501] An intentional violation of the prohibition against service as a fiduciary (among other positions) to an employee benefit plan by any person convicted of any offense specified in ERISA

Section 411(a) (see Q 2:2) is subject to a fine of $10,000, imprisonment for five years, or both. [ERISA § 411(b)]

Q 6:19 Are there other laws imposing criminal liability on a fiduciary?

Yes. The use of force or violence, or the threat thereof, or the use of fraud to restrain, coerce, or intimidate any participant or beneficiary in order to interfere with or prevent the exercise of any right under the plan may result in a $10,000 fine, imprisonment for one year, or both. [ERISA § 511]

An act of a fiduciary committed while serving as an ERISA fiduciary can also violate other criminal laws. This can include, for example, the federal crimes of mail fraud, wire fraud, or conspiracy under RICO [18 USC §§ 1341, 1343, and 1961 et seq]

> **Example.** Robert was a trustee of a union pension plan. He took kickbacks in exchange for channeling $20 million from the pension plan's assets to a Florida-based mortgage company. He was indicted and convicted of mail and wire fraud, and of engaging in a RICO conspiracy. Robert was also sued under ERISA and RICO. [US v Zauber, 857 F2d 137 (3d Cir 1988), *cert denied*, 489 US 1066 (1989) (criminal RICO), *cited in* Coar v Kazimir, 990 F2d 1413 16 EBC (BNA) 1904 (3d Cir 1993) (ERISA and civil RICO)]

Q 6:20 Do any federal crimes specifically apply to employee benefit plans?

Yes. Accepting kickbacks in connection with an ERISA plan is a federal crime punishable by a $10,000 fine, three years' imprisonment, or both. [18 USC § 1954] Knowingly making a false statement or knowingly concealing facts in connection with plan documents required by ERISA is a federal crime punishable by a $10,000 fine, five years' imprisonment, or both. [18 USC § 1027] Embezzling plan assets from an employee pension or welfare plan, as defined in ERISA, is a federal crime punishable by a $10,000 fine, five years' imprisonment, or both. [18 USC § 664]

Example. Grizzle was the President of the Grizzle Company, which employed members of the Union. A collective bargaining agreement provided that the Grizzle Company would withhold from each covered employee's wages $1.00 per hour worked and contribute these funds monthly to the Union Vacation Fund, an ERISA welfare plan. Grizzle, as President, withheld contributions and failed to contribute them. Grizzle was convicted for embezzling from an employee benefit plan, [18 USC § 664] for receiving stolen property, [18 USC § 662] and for making false statements to any department or agency of the United States. [18 USC §§ 1001, 1002; US v Grizzle, 933 F2d 943 (11th Cir), *cert denied,* 112 S Ct 271 (1991)]

Interference with ERISA Rights

Q 6:21 May a fiduciary face civil liability for interference with rights protected under ERISA?

Yes, if the fiduciary is the employer. Participants or beneficiaries may recover against any person who interferes with the exercise or attainment of any right to which they are entitled under a plan or ERISA. Interference can include discharges, fines, suspensions, discipline, or discrimination against the participants or beneficiaries. [ERISA § 510; Ingersoll-Rand Co v McClendon, 498 US 133 (1990)] This liability is generally applied to employers that discharge employees with the intent to cut off vesting under a retirement plan, and a number of courts have expressly limited this liability to employers. [Byrd v MacPapers, Inc, 961 F2d 157 (11th Cir 1992); West v Butler, 621 F2d 240 (6th Cir 1980)]

Example. An employer discharged Walter, a 62-year-old employee, a few weeks before his qualified retirement plan benefits would have become vested. The proximity of the termination date and the vesting date was sufficient to infer that the employer's purpose in discharging the employee was to deprive him of his retirement benefits. The discharge is a violation of ERISA Section 510, even though it does not constitute age discrimination. [Hazen Paper Co v Biggins, 113 SCt 1701 (1993), *vacating* Biggins v Hazen Paper Co, 953 F2d 1405 (1st Cir 1992) (vacated only as to age discrimination)]

Q 6:22 If an employer changes the terms of a health insurance plan, making it self-insured, and sharply reducing the lifetime limit for expenses related to AIDS and related illnesses, after a participant has been diagnosed with AIDS, does the change constitute interference with the exercise of rights under a plan or ERISA Section 510?

No, although if the plan remains an insured plan, state laws governing insurance may prohibit such a reduction. Medical coverage at a specific level is not an existing, enforceable obligation under ERISA; a participant or beneficiary does not "vest" in medical benefits as one vests in pension benefits. Thus, according to the Fifth Circuit, a change in the plan that effectively cuts off one and only one current participant's benefits after he made his initial claims does not constitute interference with rights under ERISA within the meaning of Section 510, even if the employer's motivation was to save the cost of benefits for that participant alone. [McGann v H&H Music Co, 946 F2d 401 (5th Cir 1991), *cert denied*, 113 SCt 482 (1992)] This holding, which the United States Supreme Court declined to review on the merits, is controversial; legislation may address these issues. In addition, other laws, such as the Americans with Disabilities Act, may limit a plan sponsor's right to cut back or restrict benefits relating to AIDS or other conditions. [42 USC §§ 12101 et seq; 29 CFR § 1630.16(f)(4)]

Protecting Against the Risk of Liability

Q 6:23 May a plan release a fiduciary from liability?

In general, no. Provisions in a plan or other agreement or instrument that would relieve a fiduciary of liability for breaching the fiduciary liability rules ("exculpatory provisions") are void as against public policy. Such provisions would relieve the fiduciary of responsibility to the plan by abrogating the plan's right to recovery from the fiduciary for breaching his or her fiduciary obligations. [ERISA § 410(a)] This prohibition, however, does not prevent a fiduciary from allocating or delegating his or her responsibilities. (See Qs 4.1 through 4:8 and Q 6:24) [ERISA Conf Comm Rep] Further, a fiduciary may be indemnified (i.e., repaid or insured against loss) by a person or entity other than the plan, as described in Q 6:31.

Planning Pointer. A statement in a plan document that a fiduciary has no liability resulting from any action he or she takes with respect to a plan is void. Also, the plan cannot indemnify a fiduciary against fiduciary liabilities. However, a statement that another fiduciary is responsible for certain fiduciary duties is valid.

Example. A provision in a trust agreement between an employee stock ownership plan (ESOP) and the trustee of the trust provided that the ESOP would indemnify the trustee for any liability the trustee would incur in responding to tender offers as long as the trustee precisely followed the plan participants' directions. The court agreed with the DOL that this indemnification agreement is not valid because it created an incentive for the trustee to breach its fiduciary duties to act in the best interests of the ESOP participants since the trustee would be unprotected by the indemnification provisions if the trustee did not precisely follow the participants' direction. [Martin v NationsBank of Georgia, NA, 16 EBC (BNA) 2138 (ND Ga 1993)]

Q 6:24 May a fiduciary be relieved from his or her fiduciary duties by delegating duties with respect to a plan to another individual?

Yes. Although ERISA prohibits exculpatory provisions in a plan, a fiduciary may, under certain conditions, delegate duties to other individuals and be held unaccountable for the other person's breach of duties. (See the discussion of the rules regarding delegation of fiduciary duties and co-fiduciary liability at Questions 4.1 through 4.8.) However, a trustee may not allocate or delegate his or her responsibility to manage and control plan assets (see Q 8:44).

Planning Pointer. A delegation of duties under which no fiduciary (i.e., the delegator or delegatee) is liable for a breach is most likely either an exculpatory provision that is void as against public policy or a breach of duties of the delegating fiduciary.

Q 6:25 May a plan fiduciary indemnify its employees who actually perform the fiduciary services for the plan?

Yes. This indemnification is permissible since it does not relieve the fiduciary of responsibility or liability under ERISA. [DOL Reg § 2509.75-4]

Q 6:26 What is the effect of a provision in a plan that purports to free a fiduciary from liability for breaching his or her fiduciary duties?

Such a provision would be void as against public policy. Thus, the fiduciary purported to be relieved of his or her fiduciary duties would in fact be subject to such duties.

Note. The prudence of other fiduciaries who deal with fiduciaries who do not recognize their statutory responsibilities could also be called into question.

Q 6:27 Is a release from a plan participant that frees a fiduciary from liability for fiduciary breaches valid?

Yes. This situation is analogous to a fiduciary being indemnified by an employer, which is permissible. (See Q 6:31)

Example. Company *A* acquired Company *B*. Employees of Company *A* were given a choice of either receiving a special severance allowance from Company *A* equal to one year's salary or to transfer to Company *B*. Employees transferred to Company *B* were given the opportunity to purchase stock of Company *A* at a substantial discount. Employees accepting the offer to purchase the stock were required to release Company *A* and Company *B* from all claims relating to his or her transfer. Certain individuals, who transferred to Company *B* accepted the stock purchase offer and signed the release, thereafter brought a suit against Company *A* claiming breach of fiduciary duties in connection with the transfer and misrepresentation concerning their entitlement to severance pay from Company *A*.

The court held that the release operated to insulate Company A from any liability with respect to these claims. Thus, ERISA's prohibition against plan exculpatory provisions would not prohibit an employer from obtaining a release from employees against a claim of breaching an employment contract and its obligation to provide severance benefits, in consideration of a grant of stock. [Miller v Gen Motors Corp, 845 F2d 326 (6th Cir 1988)]

Fiduciary Liability Insurance

Q 6:28 May a plan purchase insurance for itself or for plan fiduciaries to cover liability or losses resulting from the acts or omissions of plan fiduciaries?

Yes. However, the insurance contract must permit recourse by the insurer against the fiduciary for the loss resulting from a breach of a fiduciary obligation by such fiduciary. [ERISA § 410(b)]

Note. An issue that is unresolved is whether fiduciary liability insurance may cover fiduciaries for the 20 percent excise tax for fiduciary breaches under ERISA § 502(l).

The fiduciary who is involved in purchasing insurance against fiduciary breaches for the plan must do his or her best to secure the most suitable coverage for the plan at no greater expenditure of plan assets than is necessary. [DOL News Rel 75-127 (Mar 4, 1975)]

Q 6:29 May a fiduciary or an employer purchase insurance for the plan fiduciary to cover liability or losses resulting from the acts or omissions of the plan fiduciary?

Yes. A fiduciary may purchase insurance to cover his or her liability resulting from a breach of fiduciary duties, and an employer or an employee organization may purchase insurance for the plan fiduciary. However, in these cases (unlike the situation where the *plan* purchases the policy (see Q 6:28), the policy need not provide for recourse against the fiduciary. [ERISA § 410(b)]

Q 6:30 May plan fiduciaries purchase, from the same insurance company that insures the plan against fiduciary breaches, a policy that protects the fiduciary from recourse lawsuits that the insurer can bring against the fiduciary?

Yes. A "linked" insurance policy, that is, an insurance policy that links low-cost insurance for individual fiduciaries purchased by the fiduciary (which protects the fiduciary against recourse lawsuits that the insurer can bring against the fiduciary) with high-cost insurance (which protects the plan against a fiduciary's breach) purchased by the plan is legal as long as the plan fiduciary purchases the insurance policy prudently and solely in the interest of plan participants and beneficiaries. [DOL News Rel 75-127 (Mar 4, 1975)] The plan may not pay for this coverage (see Q 6:28).

Indemnity by Sponsor

Q 6:31 May an employer who sponsors a plan, or an employee organization whose members are covered by the plan, indemnify a fiduciary?

Yes. Although ERISA prohibits the indemnification and exculpation of the fiduciary by the plan, ERISA permits the indemnification of the fiduciary by an employer who sponsors the plan or by an employee organization whose members are covered by the plan. This indemnification does not relieve the fiduciary of responsibility or liability for fiduciary breaches. Rather, this indemnification leaves the fiduciary fully responsible and liable, but permits another party to satisfy any liability incurred by the fiduciary. Therefore, this indemnification is not void as against public policy under ERISA § 410. [DOL Reg § 2509.75-4]

> **Note.** An issue that is not resolved is whether a fiduciary may obtain indemnity from an employer for the 20 percent civil penalty assessed under ERISA § 502(1). Since the purpose of the 20 percent mandatory penalty for fiduciary breaches is to deter violations of the fiduciary responsibility provisions, the payment of the penalty must arguably be borne by the individual who incurred the breach.

Co-Fiduciaries and Contribution

Q 6:32 Does a fiduciary who is sued for a breach of fiduciary duty have an implied right of contribution and/or indemnity against a co-fiduciary who participated in the breach?

The courts are divided on this issue. The Second and Seventh Circuit Courts of Appeals have held that a fiduciary whose alleged breach caused a loss to a plan has the right to bring an action for contribution and/or indemnity against other fiduciaries.

Example 1. The current plan trustee sued the previous plan trustee to recover for losses to the plan caused by the previous trustee's lack of prudence and due diligence with respect to certain plan investments. The former trustee then counterclaimed that the current trustee had failed to adequately evaluate and pursue claims of the plan and that such failure contributed to the plan losses that were the subject of the lawsuit. The court held that since ERISA is silent as to the contribution issue, it is appropriate to incorporate the traditional trust law doctrine of contribution in the law of ERISA. [Chemung Canal Trust Co v Sovran Bank/Maryland, 939 F2d 12 (2d Cir 1991) *cert denied,* 112 S Ct 3014 (1992)]

Example 2. A trustee misused plan assets resulting in losses to the plan. The district court held that the co-trustee was jointly and severally liable with the trustee to the plan for the losses and denied the co-trustee's claim for contribution against the more culpable trustee. The Court of Appeals for the Seventh Circuit reversed the district court and held that it was within the court's equitable power under ERISA to have the more culpable fiduciary indemnify the passive co-trustee who was found liable for losses incurred by the plan as a result of the other trustee's misconduct. [Free v Briody, 732 F2d 1331 (7th Cir 1984)]

By contrast, other courts have not recognized a right of contribution or indemnity among ERISA fiduciaries. The Ninth Circuit has applied the reasoning of the U.S. Supreme Court in *Massachusetts Mut Life Ins Co v Russell,* 473 US 134 (1985), and has held that ERISA Section 409 only establishes remedies for the benefit of the plan and, therefore, could not be read as providing for an equitable remedy of contribution in favor of a breaching fiduciary. There was no indication in ERISA's legislative history that "Congress was concerned with softening the blow on joint wrongdoers." [Kim v Fujikawa, 871 F2d 1427 (9th Cir 1989)]

Example 3. An assignee of a liquidated ERISA trust brought a breach of fiduciary responsibility suit against the plan trustees, and one trustee asserted a counterclaim for contribution against the assignee and against the trustee's co-fiduciaries. The court held that the federal right to contribution may only arise when Congress has expressly stated such a right, clearly implied such a right, or has given the federal courts the power to fashion such a right under federal common law. Since Congress did not grant such a right, there is no basis for a fiduciary's right to contribution under ERISA. The court also stated that the Seventh Circuit's opinion in *Free* that there is a right of contribution against co-fiduciaries under ERISA may have been undercut by the Supreme Court's subsequent decision in *Russell*. [Mut Life Ins Co v Yampol, 706 FSupp 596 (ND Ill 1988)]

Q 6:33 Does a fiduciary who is sued for a breach of fiduciary duty have an implied right of contribution and/or indemnity against a nonfiduciary who participated in a breach?

No. The courts that have addressed this issue have concluded that ERISA's overall scheme does not support a fiduciary's claim for contribution or indemnification from a nonfiduciary.

Example. A plan sued the trustees and administrators of the plan, as well as the plan's accountant, bank, clearing broker, and certain other plan service providers in federal court for losses to the plan resulting from fraud committed, and speculative investments made, by the plan's investment manager. The trustees (who were plan fiduciaries) then asserted crossclaims for contribution and indemnification against the plan's accountants, bank, and clearing brokers (who were *not* plan fiduciaries) under ERISA. The court held that ERISA's text and stated purpose negate the inference that courts may create a common law to permit a fiduciary to seek contribution or indemnification from a nonfiduciary. [Glaziers & Glassblowers Union Local 252 Indemnity Fund v Newbridge Securities, Inc, 16 EBC (BNA) 1966 (ED Pa 1993)]

Attorneys' Fees

Q 6:34 May a plan reimburse a fiduciary's legal expenses incurred in defending a lawsuit charging breach of fiduciary duties?

Yes. A plan can provide for reimbursing a fiduciary or for advancing funds to the fiduciary to enable the fiduciary to defend against a claim that he or she breached fiduciary duties. Such a provision does not violate Section 410(a) of ERISA if the indemnification agreement also provides that if a court ultimately determines that the fiduciary breached his or her fiduciary duties, the fiduciary will be required to reimburse the plan for the advances along with reasonable interest. [DOL Adv Op Ltr No 77-66/67A (Sept 9, 1977)]

Where a plan provided for the indemnification of fiduciaries for any and all expenses incurred in the course of the performance of their duties, the plan fiduciary was entitled to compensation for expenses incurred in successfully defending himself against claims that he violated his fiduciary duties. [Packer Eng'g, Inc v Kratville, 965 F2d 174 (7th Cir 1992)]

However, the DOL held that a broad plan provision that authorizes the reimbursement of legal fees incurred by a fiduciary in any lawsuit arising in the performance of his duties would violate Section 410(a) of ERISA. [DOL Adv Op Ltr No 78-29A (Dec 1, 1978)]

Q 6:35 If a fiduciary is found liable for breaching his or her fiduciary duties, can the fiduciary be held liable for attorneys' fees?

Yes. A court may, in its discretion, award reasonable attorneys' fees and costs in a litigation claiming breach of fiduciary duties under ERISA.

Most circuit courts have examined the following five factors in deciding whether to award fees and costs:

1. The degree of the offending parties' bad faith;
2. The offending parties' ability to pay an award of fees;

Fiduciary Liability   Q 6:35

3. Whether an award of fees would have a deterrent effect on others in similar circumstances;
4. Whether the action benefitted all plan participants or the action was brought to resolve a significant legal question regarding ERISA; and
5. The relative merits of the parties' positions.

[Gray v New England Tel and Tel Co, 792 F2d 251 (1st Cir 1986); Eaves v Penn, 587 F2d 453 (10th Cir 1978)]

Under this five-factor approach, no one factor is determinative. Attorneys' fees may be granted where one factor alone is present. [Bishop v Osborn Transp, Inc, 687 FSupp 1526 (ND Ala 1988)] It is an abuse of discretion for a trial court to deny attorneys' fees without applying the five *Eaves v Penn* factors. [Graphic Communications Union, No 2 v GCIU-Employer Retirement Benefit Plan, 917 F2d 1184 (9th Cir 1990)]

Example 1. An employee was granted attorneys' fees where he brought suit to obtain early payment of benefits after his termination. The court held the employer had no legitimate reason for denying him prompt payment of his vested benefits subsequent to his discharge. [Morales v Plaxall, Inc, 541 FSupp 1387 (ED NY 1982)]

Example 2. A retiree was awarded attorneys' fees in an action against plan trustees for the erroneous calculation of monthly benefits where the trustees engaged in delaying tactics before litigation, had the employer's accountant provide testimony that was not credible, and had made arbitrary and capricious decisions regarding several issues. [Korn v Levine Bros Iron Works Corp, 574 FSupp 836 (SD NY 1983)]

Example 3. Management trustees sued by union trustees were liable for attorneys' fees because they had breached their fiduciary duties by refusing to authorize a suit that included wilful misconduct charges after an arbitrator's decision. [Iron Workers Local No 272 v Bowen, 624 F2d 1255 (5th Cir 1980)]

Example 4. A widow was awarded attorneys' fees in a suit against a plan fiduciary who did not exercise a reasonable degree of diligence in determining that she was not entitled to a joint and survivor benefit under the plan. [Mendez v Teachers Ins & Annuity Ass'n, 789 FSupp 139 (SD NY, *aff'd*, 982 F2d 783 (2d Cir 1992)]

Q 6:36 May attorneys' fees be recovered by a defendant in an ERISA action?

Yes. A court may, in its discretion, award reasonable attorneys' fees to either party in an ERISA litigation. The majority of circuit courts apply the same five-factor approach in determining entitlement to attorney fees to defendants as they do to plaintiffs. [*See, e.g.*, Gray v New England Tel & Tel Co, 792 F2d 251 (1st Cir 1986)]

Example. An employer that prevailed in a former employee's claim for pension benefits was awarded attorneys' fees and costs since the former employee's claim was time barred. Also, the former employee's claim was substantially without merit since the employee's benefits would not have vested for another five years after being discharged by the employer. The court believed that the employee could afford the fees and that the award would deter others from speculative litigation. [Monkelis v Mobay Chem, 827 F2d 935 (3d Cir 1987)]

Note. Certain types of litigants are more likely than others to recover attorneys' fees when the court applies the five-factor approach. For example, plan participants or trustees of benefit plans are more likely to be able to satisfy the five-factor requirement. To illustrate, while a defendant employer will often be able to pay its own fees, a plaintiff trustee may find it difficult to pay without injuring the beneficiaries of a plan. Also, deterrence very likely will be more justified for employers than for employees or trustees.

By contrast, the Seventh Circuit, while applying the five-factor standard for prevailing plaintiffs, applies a different standard to prevailing defendants. The Seventh Circuit automatically awards attorneys' fees to a prevailing defendant unless the court finds that the position of the plaintiff was substantially justified or that special circumstances make an award unjust. [Bittner v Sadoff & Rudoy Indus, 728 F2d 820 (7th Cir 1984)]

Fiduciary Liability   Q 6:39

Q 6:37 May attorneys' fees be awarded to a losing party in an ERISA action?

Yes. Attorneys' fees were awarded to an employee in an ERISA action for costs incurred at the appellate level, even though the employee did not succeed on the merits of his claim that punitive damages could be recovered in an ERISA action. The court applied the five-factor test and held that, in view of the employer's culpability (i.e., the employer purposely altered the employee's date of discharge in order to interfere with the employee's entitlement to medical benefits), the employer's greater ability to pay attorneys' fees, the interest in deterrence, the potential benefit to other participants, and the merits of the employee's claims despite his ultimate lack of success, the employee was entitled to attorneys' fees. [Bishop v Osborn Transp, Inc, 687 FSupp 1526 (ND Ala 1988)]

Q 6:38 How is the amount of attorneys' fees to be awarded in an ERISA action determined?

Certain jurisdictions have used the "lodestar/multiplier" method to determine the amount of attorneys' fees to be awarded. The lodestar is a reasonable hourly rate multiplied by the number of hours reasonably spent on the case. The multiplier is then applied to increase or decrease the lodestar amount on the basis of other relevant factors. [D'Emanuele v Montgomery Ward & Co, 904 F2d 1379 (9th Cir 1990)] Although reasonable attorneys' fees must be based on prevailing market rates, it has been held that a district court judge has discretion to award such fees based on his or her own knowledge and other evidence of private firm hourly rates in the community. [Miele v New York State Teamsters Conf Pens & Ret Fund, 831 F2d 407 (2d Cir 1987)]

Standard of Judicial Review

Q 6:39 What standard does a court use in reviewing a fiduciary's actions?

When a fiduciary's actions have been challenged and a breach alleged, the court applies a standard of deference to the judgment of

Q 6:39   **Fiduciary Responsibility Answer Book**

the fiduciary. The two standards for review that have evolved in the courts are the "de novo" standard and the "arbitrary and capricious" standard.

    The de novo standard accords a low degree of deference; the court reviews the merits with no special deference to the fiduciary's decisions or reasoning. By contrast, if a court applies the arbitrary and capricious standard, it is according a high degree of deference to the judgment of the fiduciary. The fiduciary's decision is overridden by the court only if the decision is an "abuse of discretion," "arbitrary and capricious," or "in violation of law." The court under this standard defers to the decision of the fiduciary if it is based on substantial evidence, even if the court itself would have reached a different result. [Firestone Tire & Rubber Co v Bruch, 489 US 101 (1989)]

> **Planning Pointer.** A fiduciary's actions are accorded less deference by a reviewing court if the fiduciary has an inherent conflict of interest, since "[a] conflicted fiduciary may favor, consciously or unconsciously, its interests over the interests of the plan beneficiaries." [Brown v Blue Cross & Blue Shield of Ala, Inc, 898 F2d 1556, 1565 (11th Cir 1990), *cert denied*, 498 US 1040 (1991)]
>
> **Example**. John, Robert, and Carl were the trustees of Corporation G's pension plan, and were the CEO, CFO, and treasurer of G, a publicly traded corporation. Corporation L made a hostile tender offer for a controlling interest in G at a price of $45 per share. The trustees determined not to tender any of the plan's shares, even though the prevailing market price was $36 to $39.75 a share (the price having risen from $26.75 to $35.88 a share when the tender offer was announced). The courts reviewing the decision gave no deference to the trustee's decision, because the independent judgment of the trustees for the benefit of plan participants and beneficiaries by all appearances was compromised by their interest in preserving their control as executives of G. [Donovan v Bierwirth, 538 FSupp 463 ED NY 1981), *modified*, 680 F2d 263 (2d Cir), *cert denied*, 459 US 1069 (1982)]

    A fiduciary is well advised to remain alert to conflicts of interest, and remove all appearance of such a conflict (by recusal or otherwise). (See the discussion of recusal and resignation at Qs 6:46 through 6:49.)

Q 6:40 In general, does a court apply a de novo standard or the arbitrary and capricious standard?

In general, a denial of benefits by an ERISA fiduciary is reviewed by a federal court under the de novo standard of review, unless the plan documents give the fiduciary authority to determine eligibility for benefits (or to rule on appeals of denied claims), and to construe the terms of the plan. [Firestone Tire & Rubber Co v Bruch, 489 US 101 (1989)]

Q 6:41 What exceptions are there to the general rule under the *Firestone* case?

Because of ambiguous language in the *Firestone* case, the federal courts have not consistently applied the general rule of applying a high degree of deference to a fiduciary's determinations of fact (as opposed to a fiduciary's interpretation of plan provisions) even if the plan documents expressly give the fiduciary the power to make such determinations.

Example. Life Insurance Company issued a group insurance policy to a multiple employer trust. A real estate partnership, *M*, joined the trust and was issued a "master certificate" under the policy. Life Insurance Company issued individual life insurance policies under the master certificate to *M*'s employees and to Roy, a 76-year-old general partner in *M*. *M* was Roy's named beneficiary.

On September 15, 1985, Roy suffered a heart attack, which ultimately led to his death on March 21, 1986. Roy was frequently hospitalized between those dates, and stopped working full-time for the partnership. He continued to participate in the partnership's business decisions, however, and he received distributions.

Life Insurance Company denied a claim under the individual policy on Roy's life, on the grounds that *M* terminated Roy's "employment" before he died. The Sixth Circuit held that the decision of fact (whether Roy was still an "employee") was a matter for de novo review. [McMahan v New England Mut Life Ins Co, 888 F2d 426 (6th Cir 1989)]

Q 6:42 Can plan documents be drafted to raise the standard of deference that a court will give to a fiduciary's determination of a benefit claim?

Yes. Plan documents can be drafted to specify that the plan fiduciary has the right, in the fiduciary's sole and absolute discretion, to make benefit determinations and interpret the terms of the plan. Such determinations and interpretations can be made final and binding on all affected persons.

Planning Pointer. Language to this effect should also appear prominently in summary plan descriptions and employee communications.

Steps to Reduce Risks

Q 6:43 How can maintaining records and minutes reduce the risk of fiduciary liability?

Every action of a fiduciary might someday be reviewed in court. If the prudence of an act is at issue, a fiduciary may need to document "procedural" prudence (e.g., responsibly selecting and monitoring the performance of an investment manager). For a discussion of monitoring investment managers, see Qs 7:7 and 7:8.

A fiduciary may need to document compliance with claims procedures (including appeals procedures) [ERISA § 503], procedures for the determination of qualified domestic relation orders (QDROs) [ERISA § 206(d)(3); IRC § 414(p)], or 20 percent withholding and rollover procedures. [IRC §§ 401(a)(31), 402(c)] For a discussion of claims procedures, see Qs 6:52 through 6:62.

Fiduciaries may need to adopt forms and establish consistent operational policies. It may be necessary or desirable to document when a fiduciary assumes duties, is dismissed, resigns, or is recused.

Fiduciaries that are plan committees should have formal meetings and minutes. At the meetings, the plan service providers (e.g., actuary, auditor, and attorney) should provide reports to the fiduciaries. Minutes of the meetings can incorporate attachments by reference (e.g., actuarial valuations or investment reports).

Even when a court uses a lower (de novo) standard of review and examines a case on the merits, thorough documentation can provide a favorable record. Where the standard of review is high, good records can help demonstrate that a fiduciary's acts or decisions are not arbitrary and capricious and not an abuse of discretion.

Q 6:44 How can maintaining records and minutes reduce the risk of co-fiduciary liability?

If, having taken all reasonable and legal steps to prevent the action, the minority fiduciaries do not succeed in derailing a breach by their co-fiduciaries, they can protect themselves from liability for the action of the majority if their objections and the responses to the objections are recorded in the minutes of the meeting. [DOL Reg § 2509.75-5, FR-10]

Q 6:45 Does consulting an expert reduce the risk of fiduciary liability?

Yes, if the fiduciary (1) lacks the necessary expertise to make a decision, (2) hires and consults the expert responsibly, and (3) continues to monitor the expert's performance responsibly. For a discussion of the prudent expert standard of fiduciary duty, see Q 7:13.

Q 6:46 How do fiduciaries protect themselves from decisions or actions that would constitute a fiduciary breach?

ERISA imposes stringent duties of care and loyalty and specifies a fiduciary obligation to avoid prohibited transactions. The DOL, in regulations, has offered guidance on a fiduciary's voluntary, temporary removal from decision-making (recusal), in circumstances where there is a potential conflict of interest or act of self-dealing. A

Q 6:47 Fiduciary Responsibility Answer Book

fiduciary is deemed not to have engaged in a prohibited transaction if the fiduciary (1) absents himself or herself from all consideration of a proposal and (2) does not exercise any authority, control, or responsibility with respect to the proposal. [DOL Reg § 2550.408b-2(f) (Ex 7)]

> **Example**. Two members of the Finance Committee of the Board of Directors of Company C also serve as fiduciaries of the Company C ESOP. Company C is spinning off Subsidiary S, which also has an ESOP. No prohibited transaction results in connection with the Company C ESOP's corresponding exchange with the Subsidiary S ESOP of Subsidiary S stock for Company C stock if the two overlapping members abstain from participation in the fiduciary decision-making process, "physically absent themselves from all discussions . . . as well as from voting" on the transactions in question, and cease all communications with the other fiduciaries of the Company C Retirement Plan. [DOL Adv Op Ltr No 84-09A, n2 (Feb 16, 1984)]

Q 6:47 Under what circumstances can recusal be a better alternative than resignation?

Recusal can be preferable to resignation when the continued input of the fiduciary is valuable to the plan. A potential conflict can arise when the fiduciary has other business interests unrelated to the plan and the sponsoring employer (or employee organization). Yet, the ongoing input of the fiduciary may be valuable enough that the plan (and its participants and beneficiaries) would benefit more from having the fiduciary temporarily remove himself or herself from decision making on one, discrete matter, rather than resign permanently.

> **Example**. Sarah Smith is a shareholder and a member of the Board of Directors of Company C, and has been for 25 years. She is also on Employer E's Pension and Benefits Committee, which is a named fiduciary of Employer E's ERISA plans. Employer E is otherwise unrelated to Company C. Sarah is the only person with such an overlap. Sarah's financial acumen provides valuable input to the Employer E Pension and Benefits Committee. The Pension and Benefits Committee is considering a proposed purchase by the Employer E Pension Plan of Company C stock. This purchase

would comply with all ERISA requirements, except for Sarah's potential conflict. If Sarah were to remove herself from all involvement in this investment alone, she could continue to serve the Employer E Pension and Benefits Committee so as to benefit participants and their beneficiaries, without even the appearance of impropriety. If Sarah were to resign, however, the benefit of her acumen would be lost.

Q 6:48 How should a recusal be documented?

Where a committee is the fiduciary, and the conflicted individual is a member of the committee, the recusal should be reflected in the minutes of the committee meeting. The minutes should specify that the committee member cited a potential conflict and physically removed himself or herself from all consideration of the proposal that raised the potential conflict. If unrelated matters are discussed later in the committee proceedings, the minutes should expressly reflect when the member joined the discussion again.

If no committee is involved, correspondence between the recusing fiduciary and the person or persons responsible for appointing the fiduciary will be required. Separate correspondence accomplishing the temporary removal and reinstatement would generally be preferable.

Q 6:49 Is a fiduciary ever required to do more than recuse himself or herself?

Yes. Where a majority of fiduciaries appear ready to take action that would clearly breach fiduciary duty, it is incumbent on the minority trustees to take all reasonable and legal steps to prevent the action, including preparations to obtain an injunction in federal court, notify the DOL, or publicize the vote if the decision is to proceed as proposed.

If, having taken all reasonable and legal steps to prevent the action, the minority fiduciaries do not succeed, they can protect themselves from liability for the action of the majority, if their objections and the responses to the objections are recorded in the minutes of the

Q 6:49   **Fiduciary Responsibility Answer Book**

meeting. Where a fiduciary believes that a co-fiduciary has already committed a breach of fiduciary duty, a resignation in protest of the breach will not generally be considered to be reasonable efforts to remedy the breach. Mere resignation, without taking steps to prevent the action, will not suffice to avoid liability for the minority fiduciaries once they know that the action is under consideration. [DOL Reg § 2509.75-5, FR-10]

> **Example.** A pension plan is considering the construction of a building to house the administration of the plan. One trustee, Sarah, has proposed that the building be constructed on a cost-plus basis by Mitchell, a contractor, without competitive bidding. When Helene, another trustee, questioned Sarah about (1) the basis for choosing Mitchell as contractor, (2) the impact of the building on the plan's administrative costs, (3) whether a cost-plus contract would yield a better price to the plan than a fixed-price contract, and (4) why a negotiated contract would be better than a contract arrived at by competitive bidding, no satisfactory answers were provided. Several trustees, including Helene, have argued that permitting such a contract would violate their fiduciary duties.
>
> A majority of fiduciaries appear ready to approve the contract with Mitchell. Helene and the minority trustees should take all reasonable and legal steps to prevent the action, including preparations to obtain an injunction in federal court, notify the DOL, or publicize the vote if the decision is to approve the contract as proposed.
>
> If, having taken all reasonable and legal steps to prevent the action, the minority fiduciaries do not succeed, they can protect themselves by insisting that written minutes of all actions taken should be kept. The minutes in this case should describe the action taken, should include the objections of the minority and the responses to the objections, and should state how each trustee voted on each matter.
>
> If Helene believes that a co-fiduciary has already committed a breach of fiduciary duty, a resignation in protest of the breach will not generally be considered to be reasonable efforts to remedy the breach. [DOL Reg § 2509.75-5, FR-10]

Q 6:50 How can delegation of one's fiduciary duty reduce the risk of fiduciary liability?

Delegating fiduciary duty can shift the responsibility for discharging obligations under ERISA. The delegating fiduciary must insure that it hired and monitored the individual selected to discharge those obligations. For example, a named fiduciary of a pension plan who retains an investment manager can relieve itself of a large part of its responsibility for investing plan assets. See the discussion of delegation at Qs 4:1 through 4:8 and 6:24.

Compliance with Claims Procedure

Q 6:51 What is a benefits claim?

A benefits claim is a request made by or on behalf of a participant or beneficiary for plan benefits. [DOL Reg § 2560.503-1(d)]

Q 6:52 When is a benefits claim deemed filed?

A claim is considered filed when the claimant follows a reasonable procedure established by the plan for such filing. If no procedure has been established, the claim is considered filed when the claimant (or an authorized representative) makes a written or oral communication reasonably calculated to bring the claim to the attention of the officer or committee that customarily handles the employer's employee benefit matters, or to the attention of an officer of the employer. The communication is considered made when it is first received by an individual in the unit. [DOL Reg § 2560.503-1(d)]

Q 6:53 How are benefit claim decisions typically made?

In the ordinary course of operations, questions of coverage and benefit entitlements are handled routinely by employees at various levels within a framework of policies and procedures established by their supervisors. The employees' duties may very well be ministerial;

if so, the employees are not fiduciaries. See the discussion of ministerial, nonfiduciary duties at Q 2:7.

Planning Pointer. Supervisors likely are fiduciaries, and should monitor subordinates' determinations and intervene promptly to correct problems. Subordinates should be directed to follow a number of procedural rules of thumb:

- Act in conformity with the plan documents;
- Treat all similarly situated individuals uniformly;
- Contact their supervisors promptly if a new question, a conflict between the plan documents and a rule of law, a conflict among the plan documents, or other unusual circumstances come to their attention;
- Keep complete and accurate records of any determination, the reasons for making the determination, and the factual background; and
- Act promptly.

[DOL Reg § 2509.75-8, D-2]

Q 6:54 Does a plan need explicit, written procedures for processing claims for benefits and reviewing the denial of claims?

ERISA generally requires a plan to provide adequate notice in writing of the denial of a claim for benefits, and to give a reasonable opportunity for full and fair review of the decision denying the claim. [ERISA § 503(1) and (2)] The procedures for accomplishing these goals are commonly called "claims procedures." DOL regulations provide the following guidelines for determining when claims procedures are reasonable:

- The procedures must be described in the summary plan description (SPD);
- The procedures must not contain any provision, or be administered in such a way, that unduly inhibits or hampers filing or processing a claim;
- The procedures comply with the rules for claim procedures set forth in the DOL regulations; and

- The procedures specifically provide for certain written notices to participants and beneficiaries.

[DOL Reg § 2560.503-1(b)]

Q 6:55 When must a claimant be informed that a benefits claim has been denied?

A claimant whose claim is denied in whole or in part must be notified in writing within a reasonable time after the plan receives the claim, not to exceed 90 days. If an extension is required, the claimant must receive written notice of the extension before the end of the initial 90-day period. The notice must specify the circumstances requiring the extension and the date by which the plan expects to render the final decision. The extension cannot exceed 90 days from the end of the initial 90-day period.

If notice of a denial (or extension) is not furnished to the claimant within a reasonable time after the claim is filed, the claim is deemed to be denied. In that case, the claimant may proceed directly under the plan's appeals procedures. [DOL Reg § 2560.503-1(e)]

Q 6:56 What information must a claim denial contain?

A written notice of claim denial issued by the plan administrator or insurer must give the following information in a manner calculated to be understood by the claimant:

1. The specific reason(s) why the claim was denied;
2. Specific reference to the pertinent plan provisions on which the denial was based;
3. An explanation of what additional material or information is necessary, and why, for the claimant to perfect the claim; and
4. An explanation of the appeals procedure by which the claimant can submit the claim for review.

"Calculated to be understood" presumably requires furnishing the information in another language, or translating the information, as appropriate. [DOL Reg § 2560.503-1(f)]

Q 6:57 What are a claimant's procedural rights on an appeal of a claim denial?

The claimant must have at least 60 days after receipt of written notice of a claims denial to file a request for review of the denied claim. The claimant or an authorized representative must be permitted to make a written application to the plan requesting a review of the claim, and must be permitted to review pertinent documents and submit issues and comments in writing. Plan procedures need not allow the claimant or a representative to appear in person; review of denied claims can be required to be made solely upon written submissions. [DOL Reg § 2560.503-1(g)]

Q 6:58 When must an appeal be decided?

Generally, a decision on appeal must be made within 60 days after the plan receives the request for review. If an extension is required, the claimant must receive written notice of the extension before the end of the initial 60-day period. The notice must specify the circumstances requiring the extension and the date by which the plan expects to render the final decision. The extension cannot exceed 60 days from the end of the initial 60-day period.

If the named fiduciary that has responsibility for reviewing claims is a committee or board that holds meetings at least quarterly, a claim must be heard at the next meeting if it is received at least 30 days in advance of the meeting. If an extension is required, the decision must be made by the third meeting after initial receipt of the request for appeal.

If notice of a denial (or extension) is not furnished to the claimant within these time periods, the appeal is deemed to be denied. [DOL Reg § 2560.503-1(h)]

Q 6:59 What information must a decision on appeal contain?

A written notice of appeal denial issued by the named fiduciary for hearing appeals must give the following information in a manner calculated to be understood by the claimant:

1. The specific reason(s) why the appeal was denied; and
2. Specific reference to the pertinent plan provisions on which the denial was based.

"Calculated to be understood" presumably requires furnishing the information in another language, or translating the information, as appropriate. [DOL Reg § 2560.503-1(h)(3)]

Q 6:60 Can a fiduciary's compliance with claims procedures reduce the risk of fiduciary liability?

Yes. Ordinarily, if the plan documents contain reasonable claims procedures (including appeals procedures) and the plan fiduciary has complied with them, a claimant must first exhaust the administrative remedies provided under the claims procedures before suing for benefits. Absent unusual circumstances, a trial court should enter summary judgment against a plan participant or beneficiary who has failed to exhaust administrative remedies. [Kross v Western Electric Co, 701 F2d 1238 (7th Cir 1983)] By contrast, a fiduciary's failure to comply with reasonable claims procedures (for example, by failing to communicate the reasons for a benefit denial) may result in the granting of a claimant's benefits by a court, if the claimant has effectively been denied the opportunity for a full and fair review of the claim. [Halpin v WW Grainger, Inc, 962 F2d 685 (7th Cir 1992)]

Q 6:61 Are any plans exempt from the requirement of providing a reasonable claims procedure?

To the extent benefits are provided or administered by an insurance company or similar, state-regulated organization, the claims procedure for those benefits may provide for filing benefit claims with, and notice of decision by, the insurance company. [DOL Reg § 2560.503-1(c)]

> **Planning Pointer.** The person or committee designated as named fiduciary for hearing appeals (appeals committee) must have the power to reverse the denial of a claim and order payment of the benefit when the appeals committee determines it is appropriate.

The appeals committee may be, but often should not be, the same individual or committee that decided the original claim. The appointment of an appeals committee should be expressly provided for in the plan documents, and should be carefully documented so as to clearly define the appeals committee's powers and responsibilities.

If plan benefits are provided through insurance, the insurer will often require that the appeals committee (and the person determining initial claims) be the insurer or a committee designated by the insurer. This can assure uniform interpretations consistent with the insurer's practices.

Benefits plans providing only apprenticeship training benefits need not provide a claims procedure. [DOL Reg § 2560.503-1(1)]

Q 6:62 What special rules for claims procedures apply to health maintenance organizations (HMOs)?

The claims procedure of a federally qualified HMO satisfies ERISA if it satisfies the federal Health Maintenance Organization Act of 1973. Thus, the HMO's claims procedures can be made to apply to a medical plan that includes benefits under the HMO. [DOL Reg § 2560.503-1(j)]

Q 6:63 What special rules for claims procedures apply to collectively bargained plans?

In the case of a plan established and maintained pursuant to a collective bargaining agreement, if the agreement specifically incorporates by reference provisions concerning (1) filing benefit claims and their initial disposition and (2) a grievance and arbitration procedure for denied claims, then the plan satisfies ERISA's requirements for claims procedures. This special rule does not apply to plans covered by Section 302(c)(5) of the Labor Management Relations Act of 1947 (concerning joint employer-union representation on the board of trustees). [DOL Reg § 2560.503-1(b)(2)]

Nonfiduciary Liability

Q 6:64 Can a nonfiduciary be held liable for a fiduciary breach of duty?

The provision of ERISA that imposes liability for breach of fiduciary duty refers only to "any person who is a fiduciary." [ERISA 409(a)] The Supreme Court has accordingly held that a nonfiduciary has no liability under ERISA Section 409. [Mertens v Hewitt Assocs, 124 LEd2d 161 (1993); Mass Mutual Life Ins Co v Russell, 473 US 134 (1985)] Other courts have held that allowing claims against nonfiduciaries departs from the plain meaning of ERISA, even if the nonfiduciaries abetted fiduciaries in their breach of duty. [Nieto v Ecker, 845 F2d 868 (9th Cir 1988)]

Individuals controlling a fiduciary entity have been held jointly and severally liable for the fiduciary's breach of duty. [Lowen v Tower Asset Mgmt, Inc, 829 F2d 1209 (2d Cir 1987)] It is unclear whether this holding can be reconciled with the Supreme Court's holdings described above.

Section 502(a)(2) of ERISA authorizes a civil lawsuit for relief under ERISA Section 409. By implication, according to the Supreme Court, this provision does not authorize a lawsuit against a nonfiduciary. However, Section 502(a)(3) of ERISA authorizes a civil suit by a participant, beneficiary, or fiduciary "to enjoin any act or practice which violates any [ERISA fiduciary rule] or the terms of the Plan," or "to obtain other appropriate equitable relief." [ERISA § 502(a)(3)] Section 502(a)(5) of ERISA authorizes analogous lawsuits by the DOL.

Accordingly, notwithstanding the recent holding in *Mertens*, the courts apparently have the power to impose equitable relief on a nonfiduciary who knowingly participated in a fiduciary's breach of duty. [Gibson v Prudential Ins Co of America, 915 F2d 414 (9th Cir 1990)]

Q 6:65 Can a nonfiduciary be liable for a prohibited transaction?

Under the Code, the 5 percent penalty tax is imposed on a disqualified person (other than a fiduciary acting solely in that capacity) for each year or part of a year that the transaction remains uncorrected, and an additional tax equal to 100 percent of the amount involved is imposed if the transaction is not timely corrected. The disqualified person must have participated in the prohibited transaction. [IRC § 4975(a) and (b)] (For a discussion of prohibited transactions, see Chapter 5.) A disqualified person can include a variety of nonfiduciaries who may be liable for the tax.

Q 6:66 Can the 20 percent penalty tax be imposed against nonfiduciaries in connection with a fiduciary breach?

Yes. The DOL imposes a penalty of 20 percent of the amount payable pursuant to a court order or settlement agreement with DOL for any knowing participation by any person, including a nonfiduciary, in a fiduciary breach. [ERISA § 502(l)] For a discussion of the 20 percent penalty, see Qs 6:15 and 6:16.

Chapter 7

Investment Issues

ERISA imposes significant responsibilities on fiduciaries who manage, control, or otherwise have the authority to invest plan assets. The investment issues that impact plans, fiduciaries, and participants encompass virtually every aspect of ERISA's fiduciary duty requirements, including prudence, exclusive benefit, diversification, and obligation to follow plan documents, as well as the numerous tax, securities, banking, and other complex legal requirements affecting investments by ERISA plans. This chapter describes the process of selecting and monitoring investment managers and examines various investment issues including concerns relating to the purchase of annuities, guaranteed investment contracts (GICs), and bank investment contracts (BICs); investments in employer securities and employer real property; social investing; and the special restrictions that apply to other types of employee benefit plan investments.

How to Select an Investment Manager Under ERISA	7-2
How to Monitor an Investment Manager Under ERISA	7-13
Investments	7-15
Purchasing Annuities	7-21
Guaranteed Investment Contracts (GICs) and Bank Investment Contracts (BICs)	7-27
Employer Securities and Employer Real Property	7-33

| Social Investing | 7-50 |
| Other Investments | 7-55 |

How to Select an Investment Manager Under ERISA

Under ERISA, the primary test for evaluating whether a plan fiduciary exercised prudence in selecting an investment manager for plan assets focuses on the fiduciary's conduct and the procedures utilized in investigating, evaluating, and selecting the manager. The following questions address the salient issues relating to the process of selecting ERISA-plan investment managers.

Q 7:1 What is the proper method of selecting an investment manager qualified to invest plan assets under ERISA?

A named fiduciary may decide to appoint one or more investment managers (see Qs 2:24, 2:25 and 4:13 through 4:26) to whom the control and management of plan assets may be delegated. Each investment manager must agree in writing to act in accordance with the fiduciary duty requirements under ERISA. (See generally Chapter 3.) As with all other fiduciary decisions, the investment manager must be selected prudently. (See Qs 3:4 through 3:10 for a discussion of prudence.)

In exercising prudence in the selection process, the fiduciary responsible for appointing the investment manager should consider, for example, the following essential factors:

- The investment manager's ability to effectively manage the type of assets involved;
- Whether the investment manager's organization and investment philosophies are consistent with the needs of the plan;
- Whether the investment manager has performed well in managing similar investments for employee benefit plans; and
- The investment manager's track record for meeting the stated objectives of plans such manager has managed.

In short, the appointing fiduciary should consider the investment manager's experience, qualifications, and investment approach. When investment decisions—from selecting an investment manager to choosing a particular investment vehicle (such as a guaranteed investment contract)—are challenged the test of prudence is "whether the individual trustees [or other relevant fiduciaries], at the time they engaged in the challenged transactions, employed the appropriate methods to investigate the merits of the investment and to structure the investment." [Katsaros v Cody, 744 F2d 270, 279 (2d Cir), *cert denied* 469 US 1072 (1984)]

Q 7:2 How should a fiduciary responsible for appointing an investment manager investigate the investment manager's experience, qualifications, and investment approach?

Because the ERISA standard of prudence is largely based on the applicable facts and circumstances, there is no clear standard or "bright line" test set forth in the statute as to the manner in which a fiduciary should investigate a potential investment manager's experience, qualifications, and investment approach. (See generally Qs 3:4 through 3:10 regarding the prudence requirement.) The fiduciary responsible for appointing the manager should consider the appropriate substantive factors ("substantive prudence") by using the proper procedures ("procedural prudence") in selecting an investment manager qualified under ERISA. (See Qs 3:8 through 3:10 regarding the distinction between substantive and procedural prudence.)

In investigating potential investment managers, the appointing fiduciary should consider, among other things, the following set of procedures.

Identify a Range of Possible Managers. Prior to selecting a particular manager, the appointing plan fiduciary should identify a range of candidates whose expertise is consistent with the proposed investment style; the plan fiduciaries should interview each such manager (to serve as a basis of comparison with one another).

Obtain Information. The plan fiduciary should solicit all available information relating to the qualifications and experience of each potential investment manager, and in particular, the information necessary for the prudent selection of an investment manager. (See Q 7:3.)

Evaluate Experience and Qualifications. In addition to interviewing representatives of the investment manager (including those who will be primarily responsible for managing the plan's portfolio), the plan fiduciaries should evaluate the manager's specific qualifications:

1. *Manager's Experience.* Examine the manager's experience in the particular area of investments under consideration, as well as its experience with other ERISA plan assets.
2. *Qualifications.* Make an independent assessment of the manager's qualifications. This may be accomplished by:
   a. Determining that the manager is widely known and well respected (as may be the case with major financial institutions);
   b. Securing and calling existing client references; and
   c. Seeking the advice of a professional investment consultant who is an expert on such matters.
3. *Past Performance.* Evaluate the record of the manager's past performance with investments of the type contemplated, and review a sample portfolio managed by the manager for a similarly situated client (although it should be recognized that excellent past performance is not a guarantee of future success).
4. *Credentials of Principals.* Evaluate the credentials and prior investment performance of the principals of the manager.
5. *Enforcement Actions.* Check with the Department of Labor (DOL) and the Securities and Exchange Commission (SEC) as to whether any relevant enforcement actions have been initiated against the manager or any of its principals or investment professionals.

Planning Pointer. Under the Investment Advisors Act of 1940, investment advisors are generally required to disclose material legal or disciplinary events within the past ten years, which would probably satisfy any possible ERISA requirement to examine a reasonable period during which any DOL or SEC actions have been initiated. Most of this information is contained in the investment advisor's Form ADV. (See Q 7:3.)

Document Process. The appointing fiduciary (such as a board of trustees, investment committee, etc.) should retain written records of the investment manager selection process. For example, this could be in the form of written minutes of the series of meetings during which the selection process took place. Documenting the selection process is a key component of procedural prudence and demonstrates that the appointing fiduciary took appropriate and prudent action.

The above list merely provides examples of procedures to consider in selecting an investment manager. It may be necessary in certain circumstances to consider additional factors not set forth above.

Q 7:3 What specific types of information should plan fiduciaries solicit in the process of selecting investment managers?

While ERISA does not set forth any specific type of information that a fiduciary is required to review in connection with the selection of investment managers, ERISA's duty of prudence suggests that a fiduciary who selects an investment manager should obtain and review all relevant information relating to the qualifications, experience, and investment performance of the investment manager.

For example, the appointing plan fiduciary should solicit the following information from each potential candidate that is being considered for retention as an investment manager for the plan:

1. *Services.* A precise description of the services that the manager is prepared to offer.
2. *History.* A history of the manager's experience in the investment management business, including the total amount of assets under its control.
3. *Investment Approach.* A statement of the manager's investment approach or philosophy, and whether the manager has any internal investment guidelines.
4. *Number of Accounts.* The number of plan accounts and other accounts under the manager's management and their total current fair market value.

5. *Fees.* A detailed schedule of investment management fees (and a determination as to whether such fees are negotiable).
6. *Staffing.* A description of the manager's current staffing, and details as to the general experience and educational qualifications of the individuals who would be primarily responsible for the plan's account.
7. *Specific Names.* The name of any individuals who would be actively involved in handling the plan's account, and details as to their experience and educational qualifications.
8. *Availability.* A clear outline of the availability of the manager's staff for meeting with the plan fiduciaries on a regular basis.
9. *Policy.* A description of how investment policy is established by the manager and how it will be implemented with respect to the plan assets under its management.
10. *Equity Investment Performance.* A tabulation of time-weighted annual rates of total investment return on the combined results of all retirement plan equity portfolios under management for a reasonable period (for example, for each of the previous one-, three-, five-, eight-, and ten-year periods, and cumulatively for that entire period).
11. *Fixed Income Investment Performance.* A tabulation of time-weighted annual rates of total investment return on the combined results of all plan fixed income portfolios under management for a reasonable period (for example, for each of the previous one-, three-, five-, eight-, and ten-year periods, and cumulatively for that entire period).
12. *Combined Portfolio Performance.* A tabulation of time-weighted annual rates of total investment return on the combined results of all plan portfolios under management for a reasonable period (for example, for each of the previous one-, three-, five-, eight-, and ten-year periods, and cumulatively for that entire period).

Planning Pointer. Special considerations and issues will apply to newly created investments or portfolios for which historical rate information may be unavailable. Plan fiduciaries should, therefore, exercise additional caution in investing in such vehicles and, perhaps, weigh more heavily the other relevant factors.

13. *Liability Insurance and Bonding.* The dollar amount of both the manager's fiduciary liability insurance, which would protect the interests of the plan in the event of a breach of fiduciary duty, and fidelity bond policies (see Qs 6:28 through 6:30 regarding the option to obtain fiduciary liability insurance and Qs 8:68 and 8:69 regarding the requirement to obtain an ERISA fidelity bond).
14. *Litigation.* The existence of any current or past litigation involving claims against the manager (or any of its principals or investment professionals), and whether the manager (or any of its principals or professionals) has ever been held to be in violation of any federal or state laws.
15. *Bankruptcy.* Whether the manager, or any of its principals, has ever undergone bankruptcy, liquidation, reorganization, or similar proceedings; has had its registration or license revoked or activities restricted; has ever been sued by a client or the SEC; or has ever been denied fiduciary liability insurance or a fidelity bond.
16. *Registration.* Whether the manager is registered with the SEC under the Investment Advisors Act of 1940, and the date of its initial registration.
17. *Broker-Dealer Affiliates.* Whether the manager is affiliated (or has any business relationship) with the broker-dealer it uses that could affect its investment decisions.
18. *Financial Condition and Capitalization.* Financial information relating to the manager, including its most recent balance sheet.
19. *Proxies.* The manager's policy with respect to the voting of proxies appurtenant to investment securities (see Qs 4:23 and 4:24 regarding proxy voting).
20. *Business Structure.* A description of the manager's business structure, principal owners, and affiliates.
21. *Prohibited Transactions.* The procedure to be employed by the manager to comply with ERISA's prohibited transaction restrictions (see generally Chapter 5 regarding prohibited transactions), and whether the investment manager is a "qualified professional asset manager." (See Qs 4:25, 4:26 and 5:14 regarding qualified professional asset managers.)

While the foregoing is not an exhaustive list, it covers significant criteria that a fiduciary should consider in selecting an investment manager.

Planning Pointer. Much of the above-listed information can be found in the investment manager's Form ADV, which is required to be completed by investment advisors registered under the Investment Advisors Act of 1940. Form ADV gives information about the investment advisor including, for example, descriptions of advisory services and fees, types of clients (which reflects whether the investment advisor provides advice to ERISA-covered plans), types of investments, methods of analysis, sources of information, investment strategies, education and business standards and backgrounds, business and financial industry activities or affiliations, participation or interest in client transactions, conditions for managing accounts, review of accounts, investment or brokerage discretion, balance sheets, and other financial information. Form ADV also contains information relating to the advisor's (or its affiliates') disciplinary history including convictions, guilty pleas, or pleas of *nolo contendere* to felony or misdemeanor charges (within the past ten years) involving investments, fraud, false statements or omissions, wrongful taking of property, bribery, forgery, counterfeiting, extortion, or disciplinary actions taken by the SEC, the Commodity Futures Trading Commission, or any other federal or state regulatory agency.

Note. Fiduciaries should verify the information provided by the advisor with a reliable independent source to the extent appropriate. (See Q 7:8, item 8 regarding independent investment consultants.)

Example. Upon recommendation of Bedell, who was interested in managing the plan's assets, Trustee C invested plan assets with Penvest, without obtaining any firsthand knowledge of Bedell's or Penvest's track record or the educational background or employment experience of key personnel. Trustee C did not compare Penvest's performance with that of other investment firms, and did not even inquire into fees that would have to be paid to the investment manager. Trustee C did not know whether Penvest or Bedell was registered with the SEC as an investment advisor (which neither company was). Trustee C also did not know the identity of other investors who invested with Bedell or Penvest and did not receive any references regarding Penvest or Bedell. He did not make independent inquiries into the finances of Penvest, and did not review any financial statements or any other written material from Penvest. All that Trustee C knew about the investments policy was that the plan's assets were in second mortgages, which he believed were a "relatively conservative type of investment." He didn't investigate the location or specific value of the secured properties. The court held that Trustee C breached his fiduciary duty in connection with the selection of Bedell and the investment of plan assets with Penvest by failing to independently investigate and evaluate a proposed investment of plan assets.

Although the Secretary of Labor found that Trustee C breached his fiduciary duty to investigate and evaluate Bedell and Penvest adequately before investing with them, the record did not contain sufficient facts for the court to find that the investment decision was objectively imprudent and, as a consequence, Trustee C was not found liable for the loss to the plan on that basis. Nevertheless, Trustee C did not properly delegate fiduciary responsibility to Bedell or Penvest and did not monitor their performance as required under ERISA. [Whitfield v Cohen, 682 FSupp 188 (SDNY 1988)]

Q 7:4 What factors should plan fiduciaries consider in developing investment guidelines or other plan objectives for investment managers?

First, the trustees of a plan (or other plan fiduciaries responsible for the investment of plan assets), or their authorized representatives, should identify an investment style for that portion of the plan assets to be committed to the investment manager for the plan. Once an investment style has been selected, the fiduciary responsible for appointing the manager has a duty to establish a clear understanding with the manager as to:

1. *Investment Performance.* The projected investment rate of return sought through management of the plan assets.
2. *Risk/Diversification.* The level of acceptable risk tolerance and diversification latitude (see Qs 3:11 and 3:12 regarding the diversification requirement).

3. *Restrictions.* A clear delineation of investment restrictions.

   Planning Pointer. Virtually any type of restriction may be imposed on an ERISA qualified investment manager with respect to any investment. For instance, a fiduciary may restrict an investment manager by imposing a percentage limitation with respect to a particular investment (e.g., no more than 45 percent of all the plan assets may be invested in equities). A fiduciary may also choose to restrict an investment manager by completely prohibiting certain investments such as futures, venture capital, employer stock, employer real property, swaps (e.g., interest rate swaps, annuity swaps, etc.), options, commodities, synthetic equities, etc.

4. *Discretion.* The scope of the manager's discretion to acquire and maintain particular forms of assets and to determine the amounts of each type of asset.
5. *Time.* The time frame for measuring the manager's investment performance.
6. *Procedures.* The precise procedures to be used in monitoring and evaluating the performance of the manager.

In addition, the nature of the plan, the plan's funding characteristics, the size of the plan, and the plan's liquidity requirements should also be considered in establishing plan investment objectives.

Q 7:5 Is an investment manager obligated to follow the investment guidelines agreed to between the manager and the plan?

Generally, yes. Because ERISA imposes on plan fiduciaries the obligation to follow the terms of the plan documents, an investment manager must follow the investment guidelines agreed to between the manager and the plan. In one case, the failure of an investment manager to adhere to an investment management agreement, which incorporated investment guidelines limiting stock investments to no more than 50 percent of total assets, violated ERISA's fiduciary duties under Section 404(a)(1)(D); that is, the duty to act in accordance with plan documents insofar as they are consistent with ERISA. [Dardaganis v Grace Capital, Inc, 889 F2d 1237 (2d Cir 1989) (even if the investment manager's investments were prudent, the manager's failure to follow the investment guidelines violated ERISA because Section 404(a)(1)(D) of ERISA imposes an independent duty to follow the formal plan documents in addition to ERISA's other fiduciary requirements.)] However, in certain instances where an investment manager would violate ERISA if he or she followed the investment guidelines (*e.g.*, the investment guidelines permitted an imprudent investment), the investment manager should not follow the investment guidelines.

Q 7:6 How should a plan fiduciary negotiate the investment management agreement?

As with the appointment of an investment manager, ERISA does not offer specific guidance as to the manner and approach that a fiduciary should take in negotiating the investment management agreement between the fiduciary and the investment manager. At a minimum, however, the plan fiduciary (such as an investment committee of a plan, trustee, or other named fiduciary) should consider the following steps for negotiating the investment management agreement:

1. *Procure Legal Counsel.* Plan fiduciaries should have legal counsel analyze the investment management agreement, offering memorandum, subscription agreement, or other documents that set forth the terms of the relationship between the plan and the investment manager.
2. *Flexible Termination Provisions.* The agreement should generally be terminable by the plan fiduciaries on little or no advance notice (under most circumstances not more than thirty days), with any fees paid in advance to the manager prorated to the date of termination.
3. *Obtain Adequate Representations.* The agreement should also provide representations and warranties that the manager:
    a. Is an investment advisor registered with the SEC under the Investment Advisors Act of 1940 (unless the manager is a bank or insurance company, see Q 2:24 regarding the definition of investment manager);
    b. Is an investment manager within the meaning of ERISA Section 3(38);

c. Acknowledges being a fiduciary (within the meaning of Section 3(21)(A) of ERISA) with respect to the plan's assets under investment;

d. Has obtained a fidelity bond in accordance with ERISA Section 412 (see Qs 8:68 and 8:69 regarding ERISA's bonding requirements);

e. Maintains fiduciary liability insurance in an amount determined by the plan fiduciaries to be sufficient under the circumstances (whether fiduciary liability insurance should be required at all may depend on the manager's size, stature, background, and experience; while ERISA does not mandate that fiduciaries obtain liability insurance, it is highly recommended; see Q 6:28 through 6:30 regarding fiduciary liability insurance);

Planning Pointer. Fiduciaries should be aware that the total amount recoverable under an investment manager's insurance policy may be diluted as a result of the investment manager's other clients. For example, suppose a plan lost $1.5 million of its assets due to the investment manager's improper and imprudent investment. The investment manager recommended the same investment to all his other clients, who lost a total of $200 million. Although the investment manager's fiduciary liability insurance of $50 million was sufficient to cover the $1.5 million that the individual plan lost, it was insufficient to cover the total liability. In such instance, it would be difficult for any single plan to recover its entire loss.

f. Has made all necessary filings and obtained all requisite approvals from all relevant government agencies;

g. Will maintain the indicia of ownership of the plan's assets within the jurisdiction of the United States District Courts;

h. Has obtained the appropriate authorization to execute the agreement;

i. Will indemnify the plan fiduciaries for any damages arising out of a breach by the manager of its agreement and/or its investment management duties (a reciprocal indemnity, from plan fiduciaries to the manager, should be avoided wherever possible);

Investment Issues   Q 7:7

j. Will promptly advise the plan fiduciaries of any change in the ownership or management of the manager;

k. May not assign the agreement to a third party without the advance written consent of the plan fiduciaries;

l. Shall not effect any transaction that directly or indirectly will cause the plan (or any fiduciary thereof) to enter into a prohibited transaction under Sections 406 through 408 of ERISA or Section 4975(c) of the Code, including any broker/dealer transactions with an affiliate of the manager that is not the subject of a prohibited transaction exemption (see generally Chapter 5 regarding prohibited transactions); and

m. Agrees that each of the foregoing representations are to be "continuing" in nature (i.e., the manager is under a continuing obligation to advise the fiduciary of any changes in these representations during the course of the manager's retention by the plan).

4. *Reasonable Fee Requirements.* If fees are to be paid to the investment manager directly from plan assets (rather than from the employer), the plan fiduciaries have a duty to ascertain periodically the reasonableness of those fees relative to both the amount of plan assets invested with the investment manager and to fees charged by comparable advisors.

How to Monitor an Investment Manager Under ERISA

After a fiduciary selects an investment manager, ERISA requires that the appointing fiduciary must continue to monitor the performance and activities of the investment manager. While many of the concerns that apply to the selection process also apply to the monitoring process, the following questions address certain specifics regarding ERISA's "duty to monitor."

Q 7:7 Once a plan fiduciary selects an investment manager, is the appointing fiduciary relieved of ERISA fiduciary duty with respect to the delegated investment duties?

As noted in Question 4:7, a fiduciary's duties with regard to the delegation of certain fiduciary duties—such as the responsibility for the investment of plan assets—does not end once the fiduciary has delegated its duties to an investment manager. A plan fiduciary retains the duty to monitor continually the performance of the investment manager (see Q 4:7). [Hunt v Magnell, 758 FSupp 1292, 1299 (D Minn 1991) ("The court recognized that, under ERISA, a trustee's fiduciary responsibilities with respect to an investment do not terminate upon the conclusion of the preliminary investigation and purchase of the asset. ERISA fiduciaries must monitor investments with reasonable diligence and dispose of investments which are improper to keep.")]

Q 7:8 What specific actions should the appointing fiduciary undertake in monitoring the investment performance of investment managers?

As noted in Question 4:7, plan fiduciaries also have a duty to monitor periodically the investments made by, and the overall performance of, the investment manager. This duty should be satisfied by the following actions:

1. *Reports.* Reviewing periodically (at least quarterly, or more often if necessary) the reports provided by the investment manager for the purpose of confirming:

    a. The adequacy of their content;

    b. The investment manager's performance during the period;

    c. The basis on which plan assets are valued;

    d. Whether the investment manager has managed the portfolio in a manner consistent both with any investment guidelines promulgated by the investment committee, trustee, or other fiduciary authorized to appoint investment managers, and with the investment manager's stated investment philosophy;

    e. The rate of return earned by the investment manager during the period in question on an overall basis, by asset class and, where investments are in more than one industry sector, by sector; and

    f. Whether that rate is reasonable (as an absolute number, and when compared to other similar investment managers, or

to appropriate indices or benchmarks) and, if not, whether the continued retention of the investment manager is prudent.
2. *Meetings.* Meeting with the investment manager periodically (at least annually) to review the status and performance of the plan's investments, as well as to review the investment manager's performance and any significant changes in its corporate or capital structure, investment style, brokerage affiliation or practices, investment process, or professional staff.
3. *Proxy Procedures.* Reviewing periodically (at least annually) the voting procedure pursuant to which the investment manager votes proxies, the manner in which proxies were voted in specific situations, and the specific rationale for such votes (see Qs 4:23 and 4:24 regarding proxies).
4. *Brokerage Practices.* Reviewing periodically the investment manager's practices regarding brokerage and trading, including brokerage costs, use of soft dollars, quality of securities' execution, and portfolio turnover.
5. *Communications.* Establishing and reviewing, at least annually, the procedures for communicating information regarding investments and investment managers among the trustees, the plan's staff, and the plan's service providers (including the plan's attorneys, actuaries, and custodial trustees).
6. *Fees.* Verifying, at least quarterly, the accuracy of the manager's fee computations.
7. *Termination.* Terminating the investment manager's services immediately if its performance is unsatisfactory.
8. *Independent Consultants.* Retaining an independent investment consulting or monitoring firm to do all or a portion of the foregoing.

Investments

Except with respect to certain prohibited transactions, the statutory provisions of ERISA do not specifically approve or prohibit any particular investment by a plan. Nevertheless, a fiduciary must follow ERISA's fiduciary duty provisions with respect to all investment activities relating to plans, which usually would involve a "facts and circumstances" analysis of the applicable situation. The following questions review the general issues pertaining to plan investments, including the factors a plan fiduciary should consider when investing plan assets, investment strategies, and the retention of experts.

Q 7:9 Are plan fiduciaries prohibited from making certain types of investments under ERISA?

Generally, no—provided, however, that the plan fiduciary satisfies ERISA's fiduciary requirements and the investment is not a prohibited transaction. Although ERISA does not set forth any preapproved or prohibited list of investments, the application of ERISA's prudence and exclusive benefit rules will dictate whether or not a particular investment is prohibited under ERISA. A fiduciary must also be aware that certain investments will be prohibited under the prohibited transaction rules of Section 406 of ERISA. (See generally Chapter 5.)

Q 7:10 What factors must a plan fiduciary consider when investing plan assets?

As noted in Question 3:9, the following factors, among others, should be considered with respect to the investment of the plan assets:

1. Whether the particular investment or investment course of action is reasonably designed, as part of the portfolio, to further the purposes of the plan, taking into consideration the risk of loss and the opportunity for gain (or other return);
2. The composition of the portfolio with regard to diversification (see Q 3:12 regarding diversification);

   Planning Pointer. While there is no specific formula against which to test diversification, fiduciaries should be wary of disproportionately heavy investments in at least the following:
   - A security of a single issuer;
   - Securities dependent upon the success of a single enterprise;
   - Securities dependent upon conditions in one locality;
   - Stock of corporations engaged in one industry;

- Mortgages concentrated in one geographical location; and
- Mortgages on one particular class of property.

3. The liquidity and current return of the portfolio relative to the anticipated cash flow requirements of the plan; and
4. The projected return of the portfolio relative to the funding objectives of the plan. [DOL Reg § 2550.404a-1]

Example. GIW maintained a profit-sharing plan with three investment funds, Fund A, Fund B, and Fund C. Fund A is an asset allocation account invested in fixed income securities, equities of publicly traded companies, and money market instruments. In June 1986, GIW hired Trevor Stewart to provide investment management services for GIW's Fund A. Trevor Stewart divided the Fund A portfolio as follows: 70 percent in long-term government bonds, 15 percent in zero coupon bonds, 10 percent in stocks, and 5 percent in cash. In October 1987, GIW terminated the contract with Trevor Stewart. At the time of termination, Fund A had lost approximately $700,000 due to the premature sale of its holdings required to increase liquidity in response to withdrawal requests. GIW filed suit against Trevor Stewart for breach of ERISA fiduciary duties alleging that Trevor Stewart failed to provide for liquidity so that payments could be made to retiring employees without adversely affecting Fund A. In affirming the District Court's holding that Trevor Stewart breached its fiduciary duty, the court noted that Trevor Stewart did not determine the historical cash flow needs or investigate prior or anticipated withdrawal patterns of Fund A. The court concluded that if Trevor Stewart investigated the age and projected retirement plans of employee participants, it could have anticipated the need for cash and for a sale of assets to fulfill that need. [GIW Industries, Inc v Trevor, Stewart, Burton & Jacobsen, Inc, 10 EBC (BNA) 2290 (SD Ga, 1989), *aff'd* 895 F2d 729 (11th Cir 1990)]

Q 7:11 How does a fiduciary design an investment strategy for plan assets?

Fiduciaries should establish prudent investment objectives and strategies for plan assets, with the assistance of persons expert in the investment arena, if necessary.

In creating the investment strategy, the plan fiduciary should first identify the financial needs of the plan, and then prepare a written statement describing the investment objectives of the plan. In establishing plan objectives, the following factors (among others) should be considered:

- Nature of the plan
- Purpose of the plan and the employer's aim in offering the plan, taking into account the age, income levels, and investment needs of participants
- Plan funding characteristics and funding provisions
- Size of the plan
- Plan liquidity requirements
- Acceptable risk-return ratios

Q 7:12 What does it mean for a fiduciary to act prudently in connection with investment decisions impacting plan assets?

As is the case with all fiduciary actions, a fiduciary must act prudently in selecting investments and making all investment decisions concerning plan assets. There is no clear "bright line" standard that a plan fiduciary must follow in acting prudently under ERISA with regard to investments. Whether an investment or certain actions taken by a fiduciary in connection with plan investments are prudent is based on a review of applicable facts and circumstances.

However, various cases suggest that fiduciaries will have acted prudently in designing investment strategies and making investment decisions by taking the following steps:

1. Employing proper methods to investigate, evaluate, and structure the investment;
2. Acting in a manner as would others who have a capacity and familiarity with such matters; and
3. Exercising independent judgment when making investment decisions.

Investment Issues   Q 7:13

[Jones v O'Higgins, 11 EBC (BNA) 1660, 1667 (NDNY 1989), *citing, inter alia*, Kastsaros v Cody, 744 F2d 270, 279 (2d Cir), *cert denied*, 469 US 1072 (1984)]

Planning Pointer. A fiduciary should be able to establish that, in making an investment decision, he or she:

- Conducted an impartial study of the advantages and disadvantages of the transaction;
- Exercised due diligence in researching all aspects of the transaction;
- Utilized acceptable standards in retaining qualified experts and consultants; and
- Relied on complete and up-to-date information.

[See Brock v Robbins, 830 F2d 640, 648 (7th Cir 1987) (Court held that plan trustees violated the prudent person standard when they entered into a contract with the Amalgamated Insurance Agency Services, Inc. for claims administration. They approved the fee provisions of the contract, committing the plan to pay over $10 million after less than ten minutes discussion and without any study.)]

Q 7:13 Must a fiduciary retain an expert when evaluating investments for a plan?

It depends on the fiduciary's level of investment expertise. As noted in Q 3:6, ERISA's duty of prudence is based on a "prudent expert" standard, not the prudence of a lay person. Given the complexity of investments and the ever-changing investment world, ERISA may require that the plan fiduciary retain qualified experts and consultants to assist the fiduciary in investing plan assets. The retention of experts is absolutely necessary in situations where plan fiduciaries are not sufficiently expert to evaluate particular investments. [*See, e.g.,* Marshall v Glass/Metal Association and Glaziers and Glassworkers Pension Plan, 507 FSupp 378, 384 (D Hawaii 1980) (While there is flexibility in the prudence standard, it is not a refuge for fiduciaries who are not equipped to evaluate a complex investment—in this case, a real estate time-sharing project. If fiduciaries commit a pension plan's assets to investments that they do not fully understand, they will nonetheless be judged, as provided in the

Q 7:14 Fiduciary Responsibility Answer Book

statute, according to the standards of others acting in a like capacity and familiar with such matters.)]

Although fiduciaries have a duty to seek independent advice where they lack the requisite education, experience, and skill, they must make their own decisions based on that advice. [Whitfield v Cohen, 682 FSupp 188, 194-195 (SDNY 1988). See also Donovan v Cunningham, 716 F2d 1455, 1474 (5th Cir 1983), *cert denied*, 467 US 1251 (1984) ("an independent appraisal is not a magic wand that fiduciaries may simply wave over a transaction to ensure that their responsibilities are fulfilled. . . . ERISA fiduciaries . . . are entitled to rely on the expertise of others . . . [but] are responsible for ensuring that information is complete and up-to-date."); Donovan v Tricario, 5 EBC (BNA) 2057 (SD Fla 1984) ("mere retention of an expert cannot be permitted to protect defendants against claims of failure to discharge their own fiduciary responsibilities. Expert advice must be considered as carefully as any other information that the trustees have available to them when making decisions to commit plan assets.")]

Reliance on limited or inaccurate information will not relieve plan fiduciaries of the duty to investigate. [Katsaros v Cody, 744 F2d 270 (2d Cir), *cert denied*, 469 US 1072 (1984) (trustees breached ERISA's prudence standard in connection with $2 million loan to bank, where trustees considered only information presented by bank holding company president who sought loan, and failed to conduct an independent investigation); see also Dimond v Retirement Plan, 582 FSupp 892 (WD Pa 1983) (failure to seek independent advice, and reliance on a mere belief that investment is "wise," constitutes breach of the duty of prudence)]

Q 7:14 Must a plan fiduciary follow industry investment standards with respect to its investment decisions?

It is unclear whether a plan fiduciary must follow industry standards, although a court will probably consider industry standards in determining whether an investment decision is prudent.

[Jones v O'Higgins, 11 EBC (BNA) 1660, 1668 (NDNY 1989). The court found that a fiduciary's conduct in investigating the merits of a transaction must satisfy prevailing industry standards. "To find the defendant liable, this court would have to be provided with evidence that [the defendant] acted imprudently within the standards of the investment industry." A fiduciary well versed in a contrarian investment policy (that is, where the investment manager believes that there is the potential of large returns from investing in companies whose stock may be initially undervalued as a result of financial difficulties) did not violate ERISA's duty of prudence by concentrating the plan's investment heavily in this type of investment where it was shown to be within industry norms. *Compare with* GIW Indus, Inc v Trevor, Stewart, Burton & Jacobsen, Inc, 10 EBC (BNA) 2290, 2304 n.23 (BNA) (SD Ga 1989). "While [investment management industry] custom and practice enter into an evaluation of prudence, the particular obligations of a fiduciary under ERISA are not controlled by the investment management industry but by statute," *aff'd*, 895 F2d 729 11 EBC (BNA) 2737 (11th Cir 1990)]

Purchasing Annuities

The purchase of an annuity and the selection of the annuity provider are subject to ERISA's fiduciary requirements just as with any other investment. Recently, much attention has been focused on insurance companies and their products because of the financial difficulties of various insurance companies over the past few years. The following questions examine certain special concerns that apply to a plan fiduciary's purchase of an annuity and the selection of an annuity provider. Many of these concerns also apply to other investments offered by insurance companies.

Q 7:15 What is the relevance of selecting an insurance product such as an annuity?

Fiduciaries acquiring insurance products must evaluate the prudence of the decisions they make with respect to these products in the same manner as any other plan investment.

The highly publicized problems of insurance companies—particularly Executive Life Company of California, Executive Life Company of New York, and Mutual Benefit Life in New Jersey—have substantial implications for pension plans, their sponsors, plan fiduciaries, and participants in plans that have purchased insurance

Q 7:16   **Fiduciary Responsibility Answer Book**

products. Obviously, fiduciaries of plans that have investments in insurance companies experiencing economic difficulties must take action to understand all facts relating to the troubled investment (including the nature of the plan's investment and the plan's contractual rights and obligations) and, further, must evaluate and monitor the investment as well as the regulatory developments governing the insurance company and the particular investment.

In any case, fiduciaries must act prudently with respect to selecting and monitoring a plan's investment in annuity products.

Q 7:16 How should a plan fiduciary select an annuity provider (e.g., insurance company)?

The DOL has long held the view that the selection of an annuity provider is an act governed by the fiduciary responsibility provisions of ERISA, including the prudence, exclusive purpose, and prohibited transaction provisions. [See Advance Notice of Proposed Rulemaking, 29 CFR § 2510; ERISA §§ 403(c)(1), 404(a)(1)(A), 404(a)(1)(B), and 406; and Ltr from Dennis M. Kass (PWBA) to John M. Erlenborn (ERISA Advisory Council), Mar 13, 1986] The fiduciary should apply the general standards it applies for the selection and evaluation of investment managers and investment products including, for example, the factors set forth under Qs 7:1, 7:2, and 7:3. In addition, the fiduciary should check into the annuity provider's financial strength by examining the carrier's financial statements and consulting with independent rating agencies.

> **Planning Pointer.** The fiduciary should not rely solely on the ratings of one ratings service. Instead, the fiduciary should check the ratings of the insurer by reviewing the ratings of various ratings agencies. For example, the fiduciary should review several or all of the following nationally-recognized ratings services: Standard & Poor's Corp.; Moody's Investors Service, Inc.; A.M. Best Company; Duff & Phelps, Inc.; and Weiss, Inc.
>
> Generally, these ratings services assess the financial strength or claims-paying ability of insurance companies and examine various factors (such as insurance companies' profitability, capital adequacy, liquidity, investment risks, and management quality). The assessment of these factors is derived from financial statements

filed by the insurance companies with state regulatory agencies, other financial information collected by the ratings organizations, meetings with the insurance companies' management, and other sources. Although the methodologies used by the ratings services are basically similar, there are some differences among the organizations concerning their sources of information, the specific factors they consider in their assessments, and how they weigh various factors.

Note. While the coverage of the insurance industry by the nationally-recognized ratings services is basically comprehensive, fiduciaries should be aware that some insurance companies—typically those of small to medium size—may not have received a rating or may only have a rating from one ratings service.

The fiduciary should also assess the insurer's claims paying ability by investigating various aspects of the company including its operating performance, general account asset quality, and asset-to-liability cash flow matching. In any case, ERISA's prudent expert rule may militate in favor of the plan fiduciary retaining qualified experts and consultants to assist the fiduciary in selecting an insurer. The retention of experts is absolutely necessary in situations where plan fiduciaries are not sufficiently expert to evaluate an insurer's qualifications (see Q 7:13).

Q 7:17 Under what circumstances may a pension plan purchase annuity contracts?

Pension plans may purchase annuities in a variety of circumstances. For example, a plan fiduciary may purchase annuities for participants and beneficiaries in connection with the termination of a plan or, in the case of an ongoing plan, plan fiduciaries may purchase annuities for participants who retire or separate from service with accrued benefits. As noted in Q 7:16, plan fiduciaries must be prudent and comply with their fiduciary obligations under ERISA in connection with their purchase of annuities or other products from insurance companies. [See, e.g., Arakelian v National Western Life Ins Co, 680 FSupp 400 (DDC 1987), *reconsid denied*, 724 FSupp 1033 (DDC 1989) (Eight individual plaintiffs who participated in pension plans patterned after a master pension plan brought an action for violations of ERISA against National Western, the Builders, Contractors and

Employees Retirement Trust and Pension Plan, and the plan's trustees. National Western established the master plan. Without altering the terms of the master plan, employers adopted the master plan. According to the master plan document, employee benefits are provided solely through the purchase of group annuity contracts from National Western. The court held that National Western violated ERISA Section 404(a) by investing plan funds solely in National Western annuity contracts. The court concluded that "National Western failed to analyze the merits of investing all the plan's assets in National Western annuity contracts because the plan instrument requires all plan assets to be used toward the purchase of National Western annuity contracts, precluding National Western from analyzing whether that investment best suits the participants needs." The court did not hold that a plan may not use all of its assets to purchase insurance contracts, but "rather National Western failed to investigate the merits of purchasing contracts from a particular insurance company."); *Cf* Horan v Kaiser Steel Retirement Plan, 947 F2d 1412, 1416 (9th Cir 1991) (Past practice of purchasing annuities for each retiree does not deprive the plan's investment committee of its discretion and obligate it to purchase annuities for all future retirees. To hold otherwise would require a fiduciary to continue purchasing annuities when it is financially unsound to do so.)]

Q 7:18 Does the purchase of an annuity contract in connection with either the termination of a plan or distribution of benefits from an ongoing plan relieve the plan and its fiduciaries of liability regarding the payment of benefits?

Yes, provided that certain requirements are met. Annuity contracts are typically purchased by a plan fiduciary to guarantee the payment of benefits under a terminated or ongoing pension plan. (See Qs 3:18 through 3:21 regarding settlor versus fiduciary activities.) In general, liability for benefits promised under the plan is transferred from the plan to the insurance company purchasing the annuity. Once the annuity contract is issued, the individuals covered under such contract generally cease to be plan participants. [*See, e.g.*, PBGC Adv Op Ltr No 91-1 (Jan 14, 1991); 29 CFR § 2510.3-3(d)(2)(ii) (The DOL, IRS, and PBGC each have recognized that an individual ceases to be a plan participant if the full benefit rights of the individual are fully guaranteed by an insurance company, thereby extinguishing the plan fiduciary's liability to that participant for the payment of benefits.)]

Regarding a terminated plan, the PBGC has taken the position that, once a plan sponsor has purchased irrevocable commitments from an insurance company authorized to do business in a state (or the District of Columbia), the plan sponsor satisfies its obligations under ERISA's plan termination insurance provisions (Title IV). [See PBGC Adv Op Ltr No 85-9 (Apr 5, 1985); PBGC Adv Op Ltr No 85-28 (Dec 3, 1985); ERISA § 4041(b)(3)]

Note. This is so even if the insurance company is unable to pay the benefits it has guaranteed under the annuity contract. The PBGC has taken this position in connection with annuity contracts issued by Executive Life, which reduced the payments under such contracts by 30 percent. That is, Executive Life, under court order, paid only 70 percent of the amounts owed under retirement annuity policies. PBGC has opined that the plan sponsor has no liability for the difference, once the annuity contract is purchased, provided that the insurance carrier was selected prudently. [PBGC Adv Op Ltr No 91-4 1991 (May 3, 1991)]

Example. The Scary Airlines Company, Inc. (SAC) terminated its defined benefit pension plan and began to purchase annuities from True Blue Insurance Company (True Blue) to guarantee payment of all nonforfeitable accrued benefits under the plan. The plan provided that benefits would not be paid in the event of continued employment beyond the normal retirement age of 60, and would be paid only upon actual retirement. SAC was subsequently acquired by Safe Airways Co. and a formal group annuity contract was executed between Safe Airways and True Blue. Plaintiff pilots, who were about to reach age 60 and wanted to continue in Safe Airways' employ, informed Safe Airways that they anticipated receiving their annuity benefits under the annuity contract as of their normal retirement date (age 60). Plaintiffs did not receive their benefits because, although they passed age 60, they remained in Safe Airways' employ. Plaintiff pilots brought an ERISA action for their benefits against True Blue and Safe Airways under the annuity contract as an ERISA plan. The court held that the annuity contract did not constitute an ERISA plan. The court based its analysis upon the regulations. First, Title I of ERISA is inapplicable to "any plan, fund, or program . . . under which no employees are participants covered under the plan" [29 CFR

§ 2510.3-3(b)], and second, an employee is not a participant in a plan if the entire benefit rights of "the individual (1) are fully guaranteed by an insurance company . . . and are legally enforceable by the sole choice of the individual against the insurance policy . . . ; and (2) a contract, policy, or certificate describing the benefits to which the individual is entitled under the plan has been issued to the individual." [29 CFR § 2510.3-3(d)(2)(ii); Thompson v Prudential Ins Co, 795 FSupp 1337, 59 FEP Cas 263 (D NJ 1992), aff'd, 993 F2d 226 (3d Cir, 1993)]

Q 7:19 Is the Pension Benefit Guaranty Corporation (PBGC) responsible for the payment of benefits after the plan purchases an annuity contract from an insurance company?

Generally, no. The PBGC has also taken the position that, once an irrevocable annuity contract is purchased from an insurance company, if the insurance company is unable to satisfy its commitments, PBGC will not pay such benefits. [PBGC Adv Op Ltr No. 91-1 (Jan 14, 1991)] It based its analysis on the fact that the insurable event under ERISA is plan termination. The final distribution of assets (i.e., purchase of annuity contract) extinguishes the PBGC's statutory guarantee obligation.

[But see PBGC Adv Op Ltr No. 81-35 (Oct 26, 1981). (This letter reflects the PBGC's former position, which is directly contrary to the PBGC's current position. In such instance, the PBGC stated that it generally would guaranty the retirement benefit if the insurance company was unable to pay the benefit under the annuity.)]

> **Planning Pointer.** Assuming the plan fiduciary was prudent in its selection of the insurance company, the plan sponsor should be relieved from any further benefit plan liabilities after purchase of an annuity. But, if the plan fiduciary was not prudent in selecting an annuity provider, the fiduciary may be liable.

Q 7:20 Are there other special considerations that apply when a plan purchases an annuity contract in connection with a plan termination?

Yes. Various technical and complex requirements apply to the purchase of annuity contracts upon a plan's termination. The DOL requires that an annuity provider selected to fulfill ERISA's plan termination requirements satisfy ERISA's general fiduciary requirements. In addition, the PBGC provides that a plan could not terminate in a standard termination unless the plan complies with the PBGC's requirements relative to the notice of intent to terminate, as well as with other applicable requirements. [PBGC Reg § 2617.1 through 2617.28]

> **Planning Pointer.** If the plan purchases irrevocable commitments from an insurer in order to wholly or partially provide for the distribution of benefits, the notice of intent to terminate must include the name and address of the insurers from whom the plan administrator intends to purchase the annuity contracts. [PBGC Reg § 2617.22(d)(9)] If, at the time the notice of intent is issued, the plan administrator has not identified the potential annuity providers, the notice must contain a statement that such identification will be provided at a later date, but no later than 45 days prior to the "date of distribution." [PBGC Reg § 2617.22(d)(9)(ii)(C)]

In the event that the plan administrator decides to select a different annuity provider than those set forth in the initial notice, a supplemental notice is required (no later than 45 days prior to the date of distribution). [PBGC Reg § 2617.22(e)] In addition, the regulations provide rules under which the plan administrator must notify PBGC of the selection of an annuity provider. [PBGC Reg § 2617.25(b)]

Guaranteed Investment Contracts (GICs) and Bank Investment Contracts (BICs)

Guaranteed investment contracts (GICs) have been one of the most popular investment options for defined contribution plans. Since GICs are issued by insurance companies, many of the concerns discussed in Questions 7:15 through 7:20 relating to the purchase of annuities and the selection of annuity providers also apply to an investment in a GIC and selection of the GIC provider. Similar concerns also apply to bank investment contracts (BICs).

Q 7:21 What is a "guaranteed investment contract" (GIC), and what is a "bank investment contract" (BIC)?

A GIC is a contract issued by an insurance company, and a BIC is a contract issued by a bank, under which the return of principal is specifically stated and "guaranteed," and a fixed rate of interest is paid for a specific period of time. A "fixed rate of interest" generally means that the insurance company or the bank, as the case may be, credits or pays a predetermined rate of return, which can be paid periodically or compounded. Under the most common type of GIC, at the specified maturity date, the principal and all unpaid interest is paid in a lump sum (scheduled payouts exist but are less common). There are various types of GICs, including, for example:

- *"General Account" GICs*—Under these instruments, the GIC contractholder does not have an interest in specific assets held by the insurance company. If the insurance company becomes insolvent and is liquidated, a GIC contractholder has a claim against the insurer's general assets, subject to the liquidation "priority" status assigned to the GIC contractholder. (See Qs 8:31 through 8:32 regarding general accounts.)

- *"Separate Account" GICS*—These instruments (which are usually fixed rate obligations) generally provide that, upon liquidation of the insurer, the contractholder would have a legally enforceable right to have the obligation owed to it satisfied out of specified assets held in a "separate account" that generally will not be subject to the creditors of the insurance carrier. (See Q 8:32 regarding separate accounts.) Note that the enforceability of this provision (granting a contractholder the right to have any obligation owed to it by the insurance company satisfied through assets held in a separate account) is generally a question of state insurance law. Although separate accounts are basically intended to be insulated from the reach of general creditors, certain state laws may lack specificity as to the extent of any protection from general creditors, or these laws may necessitate the inclusion of specific language in the insurance contract to insulate the separate account.

- *Participating GICs*—These are GICs without a fixed maturity. The interest guarantee generally is no greater than one year.

BICs are generally structured as bank deposits that replicate the contract features of GICs.

Note. Although the GIC acquired by a plan may be guaranteeing the return of principal and a set interest rate, the word "guarantee" in GIC is actually a misnomer. The sole guarantor of the guaranteed investment contract is the insurance company issuing the contract. As noted in Q 7:25, the term "guaranteed" should probably be eliminated from employee communications and the precise nature of the GIC investment should be properly communicated to plan participants.

Q 7:22 What factors should a plan fiduciary consider when selecting a GIC?

As with any plan investment, in deciding whether to invest plan assets in a GIC or BIC, or which insurer or bank to use, a plan fiduciary must act prudently and investigate the various investment alternatives. In addition, the fiduciary has a duty to undertake an adequate investigation into the soundness and stability of the insurance company or the bank. [See Whitfield v Tomasso, 682 FSupp 1287 (EDNY 1988) (Trustees breached fiduciary duties of prudence and diversification by investing a substantial amount of plan assets in CDs of a questionable insurance company; trustees did not investigate the financial soundness of the company, review ratings, or consult an expert.)]

In choosing a GIC as an investment option, plan fiduciaries should consider the following points:

- GICs are simply another type of investment; they are not guaranteed by the federal or any state government.
- The security of a GIC depends solely on the financial stability of the issuer. Thus, GICs are subject to default risks. In the event that the issuer fails, participants and beneficiaries may not receive the stated interest rate and may lose all or part of the investment.
- Like other investments, GICs have investment risks that will affect whether participants receive the benefits to which they are entitled.

- The investments underlying GICs are typically private-placement bonds, mortgages, and real estate (in many cases, the underlying investments are linked to the real estate industry). Given the present depressed state of the real property market, extra caution should be applied in evaluating these investments. Further, over a long period of time, the fixed-income return on GICs may not compare with the return that may be obtained from equity investments.

- Many GICs impose penalties for early withdrawal. Certain events, such as employment terminations (e.g., in the event of a mass layoff or division shutdown), may require an increased amount of plan distributions, which may create cash flow problems for the plan. In such a case, the plan may need to unexpectedly liquidate investments (i.e., early withdrawal). It is important to review GIC provisions and clarify the events that trigger the application of early withdrawal penalties. In addition, participants should be advised about situations in which they will bear the penalty.

Q 7:23 What factors should a plan fiduciary consider when selecting a BIC?

Since BICs are generally structured in the same manner as GICs except that the issuer is a bank rather than an insurance company, the same general concerns apply to BICs (see Q 7:22). It may be possible, however, in certain limited circumstances, that federal insurance coverage under the Federal Deposit Insurance Corporation (FDIC) may be available to certain BICs that resemble bank deposits. (See Q 7:46 regarding special concerns applicable to investments in a bank).

Q 7:24 What actions may a plan fiduciary take in connection with a plan investment—such as a GIC—that is issued by a troubled insurance company?

There is no specific course of action that a plan fiduciary must take in connection with a plan investment issued by a troubled insurance company. However, as demonstrated throughout this chapter, any investment decision or action requires the plan fiduciary to act in accordance with ERISA's fiduciary duty requirements.

In reaction to the recent financial difficulties experienced by some members of the insurance industry, plan fiduciaries may wish to consider reviewing their plans' GICs and/or substituting GICs with other investment options. However, rather than eliminate GICs entirely, plan fiduciaries should, for example:

1. Investigate methods to enhance GIC returns;
2. Engage in the prudent selection of GICs and other insurance products; and
3. Implement guidelines to ensure the prudent selection of annuity providers and GIC issuers.

Although fiduciaries must consider the default risk associated with GICs, a fiduciary should not necessarily replace the GIC with an alternate investment, which may pose an increased investment risk.

Q 7:25 How should plan fiduciaries communicate the special nature of GICs to the plan participants?

In exercising prudence, plan fiduciaries should review for accuracy all plan communications and materials that contain descriptions of the plan's GICs and other investment options. In doing so, fiduciaries should consider the following points:

- Eliminating the term "guaranteed" in order to avoid any suggestion of guaranteed rates of return or return of principal. More accurate terms such as "fixed income fund" or "stable value fund" should be used. This should minimize participants' misinterpretation of the potential risk of default and other possible investment risks inherent in GICs, and any misperception that the fund (or the income generated by it) is guaranteed by the plan sponsor or plan fiduciaries.
- Plan fiduciaries also should identify any alternative investment vehicles to GICs that are offered by the plan, and explain how and when transfers may be made from a GIC to such other

alternative, as well as a description of any risks associated with such a transfer.

- Plan language may have to be revised so as to permit other high quality, stable value investments (in addition to GICs) that are consistent with the plan's investment objectives.
- When projecting annual rates for a GIC, plan fiduciaries should communicate to participants both a rate history and the rates of other similar investments.
- If plan fiduciaries do not fully understand the terms and conditions of the GICs held by the plan, ERISA's "prudent expert" standard requires plan fiduciaries to retain experts to assist participants in understanding the relative security of their GIC portfolio. Participants should also be made aware of the action that will be taken in the event that the issuer fails.

Q 7:26 What information regarding a GIC should a plan fiduciary provide to participants?

Information should also be made available to participants regarding the quality of the underlying securities in the portfolio of the GIC offered by the plan. For example, participants should be advised as to:

- The number and types of issuers of securities represented in the portfolio;
- The percentage of the portfolio comprised of any single issuer, and the quality rating assigned by the rating agencies to each issuer's fixed income securities;
- The average maturity of all fixed income securities in the portfolio; and
- The overall quality standards used to determine whether an issuer may be included in the portfolio.

Although the regulations under Section 404(c) of ERISA pertaining to participant-directed accounts are not controlling with respect to certain general ERISA requirements, they do, however, offer some guidance as to the type of information that could be provided to participants regarding an investment such as a GIC (see Qs 4:40 and 4:41).

Employer Securities and Employer Real Property

Perhaps one of the most complex areas under ERISA regarding plan investments involves employer securities and employer real property. These investments are subject to various restrictions including, for example, restrictions on the type of employer securities or employer real property that may be held by the plan, the type of plan that may hold these investments, and the applicable percentage of plan assets that may hold these investments. The following questions examine these restrictions as well as the other ERISA fiduciary duty concerns that apply to a plan that acquires or holds employer stock or employer real property.

Q 7:27 May a plan invest in employer securities or employer real property?

Generally, yes, though subject to various restrictions and requirements. First, a plan may invest only in certain types of employer securities or employer real property. An ERISA plan that invests in employer securities or employer real property may only invest in "qualifying" employer securities (QES) (see Q 7:28) or "qualifying" employer real property (QERP) (see Q 7:29). Second, a plan subject to ERISA (other than an eligible individual account plan) may not acquire or hold QES or QERP if the total fair market value of such assets exceeds 10 percent of the total fair market value of all the plan's assets at the time of acquisition. [ERISA § 407(a)(1) and (2)] However, an eligible individual account plan may acquire or hold more than 10 percent of the value of the plan's assets in QERP and QES without violating ERISA's diversification requirement. [ERISA § 407(b)(1)] (See Q 3:25 regarding diversification and investment in QES and QERP, and Q 7:30 defining the term "eligible individual account plan.") Third, a plan's sale or acquisition of QES, or sale, acquisition, or lease of QERP, must be for "adequate consideration" (or at a price no less favorable than the price described in Q 7:28 for

Q 7:28   **Fiduciary Responsibility Answer Book**

marketable obligations) and no commission may be charged. [ERISA § 408(e)] (See Q 7:34 regarding adequate consideration.)

A plan fiduciary engages in a prohibited transaction if he or she causes a plan to acquire or hold employer securities or employer real property and does not follow these requirements. [ERISA §§ 406(a)(1)(E), 406(a)(2), and 408(e)] (See Qs 3:25, 6:12, and 5:29.) Furthermore, even if a plan fiduciary follows these rules, he or she might still violate ERISA's fiduciary requirements to act prudently and to act for the exclusive benefit of plan participants and beneficiaries. For example, although a plan fiduciary may not engage in a prohibited transaction by doing so, he or she may still violate ERISA's fiduciary duty requirements by acting in a manner that furthers his or her own self-interest, such as voting or tendering employer stock held in a plan in a manner not in the best interests of participants, purchasing or holding employer real property or employer stock when it is no longer financially appropriate to do so, etc. The potential for a conflict of interest and a breach of fiduciary duty becomes exacerbated when the fiduciary has a personal stake in the outcome of a hostile takeover or other type of control contest and the plan holds significant amounts of employer stock (see Q 7:38).

Q 7:28   What are qualifying employer securities (QES)?

For a given plan, QES means any security issued by an employer (or any of its affiliates) of employees covered by that plan and that is stock, marketable obligations, or interests in certain publicly traded partnerships. [ERISA § 407(d)(1) and (5)]

Stock or publicly traded partnership interests acquired by a plan (other than an eligible individual account plan) after December 17, 1987, will be a QES only if, immediately following the acquisition of such stock:

1. No more than 25 percent of the aggregate amount of stock of the same class issued and outstanding at the time of acquisition is held by the plan; and
2. At least 50 percent of such aggregate amount is held by persons independent of the issuer [ERISA § 407(f)(1)].

Plans holding stock that failed to meet these requirements had until January 1, 1993 to divest themselves of such stock (provided that the stock was held since December 1, 1987, or acquired after December 17, 1987 but pursuant to a legally binding contract in effect on December 17, 1987 and so held at all times since). [ERISA § 407(f)(2)] After December 17, 1987, plans must satisfy these requirements unless the acquisition is pursuant to a legally binding contract in effect on such date. [ERISA § 407(f)(3)]

Also included as a QES would be a "marketable obligation;" that is, a bond, debenture, note, certificate, or other evidence of indebtedness, if the following conditions are met:

1. The obligation is acquired: on the market either at the price prevailing on a national securities exchange (registered with the SEC) or, if not traded on such exchange, at a price not less favorable to the plan than the offering price as established by the current bid and asked prices (quoted by persons independent of the issuer); from an underwriter at a price not in excess of the public offering price and at which a substantial portion of the same issue is acquired by persons independent of the issuer, or; directly from the issuer at a price not less favorable to the plan than the price paid currently for a substantial portion of the same issue by persons independent of the issuer.
2. Immediately after the obligation is acquired, no more than 25 percent of the aggregate amount of obligations issued in such issue and outstanding is held by the plan and at least 50 percent of the aggregate amount is held by persons independent of the issuer.
3. Immediately after the obligation is acquired, not more than 25 percent of the assets of the plan is invested in obligations of the employer or its affiliate. [ERISA § 407(e)]

Example 1. The ABC Corporation issues a new class of stock, $10 million of convertible preferred stock. Plan X, a defined benefit plan sponsored by the ABC Corporation, with assets totalling $25 million, acquires $2 million of ABC Corporation's convertible preferred stock. The remaining $8 million of convertible preferred stock is sold in a public offering. The convertible preferred stock of ABC Corporation is QES since (1) the convertible preferred stock is stock; (2) Plan X does not hold more than 25 percent of the aggregate amount of stock of the same class issued and outstanding at the time of Plan X's acquisition; and (3) at least 50 percent of the stock (at least $5 million) is held by persons independent of the issuer (the public). In addition, less than 10 percent of Plan X's assets are QES and, therefore, Plan X's acquisition of the convertible preferred stock would not be a prohibited transaction. Note, however, that Plan X's investment in QES must still satisfy ERISA's general fiduciary standard—in particular, the prudence requirement and exclusive benefit rule.

Example 2. Assume the same facts as in Example 1, except that instead of the $8 million public offering of ABC Corporation convertible preferred stock, that stock is purchased by or given to several senior ABC executives. Here, the convertible preferred stock would not be QES because at least 50 percent of the stock would not be held by persons "independent of the issuer."

Note. There is little guidance interpreting the term "independent of the issuer." A few DOL advisory opinion letters, however, state that such determination is based upon the surrounding facts and circumstances. [DOL Adv Op Ltr No 92-27A (Dec 18, 1992; DOL Adv Op Ltr 78-25A (Nov 13, 1978)] These sources refer to regulations under Section 503(e) of the Internal Revenue Code of 1954 (this section was virtually identical to Section 407(e) of ERISA), which set forth a number of specific relationships that are not, by their very nature, "independent of the issuer." Although other persons may also fit the category, the following persons are clearly not independent of the issuer:

1. A corporation that directly or indirectly controls or is controlled by the issuer;

2. A controlling shareholder of the issuer or of a corporation that controls the issuer;

3. An officer, director or other employee of the issuer, of a corporation controlled by the issuer or of a corporation controlling the issuer;

4. A fiduciary of any trust created by the issuer for such other corporations; and

5. A corporation controlled by any person that in turn controls the issuer. [Treas Reg § 1.503(e)-1(b)(3)(i)(c)-(g)]

Control is defined as direct or indirect ownership of 50 percent or more of total combined voting power of all voting stock or total value of all classes of stock. For purposes of determining control, an individual's ownership is aggregated with that of a spouse, ancestors, lineal descendants, and brothers and sisters, and each such individual is deemed to be a controlling shareholder if any of them is.

Example 3. Assume the same facts as in Example 2, except that Plan X is a profit-sharing plan (which under ERISA § 407(d)(3) is an eligible individual account plan) instead of a defined benefit plan (which under ERISA § 407(d)(3) is not an eligible individual account plan). (See Q 7:25.) Here, the convertible preferred stock is QES since the requirements under ERISA § 407(f)(1) (that no more than 25 percent of the stock is held by the plan and that at least 50 percent is held by persons independent of the issuer) does not apply to an eligible individual account plan, such as a profit-sharing plan. In addition, Plan X, as an eligible individual account plan, may acquire more than $25 million of the stock and exceed the 10 percent limitation. It may also be possible for the eligible individual account, Plan X, to hold as much as 100 percent of its assets in QES—particularly if it is an employee stock ownership plan (ESOP). (See Q 7:31 regarding restrictions on investments in QES and Q 7:32 regarding ESOPs.)

Note. Usually these issues arise in connection with the investment by a pension plan in QES. It is possible, however, for a welfare plan—such as a voluntary employees' beneficiary association (VEBA) that provides for health, life and certain other benefits—to invest in QES. Since a VEBA (or any other welfare plan) is not an eligible individual account plan, fiduciaries of welfare plans should be aware that the 10 percent limitation on plan investments in QES applies (in addition to the general ERISA rules applicable to QES).

Q 7:29 What is "qualifying employer real property" (QERP)?

In a given plan, QERP consists of any parcels of real property (and related personal property) that are leased to an employer of employees covered by the plan (or affiliate) and that satisfy the following requirements:

1. A substantial number of the parcels are dispersed geographically;
2. Each parcel of real property and the improvements on the property are suitable (or adaptable without excessive cost) for more than one use, even if all such real property is leased to one lessee (which may be an employer or its affiliate); and
3. The acquisition and retention of such property complies with ERISA's fiduciary rules (except the diversification and prohibited transaction rules, which do not apply). [ERISA §§ 406(d)(2) and (4)]

Q 7:30 What is an "eligible individual account plan"?

An "eligible individual account plan" is an individual account plan (e.g., a defined contribution plan) that is:

- A profit-sharing, stock bonus, thrift, or savings plan (e.g., a 401(k) plan);
- An employee stock ownership plan (ESOP); or
- One of certain pre-ERISA money purchase pension plans.

[ERISA § 407(d)(3)(A)]

An eligible individual account plan is not subject to the 10 percent limitation regarding investments in QES or QERP, nor to the 25 percent/50 percent limit regarding whether stock or a partnership interest is QES, but is subject to the 25 percent/50 percent limit regarding whether a marketable obligation is QES.

Q 7:31 Are there any restrictions on an eligible individual account plan's investment in QES or QERP?

Yes. An eligible individual account plan may invest in QES or QERP only if the plan explicitly provides for the acquisition and holding of QES or QERP (as the case may be). [ERISA § 407(d)(3)(B)] Although ERISA restricts plans other than eligible individual account plans

Investment Issues   Q 7:31

(such as defined benefit pension plans) to a 10 percent investment in QES or QERP, no statutory restriction applies to eligible individual account plans. An ESOP—a form of tax-qualified retirement plan—is, by its very nature, an employee benefit vehicle specifically designed to invest primarily in employer securities. (See Q 7:32 regarding ERISA's definition of an ESOP.) An ESOP could invest as much as 100 percent of its assets in qualifying employer securities. Other eligible individual account plans (such as a profit-sharing plan) are neither specifically designed to invest in employer securities nor expressly prohibited from or limited in making such investment.

While there is no express limitation on the amount of assets of an eligible individual account plan that may be invested in QES or QERP, ERISA's standard of prudence and exclusive benefit rule must be satisfied when a plan invests in QES or QERP. [See, e.g., Eaves v Penn, 587 F2d 453 (10th Cir 1978) (fiduciaries violated the exclusive benefit rule and prudence requirement under ERISA when a profit-sharing plan was converted into an ESOP, an advance cash contribution was made to the plan causing significant devaluation of the stock, and the trustees mismanaged the plan); Baker v Smith, 2 EBC (BNA) 1380 (ED Pa 1981) (trustees violated the prudence requirements when they converted a profit-sharing plan into an ESOP and used profit sharing assets to purchase employer stock)]

No bright-line test or safe harbor governs whether (and to what extent) an eligible individual account plan may invest in QES or QERP. Whether a fiduciary breaches his or her fiduciary duties under ERISA in connection with such investments depends largely on the applicable facts and circumstances.

For instance, where an ESOP is established solely (or even primarily) for corporate reasons (e.g., purely to fend off a hostile takeover or to entrench incumbent management) and where fiduciaries (e.g., the trustee or administrator) act in their own or the sponsoring corporation's interest, the fiduciaries' actions will not be considered to be for the exclusive benefit of participants and, therefore, in violation of ERISA's fiduciary standard. Although it is possible for corporate officials to act as plan fiduciaries, independent fiduciaries (or independent legal and financial advisors to nonindependent fiduciaries) may be appointed in order to minimize possible conflicts of interest that give rise to breaches of fiduciary duties. This becomes particularly important in the context of certain corporate control contests and transactions (e.g., corporate governance matters, hostile takeovers, proxy contests, and responses to tender offers). (See Q 7:38 regarding special ERISA fiduciary concerns in the context of tender offers, hostile takeovers, and other corporate events.) In addition, if trustees continue to purchase and hold employer stock that becomes significantly devalued (e.g., the employer is headed toward reorganization or insolvency), the employer stock will probably no longer be a prudent investment. But see Ershick v United Missouri Bank, NA, 948 F2d 660 (10th Cir 1991) (ESOP purchase of employer stock was not imprudent merely because of declining stock value. Plaintiff, a Greb X-Ray ESOP participant, filed an action against the trustee of the ESOP, alleging it had imprudently caused the purchase of Greb X-Ray stock. The court held that United Missouri Bank (UMB) did not violate ERISA. The ESOP expressly provided that "it was intended to invest primarily in company stock" and that the administrator, Greb X-Ray, would administer the plan, including directing the trustees with regard to purchases of company stock and the fair market value thereof. The court concluded that UMB, as a directed trustee, was subject to the proper directions of the administrator and did not violate ERISA when it purchased company stock at the administrator's direction.)]

In addition to the ERISA fiduciary concerns applicable to the establishment of a plan that invests in QES or QERP, the decision to establish plans investing in QES (particularly ESOPs) is also subject to corporate law considerations—namely, the business judgment rule. Generally, the business judgment rule serves to uphold decisions of a board of directors that acts on an informed basis, in good faith, and in the honest belief that the action taken by the board (such as with respect to an ESOP) was in the best interest of the company. [See NCR Corp. v American Telephone and Telegraph Company, 761 FSupp 475, 495 (SD Ohio 1991) (The court ruled as to whether the NCR board's adoption of an ESOP as a defensive measure in response to a takeover attempt is protected by the business judgment rule under Maryland law. The court held that, although the NCR board did not act in bad faith in adopting the ESOP, the transaction is not protected by the business judgment rule because the board was not acting in an informed capacity.)] Whether or not the business judgment rule is available, courts will generally evaluate the following factors:

- Timing of the formation of the ESOP (e.g., was the plan established when the plan sponsor became faced with a hostile takeover?);
- Degree of consideration given to the ESOP's establishment (by reviewing corporate resolutions, committee minutes);
- History of employee participation in the company;
- Shareholder neutrality of the ESOP; and
- Other legitimate business reasons to form and maintain an ESOP.

[See Shamrock Holding, Inc v Polaroid Corp, Slip op 10,075 and 10,079 (Del Ch Jan 6, 1989) (Polaroid established an ESOP after Shamrock announced that it was interested in meeting with the Polaroid board of directors and owned a substantial percentage of Polaroid stock. Although the parties argued at length about the applicability of the business judgment rule, the court never resolved this issue because the court upheld Polaroid's ESOP as fair in the context of an attempted takeover, despite Shamrock's and the other defendants' allegations that Polaroid's board adopted the ESOP at the "eleventh hour" mainly to entrench management, and that the directors were both misinformed and uninformed as to material facts relating to their adoption of the ESOP). But see Norlin Corp v Rooney, Pace, Inc, 744 F2d 255 (2d Cir 1984) (Within five days after Norlin Corp. lost a federal securities action in connection with the raider's purchase of 32 percent of Norlin Corp. stock, the board took a series of "defensive" actions including transferring a substantial block of stock to an ESOP whose trustees consisted of Norlin insiders. The directors of Norlin Corp. failed to demonstrate that the ESOP was fair and reasonable since the ESOP's purpose was defensive, as evidenced by the timing of the ESOP's creation, lack of a demonstrable employee benefit purpose, the financial impact on the target, use of insider trustees, lack of any cash consideration for ESOP shares, and voting control of the shares.) Accord Buckhorn, Inc v Ropak Corp, 656 FSupp 209 (SD Ohio 1987), aff;d, 815 F2d 76 (6th Cir 1987); Podesta v Calumet Indus, Inc, Fed Sec L Rep (CCH) 96,433 (ND Ill 1978)]

Q 7:32 What is an employee stock ownership plan (ESOP)?

Under ERISA, an ESOP is an individual account plan (e.g., a defined contribution plan) that is a stock bonus plan (or a stock bonus and money purchase pension plan) qualified under Section 401 of the Internal Revenue Code, that is designed to invest primarily in QES, and that meets the requirements of the Treasury regulations applicable to ESOPs. [ERISA § 407(d)(6)]

Q 7:33 How does an ESOP acquire employer securities?

QES may be acquired through direct employer contributions or with the proceeds of a loan to the ESOP trust (i.e., a leveraged ESOP). A leveraged ESOP typically borrows funds from a financial institution in return for a promissory note, which is usually guaranteed by the employer corporation sponsoring the ESOP. The ESOP trustee uses the loan proceeds to purchase QES of the employer. The purchased stock is then held in the ESOP trust in a suspense account and may be used for the leveraged ESOP's so-called acquisition loan. The loan is paid off with contributions or dividends paid to the ESOP by the corporation. As the loan is paid off, shares are allocated from the suspense account to participants' accounts. [Treas Reg §§ 54.4975-7 and 11; and DOL Reg § 2550.408b-3] Loans to an ESOP that are used to purchase QES are exempt from ERISA's prohibited transaction rules, which prohibit loans between plans and parties-in-interest, provided that various statutory and regulatory requirements are satisfied. (See Q 5:14.) [ERISA § 408(b)(3); IRC § 4975(d)(3)] The acquisition and holding of QES are subject to various prohibited transaction exemptions. Nevertheless, any investment in QES must satisfy ERISA's general fiduciary requirements (i.e., prudence and exclusive benefit).

Q 7:34 What does it mean for a plan to purchase or sell QES for "adequate consideration" from a party-in-interest?

As noted above, the acquisition or sale of QES is exempt from the prohibited transaction rules if the acquisition or sale is for adequate consideration and no commission is charged. [ERISA § 408(e); IRC § 4975(d)(13)] In the case of a security for which there is a generally recognized market, adequate consideration means either the price of the security prevailing on a national securities exchange registered under Section 6 of the Securities Exchange Act of 1934; if the security is not traded on such a national securities exchange, a price not less favorable to the plan than the offering price for the security as established by the current bid and asked prices quoted by persons independent of the issuer and any party-in-interest. [ERISA § 3(18)(A)] (See Q 7:28 for a discussion regarding the meaning of "independent of the issuer.")

In the case of a security not freely tradable, adequate consideration means the fair market value of the security as determined in good faith by the trustee or named fiduciary, pursuant to the terms of the plan and the DOL regulations. For this purpose, fair market value must be (a) the price of a willing buyer and a willing seller in an arm's-length transaction; (b) determined as of the applicable date; and (c) reflected in a written document meeting the requirements of the DOL regulations. For this purpose, the good-faith component requires (a) objective standards of conduct; (b) prudent investigation of circumstances prevailing at the time of the valuation; (c) application of sound business principles of valuation; and (d) the fiduciary making the valuation either to be independent of all parties (other than the plan), or to rely on the report of an appraiser who is independent of all parties (other than the plan). [Prop DOL Reg § 2510.3-18; See, e.g. Leonard v Drug Fair, Inc, Fed Sec L Rep (CCH) 97, 114 (Oct 19, 1979) (Plaintiffs argued that the sale was not for "adequate consideration" because the QES might have been sold on the open market, over time, to obtain a higher price, and that the sale of 4 percent of the company's voting stock might have resulted in a premium on the stock for the control involved. Since the stock was registered and traded on the American Stock Exchange (Amex) and since the contract of sale agreed to use the price prevailing on the Amex on the previous day, the court held that the sale of stock at the prevailing market price with a net gain to the plan constituted adequate consideration. The court stated that ERISA does not require the plan to sell stock in small lots or to obtain a premium for the 4 percent of the stock.)]

Q 7:35 How are the shares of QES that are allocated to participants' accounts voted in an ESOP?

If an employer has securities that are readily tradable on an established securities exchange, the Internal Revenue Code (Code), not ERISA, requires that the vote on allocated shares be passed through to plan participants. [IRC §§ 4975(e)(7); 409(e)(2)] If the employer has securities that are not readily tradable, the Code requires that the vote on allocated shares be passed through to participants only with respect to generally significant corporate transactions (e.g., merger, recapitalization, liquidation or sale of substantially all of the assets). [IRC § 409(e)(3)]

For a non-registration type class of securities, an ESOP may, but need not, satisfy the limited pass-through requirement under the Code by granting each ESOP participant one vote with respect to an issue, regardless of the actual number of shares allocated to the participant's account. [IRC § 409(e)(5)] The "one vote per participant rule" may be used only if the ESOP trustee votes the unallocated ESOP shares in proportion to the allocated shares voted by participants under the "one vote" rule [IRS § 409(e)(5)].

Planning Pointer. Because voting is an act subject to ERISA's fiduciary responsibility requirements, the DOL has questioned whether a plan fiduciary may merely follow the direction of plan participants and, instead, has stated that plan fiduciaries cannot necessarily relieve themselves of fiduciary responsibility by passing through voting rights to participants. The DOL may, therefore, find that blind adherence to the Code's "one vote per participant rule" violates ERISA's fiduciary requirements. Fiduciaries should exercise extreme caution with ESOPs that contain this rule; while the plan fiduciary is obligated under ERISA to follow the plan terms, in such a case the duty of prudence and the exclusive benefit rule will override the duty to follow the plan's terms. Depending upon the applicable facts and circumstances, a fiduciary may breach his or her fiduciary duties under ERISA if he or she follows the one vote per participant and pass-through voting rules of the plan.

The vote on allocated shares of QES acquired with the proceeds of an ESOP acquisition loan must be passed through to participants under the Code—regardless of whether the shares are readily tradable—in order for the lender to be entitled to the 50 percent interest exclusion. [IRC § 133(b)(7)]

ERISA does not specifically provide for a voting procedure, except pursuant to Section 404(c) of ERISA regarding participant direction.

(See Qs 4:40, items 7 and 9, 4:43 and 4:45.) Because the regulations under Section 404(c) of ERISA were not finalized until 1992, the DOL addressed the validity of pass-through arrangements on a case-by-case basis. According to the DOL, the voting of allocated shares is generally considered management and control of plan assets. [DOL Adv Op Ltr to Helmuth Fandl, Avon Products, Inc (Feb 23, 1988); DOL Adv Op Ltr to Robert A.G. Monks, Institutional Shareholder Services, Inc (Jan 23, 1990)] It is a fiduciary act governed by ERISA's duty of prudence and exclusive benefit rule. [O'Neill v Davis, 721 FSupp 1013 (ND Ill 1989), *summary judgment den*, O'Neill v Davis, 1990 US Dist LEXIS 1280 (ND Ill 1990) (Plaintiff alleged that by voting the company stock to reconstitute the board of directors, the trustees of the company's ESOP breached their ERISA fiduciary duties by acting to further their own interests, rather than those of the plan participants. In denying defendant's motion to dismiss for failure to state a claim, the court concluded that the voting of the plan-owned shares by the plan's trustees was a fiduciary act under ERISA, and one that the trustees were bound to exercise in the sole interests of the plan participants (absent any undue employer coercion or influence.)] Nevertheless, courts have generally approved the use of pass-through voting for allocated ESOP shares that are exercised by participants [*see, e.g.,* British Printing & Communication Corp v Harcourt Brace Jovanovich, Inc, 664 FSupp 1519 (SDNY 1987) (where the court upheld the ESOP trustees' decision to vote the allocated shares as directed by the participants).]

Q 7:36 What should a fiduciary do if an ESOP participant does not vote the shares of QES that are passed through to such participant?

The Code does not address the ESOP trustee's obligation to vote ESOP shares that are allocated to participants, but for which the trustee receives no instructions.

The old and somewhat defunct regulations on tax-credit ESOPs (TRASOPs) offer some guidance with respect to the Treasury's position on pass-through voting, although such regulations would probably be accorded limited weight in a court of law. With respect to allocated shares that are unexercised by participants, the TRASOP regulations state that the plan may not permit the trustee to vote those

Q 7:36   **Fiduciary Responsibility Answer Book**

allocated shares that a participant fails to exercise. [Treas Reg § 1.46-8(d)-8(iv)]

However, the position taken in the TRASOP regulations directly contravenes ERISA's fiduciary requirements obligating the fiduciary (usually the ESOP trustee) to vote all shares of employer stock. An abstention by a participant does not necessarily constitute a "no" vote. Even in the cases of pass-through voting of allocated shares, the trustee and other fiduciaries are obligated to monitor the proxy vote (to ensure that the participants receive necessary and accurate information, that confidentiality procedures are followed, and that the participants are free from undue pressure and coercion from the employer or other interested persons). [*See, generally,* DOL Adv Op Ltr to Helmuth Fandl, Avon Products, Inc (Feb 23, 1988); DOL Adv Op Ltr to John Welsh, Carter Hawley Hale Stores, Inc Profit Sharing Plan (Apr 30, 1984)] In the event that the participants are subject to undue coercion, the trustee is required under ERISA to ignore the participant's decisions and act in the best interest of the participants. [See, e.g., Central Trust Co, NA v American Avents Corp, 771 FSupp 871, 874, 875 (SD Ohio 1989) (ESOP trustees must discharge their duties by evaluating the best interests of the beneficiaries in the abstract as beneficiaries, not as directors who may lose control of the company, nor as employees some of whom may lose their jobs if control of the company changes hands. "Pass-through voting is not improper per se, but is inappropriate when the exercise thereof conflicts with the fiduciary obligations imposed by ERISA." This case recognized that in certain circumstances, trustees should not follow the directions of plan participants.)]

> **Note.** Most troublesome for an ESOP trustee is the DOL position that a trustee remains responsible for determining whether an ERISA violation would occur if the participants' directions were followed, even in the case of allocated shares. [DOL Op Ltr on Tender Offers, Polaroid (February 23, 1989), footnote 2]
>
> **Example.** In the 1989 South Bend Lathe, Inc. (SBL) shareholder election, SBL's ESOP committee decided not to solicit proxies from SBL retirees, believing that the ESOP documents did not require such solicitation. Furthermore, the committee decided to direct the voting trustee to abstain from voting the ESOP's unallocated shares, as well as shares that were not voted by individual participants. As a result, 15,500 ESOP-held shares were not voted

in 1989. The plaintiffs alleged that the committee and Mr. Van Otterloo manipulated the voting of these shares and breached their fiduciary duties in their effort to pass management proposals, and thereby failed to act solely in the ESOP participants' interest as required under ERISA.

The court held that under the plan document and applicable law, the retirees did not have a right to be solicited to vote in the shareholder's meeting. The court concluded that "to say that all SBL retirees are participants in the ESOP" is not to say that all must be solicited to vote. . . . "Neither ERISA nor the committee's customs or traditions required the committee to solicit proxies from all participants."

Furthermore, the court held that it has not been persuaded that anything would forbid instructing the shares' abstention under appropriate circumstances. The court stated that the decision to abstain rather than to vote was not, standing alone, a breach of fiduciary duty. Nevertheless, the court agreed with plaintiffs that the manner in which the committee defendants exercised their discretion concerning solicitation and voting violated its fiduciary duties under ERISA. The court held that "[b]ecause the committee defendants did not engage in the sort of inquiry required of them for decisions in which their loyalties were divided . . . the plaintiffs are entitled to judgment as a matter of law against those defendants as a result of those decisions." [Newton v Van Otterloo, 756 FSupp 1121 (ND Ind 1991)]

Planning Pointer. Plan and trust documents may be drafted in various different ways to provide how unexercised but allocated shares should be voted. The following approaches have been utilized:

- Vote allocated but unexercised shares in proportion to voting of allocated and exercised shares.
- Treat unexercised as an abstention by the participant.
- Have the trustee exercise discretion under ERISA in voting unexercised allocated shares.

In instances where the first or second approach are incorporated into plan and trust documents, fiduciaries should be aware that the general rules of prudence and exclusive benefit will override the plan terms requiring a proportionate vote or total abstention. While the documents could specifically state how the shares should be voted, such documents should also state that such specific voting requirement is "subject to ERISA."

Q 7:37 How does a fiduciary vote the shares of QES held in the ESOP's loan suspense account that are not allocated to participants?

As explained above with respect to allocated shares (regardless of whether actually voted by participants), a fiduciary is obligated to vote shares of QES in accordance with the duty of prudence and the exclusive benefit rule. In fact, even if the plan document instructs the fiduciary as to how the shares should be voted, the duty of prudence and the exclusive benefit rule will override the duty to follow the written terms of the plan. Since the shares are unallocated, the fiduciary is obligated to vote in the best interest of participants (since there is no participant direction).

Q 7:38 What must a fiduciary of a plan that contains QES do when confronted with a tender offer, hostile takeover, corporate control contest, or other potential conflict of interest?

There are no specific requirements under ERISA's fiduciary responsibility rules regarding what a fiduciary (who is vested with the power to vote or tender shares of QES) must do when confronted with a tender offer, hostile takeover, corporate control contest, or other corporate event involving a potential conflict of interest. However, courts have held that where the interests of fiduciaries irreconcilably conflict with the interests of participants, the fiduciaries should seek the advice of independent legal, financial, and investment counsel. [Donovan v Bierwirth, 680 F2d 263 (2d Cir 1982), *cert denied*, 459 US 1069 (1982)] Certain situations may be so egregious as to virtually necessitate that fiduciaries resign or recuse themselves and be replaced by independent fiduciaries—even in situations where the fiduciaries already obtained independent advice (see Qs 6:46–6:49 regarding recusal and conflicts of interest).]

Note. If fiduciaries with conflicts do not resign, they may face the difficult task of proving that they complied with ERISA fiduciary requirements. Although certain facts and circumstances may dictate otherwise, it is generally advisable to utilize independent fiduciaries, appraisers (which the Code requires for annual valuations) and consultants. [*See, e.g.,* Donovan v Cunningham, 541 FSupp 276 (SD Tx 1982), *aff'd in part and rev'd in part*, 716 F2d 1455 (5th Cir 1983), *cert denied,* 467 US 1251 (1984); Leigh v Engel, 727 F2d 1113 (7th Cir 1984) *remanded,* 669 FSupp 1390 (ND Ill 1985), *aff'd,* 858 F2d 361 (7th Cir 1988), *cert denied,* 489 US 1078 (1989)]

With regard to tender offers, ERISA requires plan fiduciaries to make investment decisions—such as tender offer decisions—based on the facts and circumstances applicable to the investment and the plan. Fiduciaries are required to take the course of action that is in the economic best interest of the plan, recognizing that the plan is a legal entity designed to provide retirement income and is *not* designed to make a "quick buck" if they believe (based on an appropriate and objective analysis) the plan can achieve a higher economic value by holding the shares than by tendering the shares and reinvesting the proceeds. [Opening Statements by M. Peter McPherson (Deputy Secretary of the Treasury) and David Walker (Asst. Secretary, PWBA), DOL Press Briefing on ERISA and Takeovers (Jan 31, 1989) and Joint DOL/Dept. of Treasury Statement on Pension Investments (Jan 31, 1989)] For example, fiduciaries may weigh the long-term value of the target company, including the company's long-term business plan. A similar analysis would be involved in evaluating whether to support or oppose a merger that offered the possibility of an immediate gain.

In addition, as noted in the case of voting, there may be situations where the plan fiduciary may be required to override the actions (i.e., voting or tendering decisions) of participants. [See Danaher Corp, DH v Chicago Pneumatic Tool Co, 635 FSupp 246, 249 (SDNY 1986) (It would be inappropriate (and perhaps a breach of fiduciary obligation) for an ESOP trustee to put aside his personal judgment in favor of carrying out the wishes of the ESOP participants. "It appears that the trustees must discharge their duties by evaluating the best interests of beneficiaries in the abstract as beneficiaries. The duty cannot be discharged simply by consulting and carrying out the expressed wishes of those whose present position makes them the presumptive beneficiaries.")] For example, participants may direct the fiduciary not to tender shares because of their fear of losing their jobs. It may be inappropriate in certain circumstances, however, for a fiduciary to follow those instructions.

Social Investing

Certain plans have questioned whether they may consider investments and make investment decisions that utilize social, moral, and other noneconomic criteria. The following questions address the ERISA fiduciary issues that may be considered when a plan wants to implement a policy of "social investing."

Q 7:39 What is "social investing"?

As noted in Question 3:34, social investing has been defined as investing where the principal impetus is not the maximization of investment returns to benefit plan participants or their beneficiaries, but to further some social or other noneconomic policies or goals. While there is no single definition of this concept, the term "social investing" is generally used to describe an investment strategy or decision pursuant to which a plan fiduciary chooses or avoids certain investments primarily for their potential to affect the community at large or a targeted group of people or region, rather than for the purpose of maximizing monetary return for the plan.

Q 7:40 What are examples of social investing?

Examples of social investments range from community projects (such as low income housing or below market interest rate mortgages) to investments in environmentally sound products. Social investments may include those designed to spur local economies, increase the use of union labor, and to provide jobs to certain groups (including groups potentially comprised of participants in the plan that is making the investment). A social investment strategy may also take the form of abstaining from investing in a particular opportunity, such as a company doing business in a country that supports political (or other) policies with which the fiduciaries of the plan do not agree, or companies that manufacture products which are deleterious to human health (e.g., cigarettes) or environmentally harmful (e.g., certain sectors of the chemical industry).

Q 7:41 May fiduciaries of a plan implement an investment policy that has social underpinnings?

Generally it may not, unless the policy also satisfies ERISA's fiduciary requirements of loyalty to plan participants (e.g., the exclusive benefit rule), prudence and diversification. [ERISA § 404(a)(1)] (See Qs 3:2 through 3:12.) There are no statutory provisions in ERISA or regulations promulgated under ERISA by the DOL that specifically address whether plan fiduciaries may make investment decisions based entirely or partially on social policy concerns.

The DOL has approved social investing in at least one context. [See DOL Adv Op Ltr No 85-36A (Oct 12, 1985) ("A decision to make an investment may not be influenced by a desire to stimulate the construction industry and generate employment, unless the investment, when judged solely on the basis of its economic value to the plan, would be equal or superior to alternative investments available to the plan.")] In most situations, however, a fiduciary who pursues an investment strategy that forgoes maximization of investment return in favor of furthering a social policy or goal violates his or her fiduciary duties under ERISA. In other words, the establishment of an investment strategy that utilizes social or moral criteria in choosing investment opportunities, and does not utilize economic factors as a primary consideration in making investment decisions, probably violates ERISA. [See DOL Reg § 2550.404a-1(b)(2).]

Under limited circumstances, it may be possible for fiduciaries to implement a policy of social investing and select an investment course that reflects noneconomic factors, provided that the application of such noneconomic factors follows a financial and economic based search and analysis that uncovers a number of potential investment opportunities that are ostensibly equally advantageous from an economic perspective. [DOL Adv Op Ltr No 85-36A (Oct 23, 1985)]

Note. Despite the possibility that a policy of social investing may be permissible if plan fiduciaries give primary weight to the economic benefit to the plan of such investments, comments made during the last few years by senior staff members of the DOL and the Pension Benefit Guaranty Corporation indicate that these individuals do not believe that utilization of a social investment strategy comports with the ERISA obligations to invest plan assets for the "exclusive benefit of plan participants" or with their interpretation that ERISA requires plan fiduciaries to maximize investment returns for the sole benefit of plan participants. [*See, e.g.*, "Winning Pending Cases is Main Way to Cut Deficit, New Agency Head Says," *BNA Pension Reporter*, Aug 7, 1989 (reporting James B. Lockhart III, Executive Director of PBGC, as saying that "social investing . . . is contrary to ERISA"); "PWBA Plans to Speak Out on OIG Charges, Ball says," *BNA Pension Reporter*, Dec 18, 1989 (reporting David George Ball, Assistant Secretary of Labor for Pensions and Welfare Benefits, as saying that "ERISA mandates that fiduciaries maximize investment return").]

Since there is little guidance regarding social investing, fiduciaries should proceed very cautiously in pursuing a strategy of social investing. Fiduciaries that implement investment policies that incorporate social or moral criteria as a primary or material consideration (ahead, or in lieu, of prudent economic analyses), could be subject to legal challenge by the DOL or by plan participants and their beneficiaries. [See, e.g., Martin v Rylands, No. 91-157 (D Colo 1991) (complaint filed by the DOL against trustees of Centennial State (Colorado) Carpenters Pension Fund who invested 23 percent of plan assets with an investment manager making investments in construction loans, which investments provided employment for plan participants); Martin v Rocky Mountain Investors, Inc, No. 91-S-1951 (D Colo 1991) (complaint filed by the DOL charging investment manager with violating "exclusive purpose" and "prudent person" requirements of ERISA Section 404 by investing in construction projects with union-only restriction, later settled by consent order entered Nov 12, 1991).] Thus, after consideration of all economic factors necessary for prudence, it is especially important to document the analysis behind a fiduciary's decision to implement a policy of "social investing." Absence of documentation regarding such investments will, in most instances, violate ERISA's "procedural" prudence requirement and will leave the investments open to challenge by the DOL and plan participants.

Example. The trustees of a multiemployer pension plan approved the expenditure of $2.7 million of plan assets for the purchase, development, and leaseback of a parcel of real estate as a site for a shopping mall. The lease between the plan and the developer required the use of a particular union in the construction of the mall. The trustees entered into the transaction without obtaining a feasibility study, checking the developer's credibility, requiring typical and adequate lease commitments, obtaining a market rate of return on the investment, or taking other prudent steps. The DOL filed an action against the trustees for failing to act prudently with respect to this investment despite the fact that the investment would create additional jobs for union members who were also plan participants. The consent order required the trustees to pay $1.6 million to the plan, appointed an investment manager for 15 years, and enjoined the trustees from acting as fiduciaries for a period of ten years. [Dole v Jones, Civ No C-89-96-D (DCNH 1989)]

Q 7:42 Is a plan prohibited from investing in a single geographic area?

Probably, yes. While there is no clear prohibition on such investments, a fiduciary's decision to concentrate plan investments within a single geographic area raises various concerns. While the investment in a plan's own geographic region could spur the local economy, the plan fiduciary must consider all economic and financial factors from the plan's perspective and review alternative investment vehicles without regard to geographic region. Clearly, the investment must be prudent and satisfy the exclusive benefit rule. In addition, even where investments are individually prudent and satisfy the exclusive benefit rule, investments concentrated in a single geographic region in most cases will be held to violate ERISA's diversification requirement (see Q 3:11). [Brock v Citizens Bank of Clovis, 841 F2d 344 (10th Cir 1988), *cert denied*, 488 US 829 (1988) (a high proportion of plan assets invested in mortgage loans within a limited area of New Mexico violated ERISA); Donovan v Guaranty National Bank, 4 EBC (BNA) 1686 (SD WVa 1983) (plan violated diversification requirement when plan invested over 80 percent of its assets in mortgage loans secured by property in and near Huntington, West Virginia).]

Q 7:43 What type of plans have generally followed a strategy of social investing?

A policy of social investing has been implemented by a number of employee benefit funds that are not covered by the requirements of ERISA, such as public pension funds. (See Q 1:3 and 8:1 through 8:14 regarding whether a plan is subject to ERISA) [See, e.g., Barrington Police Pension Fund Trustees v Illinois Ins Dep't, 13 EBC (BNA) 1999 (Ill App Ct 1991) (public pension fund may invest in residential real estate mortgages that benefit fund participants and the local community).] Indeed, some states have enacted statutes that actually require pension plans to implement and follow a policy of social investing. Plans that are not subject to ERISA's fiduciary requirements may implement social investing.

Example 1. Some public funds that are not covered by ERISA have instituted the following social investment actions:

- Divested their holdings in U.S. companies doing business in South Africa or Northern Ireland.

- Bailed out New York City [Withers v Teachers' Retirement Sys of City of New York, 447 FSupp 1248 (SDNY 1978), *aff'd*, 595 F2d 1210 (2d Cir 1979) (Trustee's decision to buy highly speculative city bonds to stave off city's potential bankruptcy was prudent.)]

- Made investments to reduce the state of Massachusetts' deficit as a means to balance the state budget.

- Made investments in low-cost housing and provided loans at interest rates lower than market rates.

Example 2. Baltimore City passed an ordinance mandating that the city's pension systems remove all funds invested in companies and banks that make loans to (or do business in or with) South Africa or Namibia. Beneficiaries filed suit alleging, among other things, that the divestment impaired the trustees' contractual obligation with the trust fund beneficiaries. The court upheld the ordinance because:

1. The trustees were only required to ensure that beneficiaries earned a reasonable (not optimal) rate of return on plan investments;

2. The trustees were not in violation of their duty of loyalty to the beneficiaries because they could reasonably determine that the social investing best served the beneficiaries' long-term interest; and
3. Divestment did not impair the trustees' duty of prudence, because the trustees still retained a variety of other investment options.

[Board of Trustees of the Employees' Retirement Sys v Mayor of Baltimore City, 11 EBC (BNA) 1521 (Sept 1, 1989), *cert denied*, 493 US 1093 (1990)]

Given the fiduciary and prohibited transaction rules of ERISA, an ERISA-covered plan could not make similar investments as set forth in Example 2, unless they were determined to be prudent under a purely economic investment analysis.

Other Investments

Except as set forth in the prohibited transaction rules (see generally, Chapter 5), ERISA does not generally restrict plans as to the type of investments that they may make with plan assets. A plan may be drafted, however, to restrict the type of investments that a fiduciary may make. Even without any plan-imposed restriction, ERISA requires that plan fiduciaries apply the general fiduciary requirements of prudence, diversification, and exclusive benefit to investment decisions. The following questions set forth additional examples of issues that a plan fiduciary should consider when making certain types of investments.

Q 7:44 Are there any restrictions on a plan's investment in securities?

Generally, no. ERISA does not set forth any specific limit on the amount or percentage of plan assets that may be invested in particular securities, except with respect to employer securities where certain limitations apply. (See Qs 5:29 and 7:27.) In addition, because of the diversification requirement, ERISA may compel—depending upon the applicable facts and circumstances—fiduciaries to diversify plan

Q 7:45   Fiduciary Responsibility Answer Book

assets by investing in funds, vehicles, and financial instruments other than securities.

Q 7:45   Are there special considerations or restrictions that apply to a plan's investment in real estate?

Yes. A number of unique issues arise in connection with a plan's investment in real estate. Real estate investments can take many different forms, such as certain direct investments where the plan holds the real property (e.g., limited partnerships, tax-exempt holding companies, convertible mortgages, or direct ownership) or certain indirect investments, where the investment is not directly related to any particular parcel of real property but derives its value from some underlying interest in real property (e.g., insurance company separate accounts, common trusts, group trusts, or real estate investment trusts (REITs) that invest in real property). Each different form raises varying ERISA fiduciary and other legal concerns.

When a plan intends to invest in real estate, the following areas must be analyzed for potential liabilities and issues:

- *Prohibited transactions*—Certain real estate transactions between a plan and a party-in-interest including, among other things, the sale, exchange, or leasing of property between a plan and party-in-interest, are prohibited under ERISA (see generally Chapter 5 regarding prohibited transactions). Certain routine real estate investment activities are exempt, however, from the prohibited transaction rules. These include, for example, investments in QERP (qualifying employer real property) and situations where plans contract with a party-in-interest for office space necessary for the establishment and operation of the plan if no more than reasonable compensation is paid for the space or the services. [ERISA § 408(b)]

- *Plan assets*—The DOL considers certain investments—particularly real estate partnerships structured with significant ownership by benefit plans—to be "plan assets." If a property interest is a plan asset, it must be held in trust, which may raise some practical problems. [ERISA § 403(a)] Also, if a property interest is a plan asset, the person who exercises any authority or control over that property interest is a fiduciary under ERISA

Investment Issues Q 7:46

[ERISA § 3(21)(A)(i)] Many real estate transactions are structured in a manner so that the entire investment is not deemed to be a plan asset. (See generally Chapter 8 regarding plan assets.)

- *Trust requirements*—Generally, all plan assets must be held in trust (or insurance contracts). This does not necessarily mean that the real property investment must be held in trust; in certain circumstances only the stock of a company that holds the property must be held in trust (or only the plan's interests in the entity must held in trust). [ERISA § 403(a); DOL Reg § 2550.403a-1(b)(2) and (3)]
- *Fiduciary duties*—As noted above under "Plan Assets," it may be possible for certain persons who operate or develop real estate investments to become fiduciaries with respect to a plan if the entire real estate investment is deemed to be a plan asset. In addition, all the ERISA fiduciary concerns relating to the duty of prudence, diversification, and exclusive benefit apply to a plan fiduciary who decides to invest in real estate.
- *Tax considerations*—Special tax consequences—namely, unrelated business income tax (UBIT)—may apply to certain real property investments by qualified plans.

Q 7:46 Are there special considerations or restrictions that apply to a plan's investment in a bank?

Yes. The following special considerations apply to a plan's investments in a bank:

1. *Prudence and diversification.* The requirements of prudence and diversification may not be violated if all plan assets are invested in a federally-insured account, so long as the investments are fully insured. [HR Conf Rep No 1280, 93d Cong, 2d Sess 313 (1974) *reprinted in* 1974 US Code Cong & Admin News 5038, 5094] The DOL has taken the position that the diversification requirement under ERISA permits the investment of all the assets of an individual account plan in savings accounts of a mutual savings bank where the account balance exceeds the amount covered by federal (FDIC) insurance, assuming that the bank invested its assets in a diversified manner. To the extent

that investments are not in excess of the amount covered by federal insurance, the diversification standard will not be violated, as there cannot be large losses. [DOL Adv Op Ltr No 77-46, National Ass'n of Mutual Savings Banks (June 7, 1977)]

2. *Federal insurance coverage.* Federal Deposit Insurance Corporation (FDIC) coverage provides federal insurance for certain deposits held by certain plans in federally-insured institutions. FDIC coverage is available—on a "pass-through" basis—to all interests of participant account balances or their accrued benefits held through the plan that are aggregated and subject to the maximum average insurance available, which is $100,000. This means that "pass-through" insurance coverage is generally $100,000 per participant and not $100,000 per plan. Accounts that are owned in different manners (*e.g.*, a personal savings account and an individual account under a defined contribution plan) are insured separately (provided that certain requirements are met) and accounts owned in the same way (*e.g.*, two separate accounts under a defined contribution plan) are added together and insured up to $100,000 in the aggregate. [FDIC Reg 12 CFR § 330.12 (May 25, 1993)] Only vested interests of participants in certain plans are insured (this differs from the prior rules, which insured both vested and unvested amounts). Deposits held by a trust under a defined benefit plan (or a defined contribution plan) are allocated *pro rata* based on the present value of their interests in the plan (or account values) as of the date of the insured institution's default. [FDIC Regulation § 12 CFR § 330.12(a) (May 25, 1993)]

Example. Howard has an account balance of $20,000 in the Swan USA Company's profit-sharing plan, which has assets totalling $2 million. The First National Sleazy Bank, in which the plan has an account with a balance of $100,000, defaults. Howard's account balance is divided by the total plan assets. The resulting percentage (1 percent) is multiplied by the account balance of the defaulted Sleazy Bank. The resulting sum ($1,000) is the value attributable to Howard. [FDIC Int Rel FDIC 90-14 (Mar 27, 1990)]

FDIC insurance coverage is unavailable on a "pass-through" basis for certain contingent interests (e.g., those not capable of determination without evaluation for contingencies) in plans or for deposits allocable to the overfunded portion of a pension plan. [12 CFR § 330.12(g) (May 25, 1993)] FDIC insurance for such funds in the aggregate is $100,000. However, due to recent changes, FDIC "pass-through" deposit insurance is available to plans qualifying under Section 457 of the Code (a deferred compensation plan established by certain state and local governments and not-for-profit organizations) even if participants in these plans are deemed to have contingent interests.

Deposits in undercapitalized institutions and certain adequately capitalized institutions not authorized by the FDIC to accept brokered deposits will be covered only to $100,000 per plan, not $100,000 per participant. There are certain ways that the $100,000 per participant coverage can apply to an institution that cannot accept brokered deposits.

Note. The FDIC does not publicize its list of insured institutions that are ineligible to accept brokered deposits, but the FDIC staff is considering ways to inform depositors when an institution becomes undercapitalized and, therefore, cannot provide pass-through insurance coverage. [FDIC, Gen Counsel's Ltr Re: Final Rules Affecting Insurance Coverage of Certain Retirement and Other Employee Benefit Plan Accounts (May 28, 1993)]

3. *Bank Investment Contracts (BICs).* The FDIC recently amended its regulations to provide that BICs with "benefit-responsive" features (e.g., any withdrawal or transfer of funds during the period the guaranteed rate is in effect, without substantial penalty or adjustment, to pay benefits provided by the plan or to permit a participant to redirect the investment of his or her account balance) do not receive FDIC coverage, while BICs without benefit-responsive features and other types of deposit instruments (e.g., regular CDs) acquired by plans would still be insured. [FDIC Reg § 12 CFR 330.13 (May 25, 1993)]

Q 7:47 May a plan fiduciary invest in futures?

Generally, yes. However, plans that engage in futures contract trading (e.g., financial futures such as Treasury bonds and notes,

GNMA certificates, commercial paper, etc.) must be wary of potential prohibited transactions. [DOL Adv Op Ltr No 82-049A (Sept 21, 1982)]. In addition, as is the case with all investments, they must be prudent.

Q 7:48 Are there special considerations and restrictions on investing in foreign securities?

Yes. Although ERISA Section 404(b) provides that plan fiduciaries may not maintain or transfer the indicia of ownership of plan assets outside the jurisdiction of U.S. district courts, investments in the securities of foreign companies and governments may be an appropriate plan investment. If assets are managed and controlled by a corporation or partnership that is a bank, insurance company, or registered investment advisor, is organized under state or federal law, that meets certain net worth and financial responsibilities, and has its principal place of business in the U.S., a plan can maintain a broad indicia of ownership of the following:

- Securities issued by a person that is not organized under state or federal law and does not have its principal place of business in the U.S.
- Securities issued by a foreign government (or its agencies).
- Securities where the principal trading market is outside the U.S.
- Foreign currency kept outside of the U.S. jurisdiction. [DOL Reg § 2550.404b-1]

The indicia of ownership may be in the physical possession of, or in transit to, the fiduciary described above, or may be maintained by a broker or dealer that meets SEC requirements, or a foreign securities depository, clearinghouse, or government regulated bank. [DOL Reg § 2550.404b-1; DOL Adv Op Ltr No 84-14A (Mar 16, 1984) (clearinghouse system for foreign-traded securities qualifies as a "foreign clearing agency which acts as a securities depository," which plan fiduciaries may use without violating Section 404(b) of ERISA, subject to certain requirements)]

Q 7:49 Are there any special concerns that apply to investments made by very large pension plans?

Given the size of certain pension trusts (e.g., those with asset bases in the several billion dollar range), prudence under ERISA may require fiduciaries of such plans to seek out and consider nontraditional investments in addition to its more traditional trust investments, especially if other large ERISA plans maintain similar investments. [See, e.g., PTE 90-42, 55 Fed Reg 28,956 (General Motors Retirement Program for Retired Employees, July 16, 1990).] This does not mean that every investment in which other large ERISA plans invest is *per se* prudent. Rather, consideration of each particular investment should be based on the procedural and substantive requirements of prudence under ERISA.

The fiduciary of a large plan with access to sophisticated investment and legal advice can be expected to have access to the same techniques—including sophisticated, nontraditional techniques of enhancing return and reducing risk—to which fiduciaries of similar ERISA plans have access. Indeed, an argument could be made that the fiduciary of a large plan may be obligated under the ERISA standard of prudence to use such sophisticated, nontraditional techniques as the "alternative" investments against which the prudence of more traditional investments is measured.

Q 7:50 Are there any special rules that apply to investments by small plans?

No, there are no special rules that apply. However, given ERISA's diversification requirements, it may make sense for plans with a small amount of assets to invest in "look-through" vehicles (e.g., mutual funds) in order to better diversify the plan. (See Q 4:33 regarding ERISA Section 404(c)'s requirement for small plans to invest in look-through vehicles.)

Chapter 8

Plan Trusts and Plan Assets

Determining fiduciary responsibility under ERISA depends heavily on the definitions of key terms such as ERISA plan, plan assets, and control over plan assets. This chapter covers the issues surrounding such definitions and how they relate to fiduciary responsibility. Also covered in this chapter are the ERISA trust requirements, including the powers and duties assigned to plan trustees, and a discussion of the important look-through rule and the exceptions to it.

Plans Subject to ERISA Fiduciary Rules	8-2
Plan Assets	8-13
Plan in Writing	8-17
General Trust Requirements	8-19
Powers and Duties of Trustees	8-29
Exclusive Benefit and Anti-Inurement	8-33
Look-Through Rule	8-37
Operating Companies	8-42
Joint Ownership and Investment Pools	8-47
Miscellaneous Plan Asset Issues	8-49
Bonding	8-51

Plans Subject to ERISA Fiduciary Rules

Q 8:1 In general, what types of plan are subject to fiduciary rules under ERISA?

In general, the fiduciary rules under ERISA apply to any plan, fund, or program, whether formally a plan in writing or not (see Qs 8:24 through 8:26), that is an "employee welfare benefit plan" (see Qs 8:8 through 8:11) or "employee pension benefit plan" (see Qs 8:4 through 8:7) maintained by an employer (or a union, or both) engaged in interstate commerce, for its employees (or members), unless expressly exempted. [ERISA §§ 3(1) through (3), 4(a) and (b), 401(a)]

Q 8:2 What other fiduciary rules apply if an employee benefit arrangement is not subject to the ERISA fiduciary responsibility rules?

Fiduciary rules under state law, federal common law (or statutes other than ERISA), or foreign law may apply; it is possible that no fiduciary rules will apply. If a plan is not subject to ERISA, however, the advantage of preemption is lost. [ERISA § 514] (See the discussion of preemption at Qs 3:32 and 3:33.)

Q 8:3 Is a plan without common law employees subject to the ERISA fiduciary rules?

No. A plan such as a Keogh or H.R. 10 plan whose participants include only self-employed individuals such as partners is not subject to Title I of ERISA. An individual and his or her spouse are not treated as employees of any incorporated or unincorporated trade or business wholly owned by the individual, or wholly owned by the couple. Partners and their spouses are also not considered employees of the partnership for ERISA's fiduciary responsibility rules. If common-law employees other than the spouses of self-employed individuals are also participants in a plan, the plan covers employees and is therefore subject to the ERISA fiduciary rules. [ERISA 3(3); DOL Reg § 2510.3-3(b) and (c)]

Example. Helene owns her business as a sole proprietor, and pays her husband a salary for bookkeeping. She treats her husband as an employee for all tax purposes, but she has no other employees. Helene and her husband are the only participants in a money purchase pension plan. The plan does not cover any employees and so is not subject to the fiduciary responsibility rules of ERISA.

Q 8:4 What is an employee pension benefit plan?

In general, an employee pension benefit plan, or pension plan, subject to ERISA is any plan, fund, or program established or maintained by an employer or employee organization (or both) to the extent that it:

- Provides retirement income to employees; or
- Defers employees' compensation at least until covered employment is terminated.

[ERISA § 3(2)(A)]

The DOL has provided a number of significant exemptions and exceptions, as summarized in this chapter. For example, bonus arrangements are not pension plans, unless payments are systematically deferred until the termination of covered employment. [DOL Reg § 2510.3-2(c)]

Q 8:5 Is a severance pay plan a pension plan or a welfare plan subject to ERISA or is it a non-ERISA plan?

A severance pay plan is an ERISA pension plan unless it either satisfies a safe harbor making it a welfare plan (subject to ERISA), or is an individual employment arrangement or a one-time payment arrangement that is not subject to ERISA.

Also, as discussed in Q 8:13, there are several types of employee pension and welfare plans (including severance pay plans) that are not subject to ERISA.

If the severance pay plan is not subject to ERISA, it is, of course, not subject to any of the requirements under ERISA, including ERISA's fiduciary responsibility rules. If the severance pay plan is a welfare plan and not a pension plan, it is subject to ERISA's reporting and disclosure, fiduciary responsibility and administration and enforcement rules; however, it is not subject to ERISA's participation, vesting, trust and funding rules. If the severance pay plan is a pension plan, it is subject to all of ERISA's requirements, including the participation, vesting, trust and funding rules. [ERISA §§ 4, 201, 301, and 401]

This is a developing area of the law. The DOL has found a severance pay plan to be governed by ERISA when an employer entered into a severance arrangement with only one individual. The arrangement was with the employer's general counsel as consideration for acceptance of employment and an accompanying move across the country. [DOL Adv Op Ltr No 91-02A (July 2, 1991)] However, a severance pay plan offering a one-time payment does not constitute an ERISA plan if there is no need for an ongoing administrative program. [Fort Halifax Packing Co v Coyne, 482 US 1 (1987)]

Example. In May 1990, an employer informed employees at one location that it was consolidating operations and would discharge employees at that location. On September 15, 1990, the employer orally announced that employees who continued to work until the consolidation was complete would receive 60 days' additional pay following their last day of work. On November 15, 1990, the employer canceled the arrangement. Employees were told they could continue to work for 60 days more at their regular pay. All employees were terminated on January 15, 1991.

The employees asserted state law claims for breach of contract, negligent misrepresentation, and wage violations, as well as a federal claim of ERISA violations.

The Second Circuit Court of Appeals held that state law was not preempted, because the offer of 60 days' severance pay did not constitute an employee welfare plan under ERISA. According to the court, the employer did not have to engage in any "ongoing administrative program" to make the severance payments. [James v Fleet/Norstar Financial Group, 992 F2d 463 (2d Cir 1993), quoting Fort Halifax Packing Co v Coyne, 482 US 1, 11 (1987)]

Q 8:6 Is an individual retirement account or annuity (IRA) a pension plan subject to the fiduciary rules of ERISA?

No. An IRA is exempt from ERISA's fiduciary rules, if the following conditions are met:

1. No contributions are made by the employer or employee organization;
2. Participation is completely voluntary for employees or members;
3. The employer or employee organization does not endorse any part of the program (but may publicize the program, collect contributions, and remit them); and
4. The employer or employee organization receives no form of consideration other than reasonable compensation for services actually rendered in connection with payroll deductions or dues checkoffs.

[DOL Reg § 2510.3-2(d)]

Q 8:7 When is a tax-sheltered annuity program maintained by a tax-exempt employer under Section 403(b) of the Code a pension plan subject to the fiduciary rules of ERISA?

A tax-sheltered annuity program maintained by a tax-exempt employer under Section 403(b) of the Code is a pension plan subject to ERISA's fiduciary rules unless all of the following are satisfied:

1. The purchase of an annuity contract is pursuant to salary reduction agreements;
2. Participation is completely voluntary;
3. All rights can only be enforced by employees, beneficiaries, or their representatives;
4. The employer does not endorse any of the funding media, or receive any payment (other than reasonable reimbursement of actual expenses incurred in performing its duties under the salary reduction agreements);
5. The employer's other involvement is limited to:

Q 8:8 **Fiduciary Responsibility Answer Book**

a. Permitting agents, brokers, and other annuity contractors to publicize their products to employees;
b. Requesting, summarizing, or compiling the information concerning the funding media, products, or annuity contractors;
c. Collecting salary reduction amounts, remitting the amounts to the annuity contractors, and keeping records of collection and remittance;
d. Holding group annuity contracts in its own name; or
e. Limiting the funding media, products, or annuity contractors to a number and selection designed to give employees a reasonable choice in light of all relevant circumstances (including the number of employees affected, the number of contractors who have indicated interest, the variety of available products, the terms of the available arrangements, the administrative burdens and costs to the employer, and the possible interference with employee performance resulting from direct solicitation by contractors); and

6. The employer receives no compensation.

[DOL Reg § 2510.3-2(f)]

Planning Pointer. Agreements with annuity contractors and employee communications should be carefully reviewed by someone independent of the contractor who is familiar with the scope of ERISA. Form letters and boilerplate documents offered by annuity contractors could contain language that would subject an annuity program to ERISA and its fiduciary responsibility rules. Even if the annuity program appears to satisfy all the foregoing requirements, it may also be wise to insert a standard disclaimer stating that the employer does not endorse any annuity product or contractor and is not a fiduciary under ERISA.

Q 8:8   What is an employee welfare benefit plan that is subject to ERISA's fiduciary rules?

In general, an employee welfare benefit plan or welfare plan subject to ERISA's fiduciary rules is a plan, fund, or program providing any of the following:

- Medical, surgical, or hospital care or benefits
- Benefits in the event of sickness, accident, disability, death, or unemployment
- Vacation benefits
- Apprenticeship or other training programs
- Day care centers
- Scholarship funds
- Severance pay (see Q 8:5)
- Prepaid legal services
- Similar benefits, other than retirement income protection

[ERISA § 3(1); DOL Reg § 2510.3-1(a)(2)]

Example 1. An employer provides health coverage for its employees on a self-insured basis. Employees are required to make contributions, by means of pre-tax salary reductions, through a separate cafeteria plan. The health coverage and the separate cafeteria plan are welfare plans subject to ERISA.

Example 2. An employer provides a system of payroll deductions for deposit in savings accounts owned by its employees. This system is not a welfare plan. [DOL Reg § 2510.3-1(a)(2)]

Example 3. An employee assistance program provides referrals for employees to health providers, who then provide treatment of drug and alcohol abuse, stress, anxiety, depression, and similar health and medical problems. According to the DOL, such a program is not a welfare benefit plan subject to ERISA because the employer employs no trained counselors and only provides referrals that an employee could obtain free of charge from other sources. [DOL Adv Op Ltr No 91-26A (July 9, 1991)]

Q 8:9 Are payroll practices treated as welfare plans subject to the fiduciary rules of ERISA?

No. A payroll practice that is not of one of the types described in Q 8:8 is not a welfare plan and is not subject to ERISA. These include:

- Overtime pay

Q 8:10   Fiduciary Responsibility Answer Book

- Shift premiums
- Holiday premiums
- Weekend premiums
- Salary continuation programs paid out of general assets (e.g., paid military or parenting leave, paid vacations and holidays, paid jury duty, paid training periods, and paid sabbaticals)

[DOL Reg § 2510.3-1(b)]

Q 8:10 What types of fringe benefits or welfare programs are not treated as welfare plans?

DOL regulations provide a number of specific exceptions for welfare programs that are not treated as welfare plans, and that are therefore not subject to ERISA:

1. *On-premises facilities.* Facilities such as fitness centers, cafeterias, or first aid stations, for the use of employees (or members of the employee organization). This does not include day-care centers. [DOL Reg § 2510.3-1(c)]

2. *Holiday gifts.* Gifts (such as turkeys) at holiday seasons. [DOL Reg § 2510.3-1(d)]

3. *Sales to employees.* Sales of articles or commodities, whether or not at a discount, that an employer offers for sale in the regular course of business. [DOL Reg § 2510.3-1(e)]

4. *Hiring halls.* A hiring hall facility maintained by one or more employers, employee organizations, or both. [DOL Reg § 2510.3-1(f)]

5. *Remembrance funds.* Contributions to provide flowers, obituary notices, small gifts, and similar remembrances upon occasions such as the sickness, hospitalization, death, or termination of employment of employees (or members of an employee organization) or their family members. [DOL Reg § 2510.3-1(g)]

6. *Strike funds.* Funds by employee organizations for providing payments to their members during strikes and for related purposes. [DOL Reg § 2510.3-1(h)]

7. *Industry advancement programs.* Programs maintained by employers or employer groups, with no employee participants, that do not provide benefits to employees or their dependents (even if the programs serve as a conduit to channel funds to pension or welfare plans covered under ERISA). [DOL Reg § 2510.3-1(i)]

8. *Employee-pay-all insurance.* Group insurance programs offered by an insurer to employees (or members of an employee organization), if:

   a. The employer (or employee organization) makes no contributions;

   b. Participation is completely voluntary;

   c. The employer (or employee organization) does not endorse the program or receive any payment other than reasonable reimbursement for administrative services actually rendered in connection with payroll reductions (dues check-offs); and

   d. The employer's (or employee organization's) involvement is limited to permitting the insurer to publicize the program to employees (or members), collecting premiums through payroll deductions (or dues checkoffs), and remitting them to the insurer. [DOL Reg § 2510.3-1(j)]

Example. An employer provided accidental death and dismemberment insurance to its employees on an employee-pay-all basis. Participation was voluntary. The employer collected and remitted premiums to the insurance company, and received no prohibited consideration from the insurance company. The employer also hired an employee benefits administrator to forward employee claims to the insurance company, publicized the plan as a supplement to the rest of its benefits program, and distributed a "Summary Plan Description" booklet describing the program. The booklet, which had the employer's own name and logo on it, encouraged employees to consider carefully participation in the plan, because it could be a "valuable supplement to . . . existing coverages." In this case, the court held that the employer endorsed the plan, making it ineligible for the employee-pay-all exception. The plan was an ERISA plan. [Hansen v Continental Ins Co, 940 F2d 971 (5th Cir 1991)]

Q 8:11   **Fiduciary Responsibility Answer Book**

9. *Unfunded scholarship programs.* Scholarship programs, including tuition and education expense refund programs, if payments are made solely from the general assets of the employer or employee organization. [DOL Reg § 2510.3-1(k)]

Q 8:11 Are dependent care assistance programs (DCAPs) welfare plans subject to the fiduciary rules of ERISA?

Not unless they are part of a larger plan that is an ERISA welfare plan. A dependent care assistance program provides employees with reimbursement (or direct payment) of eligible dependent care expenses as a benefit excluded from their taxable income. [IRC § 129] The reimbursements or payments may be through a flexible spending account (FSA), as an add-on bonus, or on a salary reduction basis. If the DCAP is done on a pre-tax salary reduction basis, or if there is any alternative taxable benefit, the DCAP must comply with tax law provisions concerning cafeteria plans. [IRC § 125] Whether or not a DCAP is part of a cafeteria plan, the IRS requires annual reporting. [IRC § 6039D]. A DCAP is not subject to ERISA's fiduciary responsibility rules unless it is part of a welfare plan that is subject to those rules.

> **Example.** Tropical Plant Rentals, Inc. provides a DCAP to its employees. The employer pays, out of its general assets, a portion of the child care expenses that employees incur in order to work for the employer. Employees choose the specific day-care arrangements, and the employer then either reimburses valid dependent care expenses or pays the care provider directly; the employer does not itself provide or sponsor a care center. The program is not a welfare benefit plan. [DOL Adv Op Ltr No 88-10A (Aug 12, 1988)]

Q 8:12 Do ERISA's fiduciary responsibility rules apply if a plan is not maintained by an employer or an employee organization?

No. A benefit plan is an employee pension or welfare benefit plan subject to ERISA only if it is maintained by:

1. An employer engaged in commerce or in any industry or activity affecting commerce;

2. Any employee organization(s) representing employees engaged in commerce, or in any industry or activity affecting commerce; or
   3. Both.

[ERISA § 4(a)]

Example. A fraternal lodge without any employees sponsors both a group term life insurance program and a group medical program for its members. The programs are not covered by ERISA or its fiduciary responsibility rules.

Q 8:13 Are any employee pension or welfare benefit plans not subject to ERISA?

Yes. The following types of plans are not subject to ERISA:

1. *Governmental plans.* Plans sponsored by the government of the United States, any state or political subdivision, any agency or instrumentality of the above, or an international organization; or plans covered by the Railroad Retirement Act of 1935 or 1937. [ERISA §§ 3(32), 4(b)(1)]
2. *Church plans.* Plans sponsored by a church or a tax-exempt convention or association of churches for employees not involved in an unrelated (taxable) business, unless the sponsor has made a special coverage election. [ERISA §§ 3(33), 4(b)(2)]
3. *Workers' Compensation.* Plans maintained solely to comply with applicable workers' compensation, unemployment compensation, or disability insurance laws. [ERISA § 4(b)(3)]
4. *Foreign plans.* Plans maintained outside the United States primarily for nonresident aliens. [ERISA § 4(b)(4)]

Example. A pension plan covered 1,564 employees of a business based in England. Only 154 participants (slightly fewer than 10 percent) were U.S. citizens. The DOL ruled that the plan qualified as a foreign plan and was exempt from ERISA. [DOL Adv Op Ltr No 82-38A (Aug 2, 1982)]

5. *Excess benefit plans.* Unfunded plans, or unfunded separable parts of plans, maintained to provide retirement benefits for

Q 8:13 Fiduciary Responsibility Answer Book

certain employees in excess of the limitations on contributions and benefits imposed by Section 415 of the Code.

[ERISA §§ 3(36), 4(b)(5)]

Example 1. An airline had a multibenefit welfare benefit plan that provided some disability benefits required by state law, as well as a variety of other welfare benefits. The U.S. Supreme Court held, among other things, that the plan was a welfare plan and was not exempt from ERISA under Section 4(b)(3) of ERISA because it did not *solely* provide the disability benefits required under state law. Nor was any portion of the plan exempt under Section 4(b)(3). [Shaw v Delta Air Lines, Inc, 463 US 85, 106-108 (1983)]

Example 2. *M* Corporation provides employees located in California with a voluntary disability insurance plan as an alternative to the state-administered plan. California law permits such voluntary disability plans, but only if participants' benefits are greater, and charges to participants are not greater, than those under the state-administered plan; also, any cost savings from operating the alternative plan must be used for the benefit of participants (by reducing future premiums or increasing benefit rates). *M*'s plan provides a higher maximum weekly benefit and charges participants one-sixth less than the state-administered plan. The DOL took the position in an opinion letter that since any cost savings must be used for additional disability benefits, the alternative plan was excluded from ERISA Title I coverage by reason of Section 4(b)(3). [DOL Adv Op Ltr No 90-03A (Feb 13, 1990)]

Example 3. Cheesy Gadget Corporation maintains a retirement plan for its full-time employees. The plan is a defined benefit pension plan. The benefit formula has two separate parts: Part A is funded by a trust, and has a defined benefit formula of 3 percent of high five-year compensation multiplied by years of service up to 30, subject to the limitations of Code Section 415; Part B is an unfunded supplementary employee retirement plan (SERP), and uses the same benefit formula, but minus any benefits made available under Part A. Part B is a pension plan exempt from ERISA. [ERISA § 4(b)(5)]

Q 8:14 Are any employee pension or welfare benefit plans that are subject to ERISA exempt from ERISA's fiduciary responsibility rules?

Yes. Two types of plans are exempt from the fiduciary responsibility rules of ERISA, though they may be subject to other ERISA requirements, such as reporting or disclosure:

1. *Unfunded top hat pension plans.* Unfunded plans maintained primarily for the purpose of providing deferred compensation for a select group of management or highly compensated employees ("top hat" plans). [ERISA § 401(a)(1)]
2. *Partnership retirement agreements.* Agreements described in Code Section 736, providing payments to retired or deceased partners, or deceased partners' successors in interest.

[ERISA § 401(a)(2)]

Example. Cheesy Gadget Corporation maintains an unfunded supplementary executive retirement plan for its CEO, CFO, and 21 out of 68 vice presidents. Without reference to any other benefits under any other plan, and subject only to certain provisions concerning "golden parachutes" [IRC §§ 280G, 4999], the plan provides to any participant a lump sum upon termination or retirement equal to 25 percent of high five-year compensation multiplied by years of service up to ten. The plan is an ERISA plan and is subject to certain reporting requirements, but is not subject to the fiduciary responsibility rules of ERISA. [ERISA § 401(a)(1)]

Plan Assets

Q 8:15 Of what significance is it whether a plan's investment in another entity is a plan asset?

First, plan assets must be segregated from an employer's (or employee organization's) assets, and held in trust. [ERISA § 403(a)] If a plan invests in (or through) an entity that in turn is deemed to be holding plan assets, then DOL regulations would permit the plan to hold the evidence of ownership of the entity (e.g., limited partnership or stock certificates) in trust. [DOL Reg §§ 2509.75-2, 2550.403a-1]

Second, in general, the trustee remains responsible for the investment of plan assets. Except if the trustee is subject to the proper directions of a named fiduciary as designated in the plan documents, or if the trustee's authority has been duly and expressly delegated to an investment manager, the trustee is responsible to manage and control all plan assets. [ERISA §§ 403(a), 405(b)] (See the discussion of delegation in Chapter 4.) To the extent the trustee has delegated authority over plan assets to another entity (e.g., fund managers), the trustee remains responsible for imprudent investment losses relating to assets, including those assets over which the trustee has no practical control.

Third, to the extent the trustee has given authority over plan assets to another entity, the trustee may also bear co-fiduciary liability for actions of the other entity, or may have breached the trustee's own fiduciary duty through improper delegation. [ERISA § 405(a)]

Fourth, plan fiduciaries generally must be bonded. [ERISA § 412] (See the discussion of bonding at Qs 8:68 and 8:69.) An entity holding plan investments is unlikely to obtain the required bonding if it did not contemplate being a fiduciary with respect to plan assets.

Finally, there are certain restrictions on the payment of plan expenses from plan assets. (See the discussion of plan expenses at Qs 8:18 through 8:22.)

Q 8:16 In general, when are participant contributions considered plan assets?

Amounts (other than union dues) paid by a participant or beneficiary or withheld from wages for contribution to a plan are generally treated as plan assets as of the earliest date on which such contributions can reasonably be segregated from the employer's general assets. That date will be not more than 90 days after such amounts are received by the employer, or would otherwise have been paid to the participant in cash. [DOL Reg § 2510.3-102(a)]

Q 8:17 Are participant contributions to a cafeteria plan or contributory welfare plan treated as plan assets?

Yes, but the DOL has suspended enforcement of certain of the consequences. In theory, participant contributions to a cafeteria plan or contributory welfare plan become plan assets when they can be segregated from the employer's general assets (see Q 8:16), and then become subject to the requirement that plan assets be held in trust. [ERISA § 403(a)] In theory, the plan then also may become subject to the audit requirement (i.e., the requirement that, on the annual Form 5500 return of a plan with 100 or more participants, an independent certified public accountant must review and express an opinion on the plan's financial statements). [ERISA § 103(a)(3); DOL Reg § 2520.103-1(b)(5)] The DOL has suspended enforcement of the trust and audit requirements for cafeteria plans, and also for contributory welfare plans that exclusively have third-party insurance or HMO arrangements and forward contributions to the insurance or HMO companies within three months of collection or payroll reduction. [DOL Tech Rel No 92-01 (June 2, 1992), superseding DOL Tech Rel No 88-1 (Aug 12, 1988)] (See Q 8:35.)

Note that the suspension apparently does not apply to contributory self-insured welfare plans, unless they also are cafeteria plans under Code Section 125.

Q 8:18 May plan expenses be paid out of plan assets?

In general, yes. ERISA requires that plan assets be used exclusively to pay benefits to participants and their beneficiaries, and to defray the reasonable expenses of administering the plan. [ERISA § 404(a)] Accordingly, plan assets may be used to pay direct plan expenses that are reasonably related to plan administration and authorized by the plan. However, plan assets may not be used for settlor expenses. (See Q 8:20.)

Plan fiduciaries must also discharge their duties in accordance with the documents governing the plan (to the extent those documents are consistent with ERISA), must not engage in certain prohibited transactions, and must not deal with the plan as an adverse party. [ERISA §§ 404(a), 406(a) and (b)] Reasonable compensation may be paid to a party in interest (including a fiduciary) for services rendered for the plan. [ERISA § 408(b)(2)]

Q 8:19 What are the consequences if plan assets are used to pay improper expenses?

The improper payment of expenses from plan assets can result in any one or more of the following consequences:

1. A breach of fiduciary duty (e.g., prudence);
2. A prohibited transaction; and
3. A violation of the exclusive benefit requirement under the Code.

Q 8:20 What are settlor expenses?

Settlor expenses are expenses that relate to the business activities and decisions of the employer (settlor functions) and are not properly payable from plan assets. [DOL Info Ltr to Kirk Maldonado (Mar 2, 1987)] (See the discussion of settlor functions at Qs 3:18 through 3:21.)

Q 8:21 Should the plan documents provide that plan expenses may be paid out of plan assets?

Generally, yes, unless the parties have an agreement that the employer will pay expenses directly. Every plan must specify the basis upon which payments are made to and from the plan. [ERISA § 402(b)(4)] Plan fiduciaries also have a duty to act in accordance with the plan documents. [ERISA § 404(a)(1)]

Q 8:22 What are direct plan expenses?

To the extent that a plan fiduciary provides services to a plan (e.g., if an employer who is a fiduciary requests reimbursements for its own expenses relating to plan administration), only direct expenses can be reimbursed without violating the prohibited transaction rules of ERISA Section 408(b). Direct expenses do not include expenses that would have been incurred had the service not been provided, nor an allocable share of overhead costs. [DOL Adv Op Ltr No 89-09A (June 13, 1989)]

Q 8:23 Can a part of an insurance policy be a plan asset for fiduciary purposes, even though it is not a plan asset for prohibited transaction purposes?

Yes, according to the Second Circuit. An insurance contract issued to a retirement plan is a guaranteed benefit policy to the extent it provides for benefits guaranteed by the insurer. [ERISA § 401(b)(2)(B)] A guaranteed benefit policy is effectively exempt from the look-through rule. (See Qs 8:32 and 8:52.) However, an insurance contract is not exempt from the look-through rule to the extent any portion of the plan benefits funded by the contract are not guaranteed. The assets of the insurer corresponding to the nonguaranteed benefits are therefore plan assets. The insurer is a plan fiduciary with respect to those assets, even though the assets are not plan assets for purposes of the prohibited transaction rules. [Harris Trust & Sav Bank v John Hancock Mut Life Ins Co, 970 F2d 1138 (2d Cir 1992), *cert denied,* 113 SCt 1585 (as to holding that insurer was not ERISA fiduciary for guaranteed portion), *cert granted,* 113 SCt 1576 (1993) (as to holding that insurer is ERISA fiduciary for nonguaranteed portion)]

Plan in Writing

Q 8:24 Can an unwritten policy be an ERISA plan?

Yes, if the benefits provided under the unwritten policy are pension benefits (see Qs 8:4 through 8:7) or welfare benefits (see Qs 8:8 through 8:11). A failure or refusal to put an ERISA plan in writing violates ERISA, but does not remove the plan from ERISA coverage. [ERISA § 402(a) and (b); Adams v Avondale Indus, Inc, 905 F2d 943 (6th Cir) *cert denied,* 498 US 984 (1990) (unwritten severance plan enforceable under ERISA)]

Q 8:25 Can informal documents provide the terms of a plan?

The terms of an ERISA plan need not be set forth in one document that is labeled as a plan.

Example 1. James had worked for Fred's company since 1947. In 1981, James and Fred discussed retirement, and Fred presented James with a letter outlining group medical and other benefits payable out of the company's general assets to James upon retirement. In 1984 and 1985, the company stopped paying those benefits. The Eleventh Circuit held that the medical benefits constituted an ERISA welfare plan, even though only one individual was covered, and even though the terms of the plan were in the form of a letter. [Williams v Wright, 927 F2d 1540 (11th Cir 1991)]

Example 2. An employee handbook erroneously listed higher severance pay benefits than the company intended, as a result of a printer's error. The higher benefits were enforceable as an ERISA plan. [Hamilton v Air Jamaica, Ltd, 945 F2d 74 (3d Cir 1991), *cert denied* 112 S Ct 1479 (1992) (employee's claim denied on other grounds)]

Q 8:26 What risks are there if there is no written plan document?

First, a court may disagree with the employer's (or other fiduciary's) determination of what benefits are covered or excluded. Second, a court is likely to review such a determination without the high level of deference that compliance with a formal plan document can provide. (See Qs 6:39 through 6:42.)

Q 8:27 Does the employer bear the risk that written descriptions of plan benefits are incorrect or not up-to-date?

Generally, yes. In one case, for example, an employer announced orally to employees that motorcycle accidents would no longer be covered under its medical plan, but failed to amend the plan documents until after a participant had a motorcycle accident. The participant's coverage was held to include the motorcycle accident. [Confer v Custom Eng'g Co, 952 F2d 41 (3d Cir 1991)] In another case, because of a printer's error, a handbook erroneously listed higher severance pay levels than the employer intended. The higher level was held to be enforceable under ERISA. [Hamilton v Air Jamaica, Ltd, 945 F2d 74 (3d Cir 1991), *cert denied* 112 S Ct 1479 (1992) (claim denied on other grounds)]

Planning Pointer. All written documents and communications relating to any employee benefit plan should be reviewed carefully from a legal standpoint *before* they are distributed, and also periodically *after* distribution. Even if benefit communications are drafted by a professional service provider, such as an actuary or benefits consultant, the agreement with the service provider might not make the sponsor whole for the losses caused by the service provider's errors.

General Trust Requirements

Q 8:28 What is ERISA's trust requirement?

ERISA provides that, in general, all plan assets are to be held in trust by one or more trustees who are responsible for, and have exclusive authority and discretion over, their management and control. [ERISA § 403] Exceptions to the trust requirement are discussed in Qs 8:29 through 8:35. Exceptions to the trustee's exclusive authority and discretion over the management and control of plan assets are discussed in Qs 8:41 through 8:43.

The trust requirement mandates that plan assets be used for the exclusive purposes of providing benefits for participants and their beneficiaries and defraying the reasonable expenses of administering the plan. [ERISA § 403(c)] This rule and the exceptions to this rule are discussed in Qs 8:45 through 8:48.

ERISA's trust provisions also set forth the rules for allocating the assets of welfare plans and certain types of pension plans that are terminated. [ERISA § 403(d)] These rules are discussed in Qs 8:49 through Q 8:50. Discussed in Q 8:47 are the rules relating to the return of residual assets to the employer following the termination of the plan.

Q 8:29 When must assets of employee benefit plans be held in trust?

In general, all assets of employee benefit plans must always be held in trust by one or more trustees. [ERISA § 403(a)] However, the following types of assets of employee benefit plans are exceptions to this rule:

1. Plan assets that consist of insurance contracts or policies issued by an insurance company qualified to do business in a state (See Q 8:30);
2. A plan investment that is considered part of the assets of an insurance company or plan assets that are held by an insurance company (See Q 8:31);
3. Mutual fund investments treated as tax-sheltered annuity contracts and held by a custodian (See Q 8:33); and
4. Assets of Keogh plans maintained for self-employed individuals and their employees, and individual retirement accounts, if the plan assets are held in a custodial account that meets certain criteria under the Internal Revenue Code. (See Q 8:34.)

The DOL has indicated that it will not enforce the trust requirement in the case of participant contributions to cafeteria plans and other contributory welfare plans. (See Q 8:35.) Further, the DOL may also exempt from the trust requirement plans that are not subject to any of ERISA's participation, vesting, funding, or plan termination insurance provisions. Finally, ERISA provides a special exemption from the trust requirements for an unfunded plan, fund, or program operated by an employer, all of whose stock is directly or indirectly owned by present or former employees or their beneficiaries, for purposes of compensating retirees for benefits forfeited under a predecessor employer's plan before it became subject to ERISA. [ERISA § 403; ERISA Tech Rel 92-01]

Q 8:30 What is ERISA's trust exemption relating to plan assets consisting of insurance contracts or policies?

Insurance companies often invest in funds consisting of specified types of securities or real property, and then issue policies and contracts (including annuity contracts) to investors who share in these investments. Plans may invest their assets in these, and plan assets consisting of such contracts or policies, including annuity contracts, issued by an insurance company qualified to do business in a state or the District of Columbia, need not be held in trust. [ERISA § 403(b)(1); ERISA Conf Comm Rep]

Although these policies and contracts need not be held in trust, the person who holds such a policy or contract is nevertheless a fiduciary and must act in accordance with ERISA's fiduciary responsibility rules. For example, this person is to prudently maintain exclusive control of the policy or contract and must use prudent care and skill to preserve this property. [ERISA Conf Comm Rep]

Q 8:31 What is ERISA's trust exemption relating to plan assets of or that are held by an insurance company?

If a plan investment is considered to be part of the assets of an insurance company, or if plan assets are held by an insurance company, they need not be held in trust by the plan. [ERISA § 403(b)(2)] However, if assets held by an insurance company are considered to be plan assets, the insurance company is to be treated as a fiduciary with respect to the plan and must satisfy the fiduciary responsibility rules under ERISA. [ERISA Conf Comm Rep] (See Q 8:32 for a discussion of whether the underlying assets of an insurance company that issues group annuity contracts in which plans invest are considered plan assets.)

Q 8:32 Are the underlying assets of an insurance company that issues group annuity contracts in which plans invest considered plan assets?

Under certain circumstances, yes. If assets of an insurance company are considered to be plan assets, the insurance company will be a plan fiduciary with respect to any of its own assets that are considered plan assets, since it exercises control over them. (See Q 2:1 for a discussion of who is a fiduciary.)

If an insurance company issues a guaranteed benefit policy, the assets of the plan include the policy but do not include any of the assets of the insurance company. A guaranteed benefit policy is an insurance policy or contract that provides for benefits in an amount guaranteed by the insurer. [ERISA § 401(b)] Thus, amounts held in an insurer's separate accounts that are maintained solely in connection with fixed contractual obligations will not be plan assets if the amount payable to the plan or the participant is not affected by the

Q 8:32   **Fiduciary Responsibility Answer Book**

investment performance of the separate account. [DOL Adv Op Ltr No 83-51A (Sept 21, 1983)] Further, if an insurer's general account policy provides payments guaranteed by the insurance company, the insurer's assets will not be plan assets. [ERISA § 401(b)]

If the assets backing a group annuity contract issued by an insurance company to a plan are placed in a separate account that provides for the crediting of income on the group annuity contract based on the investment performance of the separate account, then the assets of the separate account are considered to be plan assets. Such a separate account that is ultimately applied to provide fixed annuities to participants would not be considered to be maintained in connection with a fixed contractual obligation of the insurance company (i.e., it would not be considered a guaranteed benefit policy). Thus, plan assets do not lose their status as such merely because the ultimate use of the account may be to provide fixed annuities. [DOL Adv Op Ltr No 83-51A (Sept 21, 1983); Harris Trust and Sav v John Hancock Mut Life Ins Co, 970 F2d 1138 (2d Cir 1992) *cert denied,* 113 S Ct 1585 (as to holding that insurer was not ERISA fiduciary for guaranteed portion), *cert granted,* 113 SCt 1576 (1993) (as to holding that insurer is ERISA fiduciary for nonguaranteed portion)]

If a policy or contract guarantees basic payments, but other payments vary with, for example, investment performance, then the variable part of the policy or contract and its associated assets are not considered guaranteed and are considered plan assets subject to ERISA's fiduciary rules. [ERISA Conf Comm Rep] Even if all the assets of the group annuity contract are held in an insurer's general account and a portion of the benefits offered under the contract is guaranteed, the nonguaranteed portion of such general account (i.e., the assets of the insurance company) is considered a plan asset and the insurer is subject to ERISA's fiduciary rules. [See, e.g., Harris Trust and Sav v John Hancock Mut Life Ins Co, 970 F2d 1138 (2d Cir 1992) *cert denied,* 113 S Ct 1585 (as to holding that insurer was not ERISA fiduciary for guaranteed portion), *cert granted,* 113 SCt 1576 (1993) (as to holding that insurer is ERISA fiduciary for nonguaranteed portion)]

Note that this rule is different as to prohibited transactions. If an insurance company issues a policy or contract to a plan and places the premium or other consideration paid by the plan into its own general asset account, the general asset account would not be considered a plan asset for prohibited transaction purposes. [Harris Trust and Sav v John Hancock Mut Life Ins Co, 970 F2d 1138 (2d Cir 1992) *cert denied,* 113 S Ct 1585 (as to holding that insurer was not ERISA fiduciary for guaranteed portion), *cert granted,* 113 SCt 1576 (1993) (as to holding that insurer is ERISA fiduciary for nonguaranteed portion), and DOL Reg § 2509.75-2(b)]

See Q 7:21 for a discussion regarding the terms general account guaranteed investment contracts (GICs) and separate account GICs issued by insurance companies.

Q 8:33 What is ERISA's trust exemption relating to mutual fund investments treated as tax-favored annuity contracts?

A trust is not required in the case of plan assets invested by tax qualified plans of tax-exempt organizations described in Code Section 501(c)(3), or of public educational organizations in the stock of regulated investment companies (i.e., mutual funds). These investments are treated as amounts contributed to an annuity contract under the Internal Revenue Code. In order to be subject to this exemption, the investment must be held in a custodial account by a bank or another entity that is approved by the Secretary of the Treasury to hold the assets. [ERISA § 403(b)(5); IRC § 403(b)(7)]

The custodian of those assets is treated as a fiduciary for purposes of the Internal Revenue Code and ERISA. [IRC § 401(f) and ERISA Conf Comm Rep]

Q 8:34 What is ERISA's trust exemption relating to assets of Keogh plans and individual retirement accounts?

Assets of Keogh plans (i.e., tax qualified retirement plans covering self-employed individuals and their employees) and of individual retirement accounts (IRAs) need not be held in trust if they are held in custodial accounts that qualify under the Internal Revenue Code. [ERISA § 403(b)(3)] A custodial account is qualified if it meets the following two requirements:

1. The custodial account would be a qualified trust, if it were a trust; and
2. The assets are held by a bank or another entity that is approved by the Secretary of the Treasury to hold the assets.

The entity holding the assets of the custodial account is treated as a plan trustee and shares the same types of responsibilities as the trustees of trusts under qualified plans. [ERISA §§ 401(f) and 401(h)]

Q 8:35 Must cafeteria plans and contributory welfare plans hold participant contributions in trust?

Not under current DOL policy, which suspends the trust requirement for these types of plans. [ERISA Tech Rel No 92-01 (June 1, 1992)] In 1988, the DOL took the position that certain contributory welfare plans (such as contributory health insurance plans) and cafeteria plans should hold participant contributions in trust as plan assets. (However, a dependent care assistance plan that provides reimbursement and not direct day-care facilities is not a welfare plan, and need not have a trust.) [DOL Adv Op Ltr No 88-10A (Aug 12, 1988)] In response to widespread opposition, the DOL suspended enforcement of its position concerning the trust requirement for cafeteria plans. [ERISA Tech Rel No 88-01 (Aug 12, 1988)] The suspension left it unclear, however, whether the Form 5500 audit requirement still applied to these plans if their assets are not held in trust.

In June, 1992, the DOL clarified its suspension. Any cafeteria plan, or any contributory welfare plan that exclusively has insurance or HMO arrangements, need not hold participant contributions in trust, and if its assets are not held in trust, it generally need not satisfy the audit requirement. This policy will remain in effect until December 31, 1993, unless the DOL adopts final regulations before then. [ERISA Tech Rel No 92-01 (June 1, 1992)]

Q 8:36 May ERISA plans use custodial accounts instead of a trusteed accounts?

Yes. Custodial accounts may be used instead of trusteed accounts by plans subject to the trust requirements. A plan that uses a custodial account will still have to have a trustee, but the trustee may be the plan administrator or sponsor. The plan trustee will have the responsibility for investment decisions with regard to the assets of the plan. The custodian merely retains custody of such assets. [ERISA Conf Comm Rep]

> **Planning Pointer.** Since the plan sponsor can be the trustee, the costs of plan administration should not be higher than if only a custodial account arrangement is used. Thus, costs can be controlled while ensuring that the plan has a responsible person in charge of investment decisions. [ERISA Conf Comm Rep]

Q 8:37   Who may act as a trustee of an ERISA plan?

ERISA does not require a particular type of entity, such as a bank, to act as a trustee. In general, any person may act as a trustee. The trustee may be any individual, organization, bank, or trust company, as long as the appointment of such person does not violate ERISA. Thus, fiduciaries must act prudently in selecting trustees. [ERISA § 404(a)(1)(B)] They must make sure that the trustees are capable of ensuring that the plan assets will be invested prudently. Further, persons convicted of committing certain felonies, such as robbery, bribery, extortion, embezzlement, fraud, grand larceny, burglary, or arson, may not serve as a plan trustee. [ERISA § 411(a)]

The plan sponsor may also designate an investment committee to serve in the role of trustee. For example, the plan may provide that an investment committee consisting of the president, vice president for finance, and comptroller of the employer will direct plan investments. [ERISA Conf Comm Rep]

The advantage of using an individual (i.e., a nonprofessional) trustee is that the plan can save money on the fees that a professional corporate trustee would normally charge. However, there are several advantages to using a corporate trustee. Corporate trustees may be better equipped and will generally be more experienced in handling plan investments and performing other services to the plan. For example, the trustee may assist the company and its attorneys in establishing the plan, safekeep trust assets, maintain records, prepare reports of the fund's performance, determine benefits of participants, and make distributions to participants. Also, since banks and insurance companies (as opposed to individual trustees) are generally exempt from ERISA's bonding requirement, the expense of bonding can be avoided if such entities are used. [ERISA § 412] (See the discussion of bonding at Qs 8:68 and 8:69.)

Planning Pointer. Even smaller companies and plans can obtain professional investment services at a cost that is not prohibitive. For example, small plans can have amounts invested by its trustees on a pooled basis ("pooling" means that a sponsoring bank invests commingled funds in a group trust it holds consisting of contributions of several employers with tax qualified trusts), for which fees are far less expensive than those charged for handling assets invested in individually invested funds. Further, smaller companies may invest in mutual funds, which invest in a highly diversified list of stocks and bonds. A share in a mutual fund represents an indirect ownership interest in a cross section of securities. Pooled funds and mutual funds allow plans to have a wide variety of investment choices under competent management, and at a lower cost.

For an additional discussion regarding plan trustees, see Qs 2:15 through 2:17.

Q 8:38   How are plan trustees appointed?

Trustees may be appointed by being named in a written trust instrument or plan instrument or may be appointed by a person who is a named fiduciary. [ERISA § 403(a)] For a discussion of named fiduciaries see Qs 2:9 through 2:14.

To ensure that persons who act as plan trustees recognize their special responsibilities with respect to plan assets, trustees must accept appointment before they act in such capacity. [ERISA Conf Comm Rep]

Q 8:39   What rules govern the trust agreement, and what are examples of provisions that should be addressed in a trust agreement?

The trust instrument must be in writing. [DOL Reg § 2550 403a-1(a)]

Plan Trusts and Plan Assets   **Q 8:39**

While a detailed description of all the provisions that should be set forth in a trust agreement is beyond the scope of this book, the following are examples of provisions that should be addressed in a trust agreement:

1. An acknowledgement by the plan trustees that they accept appointment to act in such capacity.

2. Whether the trustees are to have custody of the assets in addition to deciding how the assets are to be invested.

3. The powers and duties of trustees with respect to investments. If the employer wishes to restrict the trustees' powers as to investment decisions, such provisions should be set forth in the trust agreement. For example, the trust agreement may provide that no part of the fund may be invested in equities, or that a certain percentage of the funds must be invested in U.S. government securities, or that no more than a certain percentage of the funds may be invested in the securities of any one company.

4. The ERISA standards to which the trustees are subject, such as the exclusive benefit requirement [ERISA § 404(a)(1)(A)], the requirement of prudence [ERISA § 404(a)(1)(C)], limitations on investments in employer securities and employer real property [ERISA § 407], and compliance with the other requirements of ERISA (such as the prohibited transaction rules).

5. That it is impossible for any part of the corpus or income of the trust to be used for, or diverted to, any purpose other than the exclusive benefit of employees and beneficiaries before all liabilities to participants and beneficiaries are satisfied [IRC § 401(a)(2)].

6. The method and time requirements of designating and removing trustees.

7. Representations and warranties of the trustees as to their fitness to act as such.

8. Rules regarding contributions to and disbursements from the trust fund.

9. Trustee compensation and expenses.

10. The allocation of duties among the trustees, the investment manager, the employer, and the plan administrator.
11. The maintenance of records, and the rendering of an accounting.
12. Valuation of trust assets.
13. The method of amending or terminating the agreement.

Of course, the provisions in the trust agreement cannot violate ERISA. Also, while the trustees have the duty to follow the terms of the plan and the trust agreement, they may not follow such instruments if it would result in the trustees' violation of their fiduciary obligations.

Planning Pointer. Since a trust agreement under an ERISA plan is subject to the complex legal requirements imposed by the Internal Revenue Code, ERISA, and other laws, it is prudent to have an attorney who is an ERISA specialist draft or review the trust agreement.

Q 8:40 May securities owned by a plan be held in a street name or in the name of a nominee?

Yes. Securities owned by a plan may be held in a street name or in the name of a nominee (instead of holding the securities in the name of the trustee), provided that the securities are held on behalf of the plan by:

1. A bank or trust company that is subject to supervision by the federal government or a state;
2. A broker or dealer registered under the Securities Exchange Act of 1934;
3. A clearing agency (as defined in the Securities Exchange Act of 1934); or
4. A nominee of any of the above.

[DOL Reg § 2550.403a-1]

Powers and Duties of Trustees

Q 8.41 What are the powers of a trustee as to the management and control of plan assets under ERISA?

In general, trustees have the authority and discretion to manage and control the assets of the plan to the extent provided under the plan's trust instrument. [ERISA §§ 403(a), 403(c)(3), and 404(a)(1)(D)] As discussed in Q 8:39, agreements may provide for varying degrees of control by named fiduciaries over the investment powers of the trustees, or may limit the powers of the trustees.

A trustee is not always a fiduciary. For example, a trustee is not a fiduciary if he or she exercises no discretionary authority and control over plan assets. It is necessary to examine the terms of the trust agreement to ascertain whether the trustee has the requisite management authority or discretion to make the trustee a fiduciary. Thus, where a bank's duties are limited to the simple maintenance of an account and the preparation of associated records, and payments and expenditures are made solely at the direction of the plan's other trustees, the bank generally will not be deemed a fiduciary. [See O'Toole v Arlington Trust Co, 681 F2d 94 (1st Cir 1982)] Likewise, the Department of Labor (DOL) has taken the position in a number of opinion letters that a bank or similar entity is not a fiduciary merely by acting as a custodian of pension fund assets. [See e.g., DOL Adv Op Ltr No 82-049A (Sept 21, 1982)] However, the DOL has stated generally (without rendering an opinion with respect to the status of the entities requesting advice) that a custodian may be a fiduciary to the extent it exercises investment discretion over plan assets or has discretionary authority in the administration of plan assets. [DOL Adv Op Ltr No 82-052A (Sept 28, 1982)]

If the trust agreement provides that the trustee may make only certain types of investments or is subject to the direction of another person (i.e., a named fiduciary), the trustee is bound by such terms and may not make other types of investments. If the trustee does not abide by these directions, the trustee will be liable for any losses resulting from his or her breach of duties. [ERISA § 404(a)(1)(D)] If the trustee follows the terms of the trust agreement in making investments, he or she will generally not be subject to personal liability for plan losses, unless following the terms would violate the normal fiduciary responsibility rules.

ERISA sets forth the following two exceptions to the trustee's exclusive authority and discretion to manage and control plan assets:

1. The plan expressly provides that the trustee is subject to the direction of a named fiduciary who is not a trustee (see Q 8:42 for a discussion of this exception); and
2. The authority to manage, acquire, or dispose of assets of the plan is delegated to one or more investment managers (see Q 8:43 for a discussion of this exception).

Q 8:42 What is the trustee's responsibility with respect to plan assets if the trustee is subject to the direction of a named fiduciary?

If the plan expressly provides that trustees are subject to the direction of a named fiduciary (other than a trustee), then the trustees do not have the exclusive management and control over the plan assets and must generally follow the direction of the named fiduciary. [ERISA § 403(a)(1)] If the plan sponsor wants an investment committee to direct plan investments by the trustees, the plan sponsor may provide for such an arrangement in the plan. [ERISA Conf Comm Rep] Were it not for this exception, trustees could not follow instructions from a named fiduciary without violating their fiduciary responsibility to maintain exclusive control over plan assets.

If a trustee is subject to the direction of a named fiduciary (such as an investment committee) pursuant to the terms of the plan, then the trustee must follow the named fiduciary's directions unless it is clear on their face that the directed actions would be prohibited by ERISA's fiduciary responsibility rules or would be contrary to the terms of the plan or trust. [ERISA § 403(a)(1); ERISA Conf Comm Rep]

To fall within this exception to the trustee's exclusive authority and discretion to manage and control plan assets, the following requirements must be met:

1. The plan document must *expressly* provide that the trustee is subject to the direction of the named fiduciary;
2. The named fiduciary cannot be a trustee of the plan;
3. The directions given by the named fiduciary must be proper (for example, it may be necessary that such orders be given in a prescribed manner, such as in writing, by an authorized person);
4. The directions must be given pursuant to the terms of the plan; and
5. The directions must not contravene any provisions of ERISA.

If the directions given by the named fiduciary to the plan trustee do not meet these requirements, the trustee continues to have exclusive control over the plan assets. In such a case, if the trustee follows the directions of the named fiduciary and the plan incurs a loss, the trustee can be held liable for breaching his or her fiduciary duties to the plan. [ERISA § 403(a)(1); ERISA Conf Comm Rep]

Q 8:43 What is the trustee's responsibility with respect to plan assets if the authority to manage, acquire, or dispose of plan assets is delegated to an investment manager?

If a named fiduciary appoints an investment manager or managers to manage, acquire, or dispose of any assets of the plan, the named fiduciary does not have the exclusive authority and discretion to manage and control such plan assets. [ERISA § 403(a)(2)]

An investment manager is any fiduciary (other than a trustee or named fiduciary) who:

1. Has the power to manage, acquire, or dispose of any assets of the plan;
2. Is either registered as an investment adviser under the Investment Advisors Act of 1940, a bank, or an insurance company qualified to manage plan assets under the laws of more than one state; and
3. Has acknowledged in writing that he or she is a fiduciary with respect to the plan.

[ERISA § 3(38)]

If an investment manager is appointed, the trustee is not liable for any act of the investment manager. The trustee is also relieved of the liability that would attach whenever plan assets are held by co-trustees (i.e., liability resulting from either enabling the other fiduciary to commit a breach, or failing to remedy a known breach of responsibility of the other fiduciary). Furthermore, the trustee (unless he or she is a named fiduciary with respect to management and control of plan assets) does not have the obligation to monitor the performance of the investment manager. (However, the named fiduciary who appoints the investment manager would have the duty of monitoring the performance of the investment manager.) Neither does the trustee have to consider whether the acts of the investment manager are consistent with the terms of the plan and comply with ERISA. However, the trustee would still remain liable for actions of the investment manager if the trustee breaches his or her own fiduciary duties, including knowingly participating in or attempting to conceal an act or omission of the investment manager, knowing that such act or omission is a breach. [ERISA § 405(d)]

If an investment manager is appointed, the trustee is not obligated to invest or otherwise manage (and in fact may not invest or manage, since he or she lacks the authority) any assets of the plan that are subject to the management of the investment manager. [ERISA § 405(d)]

For a further discussion regarding investment managers see Qs 7:1 through 7:8.

Q 8:44 May the responsibilities of a trustee be allocated or delegated?

In general, no. It is the trustee's responsibility to manage and control the assets of the plan. The trustee would not be relieved of his or her responsibilities by the allocation or delegation of such duties, unless such duties are allocated to an investment manager by a named fiduciary as described in Q 8:43. [ERISA § 405(c)]

See Q 3:23 for special co-trustee liability rules that apply when plan assets are held by two or more trustees.

Exclusive Benefit and Anti-Inurement

Q 8:45 What are ERISA's exclusive benefit and anti-inurement rules governing plan assets?

In general, plan assets must be held for the exclusive purposes of providing benefits to participants in the plan and their beneficiaries and defraying reasonable administrative expenses. Further, plan assets may not inure to the benefit of any employer. [ERISA § 403(c)(1)]

This is also a related tax qualification rule under the Internal Revenue Code. The trust instrument must provide that it is impossible for any part of the corpus or income of the trust under the plan to be used for, or diverted to, purposes other than the exclusive benefit of employees or their beneficiaries before all the trust's liabilities to employees and their beneficiaries are satisfied. [IRC § 401(a)(2)]

> **Example.** Plan trustees may not pay gratuitous death benefits to the widow of a plan fiduciary. Since such payment could not be characterized as either compensation for services performed or a reasonable expense of administering the plan, such payments would violate ERISA's exclusive purpose requirement. [DOL Adv Op Ltr No 81-52A (June 15, 1981)]

A violation of the exclusive benefit rule can subject the breaching fiduciary to personal liability for losses to the plan resulting from the breach, and to other appropriate equitable relief. Also, such a breach often is accompanied by a violation or violations of the prohibited transaction rules (such as the prohibition against self-dealing). Violations of these prohibited transactions can subject the breaching fiduciary to substantial excise taxes under Code Section 4975. (See the discussion of prohibited transactions in Chapter 5. For a further discussion of the exclusive benefit rule see Qs 3:2 and 3:3. For exceptions to the exclusive benefit rule see Q 8:46.)

Q 8:46 What are the exceptions to ERISA's exclusive benefit rule?

ERISA permits the return of contributions to an employer under certain circumstances and within a specified time period if:

Q 8:47   **Fiduciary Responsibility Answer Book**

1. The employer made contributions as a result of certain mistakes;
2. The contribution is conditioned on the initial qualification of the plan, and the plan does not so qualify; or
3. The contribution is conditioned upon it being tax deductible, and the IRS disallows the deduction.

Also, withdrawal liability overpayments may be returned to the employer within six months after the date of the determination of such overpayment. [ERISA § 403(c)] The details of these rules are discussed in Qs 5:46 and 5:47.

Further, if the plan so provides, an employer may receive a reversion of residual assets after a single employer pension plan is terminated and all liabilities to plan participants and their beneficiaries are satisfied. (See Q 8:47.)

Also, until the end of taxable years beginning in 1995, it is permissible to transfer excess pension assets to a retiree health account under the plan if certain requirements set forth in the Internal Revenue Code are met. (See Q 8:48.)

Q 8:47   What are the rules governing the reversion of residual plan assets to the employer following the termination of a single employer pension plan?

Upon the termination of a single employer pension plan, any residual assets of such plan that remain after all liabilities of the plan with respect to participants and their beneficiaries have been satisfied may be distributed to the sponsoring employer if the distribution does not contravene any provision of law and the plan provides for such a distribution in these circumstances. [ERISA § 4044(d)(1)]

Any provision providing for a reversion of assets to the employer, or any amendment that has the effect of increasing the amount that may be distributed to the employer, is not effective before the end of the fifth calendar year following the date of such provision or amendment. However, if the plan has been in effect for fewer than five years and the plan has provided for such a

8-34

distribution since its effective date, then the employer may receive a reversion of such excess assets. [ERISA § 4044(d)(2)]

Planning Pointer. Employers implementing a new pension plan should be sure to incorporate a provision permitting the recovery of residual assets upon plan termination. If such provision is initially incorporated into the plan, the employer would have the ability (if it wishes) to recoup the residual plan assets upon the termination of the plan without having to wait five years.

If the plan sponsor receives a reversion of plan assets upon the plan's termination, an excise tax equal to 50 percent of the amount of the reversion is imposed by the IRS upon the plan sponsor. However, the excise tax is reduced to only 20 percent if:

1. The plan sponsor is in Chapter 7 bankruptcy liquidation, or in a similar court proceeding, on the plan termination date;
2. The plan provides for certain pro rata benefit increases; or
3. The employer establishes or maintains a qualified replacement plan.

[IRC § 4980(d)]

Q 8:48 What is the rule that permits the transfer of excess pension assets to a retiree health account?

Until the end of tax years beginning in 1995 (at which time this provision will expire), the Internal Revenue Code permits certain transfers of excess assets from a defined benefit pension plan (other than a multiemployer plan) to a retiree health account that is part of the plan. The Code imposes use requirements, vesting requirements, minimum cost requirements, and several limitations and other technical requirements with respect to such transfers. If the transfer meets all of the Code's requirements, it will not result in the plan's loss of its tax qualified status and the employer will not be subject to income and excise taxes imposed on reversions as a result of the transfer. [IRC § 420] Section 403(c)(1) of ERISA provides that the transfer of excess pension assets to a retiree health account that meets all of the Code's requirements will not result in the violation of ERISA's anti-inurement or exclusive purpose rules.

Q 8:49 How are plan assets allocated following the termination of a pension plan?

ERISA sets forth priority rules for the allocation and distribution of the assets of terminating plans that are subject to ERISA's termination insurance rules. [ERISA § 4044] The same priority rules apply to the allocation of assets of ERISA pension plans that are not subject to ERISA's termination insurance provisions. [ERISA § 403(d)(1)]

Q 8:50 How are plan assets distributed following the termination of a welfare plan?

The assets of a terminated welfare plan are to be allocated according to the terms of the plan. [ERISA § 403(d)(2)] If the welfare plan is maintained pursuant to a collective bargaining agreement, the terms of the agreement can control the distribution or transfer of plan assets. [ERISA Conf Comm Rep] However, the plan or the collective bargaining agreement will not govern such distribution or transfer if their implementation would either unduly impair the accrued benefits or not be in the best interests of the plan participants. [ERISA Conf Comm Rep]

Where such a distribution or transfer is incidental to the merger of one multiemployer welfare plan with another, the Secretary of Labor would disallow the distribution or transfer only if the merger would reasonably be expected to jeopardize the ability of the plan to meet its obligations, or would otherwise not be in the best interest of the plan participants. [ERISA Conf Comm Rep]

If the plan is a tax-exempt voluntary employees benefit association (generally, a trust under an employer's plan that provides for the payment of life, health, or accident insurance, or certain other benefits, and meets certain other requirements set forth under Code Section 501(c)(9)), none of its assets may be distributed to the employer. Any excess assets after plan termination must be used to benefit employees. [Treas Reg § 1.501(c)(9)-4(d)]

Look-Through Rule

Q 8:51 What is the look-through rule?

A plan's assets generally include only the investment in another entity, and not the underlying assets of the entity. The "look-through" rule is an exception to this general rule. If the look-through rule applies, then:

1. A plan's assets include not only the plan's equity interest in another entity but also an undivided interest in each underlying asset held by the entity; and
2. Any person with authority or control over the management of the underlying assets, or any person providing investment advice for a fee concerning such assets, is a fiduciary of the plan.

[DOL Reg § 2510.3-101(a)(2)]

Q 8:52 When does the look-through rule apply?

In general, the look-through rule applies if the plan's equity interest in an entity is neither

1. A publicly offered security; nor
2. A security issued by an investment company registered under the Investment Company Act of 1940.

[DOL Reg § 2510.3-101(a)(2)]

In addition, the look-through rule does not apply to the extent the plan invests in a guaranteed benefit policy issued by an insurer. [ERISA § 401(b)(2); Harris Trust & Savings Bank v John Hancock Mut Life Ins Co, 970 F2d 1138 (2d Cir 1992) *cert denied*, 113 SCt 1585 (as to holding that insurer was not ERISA fiduciary for guaranteed portion), *cert granted*, 113 SCt 1576 (1993) (as to holding that insurer is ERISA fiduciary for non-guaranteed portion)] (See Qs 8:23 and 8:32.)

Q 8:53 What is an equity interest?

An equity interest is any interest in an entity other than a pure debt interest (i.e., an instrument treated as indebtedness under applicable local law and not having any substantial equity feature). Some examples of typical equity interests would include:

- A profits interest in a partnership
- An undivided ownership interest in property
- A beneficial interest in a trust

[DOL Reg § 2510.3-101(b)(1)]

Example Plan P acquires debentures issued by Corporation T pursuant to a private offering. T is engaged primarily in investing and reinvesting in precious metals on behalf of its shareholders, all of whom are benefit plan investors. The debenture is convertible to common stock of T at P's option. When Plan P acquires the debentures, the conversion feature is incidental to T's obligation to pay interest and principal.

Although T is not an operating company (see Qs 8:59 through 8:61), P's assets do not include an interest in the underlying assets of T because P has not agreed to acquire an *equity* interest in T. However, if P exercises its option at that time (assuming that the common stock is not a publicly offered security and that there has been no change in the composition of the other equity investors in T), P's assets would then include an undivided interest in the underlying assets of T.

[DOL Reg § 2510.3-101(b)(1)]

Q 8:54 What is a publicly offered security?

A publicly offered security is a security that is

1. Freely transferable;
2. Part of a widely held class of securities; and
3. Covered under certain federal securities registration rules.

[DOL Reg § 2510.3-101(b)(2)]

To be "widely held," a class of securities must be owned by 100 or more investors who are independent of the issuer and each other. [DOL Reg § 2510.3-101(b)(3)] Whether a security is freely transferable is generally a factual question. Where the minimum investment in an offering of the security is $10,000 or less, certain listed restrictions on transfers will be ignored. [DOL Reg § 2510.3-101(b)(4)]

Q 8:55 Which equity investments are generally exempt from the look-through rule?

Investments in operating companies (see Qs 8:59 through 8:61), and investments where equity participation in the entity by benefit plan investors is not significant (see Q 8:57) are generally exempt from the look-through rule. If the investment is exempt from the look-through rule, only the investment in the entity is treated as a plan asset, and not the underlying assets owned by the entity, even though the investment is not a publicly offered security or a security issued by a registered investment company. [DOL Reg § 2510.3-101(a)(2)]

Nevertheless, if the investment falls within an unsafe harbor, as described in Q 8:56, the investment is not exempt from the look-through rule. In that case, the plan's assets include not only the investment in the entity, but also an undivided interest in the underlying assets owned by the entity. [DOL Reg § 2510.3-101(h)]

Q 8:56 What types of investments fall within an unsafe harbor and are never exempt from the look-through rule?

Any investment that falls within any of the unsafe harbors described below is not exempt from the look-through rule, even if an exemption would otherwise apply. If a plan invests in any of these entities, the plan's assets will include not only the investment in the entity, but also an undivided interest in the underlying assets owned by the entity.

1. Any interest in an entity (other than a state-licensed insurance company) established or maintained for the purpose of offering pension or welfare benefits under ERISA to participants or

beneficiaries of the investing plan is never exempt from the look-through rule. [DOL Reg § 2510.3-101(h)(2)]

Example. A medical benefit plan, P, acquires a beneficial interest in a trust, Z, which is not an insurance company licensed to do business in a state. Under this arrangement, Z will provide the benefits to the participants and beneficiaries of P that are promised under the terms of the plan. P's assets include its beneficial interest in Z and an undivided interest in each of Z's underlying assets. Thus, persons with discretionary authority or control over the assets of Z would be fiduciaries of P. [DOL Reg § 2510.3-101(j)(12)]

2. Unless the entity is an investment company registered under the Investment Company Act of 1940, if the plan invests in a tax-exempt group trust, a bank's common or collective trust fund, or a separate account of an insurance company (subject to separate investment performance), the investment is never exempt from the look-through rule. [DOL Reg § 2510.3-101(h)(1)]

3. If a plan or a related group of plans owns all of the outstanding equity interests (other than directors' qualifying shares) in an entity, and the equity interests are not qualifying employer securities, then the investment is never exempt from the look-through rule. [DOL Reg § 2510.3-101(h)(3)] A related group of employee benefit plans consists of every group of two or more employee benefit plans, each of which

    a. Receives 10 percent or more of its aggregate contributions from the same employer or from members of the same controlled group of corporations; or

    b. Is maintained either by, or under a collective bargaining agreement negotiated by, the same employee organization or its affiliates.

[DOL Reg § 2510.3-101(h)(4)]

Q 8:57 When is equity participation in an entity by benefit plan investors considered to be significant?

Equity participation in an entity by benefit plan investors is significant on any date if, immediately after the most recent acquisition of any equity interest in the entity (see Q 8:53), 25 percent or more of the value of any class of equity interest in the entity is held by benefit plan investors (see Q 8:58). [DOL Reg § 2510.3-101(f)(1); DOL Adv Op Ltr No 89-05A (Apr 5, 1989)] Excluded from the calculation is the value of any equity interests held by persons who are insiders (i.e., persons other than benefit plan investors who have discretionary authority or control over the entity's assets, who directly or indirectly provide investment advice for a fee with respect to the entity's assets, or who are affiliated with either of these). [DOL Reg § 2510.3-101(f)(1)]

Q 8:58 What is a benefit plan investor?

A benefit plan investor is:

1. An employee benefit (pension or welfare) plan, even if exempt from Title I of ERISA (which includes the fiduciary responsibility provisions);
2. A tax qualified retirement plan, or an individual retirement account or annuity; or
3. Any entity whose underlying assets include plan assets as a result of a plan's investment in the entity.

[DOL Reg § 2510.3-101(f)(2)]

Example. Plan P acquires a limited partnership interest in Limited Partnership U, which is established and maintained by A, a general partner of U. U has only one class of limited partnership interests, and is engaged in the business of investing and reinvesting in securities. Limited partnership interests in U are offered privately pursuant to an exemption from the registration requirements of the Securities Act of 1933. P acquires 15 percent of the value of all the outstanding limited partnership interests in U, and, at the time of P's investment, a governmental plan owns 15 percent of the value of those interests. U is not an operating company because it is engaged primarily in the investment of capital. In addition, equity participation by benefit plan investors is significant because immediately after P's investment such investors hold more than 25 percent of the limited partnership interests in U. Accordingly, P's assets include an undivided interest in the underlying assets of U, and A is a fiduciary of P with respect to such assets by reason of its discretionary authority and control over *U*'s assets. [DOL Reg § 2510.3-101(j)(2)]

By contrast, if *P* acquires only 5 percent of the value of all the outstanding limited partnership interests in *U*, and benefit plan investors in the aggregate hold only 10 percent of the value of the limited partnership interests in *U*, then there is no significant equity participation by benefit plan investors in *U* and, accordingly, *P*'s assets include its limited partnership interest in *U*, but do not include any of the underlying assets of *U*. Thus, A would not be a fiduciary of *P* by reason of *P*'s investment. [DOL Reg § 2510.3-101(j)(3)]

However, if the aggregate value of the outstanding limited partnership interests in *U* is $10,000 (and the value of the interests held by benefit plan investors is thus $1000), and if an affiliate of *A* owns limited partnership interests in U having a value of $6500, then the value of the limited partnership interests held by *A*'s affiliate is disregarded for purposes of determining whether there is significant equity participation in *U* by benefit plan investors. Thus, the percentage of the aggregate value of the limited partnership interests held by benefit investors in *U* for purposes of such determination is approximately 28.6 percent ($1000/$3500), constituting a significant benefit plan investment in *U*. Accordingly, *P*'s assets include an undivided interest in the underlying assets of *U*, and *A* is a fiduciary of *P* with respect to such assets by reason of its discretionary authority and control over *U*'s assets. [DOL Reg § 2510.3-101(j)(4)]

Operating Companies

Q 8:59 What is an operating company?

An operating company, which is generally exempt from the look-through rule (see Q 8:55), is:

1. An entity that is primarily engaged, directly or through majority-owned subsidiaries, in producing or selling a product or service other than the investment of capital;
2. A real estate operating company (see Q 8:60); or

3. A venture capital operating company (see Q 8:61).

[DOL Reg § 2510.3-101(d)]

Q 8:60 What is a real estate operating company (REOC)?

An entity is a REOC if:

1. At least 50 percent of its assets (valued at cost) are invested in real estate that is managed or developed;
2. The entity has the right to substantially participate directly in the management or development of the eligible real estate; and
3. The entity actually engages directly in real estate management or development.

The measuring period for the REOC requirements is generally a 12-month annual valuation period. The first measuring period begins on the first date the entity makes an investment other than a short-term investment of funds pending long-term commitment. An entity remains a REOC for 12 months after an annual valuation period in which it no longer satisfies the REOC requirements. [DOL Reg § 2510.3-101(e)]

Even if a REOC does not satisfy the general operating company requirements (see Q 8:59), it generally still is exempt from the "look-through" rule. (See Q 8:51) [DOL Reg § 2510.3-101(c)]

Example 1. Plan P invests (pursuant to a private offering) in a Limited Partnership W that is engaged primarily in investing and reinvesting assets in equity positions in real property. The properties acquired by W are subject to long-term leases, under which substantially all management and maintenance activities with respect to the property are the responsibility of the lessee. W is not engaged in the management or development of real estate merely because it assumes the risks of ownership of income-producing real property, and W is not a real estate operating company. If there is significant equity participation in W by benefit plan investors, P will be considered to have acquired an undivided interest in each of the underlying assets of W. Accordingly, any person with effective control over *any* asset of W (including lessees

Q 8:60 **Fiduciary Responsibility Answer Book**

and their agents) will be a fiduciary of *P* with respect to such asset. [DOL Reg § 2510.3-101(j)(7)]

Example 2. By contrast, assume that *W* owns several shopping centers in which individual stores are leased for relatively short periods to various merchants (rather than owning properties subject to long-term leases under which substantially all management and maintenance activities are the responsibility of the lessee). *W* retains independent contractors to manage the shopping center properties. These independent contractors negotiate individual leases, maintain the common areas, and conduct maintenance activities with respect to the properties. *W* has the responsibility to supervise and the authority to terminate the independent contractors. During its most recent valuation period, more than 50 percent of *W*'s assets, valued at cost, are invested in such properties. *W* is a real estate operating company. The fact that *W* does not have its own employees who engage in day-to-day management and development activities is only one factor in determining whether it is actively managing or developing real estate. Thus, *P*'s assets include its interest in *W*, but do not include any of the underlying assets of *W*. Accordingly, persons with effective control over the assets of *W* (including the independent contractors) will not be fiduciaries of *P* by reason of *P*'s investment in *W*. [DOL Reg § 2510.3-101(j)(8)]

Example 3. Plan *R* acquires a limited partnership interest in *X* pursuant to a private offering. There is significant equity participation in *X* by benefit plan investors. *X* is engaged in the business of making "convertible loans," which are structured as follows: *X* lends a specified percentage of the cost of acquiring real property to a borrower who provides the remaining capital needed to make the acquisition. This loan is secured by a mortgage on the property. Under the terms of the loan, *X* is entitled to receive a fixed rate of interest payable out of the initial cash flow from the property, and is also entitled to that portion of any additional cash flow equal to the percentage of the acquisition cost that is financed by its loan. Simultaneously with the making of the loan, the borrower also gives *X* an option to purchase an interest in the property for the original principal amount of the loan at the expiration of its initial term. *X*'s percentage interest in the property, if it exercises this option, would be equal to the percentage of the acquisition cost of the property financed by its loan. The parties to the transaction contemplate that the option ordinarily will be exercised at the expiration of the loan term if the property has appreciated in value. X and the borrower also agree that, if the option is exercised, they will form a limited partnership to hold the property. X negotiates loan terms that give it rights to substantially influence, or to substantially participate in, the management of the property acquired with the proceeds of the loan. These loan terms give X significantly greater rights to participate in the management of the property than it would obtain under a conventional mortgage loan. In addition, under the terms of the loan, X and the borrower ratably share any capital expenditures relating to the property.

During its most recent valuation period, more than 50 percent of the value of X's assets (valued at cost) consisted of real estate investments of the kind described above. X, in the ordinary course of its business, routinely exercises its management rights and frequently consults with and advises the borrower and the property manager. X is a real estate operating company. Thus, R's assets include its interest in X, but do not include any of the underlying assets of X. Accordingly, persons with effective control over the assets of X (including the property manager) will not be fiduciaries of P by reason of P's investment in X.

Q 8:61 What is a venture capital operating company (VCOC)?

An entity is a VCOC if:

1. At least 50 percent of its assets (valued at cost, and excluding certain short-term investments made pending long-term commitments) are invested in venture capital investments;
2. The entity's eligible venture capital investments are in operating companies (other than a VCOC) in which the entity has contractual management rights; and
3. The entity actually exercises management rights in one or more of such operating companies.

The measuring period for the VCOC requirements is generally a 12-month annual valuation period. The first measuring period begins on the first date the entity makes an investment other than a short-term investment of funds pending long-term commitment. An

Q 8:61   **Fiduciary Responsibility Answer Book**

entity remains a VCOC for 12 months after an annual valuation period in which it no longer satisfies the VCOC requirements. [DOL Reg § 2510.3-101(d)]

Even if a VCOC does not satisfy the general requirements for an operating company (see Q 8:59), it generally still is exempt from the "look-through" rule (see Q 8:51). [DOL Reg § 2510.3-101(c)]

> **Example 1.** Plan *P* invests in Limited Partnership *V*, pursuant to a private offering. There is significant equity participation by benefit plan investors in *V*. *V* acquires equity positions in the companies in which it invests, and, in connection with these investments, *V* negotiates terms that give it the right to participate in or influence the management of those companies. Some of these investments are in publicly offered securities, and some are in securities acquired in private offerings.
>
> During its most recent valuation period, more than 50 percent of *V*'s assets, valued at cost, consisted of investments with respect to which *V* obtained management rights of the kind described above. *V*'s managers routinely consult informally with and advise the management of only one portfolio company with respect to which it has management rights, although it devotes substantial resources to its consultations with that company. *V* relies on the managers of other entities to consult with and advise the other portfolio companies' management.
>
> *V* is a venture capital operating company and therefore *P* has acquired its limited partnership investment, but has not acquired an interest in any of the underlying assets of *V*. Thus, none of the managers of *V* would be fiduciaries with respect to *P* solely by reason of its investment. In this situation, the mere fact that *V* does not participate in or influence the management of all its portfolio companies does not affect its characterization as a venture capital operating company. [DOL Reg § 2510.3-101(j)(5)]
>
> **Example 2.** Assume that *V* invests in debt securities as well as equity securities of its portfolio companies. In some cases, *V* makes debt investments in companies in which it also has an equity investment; in other cases, *V* only invests in debt instruments of the portfolio company. *V*'s debt investments are acquired pursuant to private offerings and *V* negotiates covenants that give it the right to substantially participate in or to substantially influence the

conduct of the management of the companies issuing the obligations. These covenants give *V* more significant management rights than the covenants ordinarily found in debt instruments of established, creditworthy companies that are purchased privately by institutional investors. *V* routinely consults with and advises the management of its portfolio companies.

The mere fact that *V*'s investments in portfolio companies are debt, rather than equity, will not cause *V* to fail to be a venture capital operating company if it actually obtains the right to substantially participate in or influence the conduct of the management of its portfolio companies, and if in the ordinary course of its business it actually exercises those rights. [DOL Reg § 2510.3-101(j)(6)]

Q 8:62 Can an operating company (including a REOC or a VCOC) ever be subject to the look-through rule?

Yes. An investment can be subject to the look-through rules even though it is an investment in an operating company if it falls within any of the "unsafe harbors" outlined in Q 8:56. [DOL Reg § 2510.3-101(h)]

Joint Ownership and Investment Pools

Q 8:63 In determining what are plan assets, how must an asset owned jointly by a plan and other parties be counted?

Where a plan jointly owns property with others, the property is treated as the sole property of a separate entity. [DOL Reg § 2510.3-101(g)]

Example. The Bonaparte Corporation Profit-Sharing Plan invests in an undivided 40 percent share of St. Helena Acres, an undeveloped plot of land on an island. Nelson, Ltd., owned in equal parts by three individuals, Metternich, Castlereagh, and Talleyrand, is a partnership unrelated to Bonaparte and its plan. Nelson invests in the other 60 percent. St. Helena Acres is a plan asset, and Nelson is a fiduciary with respect to the Bonaparte plan to the extent it has discretionary authority and control over this plan asset; each of Nelson's owners may also be a fiduciary.

Q 8:64 In determining what are plan assets, how must an equity interest whose value relates to identified property owned by the entity be counted?

Where the value of a plan's equity interest in an entity is related solely to identified property of the entity, the property is treated as the sole property of a separate entity. [DOL Reg § 2510.3-101(g)]

Example 1. In a private transaction, a plan, *P*, acquires a 30 percent participation in a debt instrument that is held by a bank. Since the value of the participation certificate relates solely to the debt instrument, that debt instrument is treated as the sole asset of a separate entity. Equity participation in that equity by benefit plan investors is significant since the value of the plan's participation exceeds 25 percent of the value of the instrument. In addition, the hypothetical entity is not an operating company because it is primarily engaged in the investment of capital (i.e., holding the debt instrument). Thus, *P*'s assets include the participation and an undivided interest in the debt instrument, and the bank is a fiduciary of *P* to the extent it has discretionary authority or control over the debt instrument. [DOL Reg § 2510.3-101(j)(10)]

Example 2. In a private transaction, Plan *P* acquires 30 percent of the value of a class of equity securities issued by Operating Company *Y*. These securities provide that dividends shall be paid solely out of earnings attributable to certain tracts of undeveloped land that are held by *Y* for investment. The property is treated as the sole asset of a separate entity. Thus, even though *Y* is an operating company, the hypothetical entity whose sole assets are the undeveloped tracts of land is not an operating company. Accordingly, *P* is considered to have acquired an undivided interest in the tracts of land held by *Y*, and *Y* would be a fiduciary of *P* to the extent it exercises discretionary authority or control over such property. [DOL Reg § 2510.3-101(j)(11)]

Q 8.65 If a plan acquires a guaranteed governmental mortgage pool certificate, are the underlying mortgages plan assets?

No. Where a plan acquires a guaranteed governmental mortgage pool certificate (such as one guaranteed by GNMA, FHLMC, or FNMA), the plan's assets include the certificate and all of its rights with respect to the certificate under applicable law. The plan's assets do not include any of the mortgages underlying the certificate solely because the plan holds the certificate. [DOL Reg § 2510.3-101(i)]

Miscellaneous Plan Asset Issues

Q 8:66 Is a stop-loss insurance policy purchased by an employer sponsoring a welfare benefit plan considered a plan asset?

No. The DOL has ruled that a stop-loss insurance policy under a welfare plan is generally not a plan asset for purposes of ERISA.

The stop-loss policy discussed in the DOL's letter ruling dealt with an insurance policy purchased by an employer sponsoring a welfare benefit plan under which benefits were paid exclusively out of the employer's general assets. The purpose of the policy was to protect the employer in managing risk associated with its liabilities under the plan. The insurer agreed to reimburse the employer if, during the policy year, the employer is required under the plan to pay claims in excess of a predetermined amount.

The DOL held that such policy was not a plan asset since the following conditions were present:

1. The insurance proceeds were payable only to the employer, who was the named insured under the policy;
2. The employer had all rights of ownership under the policy, and the policy was subject to the claims of the employer's creditors;
3. Neither the plan nor any participant or beneficiary of the plan had any preferential claim against the policy or any beneficial interest in the policy;

Q 8:67   **Fiduciary Responsibility Answer Book**

4. No representations were made to any participant or beneficiary of the plan that the policy will be used to provide benefits under the plan or that the policy in any way represents security for the payment of benefits;
5. The benefits associated with the plan were not limited or governed in any way by the amount of insurance proceeds received by the employer; and
6. The plan did not require or allow employee contributions.

The DOL also stated in that letter ruling than in situations outside the scope of the plan assets–plan investment regulation, the assets of a plan are generally to be identified on the basis of ordinary notions of property rights. [DOL Adv Op Ltr 92-02A (Jan 7, 1992)]

Q 8:67   Is the cash value portion of a split dollar life insurance policy considered a plan asset?

No. The DOL has ruled that the cash value in a split dollar life insurance policy is generally not a plan asset for purposes of ERISA.

A split dollar life insurance policy is a policy in which the company and the executive split the cost of the coverage. Under the split dollar life insurance policy discussed in the DOL's letter ruling, the executive carried the portion of the policy that provided for the payment of a specified death benefit to the executive's beneficiaries (the "death benefit" element). The company carried the portion of the policy relating to the increase in the proceeds payable under the policy in addition to the death benefit (the "cash value" element). Under the policy, when the insured dies, the executive's beneficiaries would receive the proceeds under the death benefit element of the policy and the company would receive the proceeds under the cash value element of the policy.

The DOL ruled that the cash value element of the policy is not a plan asset. Accordingly, the cash value element of such a life insurance policy is not required to be placed in a trust and held for the exclusive benefit of the plan participants and beneficiaries.

The DOL ruled, however, that the split dollar arrangement is subject to ERISA fiduciary rules. Specifically, the policy must be selected with due regard to both the cost of the plan of the pure insurance and the financial soundness and claims-paying ability of the insurer. [DOL Adv Op Ltr 90-22A (Oct 27, 1992)]

Bonding

Q 8:68 What is ERISA's bonding requirement?

To protect plan participants and beneficiaries against losses on account of the mishandling of employee benefit funds, ERISA sets forth strict bonding requirements for most benefit plans. ERISA provides that every fiduciary of a benefit plan, as well as each person who handles funds or other property of a plan ("plan officials"), must be bonded. [ERISA § 412(a)] Any plan official who is not so bonded may not receive, handle, or otherwise exercise control of any funds or property of an employee benefit plan. [ERISA § 412(b)] Likewise, it is illegal for any plan official to allow benefit funds to be handled by a plan official who is not properly bonded. [ERISA § 412(b)] In addition, it is unlawful for any person associated with a plan to procure a bond required by ERISA from any company or through any agent in whose business such a plan (or any party in interest to such a plan) has any control or significant financial interest. [ERISA § 412(c)]

Q 8:69 What are the exceptions to ERISA's bonding requirements?

ERISA provides several exceptions to its bonding requirements. First, where the plan pays benefits only from the general assets of a union or employer, bonding is not required. [ERISA § 412(a)(1)] In addition, no bond is required of any fiduciary (or any director, officer, or employee thereof) that:

1. Is a corporation organized and doing business under the laws of the United States or any state;

2. Is authorized under those laws to exercise trust powers or to conduct an insurance business;

3. Is subject to supervision by federal or state authority; and

4. At all times has a combined capital and surplus in excess of such minimum amount as the secretary may prescribe (which is at least one million dollars).

[ERISA § 412(a)(2)]

Appendix A

Checklists

Checklist for the Selection of an Investment Manager A-1
Checklist for Monitoring an Investment Manager A-7
Checklist for Persons Who Are Appointed as Plan Fiduciaries . . . A-10

Checklist for the Selection of an Investment Manager

The following is a suggested checklist of items that should be reviewed when selecting an investment manager for plan assets:

(1) Preliminarily, the "named fiduciary" of a plan (or other plan fiduciaries responsible for the investment of plan assets) or their authorized representatives (the "Named Fiduciary") should establish proposed investment guidelines and/or identify an investment style for that portion of the plan assets to be committed to the investment manager for the plan (the "Investment Manager"). Further, the Named Fiduciary should solicit the following information from each bank, trust company, insurance company or registered investment advisor that is being considered for retention as an investment manager for the plan:

(a) A description of the precise services that the Investment Manager is prepared to offer;

(b) A history of the Investment Manager's experience in the investment management business, including the total amount of assets under its control;

(c) A statement of the Investment Manager's investment approach or philosophy, and whether the Manager has any internal investment guidelines;

(d) The number of plan accounts and other accounts under the Investment Manager's management and their total current fair market value;

(e) A detailed schedule of investment management fees;

(f) A description of the Investment Manager's current staffing, and details as to the general experience and educational qualifications of the individuals who would be primarily responsible for the plan's account;

(g) The name of any individuals who would be actively involved in handling the pension plan's account and details as to the experience and educational qualifications of such individuals;

(h) A statement as to whether members of the staff would be available to meet with the Named Fiduciary on a regular basis;

(i) A description of how investment policy is established by the Investment Manager and how it will be implemented with respect to the plan assets in question;

(j) A summary of any investment policy the Investment Manager recommended for pension plan assets placed under its management;

(k) A tabulation of time-weighted annual rates of total investment return on the combined results of all plan equity portfolios under the Investment Manager's management for each of the previous one-, three-, five-, eight-, and ten-year periods, and cumulatively for that period;

(l) A tabulation of time-weighted annual rates of total investment return on the combined results of all plan fixed income portfolios under the Investment Manager's management for each of the previous one-, three-, five-, eight-, and ten-year periods, and cumulatively for that period;

Appendix A

(m) A tabulation of time-weighted annual rates of total investment return on the combined results of all retirement plan portfolios under the Investment Manager's management for each of the previous one-, three-, five-, eight-, and ten-year periods, and cumulatively for that period;

(n) The amount of the Investment Manager's fiduciary liability insurance that would protect the interests of the Plan in the event of a breach of fiduciary duty and fidelity bond policies;

(o) The existence of any threatened, current or past litigation involving claims against the Investment Manager or any of its principals or investment professionals, and whether the Investment Manager or any of its principals or investment professionals, has ever been held to be in violation of any federal or state laws;

(p) Whether the Investment Manager, or any of its principals, has ever undergone bankruptcy, liquidation, reorganization, or similar proceedings; has had its registration or license revoked or activities restricted; has ever been sued by a client or the Securities and Exchange Commission; or has ever been denied fiduciary liability or fidelity insurance;

(q) Whether the Investment Manager is registered with the Securities and Exchange Commission under the Investment Advisors Act of 1940, and the date of its initial registration;

(r) Whether the Investment Manager is affiliated (or has any business relationship) with the broker-dealer it uses that could affect its investment decisions;

(s) Financial information relating to the Investment Manager, including its most recent balance sheet;

(t) The Investment Manager's policy with respect to the voting of proxies appurtenant to investment securities;

(u) A description of the Investment Manager's business structure, principal owners and affiliates; and

(v) The procedure to be employed by the Investment Manager to comply with ERISA's prohibited transaction restrictions and whether the Investment Manager is a Qualified Professional Asset Manager.

(2) In addition to interviewing representatives of the Investment Manager (including the individuals who will be primarily responsible for managing the portfolio), the Named Fiduciary should evaluate the Investment Manager's qualifications by doing the following:

- (a) Examining the Investment Manager's experience in the particular area of investments under consideration, as well as its experience with other ERISA plan assets;

- (b) Making an independent assessment of the Investment Manager's qualifications. This may be accomplished by:
  - (i) determining that the Investment Manager is widely known and well respected (as is the case with a major financial institution);
  - (ii) securing and calling existing client references; and/or
  - (iii) seeking the advice of a professional third-party consultant who is knowledgeable in such matters;

- (c) Evaluating the record of the Investment Manager's past performance with investments of the type contemplated, and by reviewing a sample portfolio managed by the Investment Manager for a similarly situated client;

- (d) Evaluating the credentials and performance of the principals of the Investment Manager;

- (e) If the Investment Manager is registered under the Investment Advisors Act of 1940, examining Form ADV which details information regarding descriptions of services and fees, types of clients, types of investments, methods of analysis, sources of information, investment strategies, education and business standards and backgrounds, business and financial industry activities or affiliations, client transactions, account management, investment or brokerage discretion, financial information, litigation and investigation history and actions taken by the Securities and Exchange Commission, the Commodity Futures Trading Commission and other federal and state regulatory agencies.

(3) If fees are to be paid to the Investment Manager directly from plan assets, the Named Fiduciary has a duty to ascertain the reasonableness of the fees to be paid in relation to the amount of plan

Appendix A

assets to be invested with the Investment Manager, in comparison to fees charged by comparable advisors.

(4) The Named Fiduciary should inquire of the Secretary of Labor and the Securities and Exchange Commission as to whether any enforcement actions have been initiated during the previous five to ten years with respect to the Investment Manager, or any of its principals or investment professionals.

(5) The Named Fiduciary should identify a range of candidates and document the process by which such candidates are identified whose expertise is consistent with the proposed investment guidelines or investment style identified for the investment manager position in question, and the Named Fiduciary should interview other investment managers (to serve as a basis of comparison for one another).

(6) The Named Fiduciary has a duty to review (and, if necessary, have legal counsel analyze) the investment management agreement, offering memorandum, subscription agreement, or other documents that set forth the terms of the relationship between the plan and the Investment Manager. The investment management agreement (and arrangement) between the Named Fiduciary and the Investment Manager should generally be terminable by the Named Fiduciary on little or no advance notice (*i.e.*, under most circumstances, not more than thirty days), with any fees paid in advance to the Investment Manager prorated to the date of termination. The agreement should also provide, but should not necessarily be limited to, representations that the Investment Manager:

(a) is an investment advisor registered with the SEC under the Investment Advisors Act of 1940;

(b) is an investment manager within the meaning of ERISA Section 3(38);

(c) acknowledges being a fiduciary (within the meaning of Section 3(21)(A) of ERISA) with respect to the plan's assets under investment;

(d) has obtained a bond in accordance with ERISA Section 412;

(e) maintains fiduciary liability insurance in an amount determined by the Named Fiduciary to be sufficient under the circumstances;

(f) has made all necessary filings and obtained all requisite approvals from all relevant government agencies;

(g) will maintain the indicia of ownership of the Plan's assets in the United States;

(h) has obtained the appropriate authorization to execute the agreement;

(i) will indemnify the Named Fiduciary from any damages arising out of a breach by the Investment Manager of its agreement and/or its investment management duties;

(j) will promptly advise the Named Fiduciary of any change in the ownership or management of the Investment Manager;

(k) may not assign the agreement to a third party without the advance written consent of the Named Fiduciary; and

(l) shall not effect any transaction that directly or indirectly will cause the plan (or any fiduciary thereof) to enter into a prohibited transaction under Section 406-408 of ERISA or Section 4975(c) of the Code.

(7) Much of the information contained on this checklist can be found in the Investment Manager's Form ADV, which is required to be completed by persons registered under the Investment Advisors Act of 1940 (note, however, that a Form ADV is not required to be registered by an Investment Manager that is a bank, trust company, or insurance company).

* * *

The foregoing outline represents a summary of the measures that should be undertaken in considering and evaluating an investment manager for retention by a plan. It is not an exclusive list of all such actions.

Appendix A

Checklist for Monitoring an Investment Manager

(1) Once the Named Fiduciary has selected an Investment Manager, it has a duty to ensure that the Investment Manager prepares periodic accounting and reports (at least on a quarterly basis) of the plan's investments and to promptly review such accounting and reports. The minimal content of such accounting should include:

(a) An inventory and description of the cash and each security, debenture, and other investment held;

(b) The fair market and book value of the investments (where an investment consists of securities not regularly traded on a national securities exchange, a detailed description of the financial condition of the issuer of such securities, including applicable financial statements, should be provided);

(c) A calculation of the investment income, capital appreciation or depreciation (both realized and unrealized), and investment return for the period in question (it probably also would be useful to have the investment return computed on a quarterly, annual, and from inception basis);

(d) A list of the proxies appurtenant to the investment account, and detailed information with respect to the manner in which such proxies were voted (and the precise reasons for each such vote); and

(e) A breakdown of all fees (from whatever sources) received by the Investment Manager in connection with the investment of Trust assets, including brokerage commissions.

(2) The Named Fiduciary also has a duty to periodically monitor the investments made by, and the overall performance of, the Investment Manager. This duty should be satisfied by the following actions:

(a) Reviewing periodically (at least quarterly, or more often if necessary) the accounting and reports provided by the Investment Manager for the purpose of confirming:

(i) the adequacy of their content;

(ii) the Investment Manager's performance during the period;

(iii) the basis on which assets are valued; and

  (iv) whether the Investment Manager has managed the portfolio consistent with any investment guidelines promulgated by the Named Fiduciary and the Investment Manager's stated investment philosophy and for the purpose of generally comparing them in material respects with information provided by the plan's custodian including the custodian's statement of transactions;

(b) Determining:

  (i) the rate of return earned by the Investment Manager during the period in question on an overall basis, and by asset class and, where investments are in more than one sector, by sector; and

  (ii) whether that rate is reasonable (as an absolute number, and when compared to other comparable investment managers appropriate indices or benchmarks) and, if not, whether the continued retention of the Investment Manager is prudent;

(c) Meeting with the Investment Manager periodically (at least annually) to review the status and performance of the plan's investments, as well as to review the Investment Manager's performance and any significant changes in its corporate or capital structure, investment style, brokerage affiliation or practices, investment process or professional staff;

(d) Reviewing periodically (at least annually) the voting procedure pursuant to which the Investment Manager votes proxies, in addition to the manner in which proxies were voted in specific situations;

(e) Reviewing periodically the Investment Manager's practices regarding brokerage and trading, including brokerage costs, use of soft dollars, quality of securities, execution, and portfolio turnover;

(f) Establishing and reviewing, at least annually, the procedures for communicating information regarding investments and investment managers among the Named Fiduciary, the plan's staff, and the plan's service providers (including but not limited to the plan's attorneys, actuaries and custodial trustees);

Appendix A

(g) Verifying, at least quarterly, the fee computation;

(h) Terminating the Investment Manager's services immediately if its performance is unsatisfactory; and

(i) Retaining an independent investment consulting or monitoring firm to do all or a portion of the foregoing.

(3) While some level of precaution is always needed in connection with the selection and monitoring of an Investment Manager, the amount of precaution used should reflect in significant part the percentage of fund assets that are to be managed by the Investment Manager. Insofar as the Named Fiduciary is able to review the investment reports of an independent custodian responsible for valuing fund assets and reporting all investment transactions, an added layer of precaution is added to the monitoring process.

* * * *

The foregoing outline represents a summary of the measures that should be undertaken in evaluating and monitoring an investment manager that has been retained by a plan. It is not an exclusive list of all such actions.

Checklist for Persons Who Are Appointed as Fiduciaries

The following is a suggested checklist of items that should be reviewed when becoming a fiduciary of an ERISA plan as well as during the course of a fiduciary's tenure:

(1) *Understand ERISA.* If an individual is appointed as a fiduciary for a plan, that individual becomes immediately bound to follow the fiduciary requirements under ERISA. It is, therefore, vital that the fiduciary understands ERISA's fiduciary requirements as well as the other requirements under ERISA. This includes, for example, understanding:

- what conduct is fiduciary in nature subject to ERISA's requirements and when one is acting as a fiduciary (as opposed to, for example, when acting as an employee of an employer)
- the standard of conduct applicable to fiduciaries including the duty of prudence, duty to diversify plan assets, exclusive benefit rule, and obligation to follow plan documents (unless inconsistent with ERISA)
- what is an employee benefit plan subject to ERISA (if, for example, a person who makes determinations under an employer's severance policy will be a fiduciary of such plan even if he/she may not be formally designated as such)
- who are the other fiduciaries of the plan and what are the co-fiduciary liability rules
- what are prohibited transactions
- fiduciary liability and consequences of breaching one's fiduciary duties or engaging in prohibited transactions
- the reporting and disclosure requirements under ERISA that apply to the plan
- the ERISA-required claims procedure
- other applicable substantive requirements under ERISA (for example, vesting, benefit accrual, joint and survivor annuity rules, funding, distribution, special multiemployer pension requirements for such plans, etc.)

Appendix A

If a fiduciary is not familiar with these requirements, he or she is obligated to consult with counsel and others who are knowledgeable.

(2) *Understand the Plan*. One of ERISA's fiduciary requirements is to follow the terms of the plan documents insofar as they are consistent with ERISA. Obviously, in order to follow the plan's terms, a fiduciary must be familiar with its provisions. This means that the plan documents must be read. This includes not only the plan, but also the trust agreement, the administrative services agreement, the summary plan description, and other relevant plan documents.

(3) *Understand the Fiduciary Structure*. The responsibilities of each ERISA fiduciary (including, for example, each plan committee, members of such committees, plan administrator and all other fiduciaries) should be defined carefully in writing and the distinctions among fiduciary positions should be strictly enforced. A fiduciary should understand from whom and among who his or her fiduciary duties have been allocated or delegated and, therefore, to whom he or she is accountable and responsible. A fiduciary should also know his or her co-fiduciaries. In addition, to the extent a fiduciary has delegated fiduciary responsibility, he or she has an obligation to monitor the performance of the fiduciary to whom duties have been delegated. This may include, for example, requiring reports from and/or meetings with the appointed fiduciaries on a monthly, quarterly, semi-annual or annual basis. Allocations of responsibility among named fiduciaries and delegations to fiduciaries must be clear and in writing.

(4) *Understand Plan Investments*. If a fiduciary is involved with plan investments (including a named fiduciary appointing an investment manager, a trustee or investment manager), the fiduciary must understand the investments relating to the portion of assets for which he or she has discretion and control and/or monitor the investment manager to whom investment responsibility has been delegated.

(5) *Understand Plan Procedures*. A fiduciary must understand the operation of the plan and its procedures. If adequate procedures are not in place, a fiduciary must ensure that proper procedures are established.

(6) *Understand Other Applicable Laws*. While a fiduciary's conduct is regulated by the ERISA standard, a fiduciary may need to understand the application of other laws to the plan. This may include, for

example, the Internal Revenue Code, the Family and Medical Leave Act, Age Discrimination in Employment Act, Americans with Disabilities Act, Labor-Management Relations Act, certain securities laws, state laws not preempted by ERISA, banking requirements (*e.g.*, FDIC regulations), insurance requirements, etc. If a fiduciary is not familiar with the requirements of relevant laws, he or she is obligated to consult with counsel and others who are knowledgeable in such laws.

(7) *Prudent Decision Making.* A fiduciary must act prudently and for the exclusive benefit of participants in connection with its decisions. A fiduciary must consider the appropriate substantive factors ("substantive prudence") and must do so by using proper procedures ("procedural prudence") in order to satisfy the duty of prudence. This includes, for example, doing the following:

(a) ensuring that he or she has received all pertinent information necessary to reach a decision on a particular matter and that he or she has had adequate time to review and understand the materials presented;

(b) requesting reports from their advisors in order to make important decisions;

(c) attending meetings (such as trustee or committee meetings) where important matters are considered and evaluated by plan fiduciaries;

(d) taking an active role in its decision making (this includes expressing one's own opinions, thoughts and decisions, asking questions, and where necessary, objecting to a particular course of action proposed by his or her co-fiduciaries, (and, if the proposed action may violate ERISA's fiduciary duty requirements, he or she must take appropriate steps to avoid the violation));

(e) observing formalities and documenting actions (*e.g.*, minutes of meetings) (note that minutes of all meetings (as well as resolutions regarding plan decisions) should be maintained to reflect not only the decision reached by the fiduciaries but also to reflect the decision-making process. If advisors were consulted, the minutes should reflect their attendance at the meeting as well as their reports and recommendations.)

Appendix A

Attached to this checklist is a Sample Outline of Benefit Committee Minutes.

(8) *Seek Consultants and Legal Counsel.* A fiduciary has a duty to seek the advice of others where he or she is not sufficiently familiar with the issue or does not understand the legal, financial or other considerations relevant to the plan, the participants, and/or his or her role as fiduciary.

(9) *Understand Bonding Requirements/Insurance/Legal Protection.* ERISA requires a plan to bond any fiduciary or all other persons who handle plan assets. A fiduciary should confirm that the amount of the bond is sufficient and proper. Since fidelity bonds only reimburse the plan for losses arising out of dishonesty, a fiduciary should confirm that the plan sponsor will indemnify the fiduciary for claims brought against him or her (which indemnification obligation may be secured by a guarantee, purchase of a surety bond or letter of credit, or other available means). The indemnification provision must be set forth in the plan sponsor's articles of incorporation or by-laws as well as in the plan document and should require rather than permit indemnification to the fullest extent permitted by law (although exceptions may be made for gross negligence or willful misconduct). In addition, the fiduciary should confirm that fiduciary liability insurance has been obtained. Because bonding, indemnification and fiduciary liability insurance issues can be complex, a fiduciary should consult an expert knowledgeable in such areas.

* * * *

The foregoing outline represents a summary of the measures that should be undertaken when becoming a fiduciary of a plan. It is not an exclusive list of all such actions.

Attachment to Checklist For Persons Who Are Appointed As Plan Fiduciaries

Sample Outline of Benefit Committee Minutes

The following agenda may be followed for a meeting of a Benefits Committee:

1. Call to Order.

2. Review and acceptance of the Minutes of the prior Benefits Committee meeting.
3. Report of the Plan Administrator—
   a. Participants placed in pay status since the last meeting;
   b. Benefits paid;
   c. Review of paid invoices;
   d. Review of Plan finances;
   e. Review of status of Plan Document (and amendments);
   f. Review of status of projects worked on by service providers (*e.g.*, counsel, actuary, auditor, investment manager, custodian, trustee.)
4. *Report of Plan Actuary* (for defined benefit plans)—The Benefits Committee should receive a report from the Plan actuary as to the Plan's actuarial valuation and funded status. It may be necessary and appropriate to have the actuary present in person periodically to answer the questions raised by the Plan fiduciaries. Further, if special actuarial studies or reports are prepared, it is useful to have the actuary available to discuss such studies or reports with the fiduciaries.
5. *Auditors' Report*—The Plan's auditor should review the Plan's financial reports with the Benefits Committee. As with the Plan actuary, it is probably not necessary for the auditor to attend every meeting of the Benefits Committee. However, when the financial report is submitted for review, it is a good practice to have the Plan's auditor available to present it, discuss the report and to answer the fiduciaries' questions.
6. *Report of Counsel*—Counsel should provide a report of Plan litigations, investigations, audits and the status of the plan documents, reports and forms and relevant legal developments affecting the status or operation of the plan. Generally, fiduciaries prefer to have counsel present at each meeting since legal issues typically arise for which counsel can provide guidance. At a minimum, counsel should be present when the Plan fiduciaries are aware that legal issues will arise or where legal documents will be considered (such as Plan amendments or contracts with service providers).

Appendix A

7. *Report of Investment Managers*—Fiduciaries should receive a detailed report as to the activity on the assets under management including, for example, the trades made and the gains or losses on the account during the relevant period and proxies voted or subscription rights exercised. Fiduciaries must meet with the investment managers on a regular basis (generally quarterly). If the fiduciaries choose not to meet with the managers during any period, they should review a report of the activity on the investment account since the prior meeting.

8. *Institutional Trustee/Custodian*—The fiduciaries should receive a report on the account activity of the assets being held by the Trustee/Custodian. In many cases, the plan assets are not held physically by the Trustee/Custodian, but by another entity. Whether the Trustee/Custodian has physical custody of the assets or not, the Plan's auditors are responsible for auditing the records of the Trustee/Custodian. The Benefits Committee should review the Trustee/Custodian's written report. Absent unusual circumstances, it is generally not necessary to have the Trustee/Custodian present at the Benefits Committee meeting.

9. *Future Meeting*—Some fiduciaries prefer to set a date for the next meeting at the conclusion of the current meeting. Other fiduciaries prefer not to set an exact date, but attempt to schedule at least two meetings each year (and more frequently if issues arise requiring the attention of the fiduciaries).

* * * *

The foregoing outline represents a summary of possible actions that could occur at a Benefits Committee meeting as well as the structure of the meeting minutes. It is not an exclusive list of all possible actions.

Appendix B

Regulations Under ERISA Governing Fiduciary Responsibility

§ 2550.404a-1 Investment duties

(a) *In general.* Section 404(a)(1)(B) of the Employee Retirement Income Security Act of 1974 (the Act) provides, in part, that a fiduciary shall discharge his duties with respect to a plan with the care, skill, prudence, and diligence under the circumstances then prevailing that a prudent man acting in a like capacity and familiar with such matters would use in the conduct of an enterprise of a like character and with like aims.

(b) *Investment duties.* (1) With regard to an investment or investment course of action taken by a fiduciary of an employee benefit plan pursuant to his investment duties, the requirements of section 404(a)(1)(B) of the Act set forth in subsection (a) of this section are satisfied if the fiduciary:

(i) Has given appropriate consideration to those facts and circumstances that, given the scope of such fiduciary's investment duties, the fiduciary knows or should know are relevant to the particular investment or investment course of action involved, including the role the investment or investment course of action plays in that portion of the plan's investment portfolio with respect to which the fiduciary has investme[n]t duties; and

(ii) Has acted accordingly.

(2) For purposes of paragraph (b)(1) of this section, "appropriate consideration" shall include, but is not necessarily limited to,

(i) A determination by the fiduciary that the particular investment or investment course of action is reasonably designed, as part of the portfolio (or, where applicable, that portion of the plan portfolio with respect to which the fiduciary has investment duties), to further the purposes of the plan, taking into consideration the risk of loss and the opportunity for gain (or other return) associated with the investment or investment course of action, and

(ii) Consideration of the following factors as they relate to such portion of the portfolio:

(A) The composition of the portfolio with regard to diversification;

(B) The liquidity and current return of the portfolio relative to the anticipated cash flow requirements of the plan; and

(C) The projected return of the portfolio relative to the funding objectives of the plan.

(3) An investment manager appointed, pursuant to the provisions of section 402(c)(3) of the Act, to manage all or part of the assets of a plan, may, for purposes of compliance with the provisions of paragraphs (b)(1) and (2) of this section, rely on, and act upon the basis of, information pertaining to the plan provided by or at the direction of the appointing fiduciary, if—

(i) Such information is provided for the stated purpose of assisting the manager in the performance of his investment duties, and

(ii) The manager does not know and has no reason to know that the information is incorrect.

(c) *Definitions.* For purposes of this section:

(1) The term *investment duties* means any duties imposed upon, or assumed or undertaken by, a person in connection with the investment of plan assets which make or will make such person a fiduciary of an employee benefit plan or which are performed by such person as a fiduciary of an employee benefit plan as defined in section 3(21)(A)(i) or (ii) of the Act.

(2) The term *investment course of action* means any series or program of investments or actions related to a fiduciary's performance of his investment duties.

(3) The term *plan* means an employee benefit plan to which title I of the Act applies.

§ 2550.404c-1 ERISA section 404(c) plans

(a) *In General* (1) Section 404(c) of the Employee Retirement Income Security Act of 1974 (ERISA or the Act) provides that if a pension plan that provides for individual accounts permits a participant or beneficiary to exercise control over assets in his account and that participant or beneficiary in fact exercises control over assets in his account, then the participant or beneficiary shall not be deemed to be a fiduciary by reason of his exercise of control and no person who is otherwise a fiduciary shall be liable for any loss, or by reason of any breach, which results form such exercise of control. This section describes the kinds of plan that are "ERISA section 404(c) plans," the circumstances in which a participant or beneficiary is considered to have exercised independent control over the assets in his account as contemplated by section 404(c), and the consequence of participant's or beneficiary's exercise of control.

(2) The standards set forth in this section are applicable solely for the purpose of determining whether a plan is an ERISA section 404(c) plan and whether a particular transaction engaged in by a participant or beneficiary of such plan is afforded relief by section 404(c). Such standards, therefore, are not intended to be applied in determining whether, or to what extent, a plan which does not meet the requirements for an ERISA section 404(c) plan or a fiduciary with respect to such a plan satisfies the fiduciary responsibility or other provisions of Title I of the Act.

(b) *ERISA section 404(c) plans*—(1) *In general.* An "ERISA section 404(c) Plan" is an individual account plan described in section 3(34) of the Act that:

(i) Provides an opportunity for a participant or beneficiary to exercise control over assets in his individual account (see paragraph (b)(2) of this section); and

(ii) Provides a participant or beneficiary an opportunity to choose, from a broad range of investment alternatives, the manner in which some or all of the assets in his account are invested (see paragraph (b)(3) of this section).

(2) *Opportunity to exercise control.* (i) a plan provides a participant or beneficiary an opportunity to exercise control over assets in his account only if:

(A) Under the terms of the plan, the participant or beneficiary has a reasonable opportunity to give investment instructions (in writing or otherwise, with opportunity to obtain written confirmation of such instructions) to an identified plan fiduciary who is obligated to comply with such instructions except as otherwise provided in paragraph (b)(2)(ii)(b) and (d)(2)(ii) of this section; and

(B) The participant or beneficiary is provided or has the opportunity to obtain sufficient information to make informed decisions with regard to investment alternatives available under the plan, and incidents of ownership appurtenant to such investments. For purposes of this subparagraph, a participant or beneficiary will not be considered to have sufficient investment information unless—

(1) The participant or beneficiary is provided by an identified plan fiduciary (or a person or persons designated by the plan fiduciary to act on his behalf):

(i) An explanation that the plan is intended to constitute a plan described in section 404(c) of the Employee Retirement Income Security Act, and title 29 of the Code of Federal Regulations Section 2550.440c–1, and that the fiduciaries of the plan may be relieved of liability for any losses which are the direct and necessary result of investment instructions given by such participant or beneficiary;

(ii) A description of the investment alternatives available under the plan and, with respect to each designated investment alternative, a general description of the investment objectives and risk and return characteristics of each such alternative, including information relat-

Appendix B

ing to the type and diversification of assets comprising the portfolio of the designed investment alternative;

(iii) Identification of any designated investment managers;

(iv) An explanation of the circumstances under which participants and beneficiaries may give investment instructions and explanation of any specified limitations on such instructions under the terms of the plan, including any restrictions on transfer to or from a designated investment alternative, and any restrictions on the exercise of voting, tender and similar rights appurtenant to a participant's or beneficiary's investment in an investment alternative;

(v) A description of any transaction fees and expenses which affect the participant's or beneficiary's account balance in connection with purchases or sales of interests in investment alternatives (e.g., commissions, sales load, deferred sales charges, redemption or exchange fees);

(vi) The name, address, and phone number of the plan fiduciary (and, if applicable, the person or persons designated by the plan fiduciary to act on his behalf) responsible for providing the information described in paragraph (b)(2)(i)(B)(2) upon request of an participant or beneficiary and a description of the information described in paragraph (b)(2)(i)(B)(2) which may be obtained on request;

(vii) In the case of plans which offer an investment alternative which is designed to permit a participant or beneficiary to directly or indirectly acquire or sell any employer security (employer security alternative), a description of the procedures established to provide for the confidentiality of information relating to the purchase, holding and sale of employer securities, and the exercise of voting, tender and similar rights, by participants and beneficiaries, and the name, address and phone number of the plan fiduciary responsible for monitoring compliance with he procedures (see paragraphs (d)(2)(ii)(E)*(4)(vii), (viii)* and *(ix)* of this section); and

(viii) In the case of an investment alternative which is subject to the Securities Act of 1933, and in which the participant or beneficiary has no assets invested, immediately following the participant's or beneficiary's initial investment, a copy of the most recent prospectus provided to the plan. This condition will be deemed satisfied if the participant or beneficiary has been provided with a copy of such most

recent prospectus immediately prior to the participant's or beneficiary's initial investment in such alternative;

(ix) Subsequent to an investment in a investment alternative, any materials provided to the plan relating to the exercise of voting, tender or similar rights which are incidental to the holding in the account of the participant or beneficiary of an ownership interest in such alternative to the extent that such rights are passed through to participants and beneficiaries under the terms of the plan, as well as a description of or reference to plan provisions relating to the exercise of voting, tender or similar rights.

(2) The participants or beneficiary is provided by the identified plan fiduciary (or a person or persons designated by the plan fiduciary to act on his behalf), either directly or upon request, the following information, which shall be based on the latest information available to the plan:

(i) A description of the annual operating expenses of each designated investment alternative (e.g., investment management fees, administrative fees, transaction costs) which reduce the rate of return to participants and beneficiaries, and the aggregate amount of such expenses expressed as a percentage of average net assets of the designated investment alternative;

(ii) Copies of any prospectuses, financial statements and reports, and of any other materials relating to the investment alternatives available under the plan, to the extent such information is provided to the plan;

(iii) A list of the assets comprising the portfolio of each designated investment alterna[t]ive which constitute plan assets within the meaning of 29 CFR 2510.3–101, the value of each such asset (or the proportion of the investment alternative which it comprises), and, with respect each such asset which is a fixed rate investment contract issued by a bank, savings and loan association or insurance company, the name of the issuer of the contract, the term of the contract and the rate of return on the contract;

(iv) Information concerning the value of shares or units in designated investment alternatives available to participants and beneficiaries under the plan, as well as the past and current invest-

Appendix B

ment performance of such alternatives, determined, net of expenses, on a reasonable and consistent basis; and

(v) Information concerning the value of shares or units in designated investment alternatives held in the account of the participant or beneficiary.

(ii) A plan does not fail to provide an opportunity for a participant or beneficiary to exercise control over his individual account merely because it—

(A) *Imposes charges for reasonable expenses.* A plan may charge participants' and beneficiaries' accounts for the reasonable expenses of carrying out investment instructions, provided that procedures are established under the plan to periodically inform such participants and beneficiaries of actual expenses incurred with respect to their respective individual accounts;

(B) *Permits a fiduciary to decline to implement investment instructions by participants and beneficiaries.* A fiduciary may decline to implement participant and beneficiary instructions which are described at paragraph (d)(2)(ii) of this section, as well as instructions specified in the plan, including instructions—

(1) Which would result in a prohibited transaction described in ERISA section 406 or section 4975 of the Internal Revenue Code, and

(2) Which would generate income that would be taxable to the plan;

(C) *Imposes reasonable restrictions on frequency of investment instructions.* A plan may impose reasonable restrictions on the frequency with which participants and beneficiaries may give investment instructions. In no event, however, is such a restriction reasonable unless, with respect to each investment alternative made available by the plan, it permits participants and beneficiaries to give investment instructions with a frequency which is appropriate in light of the market volatility to which the investment alternative may reasonably by expected to be subject, provided that—

(1) At least three of the investment alternatives made available pursuant to the requirements of paragraph (b)(3)(i)(B) of this section, which constitute a broad range of investment alternatives, Permit

participants and beneficiaries to give investment instructions no less frequently than once within any three month period; and

(2)(i) At least one of the investment alternatives meeting the requirements of paragraph (b)(2)(ii)(C)(*1*) of this section permits participants and beneficiaries to give investment instructions with regard to transfers into the investment alternative as frequently as participants and beneficiaries are permitted to give investment instructions with respect to any investment alternative made available by the plan which permits participants and beneficiaries to give investment instructions more frequently than once within any three month period; or

(ii) With respect to each investment alternative which permits participants and beneficiaries to give investment instructions more frequently than once within any three month period, participants and beneficiaries are permitted to direct their investments from such alternative into an income producing, low risk, liquid fund, subfund, or account as frequently as they are permitted to give investment instructions with respect to each such alternative and, with respect to such fund, subfund or account, participants and beneficiaries are permitted to direct investments from the fund, subfund or account to an investment alternative meeting the requirements of paragraph (b)(2)(ii)(C)(*1*) as frequently as they are permitted to give investment instructions with respect to that investment alternative; and

(3) With respect to transfers from an investment alternative which is designed to permit a participant or beneficiary to directly or indirectly acquire or sell any employer security (employer security alternative) either:

(i) All of the investment alternatives meeting the requirements of paragraph (b)(2)(ii)(C)(*1*) of this section must permit participants and beneficiaries to give investment instructions with regard to transfers into each of the investment alternatives as frequently as participants and beneficiaries are permitted to give investment instructions with respect to the employer security alternative; or

(ii) Participants and beneficiaries are permitted to direct their investments from each employer security alternative into an income producing, low risk, liquid fund, subfund, or account as frequently as they are permitted to give investment instructions with respect to

such employer security alternative and, with respect to such fund, subfund, or account, participants and beneficiaries are permitted to direct investments from the fund, subfund or account to each investment alternative meeting the requirements of paragraph (b)(2)(ii)(C)(1) as frequently as they are permitted to give investment instructions with respect to each such investment alternative.

(iii) Paragraph (c) of this section describes the circumstances under which a participant or beneficiary will be considered to have exercised independent control with respect to a particular transaction.

(3) *Broad range of investment alternatives.* (i) A plan offers a broad range of investment alternatives only if the available investment alternatives are sufficient to provide the participant or beneficiary with a reasonable opportunity to:

(A) Materially affect the potential return on amounts in his individual account with respect to which he is permitted to exercise control and the degree of risk to which such amounts are subject;

(B) Choose from at least three investment alternatives:

(1) Each of which is diversified;

(2) Each of which has materially different risk and return characteristics;

(3) Which in the aggregate enable the participant or beneficiary by choosing among them to achieve a portfolio with aggregate risk and return characteristics at any point within the range normally appropriate for the participant or beneficiary; and

(4) Each of which when combined with investments in the other alternatives tends to minimize through diversification the overall risk of a participant's or beneficiary's portfolio;

(C) Diversify the investment of that portion of his individual account with respect to which he is permitted to exercise control so as to minimize the risk of large losses, taking into account the nature of the plan and the size of participants' or beneficiaries' accounts. In determining whether a plan provides the participant or beneficiary with a reasonable opportunity to diversify his investments, the nature of the investment alternatives offered by the plan and the size of the portion of the individual's account over which he is permitted to exercise control must be considered. Where such portion of the account of any participant or beneficiary is so limited in size that the opportunity to invest in look-through investment vehicles is the only prudent means to assure an opportunity to achieve appropriate diversification, a plan may satisfy the requirements of the paragraph only by offering look-through investment vehicles.

(ii) *Diversification and look-through investment vehicles.* Where look-through investment vehicles are available as investment alternatives to participants and beneficiaries, the underlying investments of the look-through investment vehicles shall be considered in determining whether the plan satisfies the requirements of subparagraphs (b)(3)(i)(B) and (b)(3)(i)(C).

(c) Exercise of control. (1) *In general.* (i) Sections 404(c)(1) and 404(c)(2) of the Act and paragraphs (a) and (d) of this section apply only with respect to a transaction where a participant or beneficiary has exercised independent control in fact with respect to the investment of assets in his individual account under an ERISA section 404(c) plan.

(ii) For purposes of sections 404(c)(1) and 4040(c)(2) of the Act and paragraphs (a) and (d) of this section, a participant or beneficiary will be deemed to have exercised control with respect to the exercise of voting, tender and similar rights appurtenant to the participant's or beneficiary's ownership interest in an investment alternative, provided that the participant's or beneficiary's investment in the investment alternative was itself the result of an exercise of control, the participant or beneficiary was provided a reasonable opportunity to give instruction with respect to such incidents of ownership, including the provision of the information described in paragraph (b)(2)(i)(B)*(1)(ix)* of this section, and the participant or beneficiary has not failed to exercise control by reason of the circumstances described in paragraph (c)(2) with respect to such incidents of ownership.

(2) *Independent control.* Whether a participant or beneficiary has exercised independent control in fact with respect to a transaction depends on the facts and circumstances of the particular case. However, a participant's or beneficiary's exercise of control is not independent in fact if:

Appendix B

(i) The participant or beneficiary is subjected to improper influence by a plan fiduciary or the plan sponsor with respect to the transaction;

(ii) A plan fiduciary has concealed material non-public facts regarding the investment from the participant or beneficiary, unless the disclosure of such information by the plan fiduciary to the participant or beneficiary would violate any provision of federal law or any provision of state law which is not preempted by the Act; or

(iii) The participant or beneficiary is legally incompetent and the responsible plan fiduciary accepts the instructions of the participant or beneficiary knowing him to be legally incompetent.

(3) *Transactions involving a fiduciary.* In the case of a sale, exchange or leasing of property (other than a transaction described in paragraph (d)(2)(ii)(E) of this section) between an ERISA section 404(c) plan and a plan fiduciary or an affiliate of such a fiduciary, or a loan to a plan fiduciary or an affiliate of such a fiduciary, the participant or beneficiary will not be deemed to have exercised independent control unless the transaction is fair and reasonable to him. For purposes of this paragraph (c)(3), a transaction will be deemed to be fair and reasonable to a participant or beneficiary if he pays no more than, or receives no less than, adequate consideration (as defined in section 3(18) of the Act) in connection with the transaction.

(4) *No obligation to advise.* A fiduciary has no obligation under part 4 of Title I of the Act to provide investment advice to a participant or beneficiary under an ERISA section 404(c) plan.

(d) *Effect of independent exercise of control*—(1) *Participant or beneficiary not a fiduciary.* If a participant or beneficiary of an ERISA section 404(c) plan exercises independent control over assets in his individual account in the manner described in paragraph (c), then such participant or beneficiary is not a fiduciary of the plan by reason of such exercise of control.

(2) *Limitation on liability of plan fiduciaries.* (i) If a participant or beneficiary of an ERISA section 404(c) plan exercises independent control over assets in his individual account in the manner described in paragraph (c), then no other person who is a fiduciary with respect to such plan shall be liable for any loss, or with respect to any breach

of part 4 of Title I of the Act, that is the direct and necessary result of that participant's or beneficiary's exercise of control.

(ii) Paragraph (d)(2)(i) does not apply with respect to any instruction, which if implemented—

(A) Would not be in accordance with the documents and instruments governing the plan insofar as such documents and instruments are consistent with the provisions of Title I of ERISA;

(B) Would cause a fiduciary to maintain the indicia of ownership of any assets of the plan outside the jurisdiction of the district courts of the United States other than as permitted by section 404(b) of the Act and 29 CFR 2550.404b-1;

(C) Would jeopardize the plan's tax qualified status under the Internal Revenue Code;

(D) Could result in a loss in excess of a participant's or beneficiary's account balance; or

(E) Would result in a direct or indirect:

(1) Sale, exchange, or lease of property between a plan sponsor or any affiliate of the sponsor and the plan except for the acquisition or disposition of any interest in a fund, subfund or portfolio managed by a plan sponsor or an affiliate of the sponsor, or the purchase or sale of any qualifying employer security (as defined in section 407(d)(5) of the Act) which meets the conditions of section 408(e) of ERISA and section (d)(2)(ii)(E)(4) below;

(2) Loan to a plan sponsor or any affiliate of the sponsor;

(3) Acquisition or sale of any employer real property (as defined in section 407(d)(2) of the Act); or

(4) Acquisition or sale of any employer security except to the extent that:

(i) Such securities are qualifying employer securities (as defined in section 407(d)(5) of the Act);

(ii) Such securities are stock or an equity interest in a publicly traded partnership (as defined in section 7704(b) or the Internal Revenue Code of 1986), but only if such partnership is an existing

Appendix B

partnership as defined in section 10211(c)(2)(A) of the Revenue Act of 1987 (Public Law 100–203);

(iii) Such securities are publicly traded on a national exchange or other generally recognized market;

(iv) Such securities are traded with sufficient frequency and in sufficient volume to assure that participant and beneficiary directions to buy or sell the security may be acted upon promptly and efficiently;

(v) Information provided to shareholders of such securities is provided to participants and beneficiaries with accounts holding such securities;

(vi) Voting, tender and similar rights with respect to such securities are passed through to participants and beneficiaries with accounts holding such securities;

(vii) Information relating to the purchase, holding, and sale of securities, and the exercise of voting, tender and similar rights with respect to such securities by participants and beneficiaries, is maintained in accordance with procedures which are designed to safeguard the confidentiality of such information, except to the extent necessary to comply with Federal law or state laws no preempted by the Act;

(viii) The plan designates a fiduciary who is responsible for ensuring that the procedures required under subparagraph (d)(2)(ii)(E)*(4)(vii)* are sufficient to safeguard the confidentiality of the information described in that subparagraph, such procedures are being followed, and the independent fiduciary required by subparagraph (d)(2)(ii)(E)*(4)(ix)* is appointed; and

(ix) An independent fiduciary is appointed to carry out activities relating to any situations which the fiduciary designated by the plan for purposes of subparagraph (d)(2)(ii)(E)*(4)(viii)* determines involve a potential for undue employer influence upon participants and beneficiaries with regard to the direct or indirect exercise of shareholder rights. For purposes of this subparagraph, a fiduciary is not independent if the fiduciary is affiliated with any sponsor of the plan.

(iii) The individual investment decisions of an investment manager who is designated indirectly by a participant or beneficiary or who manages a look-through investment vehicle in which a participant or beneficiary has invested are not direct and necessary results of the designation of the investment manager or of investment in the look-through investment vehicle. However, this paragraph (d)(2)(iii) shall not be construed to result in liability under section 405 of ERISA with respect to a fiduciary (other than the investment manager) who would otherwise be relieved of liability by reason of section 404(c)(2) of the Act and paragraph (d) of this section.

(3) *Prohibited Transactions.* The relief provided by section 404(c) of the Act and this section applies only to the provisions of part 4 of title I of the Act. Therefore, nothing in this section relieves a disqualified person from the taxes imposed by sections 4975 (a) and (b) of the Internal Revenue Code with respect to the transactions prohibited by section 4975(c)(1) of the Code.

(e) *Definitions.* For purposes of this section:

(1) *Look-through investment vehicle* means:

(i) An investment company described in section 3(a) of the Investment Company Act of 1940, or a series investment company described in section 18(f) of the 1940 Act or any of the segregated portfolios of such company;

(ii) A common or collective trust fund or a pooled investment fund maintained by a bank or similar institution, a deposit in a bank or similar institution, or a fixed rate investment contract of a bank or similar institution;

(iii) a pooled separate account or a fixed rate investment contract of an insurance company qualified to do business in a State; or

(iv) Any entity whose assets include plan assets by reason of a plan's investment in the entity;

(2) *Adequate consideration* has the meaning given it in section 3(18) of the Act and in any regulations under this title;

(3) An *affiliate* of a person includes the following:

(i) Any person directly or indirectly controlling, controlled by, or under common control with the person;

Appendix B

(ii) Any officer, director, partner, employee, an employee of an affiliated employer, relative (as defined in section 3(15) of ERISA), brother, sister, or spouse of a brother or sister, of the person; and

(iii) Any corporation or partnership of which the person is an officer director or partner.

For purposes of this paragraph (e)(3), the term "control" means, with respect to a person other than an individual, the power to exercise a controlling influence over the management or policies of such person.

(4) *A designated investment alternative* is a specific investment identified by a plan fiduciary as an available investment alternative under the plan.

(f) *Examples.* The provisions of this section are illustrated by the following examples. Examples (5) through (11) assume that the participant has exercised independent control with respect to his individual account under an ERISA section 404(c) plan described in paragraph (b) and has not directed a transaction described in paragraph (d)(2)(ii).

(1) Plan A is an individual account plan described in section 3(34) of the Act. The plan states that a plan participant or beneficiary may direct the plan administrator to invest any portion of his individual account in a particular diversified equity fund managed by an entity which is not affiliated with the plan sponsor, or any other asset administratively feasible for the plan to hold. However, the plan provides that the plan administrator will not implement certain listed instructions for which plan fiduciaries would not be relieved of liability under section 404(c) (see paragraph (d)(2)(ii). Plan participants and beneficiaries are permitted to give investment instructions during the first week of each month with respect to the equity fund and at any time with respect to other investments. The plan provides for the pass-through of voting, tender and similar rights incidental to the holding in the account of a participant or beneficiary of an ownership interest in the equity fund or any other investment alternative available under the plan. The plan administrator of plan A provides each participant and beneficiary with the information described in subparagraphs *(i), (ii), (iii), (iv), (v), (vi)* and *(vii)* of paragraph (b)(2)(i)(B)*(1)* upon their entry into the plan, and provides

updated information in the event of any material change in the information provided. Immediately following an investment by a participant or beneficiary in the equity fund, the plan administrator provides a copy of the most recent prospectus received from the fund to the investing participant or beneficiary. Immediately following any investment by a participant or beneficiary in any other investment alternative which is subject to the Securities Act of 1933, the plan administrator provides the participant or beneficiary with the most recent prospectus received from that investment alternative (see paragraph (b)(2)(i)(B)*(1)(viii)*). Finally, subsequent to any investment by a participant or beneficiary, the plan administrator forwards to the investing participant or beneficiary any materials provided to the plan relating to the exercise of voting, tender or similar rights attendant to ownership of an interest in such investment (see paragraph (b)(2)(i)(B)*(1)(ix)*). Upon request, the plan administrator provides each participant or beneficiary with copies of any prospectuses, financial statements and reports, and any other materials relating to the investment alternatives available under the plan which are received by the plan (see paragraph (b)(2)(i)(B)*(2)(ii)*). Also upon request, the plan administrator provides each participant and beneficiary with the other information required by paragraph (b)(2)(i)(B)(2) with respect to the equity fund, which is a designated investment alternative, including information concerning the latest available value of the participant's or beneficiary's interest in the equity fund (see paragraph (b)(2)(i)(B)*(2)(v)*). Plan A meets the requirements of paragraphs (b)(2)(i)(B)*(1)* and *(2)* of this section regarding the provision of investment information.

Note: The regulation imposes no additional obligation on the administrator to furnish or make available materials relating to the companies in which the equity fund invests (e.g., prospectuses, proxies, etc.).

(2) Plan C is an individual account plan described in section 3(34) of the Act under which participants and beneficiaries may choose among three investment alternatives which otherwise meet the requirements of paragraph (b) of this section. The plan permits investment instruction with respect to each investment alternative only on the first 10 days of each calendar quarter, i.e. January 1-10, April 1-10, July 1-10 and October 1-10. Plan C satisfies the condition of paragraph (b)(2)(ii)(C)*(1)* that instruction be permitted not less

Appendix B

frequently than once within any three month period, since there is not any three month period during which control could not be exercised.

(3) Assume the same facts as in paragraph (f)(2), except that investment instruction may only be given on January 1, April 4, July 1 and October 1. Plan C is not an ERISA section 404(c) plan because it does not satisfy the condition of paragraph (b)(2)(ii)(C)*(1)* that instruction be permitted not less frequently than once within any three month period. Under these facts, there is a three month period e.g., January 2 through April 1 during which control could not be exercised by participants and beneficiaries.

(4) Plan D is an individual account plan described in section 3(34) of the Act under which participants and beneficiaries may choose among three diversified investment alternatives which constitute a broad range of investment alternatives. The plan also permits investment instruction with respect to an employer securities alternative but provides that a participant or beneficiary can invest no more than 25% of his account balance in this alternative. This restriction does not affect the availability of relief under section 404(c) inasmuch as it does not relate to the three diversified investment alternatives and, therefore, does not cause the plan to fail to provide an opportunity to choose from a broad range of investment alternatives.

(5) A participant, P, independently exercises control over assets in his individual account plan by directing a plan fiduciary, F, to invest 100% of his account balance in a single stock. P is not a fiduciary with respect to the plan by reason of his exercise of control and F will not be liable for any losses that necessarily result f[ro]m P's investment instruction.

(6) Assume the same facts as in paragraph (f)(5), except that P directs F to purchase the stock from B, who is a party in interest with respect to the plan. Neither P nor F has engaged in a transaction prohibited under section 406 of the Act: P because he is not fiduciary with respect to the plan by reason of his exercise of control and F because he is not liable for any breach of part 4 of Title I that is the direct and necessary consequence of P's exercise of control. However, a prohibited transaction under section 4975(c) of the Internal Revenue Code may have occurred, and, in the absence of an exemp-

tion, tax liability may be imposed pursuant to sections 495(a) and (b) of the Code.

(7) Assume the same facts as in paragraph (f)(5), except that P does not specify that the stock be purchased from B, and F chooses purchase the stock from B. In the absence of an exemption, F has engaged in a prohibited transaction described in 406(a) of ERISA because the decision to purchase the stock from B is not a direct or necessary result of P's exercise of control.

(8) Pursuant to the terms of the plan, plan fiduciary F designates three reputable investment managers who participants may appoint to manage assets in their individual accounts. Participant P selects M, one of the designated managers, to manage the assets in his account. M prudently manages P's account for 6 months after which he incurs losses in managing the account through his imprudence. M has engaged in a breach of fiduciary duty because M's imprudent management of P's account is not a direct or necessary result of P's exercise of control (the choice of M as manager). F has no fiduciary liability for M's imprudence because he has no affirmative duty to advise P (see paragraph (c)(4)) and because F is relieved of co-fiduciary liability by reason of section 404(c)(2) (see paragraph (d)(2)(iii)). F does have a duty to monitor M's performance to determine the suitability of continuing M as an investment manager, however, and M's imprudence would be a factor which F must consider in periodically reevaluating its decision to designate M.

(9) Participant P instructs plan fiduciary F to appoint G as his investment manager pursuant to the terms of the plan which provide P total discretion in choosing an investment manager. Through G's imprudence, G incurs losses in managing P's account. G has engaged in a breach of fiduciary duty because G's imprudent management of P's account is not a direct or necessary result of P's exercise of control (the choice of G as manager). Plan fiduciary F has no fiduciary liability for G's imprudence because F has no obligation to advise P (see paragraph (c)(4)) and because F is relieved of co-fiduciary liability for G's actions by reason of section 404(c)(2) (see paragraph (d)(2)(iii)). In addition, F also has no duty to determine the suitability of G as an investment manager because the plan does not designate G as an investment manager.

Appendix B

(10) Participant P directs a plan fiduciary, F, a bank, to invest all of the assets in his individual account in a collective trust fund managed by F that is designed to be invested solely in a diversified portfolio of common stocks. Due to economic conditions, the value of the common stocks in the bank collective trust fund declines while the value of publicly-offered fixed income obligations remains relatively stable. F is not liable for any losses incurred by P solely because his individual account was not diversified to include fixed income obligations. Such losses are the direct result of P's exercise of control; moreover, under paragraph (c)(4) of this section F has no obligation to advise P regarding his investment decisions.

(11) Assume the same facts as in paragraph (f)(10) except that F, in managing the collective trust fund, invests the assets of the fund solely in a few highly speculative stocks. F is liable for losses resulting from its imprudent investment in the speculative stocks and for its failure to diversify the assets of the account. This conduct involves a separate breach of F's fiduciary duty that is not a direct or necessary result of P's exercise of control (see paragraph (d)(2)(iii)).

(g) Effective date. (1) *In general.* Except as provided in paragraph (g)(2), this section is effective with respect to transactions occurring on or after the first day of the second plan year beginning on or after October 13, 1992.

(2) This section is effective with respect to transactions occurring under a plan maintained pursuant to one or more collective bargaining agreements between employee representatives and one or more employers ratified before October 13, 1992 after the later of the date determined under paragraph (g)(1) or the date on which the last collective bargaining agreement terminates. For purposes of this paragraph (g)(2), any extension or renegotiation of a collective bargaining agreement which is ratified on or after October 13, 1992 is to be disregarded in determining the date on which the agreement terminates.

(3) Transactions occurring before the date determined under subparagraph (g)(1) or (2) of this section, as applicable, are governed by section 404(c) of the Act without regard to the regulation.

Signed at Washington, DC, this 2d day of October 1992.

David George Ball,

Assistant Secretary for Pension and Welfare Benefits, U.S. Department of Labor.

[FR Doc. 92-24357 Filed 10-9-92; 8:45 am]

BILLING CODE 4510-29-M

§ 2509.75-4 Interpretive bulletin relating to indemnification of fiduciaries

On June 4, 1975, the Department of Labor issued an interpretive bulletin, ERISA IB 75-4, announcing the Department's interpretation of section 410(a) of the Employee Retirement Income Security Act of 1974, insofar as that section relates to indemnification of fiduciaries. Section 410(a) states, in relevant part, that "any provision in an agreement or instrument which purports to relieve a fiduciary from responsibility or liability for any responsibility, obligation, or duty under this part shall be void as against public policy."

The Department of Labor interprets this section to permit indemnification agreements which do not relieve a fiduciary of responsibility or liability under Part 4 of Title I. Indemnification provisions which leave the fiduciary fully responsible and liable, but merely permit another party to satisfy any liability incurred by the fiduciary in the same manner as insurance purchased under section 410(b)(3), are therefore not void under section 410(a).

Examples of such indemnification provisions are:

(1) Indemnification of a plan fiduciary by (a) an employer, any of whose employees are covered by the plan, or an affiliate (as defined in section 407(d)(7) of the Act) of such employer, or (b) an employee organization, any of whose members are covered by the plan; and

(2) Indemnification by a plan fiduciary of the fiduciary's employees who actually perform the fiduciary services.

The Department of Labor interprets section 410(a) as rendering void any arrangement for indemnification of a fiduciary of an employee benefit plan by the plan. Such an arrangement would have the same result as an exculpatory clause, in that it would, in effect, relieve the fiduciary of responsibility and liability to the plan by

Appendix B

abrogating the plan's right to recovery from the fiduciary for breaches of fiduciary obligations.

While indemnification arrangements do not contravene the provisions of section 410(a), parties entering into an indemnification agreement should consider whether the agreement complies with the other provisions of Part 4 of Title I of the Act and with other applicable laws.

[40 FR 31599, July 28, 1975. Redesignated at 41 FR 1906, Jan. 13, 1976]

§ 2509.75-5 Questions and answers relating to fiduciary responsibility

On June 25, 1975, the Department of Labor issued an interpretive bulletin, ERISA IB 75-5, containing questions and answers relating to certain aspects of the recently enacted Employee Retirement Income Security Act of 1974 (the "Act").

Pending the issuance of regulations or other guidelines, persons may rely on the answers to these questions in order to resolve the issues that are specifically considered. No inferences would be drawn regarding issues not raised which may be suggested by a particular question and answer or as to why certain questions, and not others, are included. Furthermore, in applying the questions and answers, the effect of subsequent legislation, regulations, court decisions, and interpretative bulletins must be considered. To the extent that plans utilize or rely on these answers and the requirements of regulations subsequently adopted vary from the answers relied on, such plans may have to be amended.

An index of the questions and answers, relating them to the appropriate sections of the Act, is also provided.

Fiduciary Responsibility Answer Book

INDEX

KEY TO QUESTION PREFIXES

D—Refers to Definitions.

FR—Refers to Fiduciary Responsibility.

Section No.	Question No.
3(21)	D1.
3(38)	FR-6, FR-7.
402(a)	FR-1, FR-2, FR-3.
402(b)(1)	FR-4, FR-5.
402(c)(3)	FR-6, FR-7.
404(a)	FR-10.
405(a)(3)	FR-10.
405(b)(1)(A)	FR-10.
406(a)	FR-9.
409(a)	FR-10.
412(a)	FR-8, FR-9.

D-1 Q: Is an attorney, accountant, actuary or consultant who renders legal, accounting, actuarial or consulting services to an employee benefit plan (other than an investment adviser to the plan) a fiduciary to the plan solely by virtue of the rendering of such services, absent a showing that such consultant (a) exercises discretionary authority or discretionary control respecting the management of the plan, (b) exercises authority or control respecting management or disposition of the plan's assets, (c) renders investment advice for a fee, direct or indirect, with respect to the assets of the plan, or has any authority or responsibility to do so, or (d) has any discretionary authority or discretionary responsibility in the administration of the plan?

A: No. However, while attorneys, accountants, actuaries and consultants performing their usual professional functions will ordinarily not be considered fiduciaries, if the factual situation in a particular case falls within one of the categories described in clauses (a) through (d) of this question, such persons would be considered

Appendix B

to be fiduciaries within the meaning of section 3(21) of the Act. The Internal Revenue Service notes that such persons would also be considered to be fiduciaries within the meaning of section 4975(e)(3) of the Internal Revenue Code of 1954.

FR-1 Q: If an instrument establishing an employee benefit plan provides that the plan committee shall control and manage the operation and administration of the plan and specifies who shall constitute the plan committee (either by position or by naming individuals to the committee), doe such provisions adequately satisfy the requirement in section 402(a) that a "named fiduciary" be provided for in a plan instrument?

A: Yes. While the better practice would be to state explicitly that the plan committee is the "named fiduciary" for purposes of the Act, clear identification of one or more persons, by name or title, combined with a statement that such person or persons have authority to control and manage the operation and administration of the plan, satisfies the "named fiduciary" requirement of section 402(a). The purpose of this requirement is to enable employees and other interested persons to ascertain who is responsible for operating the plan. The instrument in the above example, which provides that "the plan committee shall control and manage the operation and administration of the plan," and specifies, by name or position, who shall constitute the committee, fulfills this requirement.

FR-2 Q: In a union negotiated employee benefit plan, the instrument establishing the plan provides that a joint board on which employees and employers are equally represented shall control and manage the operation and administration of the plan. Does this provision adequately satisfy the requirement in section 402(a) that a "named fiduciary" be provided for in a plan instrument?

A: Yes, for the reasons stated in response to question FR-1. The joint board is clearly identified as the entity which has authority to control and manage the operation and administration of the plan, and the persons designated to be members of such joint board would be named fiduciaries under section 402(a).

FR-3 Q: May an employee benefit plan covering employees of a corporation designate the corporation as the "named fiduciary" for purposes of section 402(a)(1) of the Act?

A: Yes, it may. Section 402(a)(2) of the Act states that a "named fiduciary" is a fiduciary either named in the plan instrument or designated according to a procedure set forth in the plan instrument. A fiduciary is a "person" falling within the definition of fiduciary set forth in section 3(21)(A) of the Act. A "person" may be a corporation under the definition of person contained in section 3(9) of the Act. While such designation satisfies the requirement of enabling employees and other interested persons to ascertain the person or persons responsible for operating the plan, a plan instrument which designates a corporation as "named fiduciary" should provide for designation by the corporation of specified individuals or other persons to carry out specified fiduciary responsibilities under the plan, in accordance with section 405(c)(1)(B) of the Act.

FR-4 Q: A defined benefit pension plan's procedure for establishing and carrying out a funding policy provides that the plan's trustees shall, at a meeting duly called for the purpose, establish a funding policy and method which satisfies the requirements of Part 3 of Title I of the Act, and shall meet annually at a stated time of the year to review such funding policy and method. It further provides that all actions taken with respect to such funding policy and method and the reasons therefor shall be recorded in the minutes of the trustees' meetings. Does this procedure comply with section 402(b)(1) of the Act?

A: Yes. The above procedure specifies who is to establish the funding policy and method for the plan, and provides for a written record of the actions taken with respect to such funding policy and method, including the reasons for such actions. The purpose of the funding policy requirement set forth in section 402(b)(1) is to enable plan participants and beneficiaries to ascertain that the plan has a funding policy that meets the requirements of Part 3 of Title I of the Act. The procedure set forth above meets that requirement.

FR-5 Q: Must a welfare plan in which the benefits are paid out of the general assets of the employer have a procedure for establishing and carrying out a funding policy set forth in the plan instrument?

A: No. Section 402(b)(1) requires that the plan provide for such a procedure "consistent with the objectives of the plan" and requirements of Title I of the Act. In situations in which a plan is unfunded and Title I of the Act does not require the plan to be funded, there is

Appendix B

no need to provide for such a procedure. If the welfare plan were funded, a procedure consistent with the objectives of the plan would have to be established.

FR-6 Q: May an investment adviser which is neither a bank nor an insurance company, and which is not registered under the Investment Advisers Act of 1940 in reliance upon an exemption from registration provided in that Act, be appointed an investment manager under section 402(c)(3) of the Act?

A: No. The only persons who may be appointed an investment manager under section 402(c)(3) of the Act are persons who meet the requirements of section 3(38) of the Act—namely, banks (as defined in the Investment Advisers Act of 1940), insurance companies qualified under the laws of more than one state to manage, acquire and dispose of plan assets, or persons registered as investment advisers under the Investment Advisers Act of 1940.

FR-7 Q: May an investment adviser that has a registration application pending under the Investment Advisers Act of 1940 function as an investment manager under the Act prior to the effective date of registration under the Investment Advisers Act?

A: No, for the reasons stated in the answer to FR-6 above.

FR-8 Q: Under the temporary bonding regulation set forth in 29 CFR 2550.412-1, must a person who renders investment advice to a plan for a fee or other compensation, direct or indirect, but who does not exercise or have the right to exercise discretionary authority with respect to the assets of the plan, be bonded solely by reason of the provisions of such investment advice?

A: No. A person who renders investment advice, but who does not exercise or have the right to exercise discretionary authority with respect to plan assets, is not required to be bonded solely by reason of the provision of such investment advice. Such a person is not considered to be "handling" funds within the meaning of the temporary bonding regulation set forth in 29 CFR 2550.412-1, which incorporates by reference 29 CFR 464.7. For purposes of the temporary bonding regulation, only those fiduciaries who handle funds must be bonded. If, in addition to the rendering of investment advice, such person performs any additional function which constitutes the

Fiduciary Responsibility Answer Book

handling of plan funds under 29 CFR 464.7, the person would have to be bonded.

FR-9 Q: May an employee benefit plan purchase a bond covering plan officials?

A: Yes. The bonding requirement, which applies, with certain exceptions, to every plan official under section 412(a) of the Act, is for the protection of the plan and does not benefit any plan official or relieve any plan official of any obligation to the plan. The purchase of such bond by a plan will not, therefore, be considered to be in contravention of sections 406(a) or (b) of the Act.

FR-10 Q: An employee benefit plan is considering the construction of a building to house the administration of the plan. One trustee has proposed that the building be constructed on a cost plus basis by a particular contractor without competitive bidding. When the trustee was questioned by another trustee as to the basis of choice of the contractor, the impact of the building on the plan's administrative costs, whether a cost plus contract would yield a better price to the plan than a fixed price basis, and why a negotiated contract would be better than letting the contract for competitive bidding, no satisfactory answers were provided. Several of the trustees have argued that letting such a contract would be a violation of their general fiduciary responsibilities. Despite their arguments, a majority of the trustees appear to be ready to vote to construct the building as proposed. What should the minority trustees do to protect themselves from liability under section 409(a) of the Act and section 405(b)(1)(A) of the Act?

A: Here, where a majority of trustees appear ready to take action which would clearly be contrary to the prudence requirement of section 404(a)(1)(B) of the Act, it is incumbent on the minority trustees to take all reasonable and legal steps to prevent the action. Such steps might include preparations to obtain an injunction from a Federal District court under section 502(a)(3) of the Act, to notify the Labor Department, or to publicize the vote if the decision is to proceed as proposed. If, having taken all reasonable and legal steps to prevent the imprudent action, the minority trustees have not succeeded, they will not incur liability for the action of the majority. Mere resignation, however, without taking steps to prevent the imprudent action, will not suffice to avoid liability for the minority

Appendix B

trustees once they have knowledge that the imprudent action is under consideration.

More generally, trustees should take great care to document adequately all meetings where actions are taken with respect to management and control of plan assets. Written minutes of all actions taken should be kept describing the action taken, and stating how each trustee voted on each matter. If, as in the case above, trustees object to a proposed action on the grounds of possible violation of the fiduciary responsibility provisions of the Act, the trustees so objecting should insist that their objections and the responses to such objections be included in the record of the meeting. It should be noted that, where a trustee believes that a cotrustee has already committed a breach, resignation by the trustee as a protest against such breach will not generally be considered sufficient to discharge the trustee's positive duty under section 405(a)(3) to make reasonable efforts under the circumstances to remedy the breach.

§ 2509.75-8 Questions and answers relating to fiduciary responsibility under the Employee Retirement Income Security Act of 1974

The Department of Labor today issued questions and answers relating to certain aspects of fiduciary responsibility under the Act, thereby supplementing ERISA IB 75-5, (29 CFR 25555.75-5) which was issued on June 24, 1975 and published in the Federal Register on July 28, 1975 (40 FR 31598).

Pending the issuance of regulations or other guidelines, persons may rely on the answers to these questions in order to resolve the issues that are specifically considered. No inferences should be drawn regarding issues not raised which may be suggested by a particular question and answer or as to why certain questions, and not others, are included. Furthermore, in applying the questions and answers, the effect of subsequent legislation, regulations, court decisions, and interpretive bulletins must be considered. To the extent that plans utilize or rely on these answers and the requirements of regulations subsequently adopted vary from the answers relied on, such plans may have to be amended.

Fiduciary Responsibility Answer Book

An index of the questions and answers, relating them to the appropriate sections of the Act, is also provided.

INDEX

KEY TO QUESTION PREFIXES

D—Refers to Definitions.

FR—Refers to Fiduciary Responsibility.

Section No.	Question No.
3(21)(A)	D-2, D-3, D-4, D-5.
3(38)	FR-15.
402(c)(1)	FR-12.
402(c)(2)	FR-15
402(c)(3)	FR-15.
403(a)(2)	FR-15.
404(a)(1)(B)	FR-11, FR-17.
405(a)	FR-13, FR-14, FR-16.
405(c)(1)	FR-12, FR-15.
405(c)(2)	D-4, FR-13, FR-14, FR-16.
412	D-2.

NOTE: Questions D-2, D-3, D-4, and D-5 relate to not only section 3(21)(A) of Title I of the Act, but also section 4975(e)(3) of the Internal Revenue Code (section 2003 of the Act). The Internal Revenue Service has indicated its concurrence with the answers to these questions.

D2 Q: Are persons who have no power to make any decisions as to plan policy, interpretations, practices or procedures, but who perform the following administrative functions for an employee benefit plan, within a framework of policies, interpretations, rules, practices and procedures made by other persons, fiduciaries with respect to the plan:

(1) Application of rules determining eligibility for participation or benefits;

(2) Calculation of services and compensation credits for benefits;

Appendix B

(3) Preparation of employee communications material;

(4) Maintenance of participants' service and employment records;

(5) Preparation of reports required by government agencies;

(6) Calculation of benefits;

(7) Orientation of new participants and advising participants of their rights and options under the plan;

(8) Collection of contributions and application of contributions as provided in the plan;

(9) Preparation of reports concerning participants' benefits;

(10) Processing of claims; and

(11) Making recommendations to others for decisions with respect to plan administration?

A: No. Only persons who perform one or more of the functions described in section 3(21)(A) of the Act with respect to an employee benefit plan are fiduciaries. Therefore, a person who performs purely ministerial functions such as the types described above for an employee benefit plan within a framework of policies, interpretations, rules, practices and procedures made by other persons is not a fiduciary because such person does not have discretionary authority or discretionary control respecting management of the plan, does not exercise any authority or control respecting management or disposition of the assets of the plan, and does not render investment advice with respect to any money or other property of the plan and has no authority or responsibility to do so.

However, although such a person may not be a plan fiduciary, he may be subject to the bonding requirements contained in section 412 of the Act if he handles funds or other property of the plan within the meaning of applicable regulations.

The Internal Revenue Service notes that such persons would not be considered plan fiduciaries within the meaning of section 4975(e)(3) of the Internal Revenue Code of 1954.

D-3 Q: Does a person automatically become a fiduciary with respect to a plan by reason of holding certain positions in the administration of such plan?

Fiduciary Responsibility Answer Book

A: Some offices or positions of an employee benefit plan by their very nature require persons who hold them to perform one or more of the functions described in section 3(21)(A) of the Act. For example, a plan administrator or a trustee of a plan must, be the very nature of his position, have "discretionary authority or discretionary responsibility in the administration" of the plan within the meaning of section 3(21)(A)(iii) of the Act. Persons who hold such positions will therefore be fiduciaries.

Other offices and positions should be examined to determine whether they involve the performance of any of the functions described in section 3(21)(A) of the Act. For example, a plan might designate as a "benefit supervisor" a plan employee whose sole function is to calculate the amount of benefits to which each plan participant is entitled in accordance with a mathematical formula contained in the written instrument pursuant to which the plan is maintained. The benefit supervisor, after calculating the benefits, would then inform the plan administrator of the results of the calculations, and the plan administrator would authorize the payment of benefits to a particular plan participant. The benefit supervisor does not perform any of the functions described in section 3(21)(A) of the Act and is not, therefore, a plan fiduciary. However, the plan might designate as a "benefit supervisor" a plan employee who has the final authority to authorize or disallow benefit payments in cases where a dispute exists as to the interpretation of plan provisions relating to eligibility for benefits. Under these circumstances, the benefit supervisor would be a fiduciary within the meaning of section 3(21)(A) of the Act.

The Internal Revenue Service notes that it would reach the same answer to this question under section 4975(e)(3) of the Internal Revenue Code of 1954.

D-4 Q: In the case of a plan established and maintained by an employer, are members of the board of directors of the employer fiduciaries with respect to the plan?

A: Members of the board of directors of an employer which maintains an employee benefit plan will be fiduciaries only to the extent that they have responsibility for the functions described in section 3(21)(A) of the Act. For example, the board of directors may be responsible for the selection and retention of plan fiduciaries. In

Appendix B

such a case, members of the board of directors exercise "discretionary authority or discretionary control respecting management of such plan" and are, therefore, fiduciaries with respect to the plan. However, their responsibility, and, consequently, their liability, is limited to the selection and retention of fiduciaries (apart from co-fiduciary liability arising under circumstances described in section 405(a) of the Act). In addition, if the directors are made named fiduciaries of the plan, their liability may be limited pursuant to a procedure provided for in the plan instrument for the allocation of fiduciary responsibilities among named fiduciaries or for the designation of persons other than named fiduciaries to carry out fiduciary responsibilities, as provided in section 405(c)(2).

The Internal Revenue Service notes that it would reach the same answer to this question under section 4975(e)(3) of the Internal Revenue Code of 1954.

D-5 Q: Is an officer or employee of an employer or employee organization which sponsors an employee benefit plan a fiduciary with respect to the plan solely by reason of holding such office or employment if he or she performs none of the functions described in section 3(21)(A) of the Act?

A: No, for the reasons stated in response to question D-2.

The Internal Revenue Service notes that it would reach the same answer to this question under section 4975(e)(3) of the Internal Revenue Code of 1954.

FR-11 Q: In discharging fiduciary responsibilities, may a fiduciary with respect to a plan rely on information, data, statistics or analyses provided by other persons who perform purely ministerial functions for such plan, such as those persons described in D-2 above?

A: A plan fiduciary may rely on information, data, statistics or analyses furnished by persons performing ministerial functions for the plan, provided that he has exercised prudence in the selection and retention of such persons. The plan fiduciary will be deemed to have acted prudently in such selection and retention if, in the exercise of ordinary care in such situation, he has no reason to doubt the competence, integrity or responsibility of such persons.

FR-12 Q: How many fiduciaries must an employee benefit plan have?

A: There is no required number of fiduciaries that a plan must have. Each plan must, of course, have at least one named fiduciary who serves as plan administrator and, if plan assets are held in trust, the plan must have at least one trustee. If these requirements are met, three is no limit on the number of fiduciaries a plan may have. A plan may have as few or as many fiduciaries as are necessary for its operation and administration. Under section 402(c)(1) of the Act, if the plan so provides, any person or group of persons may serve in more than one fiduciary capacity, including serving both as trustee and administrator. Conversely, fiduciary responsibilities not involving management and control of plan assets may, under section 405(c)(1) of the Act, be allocated among named fiduciaries and named fiduciaries may designate persons other than named fiduciaries to carry out such fiduciary responsibilities, if the plan instrument expressly provides procedures for such allocation or designation.

FR-13 Q: If the named fiduciaries of an employee benefit plan allocate their fiduciary responsibilities among themselves in accordance with a procedure set forth in the plan for the allocation of responsibilities for operation and administration of the plan, to what extent will a named fiduciary be relieved of liability for acts and omissions of other named fiduciaries in carrying out fiduciary responsibilities allocated to them?

A: If named fiduciaries of a plan allocate responsibilities in accordance with a procedure for such allocation set forth in the plan, a named fiduciary will not be liable for acts and omissions of other named fiduciaries in carrying out fiduciary responsibilities which have been allocated to them, except as provided in section 405(a) of the Act, relating to the general rules of co-fiduciary responsibility, and section 405(c)(2)(A) of the Act, relating in relevant part to standards for establishment and implementation of allocation procedures.

However, if the instrument under which the plan is maintained does not provide for a procedure for the allocation of fiduciary responsibilities among named fiduciaries, any allocation which the named fiduciaries may make among themselves will be ineffective to relieve a named fiduciary from responsibility or liability for the

Appendix B

performance of fiduciary responsibilities allocated to other named fiduciaries.

FR-14 Q: If the named fiduciaries of an employee benefit plan designate a person who is not a named fiduciary to carry out fiduciary responsibilities, to what extent will the named fiduciaries be relieved of liability for the acts and omissions of such person in the performance of his duties?

A: If the instrument under which the plan is maintained provides for a procedure under which a named fiduciary may designate persons who are not named fiduciaries to carry out fiduciary responsibilities, named fiduciaries of the plan will not be liable for acts and omissions of a person who is not a named fiduciary in carrying out the fiduciary responsibilities which such person has been designated to carry out, except as provided in section 405(a) of the Act, relating to the general rules of co-fiduciary liability, and section 405(c)(2)(A) of the Act, relating in relevant part to the designation of persons to carry out fiduciary responsibilities.

However, if the instrument under which the plan is maintained does not provide for a procedure for the designation of persons who are not named fiduciaries to carry out fiduciary responsibilities, then any such designation which the named fiduciaries may make will not relieve the named fiduciaries from responsibility or liability for the acts and omissions of the persons so designated.

FR-15 Q: May a named fiduciary delegate responsibility for management and control of plan assets to anyone other than a person who is an investment manager as defined in section 3(38) of the Act so as to be relieved of liability for the acts and omissions of the person to whom such responsibility is delegated?

A: No. Section 405(c)(1) does not allow named fiduciaries to delegate to others authority or discretion to manage or control plan assets. However, under the terms of sections 403(a)(2) and 402(c)(3) of the Act, such authority and discretion may be delegated to persons who are investment managers as defined in section 3(38) of the Act. Further, under section 402(c)(2) of the Act, if the plan so provides, a named fiduciary may employ other persons to render advice to the named fiduciary to assist the named fiduciary in carrying out his investment responsibilities under the plan.

FR-16 Q: Is a fiduciary who is not a named fiduciary with respect to an employee benefit plan personally liable for all phases of the management and administration of the plan?

A: A fiduciary with respect to the plan who is not a named fiduciary is a fiduciary only to the extent that he or she performs one or more of the functions described in section 3(21)(A) of the Act. The personal liability of a fiduciary who is not a named fiduciary is generally limited to the fiduciary functions, which he or she performs with respect to the plan. With respect to the extent of liability of a named fiduciary of a plan where duties are properly allocated among named fiduciaries or where named fiduciaries properly designate other persons to carry out certain fiduciary duties, see question FR-13 and FR-14.

In addition, any fiduciary may become liable for breaches of fiduciary responsibility committed by another fiduciary of the same plan under circumstances giving rise to co-fiduciary liability, as provided in section 405(a) of the Act.

FR-17 Q: What are the ongoing responsibilities of a fiduciary who has appointed trustees or other fiduciaries with respect to these appointments?

A: At reasonable intervals the performance of trustees and other fiduciaries should be reviewed by the appointing fiduciary in such manner as may be reasonably expected to ensure that their performance has been in compliance with the terms of the plan and statutory standards, and satisfies the needs of the plan. No single procedure will be appropriate in all cases; the procedure adopted may vary in accordance with the nature of the plan and other facts and circumstances relevant to the choice of the procedure.

§ 2510.3-21 Definition of "Fiduciary"

(a)-(b) [Reserved]

(c) *Investment advice.* (1) A person shall be deemed to be rendering "investment advice" to an employe benefit plan, within the meaning of section 3(21)(A)(ii) of the Employee Retirement Income Security Act of 1974 (the Act) and this paragraph, only if:

Appendix B

(i) Such person renders advice to the plan as to the value of securities or other property, or makes recommendation as to the advisability of investing in, purchasing or selling securities or other property; and

(ii) Such person either directly or indirectly (e.g., through or together with any affiliate)—

(A) Has discretionary authority or control, whether or not pursuant to agreement, arrangement or understanding, with respect to purchasing or selling securities or other property for the plan; or

(B) Renders any advice described in paragraph (c)(1)(i) of this section on a regular basis to the plan pursuant to a mutual agreement, arrangement or understanding, written or otherwise, between such person and the plan or a fiduciary with respect to the plan, that such services will serve as a primary basis for investment decisions with respect to plan assets, and that such person will render individualized investment advice to the plan based on the particular needs of the plan regarding such matters as, among other things, investment policies or strategy, overall portfolio composition, or diversification of plan investments.

(2) A person who is a fiduciary with respect to a plan by reason of rendering investment advice (as defined in paragraph (c)(1) of this section) for a fee or other compensation, direct or indirect, with respect to any moneys or other property of such plan, or having any authority or responsibility to do so, shall not be deemed to be a fiduciary regarding any assets of the plan with respect to which such person does not have any discretionary authority, discretionary control or discretionary responsibility, does not exercise any authority or control, does not render investment advice (as defined in paragraph (c)(1) of this section) for a fee or other compensation, and does not have any authority or responsibility to render such investment advice provided that nothing in this paragraph shall be deemed to:

(i) Exempt such person from the provisions of section 405(a) of the Act concerning liability for fiduciary breaches by other fiduciaries with respect to any assets of the plan; or

(ii) Exclude such person from the definition of the term "party in interest" (as set forth in section 3(14)(B) of the Act) with respect to any assets of the plan.

(d) *Execution of securities transactions.* (1) A person who is a broker or dealer registered under the Securities Exchange Act of 1934, a reporting dealer who makes primary markets in securities of the United States Government or of an agency of the United States Government and reports daily to the Federal Reserve Bank of New York its positions with respect to such securities and borrowing thereon, or a bank supervised by the United States or a State, shall not be deemed to be a fiduciary, within the meaning of section 3(21)(A) of the Act, with respect to an employee benefit plan solely because such person executes transactions for the purchase or sale of securities on behalf of such plan in the ordinary course of its business as a broker, dealer, or bank, pursuant to instructions of a fiduciary with respect to such plan, if:

Neither the fiduciary nor any affiliate of such fiduciary is such broker, dealer, or bank; and

(ii) The instructions specify (A) the security to be purchased or sold, (B) a price range within which such security is to be purchased or sold, or, if such security is issued by an open-end investment company registered under the Investment Company Act of 1940 (15 U.S.C. 80a-1, *et seq.*), a price which first determined in accordance with Rule 22c-1 under the Investment Company Act of 1940 (17 CFR 270.22c-1), (C) a time span during which such security may be purchased or sold (not to exceed five business days), and (D) the minimum or maximum quantity of such security which may be purchased or sold within such price range, or, in the case of a security issued by an open-end investment company registered under the Investment Company Act of 1940, the minimum or maximum quantity of such security which may be purchased or sold, or the value of such security in dollar amount which may be purchased or sold, at the price referred to in paragraph (d)(1)(ii)(B) of this section.

(2) A person who is a broker-dealer, reporting dealer, or bank which is a fiduciary with respect to an employee benefit plan solely by reason of the possession or exercise of discretionary authority or discretionary control in the management of the plan or the management or disposition of plan assets in connection with the execution of a transaction or transactions for the purchase or sale of securities on behalf of such plan which fails to comply with the provisions of paragraph (d)(1) of this section, shall not be deemed to be a fiduciary

regarding any assets of the plan with respect to which such broker-dealer, reporting dealer or bank does not have any discretionary authority, discretionary control or discretionary responsibility, does not exercise any authority or control, does not render investment advice (as defined in paragraph (c)(1) of this section) for a fee or other compensation, and does not have any authority or responsibility to render such investment advice, provided that nothing in this paragraph shall be deemed to:

(i) Exempt such broker-dealer, reporting dealer, or bank from the provisions of section 405(a) of the Act concerning liability for fiduciary breaches by other fiduciaries with respect to any assets of the plan.

(ii) Exclude such broker-dealer, reporting dealer, or bank from the definition, of the term "party in interest" (as set forth in section 3(14)(B) of the Act) with respect to any assets of the plan.

(e) *Affiliate and control.* (1) For purposes of paragraphs (c) and (d) of this section, an "affiliate" of a person shall include:

(i) Any person directly or indirectly, through one or more intermediaries, controlling, controlled by, or under common control with such person;

(ii) Any officer, director, partner, employee or relative (as defined is section 3(15) of the Act) of such person; and

(iii) Any corporation or partnership of which such person is an officer, director or partner.

(2) For purposes of this paragraph, the term "control" means the power to exercise a controlling influence over the management or policies of a person other than an individual.

Glossary of Commonly Used Terms

The following is a glossary of commonly used terms (arranged in alphabetical order) that is intended to provide the reader with an additional guide to understanding the concepts that apply to ERISA-covered plans.

Actuary: A professional trained in actuarial science, mathematics, pensions and/or insurance, who performs various calculations relating to pension plans including the amount required to be contributed to a pension plan to provide for future benefits and the amount of distributions to be made to participants.

Adequate Consideration: In the case of a security where there is a generally recognized market either (i) the security's price on a nationally recognized exchange or (ii) if the security is not traded on a national exchange, a price not less favorable to the plan than the offering price for the security as established by the current bid and asked prices quoted by persons independent of the issuer and of any party in interest. In the case of a security not tradable on a national exchange, the fair market value of the security as determined in good faith by the trustee or named fiduciary, pursuant to the terms of the plan and the DOL regulations. In this instance, fair market value must be the price agreed upon by a willing buyer and willing seller in an arm's-length transaction, determined as of the applicable date and reflected in a written document meeting the requirements of the DOL regulations.

Administrator: Any person designated by the terms of the instrument under which the plan is operated, and if an administrator is not so designated, the plan sponsor (generally, the employer), or in the case of a plan for which an administrator is not designated and a plan sponsor cannot be identified, such other person as the Secretary of Labor may by regulation prescribe. The administrator is the fiduciary, subject to ERISA's fiduciary requirements, who is responsible for the administration, operation and management of a plan.

Annuity: A series of periodic payments, usually level in amount or adjusted according to some index (e.g., cost of living), that typically continue for the lifetime of the recipient. In contrast, an installment payment is one of a specific number of payments that will be paid whether or not the recipient lives to receive them. An annuity is usually in the form of a contract issued by an insurance company. For example, an annuity may be purchased as an investment under a plan or may be a form of benefits distributed to plan participants.

Anti-Inurement Requirement: An ERISA requirement that provides that assets of a plan may not inure to the benefit of any employer and shall be held for the exclusive purposes of providing benefits to participants in the plan and their beneficiaries and defraying reasonable expenses of administering the plan.

Bank Investment Contracts or BICs: A contract similar to a "GIC" (see "Guaranteed Investment Contracts"), but which is issued by a bank.

Beneficiary: A person designated by a participant, or by the terms of an employee benefit plan, who is or may become entitled to a benefit thereunder.

Benefit Plan Investor: Any employee benefit plan whether or not it is subject to the provisions of Title I of ERISA, a tax qualified retirement plan, or an individual retirement account or annuity, or any entity whose underlying assets include plan assets by reason of a plan's investment in the entity.

Breach of Fiduciary Duty: A fiduciary's violation of the duty owed to a plan and its participants and beneficiaries including the duty of prudence, duty to diversify, acting for the exclusive benefit of

Glossary of Commonly Used Terms

participants and their beneficiaries, and the obligation to follow plan doctrine.

Cafeteria Plan: A plan in which participants may choose among two or more benefits containing taxable or nontaxable compensation elements (i.e., cash or "qualified benefits"). The participant may choose qualified benefits by electing not to receive taxable cash compensation (or currently taxable benefits treated as cash). Many cafeteria plans are funded by salary reduction agreements. All of the participants must be either current or former employees.

Claims Procedure: The ERISA mandated procedure — which every ERISA plan must include in writing — to govern participants' (or beneficiaries') claims for benefits.

Class Exemption: An administrative exemption that applies to any parties in interest within the class of parties in interest specified in the exemption who meet the conditions of the exemption.

Code: The Internal Revenue Code of 1986, as amended.

Collectively Bargained Plan: Plans that provide benefits whose terms have been the subject of good faith bargaining between an employer or group of employers and employee representatives (such as unions). Typically, the basic terms are set forth under a collective bargaining agreement.

Co-fiduciary Liability: Under ERISA, plan fiduciaries are obligated to guard against breaches of fiduciary responsibilities by other plan fiduciaries, in addition to being responsible (and personally liable) for his or her own fiduciary breaches.

Core Alternative: Under an ERISA Section 404(c) plan, a participant must at a minimum be able to choose from among at least three investment alternatives which must constitute a broad range of alternatives. Each core alternative must be diversified and have materially different risk and return characteristics.

Defined Benefit Plan: A pension plan, other than a defined contribution plan, which provides a predetermined amount for retirement income to the participant, based on factors such as salary, length of service, and retirement age.

Defined Contribution Plan: A pension plan which provides for an individual account for each participant and for benefits based solely upon the amounts contributed to the participant's account, and any income, expenses, gains and losses, and any forfeitures of accounts of other participants which may be allocated to such participant's account.

Disqualified Person: A person who is a fiduciary, or a person providing services to the plan, or an employer any of whose employees are covered by the plan, or an employee organization any of whose members are covered by the plan, or an owner, direct or indirect, of 50 percent or more of (a) the combined voting power of all classes of stock entitled to vote or the total value of shares of all classes of stock of a corporation, (b) the capital interest or the profits interest of a partnership, or (c) the beneficial interest of a trust or unincorporated enterprise, which is an employer or an employee organization described above, or a member of the family of any individual described above, or a corporation, partnership, or trust or estate of which (or in which) 50 percent or more of (i) the combined voting power of all classes of stock entitled to vote or the total value of shares of all classes of stock of such corporation, (ii) the capital interest or profits interest of such partnership, or (iii) the beneficial interest of such trust of estate, is owned directly or indirectly, or held by persons described in subparagraph above, or an officer, director (or an individual having powers or responsibilities similar to those of officers or directors), a 10 percent or more shareholder, or a highly compensated employee (earning 10 percent or more of the yearly wages of an employer) of a person described above.

Diversification Rule: One of ERISA's fiduciary duty requirements mandating that fiduciaries diversify plan investments to avoid the risk of losses—unless circumstances make it imprudent to diversify. This rule is aimed toward minimizing investment risks by investing in many different types of vehicles.

DOL or Department of Labor: The U.S. Department of Labor which has enforcement authority over the regulatory and administrative (nontax) provisions of ERISA.

Duty to Monitor: A fiduciary's duty to monitor the actions of those individuals to whom fiduciary responsibilities have been delegated,

Glossary of Commonly Used Terms

requiring the appointing fiduciary to review and evaluate, at reasonable intervals, the performance of other fiduciaries.

Eligible Individual Account Plan: An individual account plan which is a profit-sharing, stock bonus, thrift, or savings plan, an employee stock ownership plan, or a pre-ERISA money purchase pension plan which, under the terms of the plan, invests primarily in qualifying employer securities.

Employee: Any individual employed by an employer.

Employee Organization: Any labor union or any organization of any kind, or any agency or employee representation committee, association, group, or plan, in which employees participate and which exists for the purpose, in whole or in part, of dealing with employers concerning an employee benefit plan, or other matters incidental to employment relationships; or any employees' beneficiary association organized for the purpose in whole or in part, of establishing such a plan.

Employee Welfare Benefit Plan or Welfare Plan: Any plan, fund, or program that is established or maintained by an employer and/or an employee organization, to provide for its participants or their beneficiaries, through the purchase of insurance or otherwise, the following benefits (1) medical, surgical, or hospital care or benefits, or benefits in the event of sickness, accident, disability, death or unemployment, or vacation benefits, apprenticeship or other training programs, or day care centers, scholarship funds, or prepaid legal services, or (2) any other stated benefit (other than pensions on retirement or death, and insurance to provide such pensions).

Employee Pension Benefit Plan or Pension Plan: Any plan, fund, or program which is established or maintained by an employer and/or an employee organization, to the extent that by its express terms or as a result of surrounding circumstances such plan, fund, or program provides retirement income to employees, or results in a deferral of income by employees for periods extending to the termination of covered employment or beyond.

Employee Stock Ownership Plan or ESOP: An individual account plan that is a stock bonus plan that is qualified, or a stock bonus plan and money purchase plan either of which is qualified, and that is designed to invest primarily in qualifying employer securities and that meets such other requirements as the Secretary of the Treasury may prescribe by regulation.

Employer: Any person acting directly as an employer, or indirectly in the interest of an employer, in relation to an employee benefit plan, including a group or association of employers acting for an employer in such capacity.

Employer Security: A security issued by an employer of employees covered by the plan, or by an affiliate of such employers.

Employer Real Property: Real property (and related personal property) which is leased to an employer of employees covered by the plan, or to an affiliate of such employer. For purposes of determining the time at which a plan acquires employer real property for purposes of this section, such property shall be deemed to be acquired by the plan on the date on which the plan acquires the property or on the date on which the lease to the employer (or affiliate) is entered into, whichever is later.

Equity Interests: Any interest in an entity other than an instrument that is treated as indebtedness under applicable local law and which has no substantial equity features. A profits interest in a partnership, an undivided ownership investment in property and a beneficial interest in a trust are equity interests.

ERISA: Employee Retirement Income Security Act of 1974, as amended — the federal statute that regulates employee benefit plans. It incorporates both the pertinent IRC provisions and labor law provisions and imposes fiduciary responsibilities and other standards (such as claims procedures, funding requirements, tax-qualification standards, etc.) on, and provides enforcement procedures regarding, both pension and welfare plans.

ERISA Section 404(c) Plan: A plan which is an individual account plan, such as a money purchase pension, profit sharing, 401(k), or 403(b) plan, that provides an opportunity for a participant or beneficiary to exercise control over the assets in his or her individual account, and choose, from within a broad range of investment alternatives, the manner in which some or all of the assets in his or her account are invested.

Glossary of Commonly Used Terms

ERISA Plan: See Plan.

Exclusive Benefit Rule: A fiduciary duty requirement under ERISA, whereby a plan fiduciary must exercise an unwavering duty of complete loyalty to plan participants and beneficiaries, to the exclusion of the interests of all other parties. Under ERISA, fiduciaries have a duty to administer plans solely in the interest of participants and beneficiaries and are not permitted to allow plan assets to inure to the benefit of the employer.

FDIC or Federal Deposit Insurance Corporation: A membership corporation which is sponsored by the federal government to insure repayment of savings and time deposits if a member bank becomes insolvent.

Fiduciary: A person (in the legal sense of an individual, corporation, etc.) who exercises any discretionary authority or discretionary control respecting the management of such plan or exercises any authority or control respecting the management or disposition of its assets, and who renders investment advice for a fee or other compensation, direct or indirect, with respect to any moneys or other property of such plan, or has any authority or responsibility to do so, or who has any discretionary authority or discretionary responsibility in the administration of such plan.

Fiduciary Duties or Standard of Conduct: The duties or standard of conduct that apply to a fiduciary which requires a fiduciary to discharge his or her duties with respect to a plan solely in the interest of the participants and beneficiaries and for the exclusive purpose of providing benefits to participants and their beneficiaries, and defraying reasonable expenses of administering the plan, with the care, skill, prudence, and diligence under the circumstances then prevailing that a prudent person acting in a like capacity and familiar with such matters would use in the conduct of an enterprise of a like character and with like aims, and by diversifying the investments of the plan so as to minimize the risk of large losses, unless under the circumstances it is clearly prudent not to do so, and in accordance with the documents and instruments governing the plan.

401(k) Plan: A tax-qualified defined contribution plan that allows participants to make employee contributions to the plan on a pre-tax basis, through salary reduction.

General Account GICS: A guaranteed investment contract whereby the contract holder does not have an interest in specific assets held by the insurance company. In the event that the insurance company becomes insolvent and is liquidated, the contract holder will have a claim against the insurer's general assets, but subject to the liquidation "priority" status assigned to the contract holder.

Guaranteed Investment Contracts or GICs: A contract issued by an insurance company on a negotiated basis, which specifies how and when contributions are made, when and at what rate interest is paid, and the length of the commitment. The contract is "guaranteed" by the insurance company and backed solely by its assets.

Indicia of Ownership: The bonds, stock certificates, or other evidence of ownership of plan assets.

Individual Exemption: An administrative exemption that applies only to the specific parties in interest named or otherwise defined in the exemption.

IRC: See Code.

IRS: Internal Revenue Service; the federal agency, which is part of the U.S. Department of the Treasury, that is charged with primary responsibility for administering, interpreting, and enforcing the Code. (Note, however, that the Secretary of the Treasury—and not the IRS—issues regulations under the Code.)

Investment Advisors Act of 1940: An act passed in 1940 that, by means of registration, brought persons and firms engaged in investment advisory work within regulation of the Securities and Exchange Commission (SEC).

Investment Company Act of 1940: An act designed to control many abuses associated with investment companies and investment advisors. The Securities and Exchange Commission (SEC) states that under this act, the activities of companies engaged primarily in the business of investing, reinvesting, and trading in securities and whose own securities are offered and sold to and held by the investing public, are subject to certain statutory prohibitions and to commission regulation in accordance with prescribed standards deemed necessary to protect the interests of investors and the public.

Glossary of Commonly Used Terms

Investment Manager: A person who has the power to manage, acquire, or dispose of any asset of a plan, and who is (a) registered as an investment adviser under the Investment Advisers Act of 1940, (b) is a bank, as defined in that Act, or (c) is an insurance company qualified to perform the above stated services under the laws of more than one State, and has acknowledged in writing that he is a fiduciary with respect to the plan. Generally, a plan's named fiduciary delegates investment authority over plan assets to an investment manager pursuant to an express authorization in the Plan documents.

Investment Advice: A person is deemed to be rendering "investment advice" to a plan if such person renders advice to the plan as to the value of securities or other property, or makes recommendations as to the advisability of investing in, purchasing, or selling securities or other property, and such person either directly or indirectly (e.g., through or together with any affiliate) (a) has discretionary authority or control, whether or not pursuant to agreement, arrangement or understanding, with respect to purchasing or selling securities or other property for the plan, or renders such advice on a regular basis to the plan pursuant to a mutual agreement, arrangement or understanding, written or otherwise, between such person and the plan or a fiduciary with respect to the plan, that such services will serve as a primary basis for investment decisions with respect to plan assets, and that such person will render individualized investment advice to the plan based on the particular needs of the plan regarding such matters as, among other things, investment policies or strategy, overall portfolio composition, or diversification of plan investments.

Individual Retirement Account or IRA: A trust or custodial account for the exclusive benefit of an individual or his beneficiaries. Under the Code, certain individuals can make tax-deductible contributions up to a fixed amount on an annual basis.

Keogh Plan: A qualified retirement plan, either a defined contribution plan or a defined benefit plan, that covers a self-employed person, although not excluding coverage for other employees.

Look-Through Rule: Generally, when a plan invests in another entity, the plan's assets include its investment, but do not include any of the underlying assets of the entity. However, in the event of a plan's investment in an equity interest of an entity that is neither a publicly offered security nor a security issued by an investment company registered under the Investment Company Act of 1940, its assets include both the equity interest and an undivided interest in each of the underlying assets of the entity.

Money Purchase Pension Plan: A defined contribution plan with individual accounts, subject to minimum funding requirements, whereby employer contributions, and any income, expenses, gains and losses and any forfeitures are allocated to participants' accounts.

Multiemployer Plan: A plan to which more than one employer is required to contribute, which is maintained pursuant to one or more collective bargaining agreements between one or more employee organizations and more than one employer, and which satisfies such other requirements as the Secretary of Labor may prescribe by regulation.

Named Fiduciary: A fiduciary who is named in the plan instrument, or who, pursuant to a procedure specified in the plan, is identified as a fiduciary by a person who is an employer and/or employee organization with respect to the plan and is given the express authority to control plan operations and administration.

Operating Company: An entity that is primarily engaged, directly or through a majority owned subsidiary or subsidiaries, in the production or sale of a product or service other than the investment of capital; a venture capital operating company; or a real estate operating company.

Participant: Any employee or former employee of an employer, or any member of an employee organization, who is or may become eligible to receive a benefit of any type from an employee benefit plan which covers employees of such employer or members of such organization, or whose beneficiaries may be eligible to receive any such benefit.

Person: An individual, partnership, joint venture, corporation, mutual company, joint-stock company, trust estate, unincorporated organization, association, or employee organization.

Party in Interest: Any fiduciary (including, but not limited to, any administrator, officer, trustee, or custodian), counsel, or employee of

Glossary of Commonly Used Terms

a plan, or a person providing services to such plan, or an employer any of whose employees are covered by such plan, and an employee organization any of whose members are covered by such plan. The term also includes: an indirect or direct owner of 50 percent of the combined voting power of all classes of voting stock or total value of stock, the capital interest of a partnership or the beneficial interest of a trust or unincorporated enterprise which is an employer or employee organization whose employees (or, in the case of an employee organization, members) are covered by a plan; or a relative of a fiduciary, service provider, employer (e.g., plan sponsor) or 50 percent owner; or an entity (corporation, partnership or trust or estate) of which 50 percent is owned directly or indirectly by a fiduciary, service provider, employer, employee organization or 50 percent owner; or an employee, officer, director or 10 percent or more shareholder (or 10 percent or more partner or joint venturer) of a service provider, employer (plan sponsor), employee organization, 50 percent owner, 50 percent owned entity or plan.

Pass-Through Provisions: The concept that certain rights appurtenant to a security (such as voting or tender rights) held by a plan are required to be or may be "passed through" to plan participants and beneficiaries. For example, in the ESOP context, the IRC requires that the vote on allocated shares of employer securities that are readily tradable on an established securities exchange be passed through to plan participants. If the employer has securities that are not readily tradable, the IRC requires that the vote on allocated ESOP shares be passed through to participants only with respect to generally significant corporate transactions (e.g., merger, recapitalization, liquidation or sale of substantially all of the assets). ERISA imposes fiduciary duty requirements with respect to pass-through provisions.

Plan: An employee welfare benefit plan or an employee pension benefit plan or a plan which is both an employee welfare benefit plan and an employee pension benefit plan.

Plan Administrator: See Administrator.

Plan Assets: The assets of a plan which are generally identified on the basis of ordinary notions of property rights. A plan's assets generally include only the investment in another entity, and not the underlying assets of the entity. However, the DOL has expanded the definition of a plan asset to apply the look-through rule. This means that not only is a plan's equity interest in another entity a plan asset, but in certain circumstances, so is an undivided interest in each underlying asset held by the entity considered to be a plan asset.

Plan Sponsor: The employer in the case of a plan established or maintained by a single employer, or the employee organization in the case of a plan established or maintained by an employee organization, or in the case of a plan established or maintained by two or more employers or jointly by one or more employers and one or more employee organizations, the association, committee, joint board of trustees, or other similar group of representatives of the parties who establish or maintain the plan.

Plan Investment: Generally, when a plan invests in another entity, the plan's assets include its investment, but do not, solely by reason of such investment, include any of the underlying assets of the entity. However, in the case of a plan's investment in an equity interest of an entity that is neither a publicly-offered security nor a security issued by an investment company registered under the Investment Company Act of 1940 its assets include both the equity interest and an undivided interest in each of the underlying assets of the entity unless it is established that the entity is an operating company, or equity participation in the entity by benefit plan investors is not significant.

Preemption: A broadly interpreted concept that ERISA supersedes any and all State laws to the extent that they "relate to" any ERISA plan. However, the savings clause under ERISA "saves" or "exempts" from the scope of preemption certain State laws that regulate insurance, banking or securities. For this purpose, ERISA plans are not deemed to be engaged in the insurance or banking business.

Profit Sharing Plan: A defined contribution plan where contributions are allocated among participants' accounts based on a predetermined formula and will be paid following a stated age, fixed number of years or upon an occurrence of an event (e.g., disability, retirement, death, or separation from service).

Prohibited Transaction Exemption: The DOL has the authority to issue rulings and regulations on, and grant exemptions from, the prohibited transaction restrictions. In granting exemptions from the prohibited transaction rules, the DOL requires the exemption to be

Glossary of Commonly Used Terms

administratively feasible, be in the interests of the plan, its participants and beneficiaries, and is protective of the rights of the plan's participants and beneficiaries.

Prudent Expert Rule: In the context of investing plan assets, a fiduciary charged with an investment decision must act as a prudent expert would under similar circumstances, taking into account all relevant substantive factors, as they appeared at the time of the investment decision, not upon hindsight. ERISA may require that the plan fiduciary retain qualified experts and consultants to assist in the investing of plan assets.

Prudent Person Rule: The standard under which a fiduciary must perform his duties. A fiduciary must act "with the care, skill, prudence, and diligence under the circumstances then prevailing that a prudent acting in a like capacity and familiar with such matters would use in the conduct of an enterprise of a like character and with like aims."

Prohibited Transactions: ERISA prohibits certain transactions between a plan and parties-in-interest including, for example, any direct or indirect sale or exchange, or leasing, of any property between a plan and a party-in-interest, any lending of money or other extension of credit between a plan and a party-in-interest, any furnishing of goods, services, or facilities between a plan and a party-in-interest, any transfer to, or use by or for the benefit of, a party-in-interest of the income or assets of a plan, any act by a party-in-interest who is a fiduciary whereby he deals with the income or assets of a plan in his own interest or for his own account, or any receipt of any consideration for his own personal account by any party-in-interest who is a fiduciary from any party dealing with the plan in connection with a transaction involving the income or assets of the plan.

Publicly Offered Security: A security that is freely transferable, part of a widely held class of securities, and covered under certain federal securities registration rules.

Punitive Damages: Damages which are allowed as an enhancement of compensatory damages because of the wanton, reckless, malicious, or oppressive character of the acts committed by the wrongful party. These damages are not available for a breach of fiduciary duty.

Qualifying Employer Real Property or QERP: Parcels of employer real property if a substantial number of the parcels are dispersed geographically, if each parcel of real property and the improvements thereon are suitable (or adaptable without excessive cost) for more than one use, even if all of such real property is leaded to one lessee (which may be an employer, or an affiliate of an employer), and if the acquisition and retention of such property comply with the provisions of this part to the extent it requires diversification.

Qualifying Employer Security or QES: An employer security which is stock, a marketable obligation such as a bond, debenture, note, or certificate, or other evidence of indebtedness, acquired at a fair and reasonable public offering price and which meets other standard requirements under ERISA, or an interest in a publicly traded partnership, but only if such partnership is an existing partnership.

Qualified Professional Asset Manager or QPAM: A bank, savings and loan association, insurance company, or an investment advisor which manages investment funds, and who acknowledges in writing that it is a fiduciary, and must be independent of the parties in interest. Generally, each bank, savings and loan association, and insurance company that is a QPAM must have equity capital or net worth in excess of $1 million. An investment advisor must have at least $50 million in total client assets under its management and control and either (1) shareholders' or partners' equity in excess of $750,000 or (2) payment of all its liabilities is unconditionally guaranteed by (a) affiliates with shareholders' or partners' equity in excess of $750,000, (b) a bank, savings and loan association or insurance company with equity capital or net worth of at least $1 million or (c) a broker-dealer with net worth in excess of $750,000.

Real Estate Operating Company: An operating company in which at least 50 percent of its assets (valued at cost) are invested in real estate that is managed or developed, where the entity has the right to substantially participate directly in the management or development of the eligible real estate, and where the entity actually engages directly in real estate management or development.

Right of Contribution or Indemnity: Derived from traditional trust law principles, the right to seek payment from a co-fiduciary to recover losses to the plan for the co-fiduciary's breach of ERISA's fiduciary duty. The courts are divided on the issue of whether a fiduciary who is sued for a breach of fiduciary duty has an implied right of contribution or indemnity against other fiduciaries.

SEC: Securities and Exchange Commission.

Securities Act of 1933: An act approved in 1933 that provides the process by which securities are offered to the public or by which securities are otherwise distributed to private investors, institutions or groups of investors and subsequently offered to the public. In either type of distribution, unless an exemption applies, this act requires registration of the securities.

Securities and Exchange Act of 1934: An act approved in 1934 that seeks to outlaw misrepresentation, manipulation, and other abusive practices in securities markets and to establish and maintain "just and equitable principles of trade which would be conducive to open, fair and orderly markets." It is directed at regulating all aspects of public trading of securities. The act marked the first time that the securities markets were brought under uniform regulation; in addition, it contains provisions affecting corporate practices, trading on the securities markets, and imposes various reporting requirements.

Separate Account GICS: A guaranteed investment contract that, upon the liquidation of the insurer, provides the contract holder with a legally enforceable right to have the obligation owed to it satisfied out of specific assets held in a "separate account" that generally will not be subject to the creditors of the insurance carrier.

Self-dealing: Under ERISA, prohibited activities by a plan fiduciary such as using plan assets for personal profit, accepting bribes or kickbacks from anyone dealing with the plan, or acting on behalf of a party whose interest are adverse to those of the plan.

Settlor Function: An action or decision made by the sponsoring employer (or in the case of a collectively bargained plan, the employers and the employee representatives), rather than by a fiduciary exercising discretion.

Single-Employer Plan: A plan which is not a multiemployer plan.

Social Investing: An investment strategy or decision pursuant to which a plan fiduciary chooses or avoids certain investments primarily for their potential to affect the community at large or a targeted group of people or region, rather than for the purpose of maximizing monetary return for the plan.

Split-Dollar Life Insurance: A type of life insurance in which the employer and employee share in premiums, ownership, and death benefits.

Summary Plan Description or SPD: An understandable and detailed, summary description of an employee benefit plan's provisions that must be provided to plan participants and beneficiaries, and, in most cases, filed with the U.S. Department of Labor.

Tax-Sheltered Annuity Plan or 403(b) Plan: A plan that provides for the deferral of income by employees of certain tax-exempt organizations through an annuity in accordance with Section 403(b) of the Code.

Top Hat Plan: A plan maintained by an employer primarily for the purpose of providing deferred compensation for a select group of management or highly compensated employees. A top hat plan is exempt from most of ERISA's requirements (including the fiduciary duty requirements) — although it is subject to limited reporting and disclosure and the claim procedure requirements.

Trust: The entity in which a party (the trustee) holds legal title to the assets of a plan for the benefit of the plan's participants and beneficiaries.

Trustee: Any person or group of persons that serves in a fiduciary capacity with respect to a plan, who holds all plan assets in trust and is either named in the trust document or plan document, or is appointed by a person who is a named fiduciary, and upon acceptance of being named or appointed, such trustee or trustees shall have exclusive authority and discretion to manage and control the assets of the plan, except to the extent that the plan expressly provides that the trustee or trustees are subject to the direction of a named fiduciary who is not a trustee, in which case the trustees shall be subject to proper directions of such fiduciary which are made in accordance with the terms of the plan and which are not contrary to ERISA, or authority to manage, acquire, or dispose of assets of the plan is delegated to one or more investment managers.

Glossary of Commonly Used Terms

Trustee Responsibility: Any responsibility provided in the plan's trust instrument (if any) to manage or control the assets of the plan, other than a power under the trust instrument of a named fiduciary to appoint an investment manager.

Twenty Percent (20%) Penalty: In the case of any breach of fiduciary responsibility by a fiduciary, or any knowing participation in such a breach by any other person, the DOL has the authority to assess a civil penalty of 20 percent of the amount payable pursuant to a court order or settlement agreement with the DOL against such fiduciary or other person.

VEBA: Voluntary employees' beneficiary association; a tax-exempt welfare benefit fund regulated by Code Section 501(c)(9) that pays death, sickness, accident, or other benefits to members, their dependents and/or beneficiaries.

Venture Capital Operating Company: An operating company in which at least 50 percent of its assets (valued at cost, and excluding certain short-term investments made pending long-term commitments) are invested in venture capital investments; the entity's eligible venture capital investments are in operating companies (other than a venture capital operating company) in which the entity has contractual management rights; and the entity actually exercises management rights in one or more of such operating companies.

Welfare Benefit Plan: See Employee Welfare Benefit Plan.

Tables

[*References are to question numbers.*]

Table of ERISA Sections

Section		Section	
3(1)	1:3, 8:1, 8:8	4	8:5
3(2)	8:1	4(a)	8:1, 8:12
3(2)(A)	8:4	4(b)	1:3, 8:1
3(3)	8:1, 8:3	4(b)(1)	8:13
3(7)	3:15	4(b)(2)	8:13
3(8)	3:16	4(b)(3)	8:13
3(9)	2:1, 2:11	4(b)(4)	8:13
3(14)	5:4	4(b)(5)	8:13
3(16)(A)	2:23	101(a)	3:16
3(16)(B)	2:18	101(b)	3:16, 3:17
3(18)(A)	7:34	101(d)	3:17
3(21)(A)	1:1, 2:1, 2:7, 2:16, 2:27, 7:6	101(e)	3:17
3(21)(A)(i)	7:45	103(a)(3)	8:17
3(32)	8:13	103(a)(3)(A)	2:30
3(33)	8:13	201	8:5
3(36)	1:3, 2:11	206(d)	6:6
3(37)	2:36	206(d)(3)	6:43
3(38)	1:8, 2:24, 4:20, 7:6, 8:43	301	8:5
		401	5:5, 8:5

T-1

Fiduciary Responsibility Answer Book

[References are to question numbers.]

Section		Section	
401(a)	8:1		5:41, 7:41
401(a)(1)	8:14	404(a)	8:18
401(a)(2)	8:14	404(a)(1)	1:2, 3:1, 7:41, 8:21
401(b)	8:32		
401(b)(2)	8:52	404(a)(1)(A)	3:2, 3:14, 3:36, 7:16, 8:39
401(b)(2)(B)	8:23		
401(f)	8:34	404(a)(1)(B)	3:4, 7:16, 8:37
401(h)	8:34		
402(a)	2:9, 8:24	404(a)(1)(C)	3:11, 8:39
402(a)(3)	4:4	404(a)(1)(D)	3:13, 7:5, 8:41
402(b)(1)	2:25	404(a)(2)	3:11, 3:25
402(b)(4)	8:21	404(b)	3:27, 4:3, 4:44, 7:48
402(c)(1)	2:6, 2:30	404(c)	1:8, 2:35, 3:28, 4:2, 4:4, 4:24, 4:27-4:49, 5:43, 7:26, 7:35, 7:50
402(c)(3)	2:24, 4:14		
403	5:41, 8:28, 8:29		
403(a)	2:10, 2:15, 4:13, 7:45, 8:15, 8:17, 8:28, 8:29, 8:38, 8:41	404(c)(1)(i)	4:39
		404(d)(1)	3:30
		405	2:7, 4:49
403(a)(1)	8:42	405(a)	4:10, 5:9, 8:15
403(a)(2)	4:4, 8:43	405(a)(1)	1:9, 3:22, 4:9
403(b)	5:47, 8:7		
403(b)(1)	8:30	405(a)(2)	4:11
403(b)(2)	8:31	405(a)(3)	1:9, 3:22, 4:9, 4:10
403(b)(3)	8:34		
403(b)(5)	8:33	405(a)(20)	3:22
403(b)(7)	8:33	405(b)	2:6, 8:15
403(c)	5:46, 8:28, 8:46	405(b)(1)	3:23
403(c)(1)	5:45, 7:16, 8:45, 8:48	405(b)(1)(B)	4:12
		405(b)(2)	3:23
403(c)(3)	8:41	405(c)	8:44
403(d)	5:46, 8:28	405(c)(1)	2:10, 3:24, 4:1, 4:2, 4:4
403(d)(1)	8:49		
403(d)(2)	8:50	405(c)(1)(B)	2:20
404	3:36, 5:17,	405(c)(3)	4:2, 4:3

T-2

Tables

[References are to question numbers.]

Section		Section	
405(d)	2:24, 8:43		7:45, 8:22
405(d)(1)	3:26, 4:4	408(b)(1)	5:15
405(d)(2)	3:26	408(b)(2)	5:23, 8:18
406	5:1, 5:5, 5:12, 6:16, 7:6, 7:9, 7:16	408(b)(3)	5:14, 7:33
		408(b)(6)	5:33
406(a)	3:36, 8:18	408(b)(7)	5:12
406(a)(1)(A)	5:12	408(c)	5:2, 5:3
406(a)(1)(B)	5:14	408(d)	5:16
406(a)(1)(C)	5:22	408(e)	4:44, 5:12, 5:14, 7:27, 7:34
406(a)(1)(D)	5:34		
406(a)(1)(E)	5:29, 7:27	409	6:6, 6:13, 6:15, 6:64
406(a)(2)	5:29, 7:27		
406(b)	5:23, 8:18	409(a)	1:6, 2:2, 6:1, 6:4, 6:9, 6:12, 6:64
406(b)(2)	5:35		
406(b)(3)	5:36	409(b)	6:2
406(d)(2)	7:29	410	5:38, 6:31
406(d)(4)	7:29	410(a)	6:23, 6:34
407	5:29, 7:6, 8:39	410(b)	6:28, 6:29
407(a)(1)	3:25, 7:27	411(a)	6:18, 8:37
407(a)(2)	3:25, 5:29, 7:27	411(b)	6:18
407(b)(1)	3:25, 7:27	412	2:7, 7:6, 8:15, 8:37
407(d)(1)	7:28		
407(d)(3)	7:28	412(a)	8:68
407(d)(3)(A)	7:30	412(a)(1)	8:69
407(d)(3)(B)	7:31	412(a)(2)	8:69
407(d)(5)	5:14, 7:28	412(b)	8:68
407(d)(6)	7:32	412(c)	8:68
407(e)	7:28	501	5:8, 6:18
407(f)(1)	7:28	502	5:8
407(f)(2)	7:28	502(a)	1:4
407(f)(3)	7:28	502(a)(2)	1:6, 6:1, 6:64
408	7:6		
408(a)	5:39	502(a)(3)	6:64
408(b)	5:15, 5:39,	502(c)(1)	3:17

T-3

Fiduciary Responsibility Answer Book

[References are to question numbers.]

Section		Section	
502(c)(2)	3:17	506	1:4
502(c)(3)	3:17	510	6:13, 6:21, 6:22
502(h)	1:4	511	6:19
502(i)	2:27, 5:9, 6:16, 6:17	514	8:2
		514(a)	1:7, 3:32, 3:33
502(l)	5:9, 6:28, 6:31, 6:66	514(b)(2)	3:33
		514(b)4)	3:33
502(l)(1)	1:4, 6:15	514(b)(5)	3:33
502(l)(3)	6:15	4041(a)(2)	3:30
502(l)(4)	6:16	4041(b)(3)	7:18
503	6:43	4044	8:49
503(1)	6:54	4044(d)(1)	8:47
503(2)	2:10, 6:54	4044(d)(2)	8:47
504	1:4		

Tables

[*References are to question numbers.*]

Table of Internal Revenue Code Sections

Section	
72(p)	5:16
72(p)(1)(a)	5:15
125	8:11
129	8:11
133(b)(7)	7:35
280G	8:14
401	5:6, 7:32
401(a)(2)	5:47, 8:39, 8:45
401(a)(31)	6:43
401(f)	8:33
402(c)	6:43
402(c)(3)	5:16
402(f)	3:35
404	5:46
404(a)(2)	5:6
409(e)(2)	7:35
409(e)(3)	7:35
409(e)(5)	7:35
414(g)	2:23
414(p)	6:43
415	3:35, 8:13
420	8:48
501(c)(3)	8:33
503(c)(9)	8:50
503(e)	7:28

Section	
4975	3:36, 4:48, 5:8, 5:9, 5:5, 6:16, 6:17, 8:45
4975(a)	2:27, 5:1, 5:8, 5:11, 6:17, 6:65
4975(b)	5:8, 6:17, 6:65
4975(c)	7:6
4975(c)(1)	5:12
4975(c)(1)(A)	5:12
4975(c)(1)(B)	5:14
4975(c)(1)(C)	5:22
4975(c)(1)(D)	5:34
4975(c)(1)(F)	5:36
4975(c)(2)	5:39
4975(d)(3)	5:14, 7:33
4975(d)(13)	7:34
4975(e)	5:5, 7:35
4975(e)(2)	5:4
4975(f)(1)	5:11
4975(f)(5)	5:37
4980	3:30
4980(d)	8:47
4999	8:14
6039D	3:17, 8:11
6058	3:17

T-5

[References are to question numbers.]

Table of United States Code Sections

Section

18 USC 662 . . . . 6:20
18 USC 664 . . . . 6:20
18 USC 1001 . . . . 6:20
18 USC 1027 . . . . 6:20
18 USC 1341 . . . . 6:19

Section

18 USC 1343 . . . . 6:19
18 USC 1954 . . . . 6:20
18 USC 1961 et seq 6:19
42 USC 12101 et seq 6:22

Tables

[References are to question numbers.]

Table of Treasury Regulations

Section		Section	
1.46-8(d)-8(iv)	7:36	1.503(e)-1(b)(3)(i)(c)-(g)	7:28
1.414(g)	2:23	53.4963-(1)(e)(3)	5:37
1.501(c)(9)-4(d)	8:50	54-4975-7	7:33

[References are to question numbers.]

Table of Department of Labor (DOL) Regulations

Section		Section	
2506.502i-1	6:17	2510.3-1(a)(2)	8:8
2509.75-2	8:15	2510.3-1(c)	1:3, 8:10
2509.75-2(b)	8:32	2510.3-1(d)	1:3, 8:10
2509.75-4	6:25, 6:31	2510.3-1(e)	1:3, 8:10
2509.75-5	2:2	2510.3-1(f)	1:3, 8:10
2509.75-5, D-1	2:27	2510.3-1(g)	1:3, 8:10
2509.75-5, FR-1	2:13, 3:17	2510.3-1(h)	1:3, 8:10
2509.75-5, FR-2	2:13	2510.3-1(i)	1:3, 8:10
2509.75-5, FR-3	2:11, 2:20, 3:17	2510.3-1(j)	1:3, 8:10
		2510.3-1(k)	1:3, 8:10
2509.75-5, FR-6	4:20	2510.3-2(c)	1:3, 8:4
2509.75-5, FR-7	4:20	2510.3-2(d)	1:3, 8:6
2509.75-5, FR-10	4:10, 4:12, 6:44, 6:49	2510.3-2(f)	1:3, 8:7
		2510.3-2(g)	1:3
2509.75-8	2:2, 4:7	2510.3-3(b)	1:3, 3:29, 8:3
2509.75-8, D-2	2:7, 2:31, 6:53	2510.3-3(c)	1:3, 8:3
2509.75-8, D-3	2:5, 2:29, 2:32	2510.3-3(c)(1)	3:29
		2510.3-3(c)(2)	3:29
2509.75-8, D-4	2:6, 2:7, 2:19, 2:20	2510.3-21(c)(1)	2:33, 2:34
		2510.3-21(d)(1)	2:26
2509.75-8, FR-12	2:7, 2:8	2510.3-21(d)(2)	2:26
2509.75-8, FR-13	2:14, 4:1, 4:6	2510.3-101(a)(2)	8:51, 8:52, 8:55
2509.75-8, FR-14	2:14, 4:6	2510.3-101(b)(1)	8:53
2509.75-8, FR-15	2:25	2510.3-101(b)(2)	8:54
2509.75-8, FR-16	2:7, 2:12, 4:21	2510.3-101(b)(3)	8:54
		2510.3-101(b)(4)	8:54
2509.75-9	2:30	2510.3-101(c)	8:60, 8:61

Tables

[References are to question numbers.]

Section	
2510.3-101(d)	8:59, 8:61
2510.3-101(e)	8:60
2510.3-101(f)(1)	8:57
2510.3-101(f)(2)	8:58
2510.3-101(g)	8:63, 8:64
2510.3-101(h)	8:55, 8:62
2510.3-101(h)(1)	4:22, 8:56
2510.3-101(h)(2)	8:56
2510.3-101(h)(3)	8:56
2510.3-101(h)(4)	8:56
2510.3-101(i)	8:65
2510.3-101(j)(2)	8:58
2510.3-101(j)(3)	8:58
2510.3-101(j)(4)	8:58
2510.3-101(j)(5)	8:61
2510.3-101(j)(6)	8:61
2510.3-101(j)(7)	8:60
2510.3-101(j)(8)	8:60
2510.3-101(j)(10)	8:64
2510.3-101(j)(11)	8:64
2510.3-101(j)(12)	8:56
2510.3-102(a)	8:15
2520.103-1(b)(5)	8:17
2550.403a-1	8:15, 8:40
2550.403a-1(a)	8:39
2550.403a-1(b)(2)	7:45
2550.403a-1(b)(3)	7:45
2550.404a-1	7:10
2550.404a-1(b)	3:5, 3:9
2550.404a-1(b)(2)	7:41
2550.404b-1	4:3, 4:44, 7:48
2550.404b-1(a)	3:27
2550.404c-1	3:28, 4:33, 4:34, 4:35, 4:38-4:40, 4:42, 4:45, 4:47-4:49
2550.404c-1(a)(1)	4:27
2550.404c-1(b)(1)	4:29
2550.404c-1(b)(2)(B)(2)(ii)(c)	4:31
2550.404c-1(b)(2)(i)(A)	4:30, 4:43
2550.404c-1(b)(2)(i)(B)	4:30
2550.404c-1(b)(2)(i)(B)(1)	4:40, 4:43
2550.404c-1(b)(2)(i)(B)(2)	4:41
2550.404c-1(b)(2)(ii)(B)	4:44
2550.404c-1(b)(2)(ii)(C)(2)	4:35
2550.404c-1(b)(2)(ii)(C)(2)(ii)	4:35
2550.404c-1(b)(3)	4:33
2550.404c-1(b)(3)(i)(C)	4:33
2550.404c-1(c)(1)	4:36
2550.404c-1(c)(2)	4:36
2550.404c-1(c)(3)	4:36, 4:37
2550.404c-1(c)(4)	4:46
2550.404c-1d	4:43
2550.404c-1(d)(1)	4:48
2550.404c-1(d)(2)(i)	4:49
2550.404c-1(d)(2)(ii)	4:44
2550.404c-1(d)(2)(ii)(E)(4)	4:45
2550.404c-1(d)(2)(ii)(E)(4)(vii)	4:43
2550.404c-1(d)(2)(ii)(E)(4)(viii)	4:43
2550.404c-1(d)(2)(ii)(E)(4)(ix)	4:43
2550.404c-1(f)(2)	4:31
2550.404c-1(f)(3)	4:31
2550.404c-1(f)(5)	4:49
2550.404c-1(f)(6)	4:48
2550.404c-1(f)(7)	4:49
2550.408b	5:17, 5:21
2550.408b-1(a)(1)(i)	5:17
2550.408b-1(a)(2)	5:16

Fiduciary Responsibility Answer Book

[References are to question numbers.]

Section	
2550.408b-1(b)	5:17
2550.408b-1(c)	5:17
2550.408b-1(d)	5:18
2550.408b-1(e)	5:20
2550.408b-1(f)	5:21
2550.408b-1(f)(1)	5:21
2550.408b-2(c)	5:24
2550.408b-2(e)	5:23
2550.408b-2(e)(1)	5:36
2550.408b-2(e)(2)	3:3, 5:32
2550.408b-2(f)	3:3, 5:23
2550.408b-2(f), Ex 1	5:32
2550.408b-2(f), Ex 5	5:30
2550.408b-2(f), Ex 6	5:30
2550.408b-2(f), Ex 7	5:32, 6:46
2550.408b-3	7:33
2550.408c-2(b)(1)	5:26
2550.408c-2(b)(2)	5:27, 5:28
2550.408c-2(b)(3)	5:28

Section	
2550.408c-2(b)(5)	5:26
2560.503-1(b)	6:54
2560.503-1(b)(2)	6:63
2560.503-1(c)	6:61
2560.503-1(d)	6:51, 6:52
2560.503-1(e)	6:55
2560.503-1(f)	6:56
2560.503-1(g)	6:57
2560.503-1(h)	6:58
2560.503-1(h)(3)	6:59
2560.503-1(j)	6:62
2560.503-1(l)	6:61
2570.31(b)	5:43
2570.31(e)	5:44

DOL Proposed Regulations

2510.3-18	7:34
2560.5021-1	6:15

Tables

[References are to question numbers.]

Table of Miscellaneous Releases, Exemptions, Opinions, Letters, and PBGC Material

Section

ERISA Technical Releases

88-01	8:35
92-01	8:29, 8:35

DOL Technical Releases

85-1	5:41
88-1	8:17
92-01	8:17

DOL News Releases

75-127	6:28, 6:30

Prohibited Transaction Class Exemptions (PTCE)

76-1	5:43
77-10	5:43
80-26	5:43
80-51	5:43
81-6	5:43
84-14	4:25, 4:26, 5:43
84-24	5:43
85-68	5:43
88-59	5:14

Prohibited Transaction Exemptions (PTE)

82-125	5:42

Section

83-124	5:42

Advisory Opinion Letters

77-66/67A	6:34
77-79/80A	6:4
78-25A	7:28
78-29A	6:34
79-42A	3:3
81-30A	3:20
81-52A	8:45
81-69A	5:13
82-38A	8:13
82-49A	7:47, 8:41
82-52A	8:41
83-51A	8:32
84-09A, n.2	3:3, 6:46
84-14A	7:48
85-36A	7:41
88-09A	2:17, 8:22
88-10A	8:11, 8:35
88-52A	2:17
88-02A	2:17
89-05A	8:57
89-08A	5:34
89-30A	5:17
90-03A	8:13
90-05A	5:13

Fiduciary Responsibility Answer Book

[References are to question numbers.]

Section

90-22A	8:67
91-02A	8:5
91-26A	8:8
91-28A	3:27
92-02A	8:66
92-08A	5:32
92-27A	7:28

Opinion Letters

75-80	3:27
76-20	4:20
76-95	6:3
77-46	7:46

Letters

Helmuth Fandl,
  Avon Products, Inc . . . 7:35, 7:36

Section

Kirk F Maldonado 2:19
Robert A.G. Monks, Institutional
  Shareholder Services, Inc . . . 7:35
John Welsh, Carter Hawley Hale
  Stores, Inc Profit Sharing Plan . 7:36

Pension Benefit Guaranty Corporation (PBGC)

Regulations

2616.3 . . . . 3:30

PBGC Advisory Opinion Letters

81-35	7:19
91-1	7:19

Tables

[References are to question numbers.]

Table of Cases

A

Accord Buckhorn Inc v
   Ropak Corp 7:31
Adams v Avondale Indus,
   Inc, ... 1:3, 8:24
Amalgamated Clothing & Textile
   Workers Union v Murdock . . . 6:5
American Federation of Musicians'
   & Employers' Pension Fund,
   In re: 3:33
American Federation of Unions
   v Equitable Life Assurance
   Soc'y 2:32
Anderson v Mortell 6:2
Anoka Orthopaedic Assocs, PA v
   Lechner 2:27
Arkalian v National Western Life
   Ins Co 2:15, 7:17

B

Baeten v Van Ess 6:2
Baker v Smith 7:31
Barrington Police Pension Fund
   Trustees v Illinois Ins Dep't . . 7:43
Batchelor v Oak Hill Medical
   Group 2:20
Belade v ITT Corp 3:14
Birmingham v SoGen-Swiss Int'l
   Corp Retirement Plan 2:12
Bishop v Osborne Transp
   Inc 6:35, 6:37

Bittner v Sadoff & Rudoy Indus . 6:36
Blatt v Marshall & Lassman 2:2, 2:19
Brink v DaLesio 5:36
British Printing & Communication
   Corp v Harcourt Brace
   Jovanovich, Inc 7:35
Brock v Citizens Bank of
   Clovis 5:14, 7:42
Brock v Gillikin 5:14
Brock v Robbins 7:12
Brown v Blue Cross & Blue Shield
   of Ala 6:39
Byrd v MacPapers 6:21

C

Central Trust Co, NA v American
   Avents Corp 7:36
Chemung Canal Trust Co v Sovran
   Bank/Maryland 6:32
Coar v Kazimir 6:6, 6:19
Cody v Donovan 3:7, 3:8,
   7:1, 7:12, 7:13
Comm'r v Keystone Consol
   Indus, Inc 5:13
Confer v Custom Eng'g Co 8:27
Cutaiar v Marshall 5:1, 5:35

D

Danaher Corporation, DH v Chicago
   Pneumatic Tool Co 7:38
Dardaganis v Grace Capital Inc . 6:9,

T-13

Fiduciary Responsibility Answer Book

[References are to question numbers.]

                                                  7:5
Davidson v Cook 4:9
D'Emanuele v Montgomery
  Ward & Co 6:38
Diduck v Kaszycki & Sons
  Contractors, Inc 6:14
Dimond v Retirement Plan . . . 7:14
Dole v Jones 7:41
Donovan v Bierwirth . . . 3:3, 6:10,
                          6:39, 7:38
Donovan v Cunningham 6:9,
                          7:13, 7:38
Donovan v Daugherty 5:30
Donovan v Guaranty National
  Bank 7:42
Donovan v Mazola 6:12
Donovan v Mercer 2:2
Donovan v Tricario 7:13

E

Eaves v Penn 6:8, 6:35,
                               7:31
Employees' Retirement System v
  Mayor of Baltimore City . . . 7:43
Ershick v United Missouri Bank . 7:31

F

Farm King Supply, Inc Integrated
  Profit Sharing Plan & Trust v
  Edward D Jones & Co 2:2,
                          2:26, 2:34
Farr v US West, Inc 3:35
Fink v National Sav & Trust Co . . 4:9
Firestone Tire &
  Rubber Co v Bruch 3:15,
                          6:39, 6:40

Foltz v US News & World
  Report, Inc 5:9
Fort Halifax Packing Co v
  Coyne 1:3,
                          3:32, 8:5
Free v Briody 4:11, 6:2,
                               6:32
Freund v Marshall & Ilsley
  Bank 2:19, 4:10,
                          5:35, 6:2

G

Gaskell v Harvard Coop Soc'y . . 6:13
Gibson v Prudential Ins
  Co of America 6:64
Gilliam v Edwards 6:8
GIW Indus, Inc v Trevor, Stewart,
  Burton & Jacobsen, Inc 6:9, 7:10,
                               7:14
Glaziers & Glassblowers Union
  Local 252 v Newbridge
  Securities, Inc 6:33
Graphic Communs Union, No 2 v
  GCIU-Employer Retirement Benefit
  Plan 6:35
Gray v New England Tel
  and Tel Co 6:35, 6:36
Guidry v Sheet Metal Workers Nat
  Pension Fund 1:7, 6:6
Gulf Pension Litigation, In re . . . 6:8

H

Halpin v WW Grainger, Inc . . . 6:60
Hamilton v Air Jamaica, Ltd 8:25, 8:27
Hansen v Continental Ins Co . . . 8:10

T-14

Tables

[References are to question numbers.]

Harris Trust & Sav Bank v Hancock Mut Life Ins 8:23, 8:32, 8:52
Haywood v Russell Corp 6:13
Hazen Paper Co v Biggens . . . 6:21
Hibernia Bank v Int'l Bhd of Teamsters 2:17
Horan v Kaiser Steel Retirement . 7:17
Hunt v Magnell 7:7

I

Ingersoll-Rand Co v McClendon 6:13, 6:21
Iron Workers Local No 272 v Bowen 6:35

J

James v Fleet/Norstar Financial Group 3:32, 8:5
Jones v O'Higgins 7:12, 7:14

K

Katsaros v Cody 1:9, 3:7, 3:8, 6:5, 7:1, 7:12, 7:13
Keystone Consol Indus, Inc v Comm'r 5:13
Kim v Fujikawa 6:32
Korn v Levine Bros Iron Works Corp 6:35
Kross v Western Electric Co . . . 6:60
Kyle Railways, Inc v Pacific Administration Services Inc . . 2:31

L

Lanka v Higgins 3:10

Leib v Comm'r 5:1
Leigh v Engle . 2:19, 4:43, 6:11, 7:38
Leonard v Drug Fair, Inc 7:34
Libbey-Owens-Ford Co v Blue Cross & Blue Shield of Ohio. 3:14, 3:36
Lowen v Tower Asset Management 5:35, 6:64

M

McDougall v Donovan . . . 5:9, 5:12
McGann v H&H Music Co 6:22
McLaughlin v Tomasso 5:30
McMahan v New England Mut Life Ins Co 6:41
Marshall v Craft 6:3
Marshall v Glass/Metal Assoc and Glaziers and Glassworkers Pension Plan 7:13
Marshall v Kelly 6:7, 6:12
Marshall v Snyder 3:6, 6:7
Martin v Feilen 2:1, 2:2, 2:27, 3:1
Martin v Harline 2:2, 2:3, 2:20, 4:7
Martin v Nations Bank of Georgia 6:23
Martin v Rocky Mountain Investors, Inc 7:41
Martin v Rylands 7:41
Massachusetts Mutual Life Ins Co v Russell 6:13, 6:14, 6:32, 6:64
Mazur v Gaudet 4:11
Mendez v Teachers Ins & Annuity Ass'n 6:35
Mertens v Hewitt Assocs . 1:6, 2:27,

T-15

Fiduciary Responsibility Answer Book

[References are to question numbers.]

                    5:9, 6:5, 6:13, 6:64
Miele v New York State Teamsters
    Conf Pens & Ret Fund 6:38
Miller v Gen Motors Corp 6:27
Monkelis v Mobay Chem 6:36
Morales v Plaxall Inc 6:35
Morgan Guaranty Trust Co v Tax
    Appeals Tribunal 3:33
Mutual Life Ins Co v Yampol . . 6:32

N

Nationwide Mutual Ins Co v
    Darden 3:15
NCR Corp v American Tel &
    Tel Co 7:31
Newton v Van Otterloo . . 2:20, 7:36
Nieto v Ecker 2:27, 5:9,
                        5:26, 6:64
NLRB v Amax Coal Co 3:20
Norlin Corp v Rooney, Pace, Inc . 7:31

O

Olsen v EF Hutton & Co Inc 2:26, 2:27
O'Malley v Comm'r 5:22
O'Neill v Davis 7:35
Oscar A Samos, MD v Dean Witter
    Reynolds 1:6
O'Toole v Arlington Trust Co . . 8:41

P

Packer Eng'g, Inc v Kratville . . 6:34
Painters of Philadelphia Dst Council
    No 21 Welfare Fund v Price
    Waterhouse 2:27
Pappas v Buck Consultants, Inc . 2:27

Payonk v HMW Indus . . . 2:19, 3:20
PBGC v Fletcher 5:34
Pension Plan of Public Serv Co of
    New Hampshire v KPMG Peat
    Marwick 2:1
Podesta v Calumet Industries, Inc 7:31

R

Robbins v First American Bank . 2:17
Rutland v Comm'r 5:10

S

St Mary Medical Ctr v Cristiano . 2:19
Schoenholtz v Doniger 6:14
Schoonmaker v Employee Savings
    Plan of Amoco Corp and Parti-
    cipating Companies 3:13
Schwartz v Gordon 1:3
Shamrock Holding, Inc v Polaroid
    Corp 7:31
Shaw v Delta Air Lines, Inc . . . 8:13
Sixty-Five Security Plan v Blue Cross
    & Blue Shield of New York . . 2:32

T

Thompson v Prudential Ins Co . . 7:18
Thorton v Evans 5:9
Trapani v Consolidated Edison
    Employees' Mutual Aid Society 6:8
Trenton v Scott Paper Co . . 3:19, 3:21
Tuvia Convalescent Center v National
    Union of Hospital and Health Care
    Employees 3:14

Tables

[References are to question numbers.]

U

United States v Grizzle 6:20
United States v Keystone Consol
 Indus 3:36
United States v Zauber 6:19
Useden v Acker 2:17, 2:27, 2:28

W

West v Butler 6:21
Westoak Realty and Investment
 Co, Inc 5:37

Whitfield v Cohen 3:6, 4:7, 6:7, 7:3, 7:13
Whitfield v Tomasso 5:14, 6:5, 7:22
Williams v Wright 1:3, 8:25
Withers v Teachers' Retirement
 System of City of New York . . 7:43
Wood v Comm'r 5:13

Y

Yeseta v Baima 2:27

Index

[*References are to question numbers.*]

A

Accountants
  Fiduciary status, 2:1, 2:2
Acquired Immune Deficiency Syndrome (AIDS)
  Health insurance plan, changes related to, 6:22
Acquisition of businesses
  Fiduciary rules applicable to, 3:31
Allocation and delegation of fiduciary duties. *See* **Fiduciary duties**
Annual reports
  Fiduciary duty to furnish, 3:17
Annuities
  Fiduciary liability in provider selection, 7:19
  Insurance company selection, 7:15, 7:16
  Pension plan purchase of, 7:17
  Rating services, 7:16
  Termination of plan, purchase in connection with, 7:18, 7:19, 7:20
Asset transfers
  Prohibited transaction rules applicable to, 5:35

Attorneys' Fees
  Breach of fiduciary duties, court costs
    Plan payment of, 6:34
  Fiduciary liability for, 6:35
  ERISA actions
    Amount of fees, 6:38
    Defendant recovery of fees in, 6:36
    Losing party, fees awarded to, 6:37
"Audit requirement", 8:17
Auditing firms
  Fiduciary status, 2:1

B

Bank investment contracts (BICs)
  Defined, 7:21
  FDIC coverage of, 7:46
  Fixed rate of interest, 7:21
  Selection considerations, 7:23
Banks
  Custodial banks
    Fiduciary status, 2:17
    Plan investment in, 7:46

Fiduciary Responsibility Answer Book

[References are to question numbers.]

Banks (*cont'd*)
  QPAM status, 4:25, 4:26
  Trustee status, 8:37
Beneficiary
  Contributions as plan assets, 8:16, 8:17
  Defined, 3:16
  Fiduciary as beneficiary, 5:2
  Individual control over accounts, rules applicable to, 2:35, 3:28
Benefit plan investor
  Defined, 8:58
Benefits claim
  Appeal of denied claim
    Appeal denial, required contents of, 6:59
    Claimant's right to, 6:57
    Decision, time frame for, 6:58
  Defined, 6:51
  Denial of claim
    Contents of denial, 6:56
    Notification procedure, 6:55
  Exemption from provision of claims procedure, 6:61
  Filing of, 6:52
  HMOs, rules for claims procedure, 6:63
  Method of handling, 6:53
  Plan documents stating procedures for, 6:54
  Benefits committee
  Fiduciary status, 2:3
Blind purchases
  Fiduciary liability, 5:7
Bonding
  Requirements, 8:68, 8:69
Breach of fiduciary duty
  Co-fiduciaries, 3:22, 4:9-4:12, 6:32
  Criminal liability for, 6:18, 6:19, 6:20
  Damages, recovery of, 6:9, 6:10, 6:11
  Equitable remedies for, 6:5-6:9
  Excise taxes imposed for, 6:17
  Nonfiduciary, contribution action against, 6:33

  Joint and several liability of company officers, 2:2
  Judicial review. *See* Judicial review
  Losses caused by, measure of, 6:10
  Penalties, 5:8, 6:15, 6:16
  Percent penalty, 6:15, 6:16
  Personal liability for, 6:1
  Prior breach
    Duty to remedy, 6:3
    Successor fiduciary, liability for, 6:2, 6:3
  Professional service providers, 2:27
  Profit to fiduciary resulting from, 6:12
  Prohibited transactions. *See* Prohibited transactions
  Punitive damages, recovery of, 6:13, 6:14
  Successor fiduciary, liabilities and duties regarding prior breach, 6:2, 6:3
Broker-dealers
  Fiduciary status, 2:26
Brokerage firms
  Fiduciary status, 2:2
Bonus arrangements
  Pension plans, as, 8:4

C

Cafeteria plans
  Beneficiary contributions to, 8:17, 8:29, 8:35
  Custodial accounts for, 8:34
  ERISA applicability to, 8:8
  Trust requirements applicable to, 8:29, 8:35
Church plans
  ERISA applicability to, 8:13
Co-fiduciaries
  Allocation of fiduciary responsibilities, 3:24
  Breach of fiduciary duty

Index

[References are to question numbers.]

Generally 3:22
Liability of co-fiduciary for breach of another. *See subhead:* Liability of
Contribution actions against a co-fiduciary, 6:32
Co-trustees as, 3:23, 8:15
ERISA Section 404(c) plans, liability under, 4:49
Indemnification actions against a co-fiduciary, 6:32
Liability of
  Contribution actions, 6:32
  Control and protection of plan assets, failure to assert, 4:11
  Duty to monitor a co-fiduciary, 4:11
  Indemnification actions, 6:32
  Knowledge of another's breach, 4:10, 4:12
  Participation in another's breach, 4:9
  Prudence obligation, failure to observe, 4:11
Collectively bargained plans
  Fiduciaries for, 2:36
Conflict of interest
  Fiduciary recusal to avoid, 6:46
Contributory self-insured welfare plans, 8:17
Contributory welfare plans
  Beneficiary contributions to, 8:17, 8:29, 8:35
  Trust requirements applicable to, 8:29, 8:35
Corporate control contest
  Qualifying employer securities, plans containing, 7:38
Corporate restructuring
  Fiduciary rules applicable to, 3:31
Corporate trustees, 8:37
Co-trustees
  Co-fiduciaries, as, 3:23, 8:15

Liability for breach of another, 4:11, 4:12
Credit, extension of
  Prohibited transaction rules, applicability to, 5:14
Custodial accounts
  IRAs, use in, 8:34
  Keogh plans, use in, 8:34
  Trusteed accounts, use in place of, 8:36
Custodial banks
  Fiduciary status, 2:17

D

Damages
  Fiduciary liability for, 6:9-6:11, 6:13, 6:14
Defined benefit pension plan
  ERISA applicability to, 8:13
Dependent care assistance programs (DCAPS)
  ERISA applicability to, 8:11
Direct plan expenses, 8:22 *See also* **Plan expenses**
Disability insurance plans
  Voluntary plans, ERISA applicability, 8:13
Discharge of employee
  Early discharge as violation of rights, 6:21
Disclosure requirements, 3:17
Disqualified person. *See* **Parties in interest**
Diversification requirement
  Explained, 3:11
  Factors of diversification, 3:12
Divorce
  Hold placed on participant account pending, 3:13

I-3

E

Eligible individual account plan
　Defined, 7:30
　Qualifying employer real property, investment in, 7:30, 7:31
　Qualifying employer securities, investment in, 7:30, 7:31
Employee assistance programs
　ERISA applicability to, 8:8
　Services provided by, 8:8
Employee-pay-all insurance
　ERISA applicability to, 8:10
Employee pension benefit plans
　Benefit plan investor, as, 8:58
　Defined, 8:4
　ERISA applicability to, 8:1
Employee Retirement Income Security Act of 1974 (ERISA) *See also specific headings*
　Enforcement of fiduciary rules, 1:5
　Plans subject to, 1:4, 8:1
　Preemption rules
　　Exceptions to, 3:32, 3:33, 8:10, 8:11, 8:12
　　Explained 3:32, 8:2
Employee Stock Ownership Plans (ESOPs)
　Breach of fiduciary duty, 2:2
　Defined, 7:32
　Eligible individual account plan, as, 7:30
　Exclusive benefit rule, 3:2
　Loans to, 5:14, 5:40
　Qualifying employer real property (QERP), acquisition of, 7:31
　Qualifying employer securities (QES), acquisition of, 7:31, 7:33, 7:35, 7:36, 7:37
　Special fiduciary rules applicable to, 3:25
Employee welfare benefit plans *See also specific plans*
　Benefit plan investor, as, 8:58
　Defined, 8:8
　Employee assistance programs as, 8:8
　Excepted welfare programs, 1:4, 8:10
　ERISA applicability to, 8:1, 8:8
　Payroll deduction savings accounts as, 8:8
　Prohibited transaction rules, 5:6 *See also* Prohibited transaction rules
　Termination of plan, 8:50
Employer contributions
　Encumbered property, 5:13
　Exclusive benefit rule and, 3:36
　Prohibited transaction rules, applicability to, 5:13
　Refund of
　　Exception to exclusive benefit rule, as, 8:46
　　Multiemployer plans, 5:48
　　Single employer plan, 5:47, 8:46, 8:47
Employer real property
　Acquisition on behalf of a plan, 5:29
　Qualifying. *See* Qualifying employer real property
Employer securities
　Acquisition on behalf of a plan, 5:12, 5:29
　Qualifying. *See* Qualifying employer securities
Equitable remedies
　Breach of fiduciary duty, for, 6:5-6:9
Equity interest
　Defined, 8:53
　Look-through rule and investment of, 8:55
　Property, equity interest in, treatment of, 8:64
ERISA rights, violation of, 6:21, 6:22
ERISA Section 404(c) plan
　Beneficiary control over individual assets, 4:30
　Co-fiduciary liability under, 4:49
　Core alternatives requirement, 4:32, 4:33

Index

[References are to question numbers.]

Defined, 4:29
Fiduciary involvement in investments, 4:37, 4:44
Fiduciary liability, 4:45
Fiduciary responsibilities in, 4:31, 4:43, 4:44, 4:46, 4:47
"Independent control" defined, 4:36
Information supplied to participants, requirements regarding, 4:40, 4:41, 4:42
Investment advice, 4:46
Investment alternatives offered, 4:32, 4:33, 4:34
Investment instructions, 4:31, 4:39
Partial participant control of assets, 4:38
Participant control over individual assets, 4:30
Participant liability, 4:48
Prohibited transaction, participant engagement in, 4:48
Purpose of, 4:27
Transfer of assets, 4:35

Excess benefit plans
ERISA applicability to, 8:13

Excise tax
Breach of fiduciary duty, as penalty for, 6:17
Prohibited transaction, as penalty for, 5:8, 5:9, 5:10, 5:11, 5:38

Exclusive benefit rule
Dual loyalty, 3:2, 3:3
Employer, incidental benefit of, 3:3
Employer's contribution, rejection of, 3:36
Exceptions to, 8:46
Explained, 3:1, 8:45
Violations of, 3:2, 3:3, 8:45

Expenses
Fiduciary's "direct expenses", reimbursement for, 5:28
Plan assets used to pay, 5:46
Settlor functions, for, 5:46

Experts
Fiduciary liability, use of experts as risk minimization, 6:45

F

Federal Deposit Insurance Coverage (FDIC)
Plan investments in banks covered by, 7:46

Felons
Fiduciary status, rules regarding, 2:2
Trustee status, rules regarding, 8:37

Fiduciary duties
Allocation and delegation of
  Duty to monitor, 4:7, 4:8
  Investment manager, appointment and monitoring of, 7:1-7:8
  Liability of allocating or delegating fiduciary, 4:6
  Nonfiduciaries, to, 4:2
  Other fiduciaries, to, 4:1
  Prudence requirement applied to, 4:5
  Trustee responsibilities, 4:3, 4:4
Annual reports, duty to furnish, 3:17
Common law fiduciary duty requirements differentiated, 1:8
Disclosure requirements, 3:17
Enforcement, 1:5
Exclusive benefit rule, 3:2, 3:3
Funding standards, duty to meet, 3:17
Generally, 1:6, 2:1, 2:2, 3:1
Insurance companies, plan assets of, 8:31, 8:32
Reporting requirements, 3:17
Tax information, providing, 3:35
To whom duty is owed, 3:14
Transfer of funds, duty of notification, 3:17

[*References are to question numbers.*]

Fiduciary liability *See also* **Breach of fiduciary duty,** Prohibited transactions
  Claims procedures, compliance with as risk minimizing, 6:60
  Conflicts of interest, recusal by fiduciary to avoid, 6:46
  Damages, liability for, 6:9, 6:10, 6:11
  Delegation of duties as relief from, 6:24, 6:50
  Experts, use in minimizing risk of liability, 6:45
  Equitable remedies, 6:5-6:9
  Indemnification of employees performing fiduciary functions, 6:25
  Insurance, 2:2, 6:28-6:30
  Personal liability, 1:7, 6:1
  Prior breaches, 6:2, 6:3
  Punitive damages, liability for, 6:13, 6:14
  Record-keeping, importance of, 6:43, 6:44
  Recusal by fiduciary
    Action taken in addition to, 6:49
    Conflict of interest, to avoid, 6:46
    Documentation of, 6:48
    Self-dealing, to avoid, 6:46
    Resignation, in place of, 6:47
  Release from, 6:23-6:27
  Self-dealing, recusal by fiduciary to avoid, 6:46
  Successor fiduciary, liability for prior breach, 6:2, 6:3, 6:4
  Unwitting errors or violations, liability for, 1:10
Fiduciary liability insurance
  Employer purchase of, 6:29
  Fiduciary purchase of, 6:29
  "Linked" insurance policies, 6:30
  Plan purchase of, 2:2, 6:28
Fiduciary responsibilities. *See* **Fiduciary duties**
Fiduciary status
  Activities rendering, 2:4
  Appointment of fiduciary, 2:2
  Bonded fiduciaries, 8:15
  Consent to, 1:9
  Defined, 1:2, 2:1
  ERISA laws governing, 1:3
  Functions rendering, 2:2
  Informing fiduciary of functions and liabilities, 2:2
  Nonfiduciaries allocated fiduciary responsibilities, 4:2
  Number of fiduciaries, 2:8
  Offices and positions rendering, 2:5
  Purpose of, 2:12
  Title vs. function in determination of, 2:3
  Widow of fiduciary, gratuitous death benefits paid to, 8:45
Foreign plans
  ERISA applicability to, 8:13
Foreign securities
  Plan investment in, 7:48
Funding standards
  Fiduciary duty to meet, 3:17
Futures
  Plan investment in, 7:47

G

Goods, services and facilities
  Compensation for providing, 5:26
  Fiduciary services, compensation for, 5:27
  Necessary services, 5:25
  Party in interest, furnished by, 5:23
  Prohibition against furnishing, 5:22
  "Reasonable contract or arrangement" defined, 5:24
Governmental plans
  ERISA applicability to, 8:13
Guaranteed benefit insurance policy
  Look-through rule and, 8:51
  Plan asset, as, 8:23, 8:32

Index

[References are to question numbers.]

Guaranteed governmental mortgage pool certificate
Acquisition by plan, treatment of, 8:65
Guaranteed investment contracts (GICs)
Defined, 7:21
Guarantor of, 7:21
General account GICs, 7:21
Investment risk, 7:24
Participants, providing information to, 7:25, 7:26
Participating GICs, 7:21
Selection considerations, 7:22, 7:24
Separate account GICs, 7:21
Types of, 7:21

H

Health Maintenance Organizations (HMOs)
Benefits claims procedure, rules governing, 6:63
Hiring halls
ERISA applicability to, 8:10
Holiday gifts
ERISA applicability to, 8:10
Hostile takeovers
Fiduciary rules applicable to, 3:31, 7:38
Qualifying employer securities, plans containing, 7:38
H.R. 10 plans
ERISA applicability to, 8:3
Fiduciary standards, 3:29

I

Indemnification of fiduciary, 6:31
Individual Retirement Account (IRA)
Benefit plan investor, as, 8:58
ERISA applicability to, 8:6
Trust requirements, applicability to, 8:34
Industry advancement programs
ERISA applicability to, 8:10
Insurance policies
Group annuity contracts, 8:32
Guaranteed benefit policies, 8:23, 8:32, 8:52
"Look-through" rule, 8:23
Plan asset, as, 8:23, 8:29
Prohibited transactions, insurance against losses resulting from, 5:39
Trust requirement applicability, 8:29, 8:30
Insurance companies and brokers
Annuities. *See* Annuities
Assets of, 8:30, 8:31, 8:32
Bank investment contracts. *See* Bank investment contracts
Fiduciary status, 2:32, 2:33, 8:31, 8:32
Guaranteed investment contracts. *See* Guaranteed investment contracts
QPAM status, 4:25, 4:26
"Render investment advice" defined, 2:34
Trust requirements on assets, 8:30, 8:31, 8:32
Trustees, as, 8:37
Investment Advisors Act of 1940, 7:2, 7:3
Investment diversification. *See* **Diversification requirement**
Investment managers
Appointment by fiduciary, 4:13, 4:14 *See also subhead:* Selection of
Collective, common or group trusts, 4:22
Defined, 2:24, 8:43
Fiduciary status, 2:25
Individuals precluded from serving as, 4:20

Fiduciary Responsibility Answer Book

[*References are to question numbers.*]

Investment managers (*cont'd*)
  Investment guidelines, 4:18, 7:4, 7:5, 7:9-7:15
  Investment management agreement, negotiation of, 7:5
  Monitoring
    Fiduciary liability for delegated investment duties, 7:7
    Methods of, 7:8
  Multiple investment managers, 4:21
  Plan fiduciaries serving as, 4:19
  Proxies, use of, 4:23
  QPAM status, 4:25, 4:26
  Responsibilities of, 4:17
  Selection of
    Applicant's record, collecting, 7:3
    Information required for, 7:3
    Investigation of potential managers, 7:2
    Investment guidelines, establishing, 7:4
    Methodology used in, 7:1
  Special fiduciary rules applicable to, 3:26
Investments
  Experts, use of, 7:11, 7:13
  Factors of consideration, 7:10
  Industry standards, 7:14
  Investment strategy design, 7:11
  Permissible investments, 7:9
  Prudence in decision making 7:12
Investor. *See* **Benefit plan investor**

J

Joint ownership
  Property jointly owned, treatment of, 8:63
Judicial review
  Arbitrary and capricious standard for review, 6:39, 6:40
  De novo standard for review, 6:39, 6:40
  Fiduciary actions, standard of review for, 6:39
  Firestone case, 6:41
  Plan document specification of standard of deference accorded fiduciaries, 6:42

K

Keogh plans
  Common-law employees, inclusion in, 8:3
  Custodial accounts for, 8:34
  ERISA applicability to, 8:3
  Fiduciary standards, 3:29
  Trust requirements applicability, 8:29, 8:34
Kickbacks
  Federal crime applicable to, 6:20
  Prohibition against, 5:1, 5:37

L

Limited purpose fiduciary, 2:6
Loans
  Availability requirements, 5:17
  Generally 5:15
  Information provided to participants regarding, 5:19
  Interest rate requirements, 5:20
  Minimum loans, 5:18
  Permissible plan loans, 5:15, 5:17
  Prohibited transaction exemptions and, 5:15, 5:16, 5:40
  Prohibited transaction rules regarding, 5:14
  Security requirements, 5:21
Look-through rule
  Applicability, 8:52, 8:59, 8:60, 8:61, 8:62
  Explained, 8:51

Index

[References are to question numbers.]

Operating companies, applicability to, 8:59–8:62

Prohibited transactions, liability for, 5:9, 6:65

M

Medical benefit plan, 8:56
Multibenefit plans
  ERISA applicability to, 8:13
Multiemployer plans
  Employer contributions, refund of, 5:48
Mutual fund investments
  Trust requirement applicability, 8:29, 8:33

N

Named fiduciaries
  Allocation of fiduciary duties to, 4:1, 4:5
  Appointment of, 2:11
  Defined, 2:9
  Designation in plan documents, 2:13
  Duties, 2:10
  Investment duties, delegation by, 4:13, 4:14
  Liabilities, 2:14
  Purpose of, 2:12
  Trustees
    Appointment of, 8:38
    Subject to direction of named fiduciary, 8:42
Nonfiduciaries
  Allocation of fiduciary duties to, 4:2
  Breach of fiduciary duty, contribution actions against nonfiduciaries, 6:33
  Liability of, 6:33, 6:64
  Nonfiduciary functions, 2:7 *See also* Settlor functions
  Penalty tax connected with fiduciary breach, applicability of, 6:66

O

On-premises facilities
  ERISA applicability to, 8:10
Operating companies
  Defined, 8:59
  Look-through rule applicability, 8:59–8:62
Owner-employee
  Defined, 5:16
  Loans to, 5:16

P

Participant-directed plan investments *See also* **ERISA Section 404(c) plans**
  ERISA Section 404(c) plans differentiated, 4:28
  Purpose of, 4:27
Parties in interest
  Adverse interests, parties with, 5:36
  Defined, 5:4
  Excise taxes imposed upon, 5:7, 5:8
  Extension of credit involving, 5:14
  Fiduciaries who also represent parties in interest, 5:3
  Goods, services and facilities. *See* Goods, services and facilities
  Joint and several liability, 5:11
  Loans involving, 5:14 *See also* Loans
  Plan assets, use by or for, 5:35
  Prohibited transactions with, 5:1 *See also* Prohibited transactions
  Sales, exchanges or leases between a plan and, 5:12
Parties with adverse interests
  Prohibited transactions rules applicable, 5:36

Fiduciary Responsibility Answer Book

[References are to question numbers.]

Partners and Partnerships
  Benefit plan investor, as, 8:58
  ERISA applicability to, 8:3
  Retirement agreements, 8:14

Payroll practices
  ERISA applicability to, 1:4, 8:9

Pension Benefit Guaranty Corporation (PBGC)
  Payment of benefits for annuity contracts, 7:19
  Termination of plan, role in, 7:20

Pension benefit plans
  Annuity contracts, purchase of, 7:17
  Large plans, investment considerations specific to, 7:49
  Prohibited transaction rules, 5:6 *See also* Prohibited transaction rules
  Small plans, considerations for, 7:50
  Termination of plan, 8:49

Pension plan trustees
  Fiduciary status of, 2:2

Plan administrators
  Defined, 2:22
  Failure to designate, 2:23
  Responsibilities, 2:22

Plan assets
  Anti-inurement rules, 8:45
  Beneficiary contributions as, 8:16, 8:17
  Exclusive benefit rule
    Explained, 8:45
  Expenses paid out of, 5:46
  Fiduciary with individual account dealing with total plan assets, 5:31
  Improper expenses, payment of, 8:19
  Indicia of ownership maintained outside U.S., 3:27
  Insurance policies and contracts, 8:23, 8:29, 8:30, 8:66, 8:67
  Investment of, 4:3, 8:15 *See also* Diversification requirement
  Investment managers. *See* Investment managers

  Jointly owned assets, 8:63
  Participant contributions as, 8:16, 8:17
  Party in interest, use by or for, 5:35
  Plan expenses paid from, 8:16, 8:18
  Proxies, use of, 4:23
  Regulations pertaining to, 8:15, 8:28
  Tax qualification rule, 8:45
  Termination of plan, asset allocation upon. *See* Termination of plan
  Trust requirements. *See* Trust requirements
  Trustee responsibilities regarding. *See* Trustees

Plan committee
  Fiduciary status, 2:3

Plan documents
  Amendments to, 3:19
  Errors in, 8:25
  Fiduciary adherence to, 3:13
  Informal documents, legality of, 8:25
  Oral changes to, legality of, 8:27
  Periodic review of, 8:27
  Plan administrator named in, 2:22
  Plan expenses, provisions for, 8:21
  Standard of deference accorded fiduciaries specified in, 6:42
  Termination of, 3:19
  Unwritten plans, 8:26

Plan expenses
  Direct expenses, 8:22
  Plan assets, paid out of, 8:16, 8:18, 8:21
  Provisions for, 8:21

Plan participants
  Defined, 3:15
  Individual control over accounts, 2:35, 3:28

Plan sponsors
  Board of directors as, 2:20
  Defined, 2:18
  Fiduciary status, 2:17, 2:21
  Individual members, status of, 2:21

Index

[References are to question numbers.]

Plan trustees. *See* **Trustees**
Pooled investments, 8:37
Professional service providers
  Fiduciary status of, 2:27, 2:30
  In-house, 2:29
  Professional firms, 2:28
Prohibited transaction exemptions
  Administrative exemptions, 5:41, 5:44, 5:45
  Class exemptions, 5:44
  Closely held corporations, exemptions for, 5:43
  Individual exemption, 5:45
  Loans applicable to, 5:15, 5:16
  Retroactive exemptions, 5:42
  Statutory exceptions, 5:40
Prohibited transactions
  Blind purchases, 5:7
  Correction of, 5:38
  Employer contributions, 5:13
  ERISA Section 404(c) plans, participant liability under, 4:48
  Excise taxes, imposition of, 5:8–5:11
  Exemptions. *See* Prohibited transaction exemptions
  Explained, 5:1
  Fiduciary duty to avoid, 3:36, 5:1
  Goods, services and facilities, furnishing of. *See* Goods, services and facilities
  Insurance protection against losses resulting from, 5:39
  IRC code and ERISA rules differentiated, 5:5, 5:6
  Liability of fiduciary, 5:6
  Loans, applicability to, 5:14 *See also* Loans
  Multiple infractions for single event, 5:10
  Non-fiduciary liability for, 5:9, 6:65
  Parties in interest. *See* Parties in interest
  Penalties, 5:8
  Plan assets, improper expenses paid from, 8:19
  Plans covered by, 5:6
  Prudence, factors in determining, 5:7
  Qualifying employer securities and, 5:12
  Sale of property, 5:12
  Self-dealing, 5:30
  Statutory exceptions to, 5:40
  Transfer of property, 5:12
Proxies
  Investment manager status granted by exercising, 4:24
  Use with plan securities, 4:23
Prudent man rule
  Allocation of fiduciary duties, application to, 4:5
  Expert advice, 3:7
  Explained, 3:4
  Procedural prudence, 3:8, 3:9
  Standards for determination, 3:5, 3:6
  Substantive prudence, 3:8, 3:9
Public employee plans
  Fiduciary standards applicable, 3:34
  Social investing, 3:34
Punitive damages
  Fiduciary liability for, 6:13, 6:14

Q

Qualified professional asset manager (QPAM)
  Defined, 4:25
  Investment manager, as, 4:26
  Transactions between parties in interest and, 5:14
Qualifying employer real property (QERP)
  Acquisition on behalf of a plan, 5:29, 7:27
  Defined, 7:29

[References are to question numbers.]

Qualifying employer real property (QERP) *(cont'd)*
   Eligible individual account plan investment in, 7:30, 7:31
   ESOP, acquisition by, 7:31
   Fiduciary rules applicable to, 3:25
   Restrictions on investment in, 7:31
   Trustee responsibility to invest, 4:3

Qualifying employer securities (QES)
   Acquisition on behalf of a plan, 5:29, 7:27
   Defined, 7:28
   Eligible individual account plan investment in, 7:30, 7:31
   ESOP, acquisition by, 7:31, 7:33, 7:35, 7:36, 7:37
   Fiduciary rules applicable to, 3:25
   Look-through rule applicability, 8:56
   Party-in-interest, acquisition from, 7:34
   Prohibited transaction rules and, 5:12, 5:29
   Restrictions on investment in, 7:31
   Tender offers, effect of, 7:38
   Trustee responsibility to invest, 4:3

R

Real estate
   Plan investment in, 7:45
   Real estate investment trusts (REITs) Plan investment in, 7:45

Real estate operating company (REOC)
   Defined, 8:60
   Look-through rule applicability, 8:60, 8:62

Recusal by fiduciary
   Action taken in addition to, 6:49
   Conflict of interest, to avoid, 6:46
   Documentation of, 6:48
   Self-dealing, to avoid, 6:46
   Resignation, in place of, 6:47

Remembrance funds
   ERISA applicability to, 8:10

Reporting requirements, 3:17

Retiree health account
   excess pension assets transferred to, 8:45, 8:47

S

Salary continuation programs
   ERISA applicability to, 8:9

Sale of property
   Parties in interest, sale between a plan and, 5:12

Sales to employees
   ERISA applicability to, 8:10

Savings and loan association
   QPAM, Q 4:25, 4:26

Scholarship programs
   ERISA applicability to, 8:10

Securities
   Foreign, plan investment in, 7:48
   Publicly offered securities, 8:54
   Restrictions on investment in, 7:44
   Street name or nominee's name, holdings in, 8:40

Self-dealing
   Compensation for services constituting, 5:32, 5:33
   Fiduciary recusal to avoid, 6:46
   Multiple services provided by fiduciary, 5:34
   Prohibited transaction, as, 5:30

Self-employed individuals
   Benefit plans covering, fiduciary standards for, 3:29, 8:3

Settlor functions
   Defined, 3:18
   Examples of, 3:19, 3:20
   Expenses incurred by, 5:46, 8:18, 8:20
   Fiduciary performance of
      Generally, 3:20

Index

[References are to question numbers.]

Rules of fiduciary responsibility and, 3:21
Severance pay plan
  ERISA applicability, 8:5
Shareholder-employee
  Defined, 5:16
  Loans to, 5:16
Single-employer pension plan
  Employer contributions, sponsor refund of, 5:47, 8:47
  Termination of
    Fiduciary rules applicable to, 3:30
    Refund of employer contributions upon, 8:46, 8:47
Social investing
  Examples of, 7:40
  Explained, 3:34, 7:39
  Fiduciary introduction of, 7:41
  Plans utilizing, 7:43
  Single geographic area, prohibition from investing in, 7:42
Sole proprietorship
  ERISA applicability to, 8:3
Strike funds
  ERISA applicability to, 8:10

T

Tax information
  Fiduciary responsibility in providing, 3:35
Tax qualification rule, 8:45
Tax qualified retirement plan
  Benefit plan investor, as, 8:58
Tax sheltered annuity program
  ERISA applicability to, 8:7
Tender offers
  Fiduciary rules applicable to, 3:31, 7:38
  Qualifying employer securities, plans containing, 7:38

Termination of plan
  Annuity contracts purchased in connection with, 7:18, 7:19, 7:20
  Collectively bargained plans, 8:50
  Multiemployer plans, 5:48, 8:50
  Pension plans
    Allocation of assets, 8:49
    Single-employer plans, 5:47, 8:46, 8:47
  Welfare plans
    Distribution of assets, 8:50
Third party administrators
  Employer, duty owed to, 3:14, 3:37
  Fiduciary status, 2:31
Top hat pension plans
  Voluntary plans, ERISA applicability to, 8:15
Transfer of funds
  Notice requirements regarding, 3:17
Transfer of property
  Parties in interest, transfer between a plan and, 5:12
Trust agreement
  Contents, 8:39
  Rules governing, 8:39
Trust requirements
  Exceptions to, 8:29, 8:30
  Explained, 8:28
  Insurance companies, 8:29–8:32
  Keogh plans and, 8:29
  Mutual fund investments, 8:29, 8:33
Trustees
  Appointment of, 8:38
  Corporate trustees, 8:37
  Co-trustee liability, 4:11, 4:12
  Custodial banks, 2:17
  Defined, 2:15
  Exclusive authority of
    Explained, 8:41
    Exceptions to, 8:41, 8:43
  Duties of, 8:41
  Fiduciary status, 2:16

Fiduciary Responsibility Answer Book

[*References are to question numbers.*]

Trustees (*cont'd*)
  Investment manager in control of assets, trustee responsibility in cases of, 8:43
  Limited power, trustees with, 8:41
  Losses, liability for, 8:41
  Named fiduciary, trustees subject to, 8:42
  Plan assets, management of, 8:41
  Pooled investments, 8:37
  Powers of, 8:41
  Proxies, use of, 4:23
  Requirements to becoming, 8:37
  Responsibilities of
    Allocation/delegation of, 4:4, 8:44
    Explained, 4:3, 8:15, 8:28, 8:41
  Types of, 2:15

U

Union dues, 8:16
Unfunded plans
  Trust requirement exception, 8:29

Unsafe harbors
  Investments falling within
    Explained 8:56
    Look-through rule applicability to, 8:56
Unwritten plans
  ERISA applicability, 8:24, 8:26

V

Venture capital operating company (VCOC)
  Defined, 8:61
  Look-through rule applicability, 8:61, 8:62
Voluntary employee benefit association (VEBA)
  Termination of plan, 8:50

W

Workers' compensation plans
  ERISA applicability to, 8:13